Nigeria's Christian Revolution

The Civil War Revival and its Pentecostal Progeny (1967-2006)

[Series Listing- awaiting final text from Jeremy Mudditt]

Nigeria's Christian Revolution

The Civil War Revival and its Pentecostal Progeny (1967-2006)

Richard Burgess

PATERNOSTER PRESS

First published 2008 by Paternoster Press
Paternoster Press is an imprint of Authentic Media
PO Box 300, Carlisle, Cumbria, CA3 OQS, U.K.
and PO Box 1047, Waynesboro, GA 30830-2047, USA

09 08 07 06 05 04 03 7 6 5 4 3 2 1

British Library Cataloguing in Publication Data
A catalogue record for this book is available from the British Library.

ISBN: 978-1-506477-64-0

Published by Paternoster Press,
PO Box 300, Carlisle, Cumbria CA3 9AD

Distributed by 1517 Media in the US and Canada

Series Preface

Regnum Studies in Mission are born from the lived experience of Christians and Christian communities in mission, especially but not solely in the fast growing churches among the poor of the world. These churches have more to tell than stories of growth. They are making significant impacts on their cultures in the cause of Christ. They are producing 'cultural products' which express the reality of Christian faith, hope and love in their societies.

Regnum Studies in Mission are the fruit often of rigorous research to the highest international standards and always of authentic Christian engagement in the transformation of people and societies. And these are for the world. The formation of Christian theology, missiology and practice in the twenty-first century will depend to a great extent on the active participation of growing churches contributing biblical and culturally appropriate expressions of Christian practice to inform World Christianity.

Series Editors

Preface

This study is an adaptation of my PhD thesis, which I completed in 2004. The impulse behind it is my work as a theological educator in Nigeria since 1990, my growing awareness of the importance of Pentecostalism for contemporary African Christianity, and my personal experience of the British Charismatic movement over twenty years. Between 1990 and 1996 I taught in a small theological college in Nigeria, training pastors for the Qua Iboe Church, a large denomination with roots in the 'faith missions' movement at the close of the nineteenth century. Two developments triggered my interest in African Pentecostalism. The first related to internal changes taking place within the Qua Iboe Church due to exposure to Pentecostal influences. A group calling themselves the 'revival movement' challenged the existing church structures and traditional forms of worship inherited from Western missionaries. The church elders maintained control by prohibiting the public use of spiritual gifts, but this only heightened tension and threatened to divide the church.

The discovery of two very different popular participant accounts of Nigerian revivals further stimulated my interest. The first was the 1927 'Spirit Movement' in south-eastern Nigeria, associated with the Qua Iboe Church itself.[1] This coincided with other similar movements in Nigeria, which together produced Nigeria's first wave of indigenous Pentecostal churches. The second was a revival among the Igbo people of Eastern Nigeria closely connected to events surrounding the Nigerian civil war (1967-70).[2] It is this movement and the new Pentecostal churches it generated which is the focus of the present study. The book traces the development of the movement from its origins in the civil war to the present. It shows the importance of context for understanding religious movements and the way that the local and the global can interact to produce

---

[1] J. W. Westgarth, *The Holy Spirit and the Primitive Mind. A Remarkable Account of a Spiritual Awakening in Darkest Africa*, London: Victory Press, 1946.

[2] Frances Lawjua Bolton, *And We Beheld His Glory. A Personal Account of the Revival in Eastern Nigeria in 1970/'71*, Harlow: Christ the King Publishing, 1992.

distinctive expressions of Christian spirituality. Revivals are historically and culturally situated events. Yet their shape is invariably influenced by external forces introduced via the media and through transnational exchanges of ministry.

During doctoral research I travelled widely in Nigeria, conducting interviews with former revivalists, Pentecostal pioneers and church members, collecting a variety of locally produced Christian literature, and attending as many church related meetings as possible. In 2005, I returned to Nigeria as a lecturer at the Theological College of Northern Nigeria, where I became actively involved in Redeemed People's Mission, one of the early post-civil war Pentecostal denominations. As a result I have extended the period covered by the original thesis.

Three further points concerning the scope of the book and its contemporary relevance invite further comment. Firstly, the rapid spread of African Pentecostal churches around the world, due to the migratory patterns and missionary ambitions of their members, makes a study of this kind important not only for the continent of Africa but also for Christians in the global North. It is hoped that this glimpse into the inner life of one segment of the movement will contribute to a better understanding of African Pentecostal spirituality. Secondly, increases in Christian/Muslim tensions since September 11th 2001 mean that Nigeria's contemporary religious landscape, with its particular mix of radical Christianity and Islam, may increasingly come to represent other parts of the world influenced by the two faiths. Finally, there have been recent calls by Igbos, reacting against their marginalisation within the Federation and their victimisation by militant Muslims in the North, for the creation of an independent Biafran state, echoing the sentiments of their predecessors forty years previously.[3] The reflections on the Nigerian civil war within these pages may serve as a sober reminder of the consequences of secession.

The study is structured as follows. In chapter 1, I lay some theoretical and methodological foundations. The inter-related processes of globalisation, modernisation and secularisation contributed to the Igbo identity crisis and created a favourable environment for religious innovation. Thus I reflect upon contemporary discussions of globalisation,

---

[3] See for example an article entitled 'Reviving the Rebellion' in the August 8 2005 edition of the Nigerian magazine Newswatch, which discusses the activities of MASSOB (Movement for the Actualisation of the Sovereign State of Biafra). The article claims that MASSOB has considerable popular support among Igbos. See also the following subtitle to a recent article in Nigeria's Tell magazine ('Keeping the Dream Alive', May 1 2006, 24-31): 'MASSOB mobilises the Igbo for the actualisation of the defunct Biafra Republic, but the elite describe the agitation as a utopian dream spurred by mass frustration'.

modernisation, and secularisation, and the role of conversion, narrative texts and local theologies in identity construction. In chapter 2, I explore the socio-political, economic and religious background to the revival and its Pentecostal progeny, and show how the crisis generated by colonial legacies, missionary ideologies, decolonisation and conflict created a favourable environment for religious innovation. In chapter 3, I discuss the revival's growth in terms of an economic model of supply and demand, and its relationship of continuity and rupture with existing religious landscapes. Igboland's moment of crisis not only created new religious demands, it contributed to the formation of a dynamic missionary fellowship. At the same time, I reflect upon the moral and social consequences of the revival. In chapters 4 and 5, I examine the provenance and popularity of the Igbo initiated neo-Pentecostal churches and link these to the revival's missionary impulse and the flexibility of Pentecostal spirituality. I attempt to show that the success of the new churches rested partly on their ability to adapt their message and methodology to suit local contexts increasingly affected by global and modernising processes. However, in their haste to respond to consumer demands they modified their message to the detriment of the movement's original vision and values. This had socio-political implications. In chapter 6, I trace the historical development of Igbo neo-Pentecostal socio-political theology and praxis from the revival to the beginning of the new millennium, and reflect on the movement's potential as an agent of social transformation in a pluralistic society. The concluding chapter 7 summarizes the main findings of the research before proceeding to some general conclusions concerning the movement's enduring impact and future prospects.

Acknowledgements

There are people and organisations that deserve thanks for helping to bring this book to publication. I am grateful to Mission Africa and to the Qua Iboe Church of Nigeria who made it possible for me to work in Nigeria. I would like to thank the Spalding Trust, and especially the Whitefield Institute, for helping to fund my doctoral research. My interest in African revival movements and Pentecostalism developed as I interacted with Christians in Nigeria and the UK. I am especially grateful to Ogbu Kalu and Amaechi Nwachukwu, whose idea it was to organise the 'Remembering the Seventies' Conference, which introduced me to so many key figures from the Civil War Revival.

I would like to thank those who have provided hospitality and friendship throughout the research process, and who have been willing to tell their stories and allow me to participate in their church activities, especially the communities of Amazing Love Assembly in Enugu and Redeemed People's Mission in Bukuru, Cyril and Eunice Okorocha, Rufus and Iris Ogbonna, Richard and Aureola Enwezor, Benjamin Ikedinobi, Godwin Nwosu, Akoh Abraham, David Smith, Sid and Jean Garland, and the staff and students of the Theological College of Northern Nigeria. Special thanks to Iliya Kachalla, an invaluable assistant and friend during my six months field research in Jos. I am also grateful to Peter and Margaret Robins, Trevor and Ann Luke, and Udobata Onunwe, for allowing me to stay in their homes during visits to Cambridge, Oxford, and Birmingham respectively. Former Scripture Union travelling secretary Bill Roberts provided me with hospitality on a number of occasions and allowed me access to his private papers which proved a valuable resource. Many others, too numerous to mention, have contributed to the project. Some of their names are mentioned in the text of the book itself. I hope I have captured in this work a little of their vision and experience.

The present study has benefited from interactions with other scholars. Various parts of the original thesis have been presented to seminar groups at the Whitefield Institute and the University of Birmingham, and I am grateful for the helpful comments from fellow research students and staff. In Allan Anderson I had a sympathetic and helpful supervisor to whom I owe a great deal. I would also like to acknowledge Kevin Ward for encouraging me to have my work published and agreeing to write the Foreward.

Finally, I would like to express my gratitude to Tony Gray of Regnum for his editorial advice. Above all, I thank my parents for their support in various ways over the years. This book is dedicated to them in gratitude, and to the glory of God.

Contents

Illustrations and Tables

Illustrations

Tables

Abbreviations

AACC	All Africa Conference of Churches
ACFM	All Christians Fellowship Mission
AFC	Apostolic Faith Church
AG	Assemblies of God
AICs	African Independent Churches
ALA	Amazing Love Assembly
CAN	Christian Association of Nigeria
CAPRO	Calvary Productions (Calvary Ministries)
CCN	Christian Council of Nigeria
CESM	Christian Evangelical Social Movement
CICCU	Cambridge Inter-Collegiate Christian Union
CJC	Church of Jesus Christ
CMF	Christian Missionary Foundation
CMS	Church Missionary Society
COCEN	Congress of Christian Ethics in Nigeria
COCIN	Church of Christ in Nigeria
CPM	Christian Pentecostal Mission
CSN	Catholic Secretariat of Nigeria
CU	Christian Union
ECWA	Evangelical Churches of West Africa
ECU	Evangelical Christian Union
EFAC	Evangelical Fellowship in the Anglican Communion
FCS	Fellowship of Christian Students
FESTAC	Festival of Arts and Culture
FGS	Free Gospel Society
Hour of Deliverance	Hour of Deliverance Ministry
Hour of Freedom	Hour of Freedom Evangelistic Association
ICEJ	International Christian Embassy Jerusalem
IFES	Inter-Varsity Fellowship of Evangelical Students
IMC	International Missionary Council
IMF	International Monetary Fund

IVCU	Ibadan Varsity Christian Union
IVF	Inter-Varsity Fellowship
Jesus the Way	Jesus the Way Mission
JETS	Jos ECWA Theological Seminary
JRA	*Journal of Religion in Africa*
LWM	Living Word Ministries
MVC	Master's Vessel Church
NASB	New American Standard Bible
NDP	Niger Delta Pastorate
NEM	National Evangelical Mission
NEMA	Nigerian Evangelical Missions Association
NEMI	Nigeria Evangelical Missionary Institute
NIFES	Nigerian Fellowship of Evangelical Students
NPC	Neo-Pentecostal Church
NTA	Nigerian Television Association
NYSC	National Youth Service Corps
OAIC	Organisation of African Instituted Churches
OIC	Organisation of Islamic Countries
PFN	Pentecostal Fellowship of Nigeria
Pneuma	*Pneuma: The Journal of the Society for Pentecostal Studies*
RCT	Rational Choice Theory
REPETHEC	Redeemed People's Theological College
Riches of Christ	Riches of Christ Mission
RPM	Redeemed People's Mission
SAP	Structural Adjustment Programme
SCM	Student Christian Movement
SIM	Sudan Interior Mission
SU	Scripture Union
SUM	Sudan United Mission
TCNN	Theological College of Northern Nigeria
TEKAN	Tarayar Ekklesiyoyin Kristi a Nigeria
TREM	The Redeemed Evangelical Mission
UNN	University of Nigeria, Nsukka
UPPB	Ufuma Practical Prayer Band
WATC	World Action Team for Christ
WCC	World Council of Churches

FOREWORD

Kevin Ward

This study of Revival and Pentecostalism in eastern Nigeria is an important contribution both to the history of Christianity in Nigeria and to the growing study of African Neo-Pentecostalism. The modern Pentecostal or charismatic movement is one of the most significant phenomena in the recent history of Christianity in Africa, transforming the ways in which Christianity as a whole relates to traditional African culture and helping to shape sub-Saharan Africa responses to globalisation and modernity. Richard Burgess presents a detailed and convincing account of the rise and significance of modern Pentecostalism in a particular part of Africa – the movement of renewal within the established Christian churches among the Igbo of eastern Nigeria from the 1960s. He identifies the Scripture Union in Igbo secondary schools as the seed-bed for this revival, given poignancy for many of the participants by the experience of suffering during the Biafran civil war and by the energies released in the subsequent reconstruction of Igbo society as part of a reunited Nigeria. Many of the student leaders of this period have gone on to exercise leadership in the burgeoning new pentecostal churches; others have become bishops and leaders in the older churches, such as the influential Anglican Church of Nigeria.

Much scholarship has concentrated on the external factors and inspirations of the Pentecostal explosion in Africa. Burgess' historical analysis helps to show the indigenous dynamic of the movement, particularly highlighting the agency of Igbo Christians from within the well-established Protestant Evangelical tradition. Charismatic forms of piety proved highly attractive to the growing number of young people with a prolonged exposure to education, but who faced an uncertain future in terms of job opportunities and economic security in the fragile new world that replaced the colonial era. The situation, as described by Burgess, has a resonance in other parts of Africa. The character of present-day Protestant Christianity in Uganda and Kenya, for example, traces a similar trajectory, with Scripture and Christian Unions in schools and college performing a comparable role. In both parts of the continent older forms of church life and older forms of Revivalism have been transformed by the charismatic movement. Burgess writes about the developments in eastern Nigeria with an admirable clarity, giving historical depth to the issues. The result is an account which has important implications not only for the understanding of Nigerian Christianity, but of Evangelicalism in Africa more generally.

Kevin Ward
Senior Lecturer in African Religious Studies
University of Leeds
2006

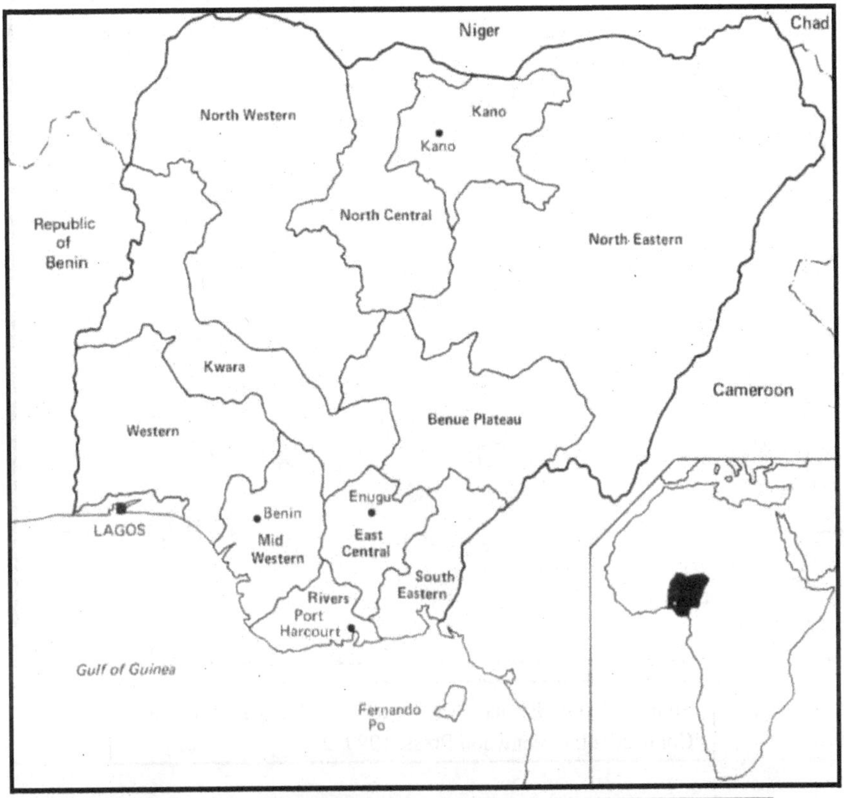

Nigeria: The Twelve States, 1967.

Source: Guy Arnold, *Modern Nigeria*, London: Longman, 1977.

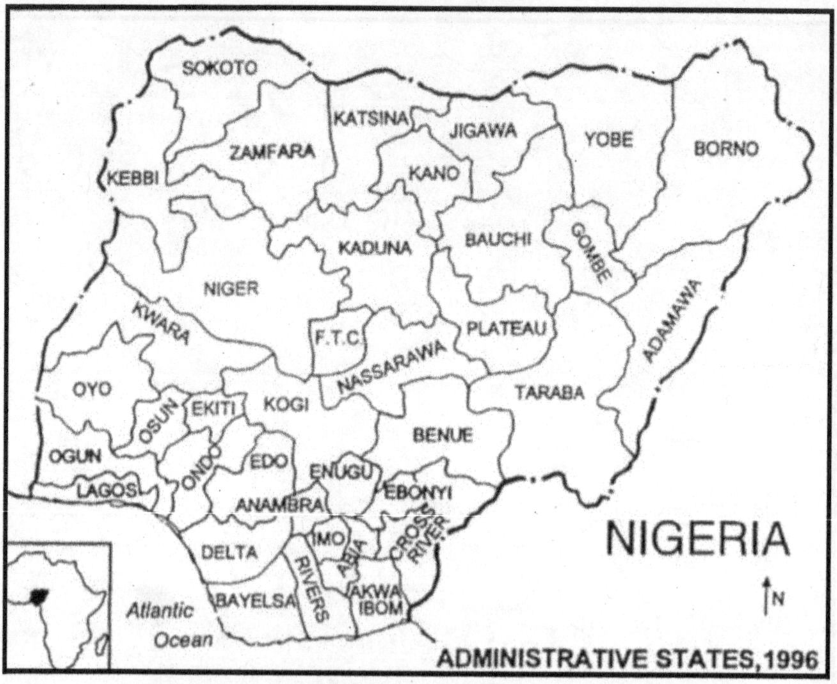

Source: Toyin Falola, *The History of Nigeria*, Westport, Connecticut: Greenwood Press. 1999. 2.

Source: Falola, *History*, 6.

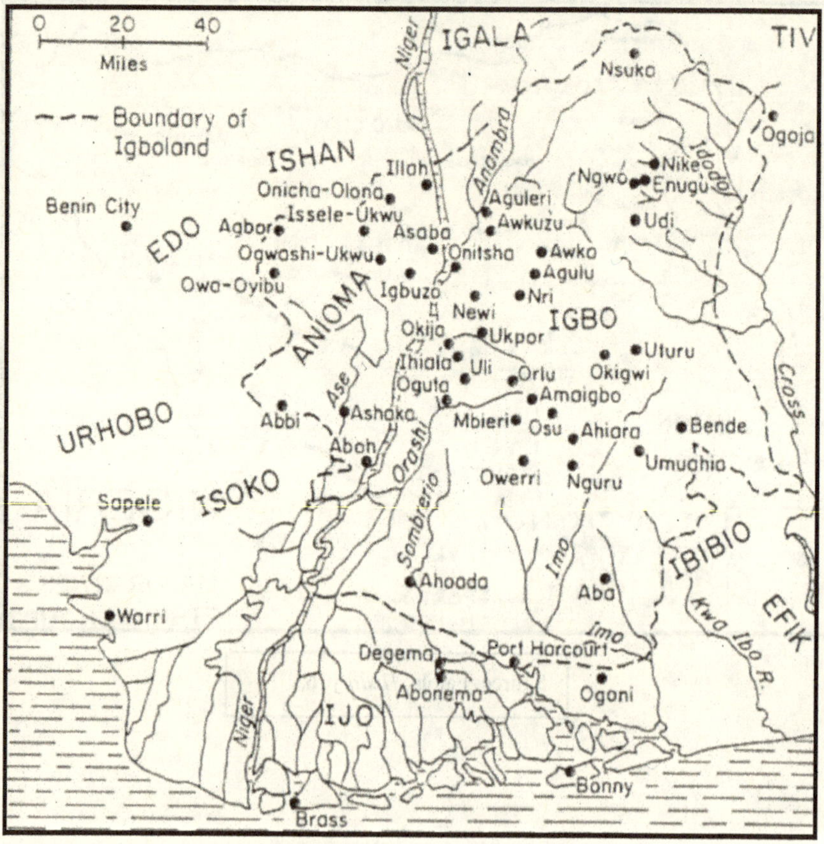

The Igbo People and their Neighbours

Source: Don C. Ohadike, *Anioma. A Social History of the Western Igbo People*, Athens: Ohio University Press, 1994, 14.

Chapter 1

Constructing African Identities

Pentecostalism in all its diversity represents the fastest-growing sector of world Christianity today. Sociologist David Martin describes it as the 'most dramatic development of Christianity' in the twentieth century and Pentecostal theologian Allan Anderson as the 'largest numerical force in world Christianity after the Roman Catholic Church'.[1] So pervasive has been its influence that the subtitle to Harvey Cox's *Fire from Heaven* refers to the 'reshaping of religion' through the 'rise of Pentecostal spirituality'. In less than one hundred years, it has attained a worldwide constituency of nearly half a billion, a growth rate described by Walter Hollenweger, the acknowledged Dean of Pentecostal studies, as unprecedented in the history of global Christianity.[2] If these statistics are to be taken as reliable then Pentecostalism represents a quarter of all Christians. One reason for this, according to Cox, is that it was 'a religion made to travel'.[3]

Pentecostal growth is especially apparent in Africa where a new wave of popular Christianity has swept across the continent since independence, bringing renewal to existing churches and generating new Pentecostal denominations. Indeed, some authorities believe that the global centre of gravity as far as dramatic church growth is concerned has shifted in the 1990s from South Korea to Nigeria, Africa's most populous nation.[4] Since the 1960s, Nigeria has experienced a religious revolution as a result of this Pentecostal impulse, which had its roots in an evangelical revival,

---

[1] David Martin, *Pentecostalism: The World Their Parish*, Oxford: Blackwell, 2002, 1; Allan Anderson, *An Introduction to Pentecostalism*, Cambridge: Cambridge University Press, 2004, 1.

[2] Walter Hollenweger, *Pentecostalism: Origins and Developments Worldwide*, Peabody, MA: Hendrickson, 1997, 1. Recent research suggests that there were over 523 million 'Pentecostal/charismatics' worldwide in 2001. See David B. Barrett and Todd M. Johnson, 'Annual Statistical Table on Global Mission: 2003', *International Bulletin of Missionary Research*, 27.1, 2003, 25. For a discussion, see Anderson, *Pentecostalism*, 10-11.

[3] Harvey Cox, *Fire From Heaven. The Rise of Pentecostal Spirituality and the Reshaping of Religion in the Twenty-First Century*, Reading, Massachusetts: Addison-Wesley, 1995, 102.

[4] See C. Peter Wagner, 'Introduction', in C. Peter Wagner and Joseph Thompson (eds.), *Out of Africa*, Ventura, California: Regal Books, 2004, 9-10.

associated with Scripture Union and the university campuses at the end of the Nigerian civil war (1967-70). It has generated a proliferation of new Pentecostal denominations, which together represent the dominant expression of Nigerian Christianity. Churches bearing names such as Deeper Life Bible Church, Grace of God Mission, and Mountain of Fire and Miracles, now litter the Nigerian religious landscape, especially in urban areas. Deeper Life Bible Church's headquarters congregation in Lagos, for example, had about 150,000 members in 2004, and it has planted more than 6,000 branches across Nigeria.[5] Living Faith Church (also known as Winners' Chapel), founded in 1983 by former architect David Oyedepo, has recently opened the largest church auditorium in the world, the 50,400 seat Faith Tabernacle in Lagos.

As well as spectacular church growth within its own borders, Nigeria is also becoming known as one of the foremost missionary sending nations of the world, exposing Christian communities in the global North to African Pentecostal spirituality. For example, two of the three largest churches in Europe today were planted by Nigerian missionaries. Embassy of God in Ukraine, founded by Sunday Adelaja in 1993, has over 20,000 members in its headquarters church and over two hundred congregations across several nations. Matthew Ashimolowo's Kingsway International Christian Centre in London, started in the 1980s with eleven people, by 2002 had approximately 5,000 members at its headquarters church, as well as several satellite churches. Nigerian-based Pentecostal denominations are also establishing churches across Africa, Europe and the USA. The Redeemed Christian Church of God, with its headquarters in Lagos, has over 6,000 churches in more than fifty nations. Indeed, the largest churches in Kenya, Tanzania, Ghana, Zimbabwe and Jamaica are led by Nigerians. Oyedepo's Winners' Chapel, for example, came to Ghana in 1997, and by 2001 its Accra congregation was attracting about 13,000 to its Sunday worship meeting.[6] All this demonstrates how important it is to study the origins and development of this movement in an era of globalisation. This book explores its progress among the Igbo people of Eastern Nigeria (one of the three main Nigerian ethnic groups) from its origins in the Nigerian civil war to the present.

One of its aims is to reflect on the movement's contribution to the growth of the church and the construction of Nigerian Christian identity.

---

[5] *Ibid.*, 10.

[6] Sunday Adelaja, 'Go to a Land that I will Show you', in Wagner and Thompson (eds.), *Out of Africa*, 37-8; Sola Fola-Alade, 'Missionary to London', in Wagner and Thompson (eds.), *Out of Africa*, 127; Wagner, 'Introduction', 14; Paul Gifford, *Ghana's New Christianity. Pentecostalism in a Globalizing African Economy*, Bloomington & Indianapolis: Indiana University Press, 2004, 56.

Since the 1960s, scholars have drawn attention to the African Christian identity crisis and the need to promote local identities in response to socio-cultural change.[7] This task has become all the more urgent now that Africa has largely rejected the Western value-setting of the Christian faith and Christianity's epicentre has shifted southwards. In theology, the quest for a distinctive African Christian identity was reflected in the publication of *African Theology en Route*, a collection of papers from the Pan-African Conference of Third World Theologians (December 17-23, 1977, Accra, Ghana), which address the African Christian identity crisis by seeking to free African theology from Euro-American influence and integrate it into local societies.[8] In historiography, it was first reflected in a dramatic movement under the influence of nationalist currents away from European missionary history to an African Christian history. History, it was said, had to reinforce the identity of Christian communities. Proponents of this new history called for an approach 'from below' which focused on African responses to the gospel rather than church institutions. The pursuit of a genuinely African Christian identity shifted in the late 1960s to the search for African initiatives. While the overwhelming focus was on the African initiated churches (AICs), there were a number of studies on revival movements within the mainline churches, which explored issues such as local agency, global influences, and the interaction between gospel and culture, all themes I discuss here.[9] The 1980s saw a renewed interest in the history and experience of the mission-founded churches, encouraged by the work of historians Terence Ranger and Andrew Walls. More recently, a shift has occurred from institutions to movements and from the study of 'official' missionary theology to popular Christianity.[10] Ranger describes religious movements as 'widespread and grassroots adherence to religious ideas, symbols and rituals, sometimes brief in duration, sometimes long-

[7] See Andrew F. Walls, 'Africa and Christian Identity', *Mission Focus*, 6.7, 1978; Terence O. Ranger, 'Religion, Development and African Christian Identity', *Neue Zeitschrift fur Missionswissenshcaft*, 42.1, 1986, 44-68.

[8] K. Appiah-Kubi and Sergio Torres (eds.), *African Theology en Route*, Maryknoll: Orbis, 1979, 193.

[9] For example, Brian Stanley, 'The East African Revival: African Initiative within a European Tradition', *The Churchman*, 92.1, 1978, 6-22.

[10] For developments in African Christian Studies, see Adrian Hastings, 'African Christian Studies, 1967-1999: Reflections of an Editor', *JRA*, 30.1, 2000, 30-44; David Maxwell, 'Introduction. Christianity and the African Imagination', in David Maxwell with Ingrid Lawrie (eds.), *Christianity and the African Imagination. Essays in Honour of Adrian Hastings*, Leiden: Brill, 2002, 1-24.

lasting; sometimes lacking and sometimes acquiring formal organizational structures', and includes AICs and revivals within this spectrum.[11]

The growing interest in contemporary African Pentecostalism is a reflection of these trends. Paul Gifford describes it as 'Africa's new Christianity' and 'undoubtedly the salient sector of African Christianity today'.[12] Ogbu Kalu calls it the 'third response' to white cultural dominance over the Church in Africa, the earlier two being 'Ethiopianism' and the Aladura or Zionist churches.[13] Matthews Ojo has examined its origins and developments in Western Nigeria, with its roots in the university campuses and the work of Scripture Union.[14] This study tells the story of the movement among the Igbo people of Eastern Nigeria and reflects on its contribution to the construction of local Christian identity. Igbo revivalists were drawn largely from the mission churches and many chose to remain within their ranks. My study limits itself to the revival itself and the Igbo-founded Pentecostal churches it generated. It reflects on the encounter between a particular brand of Christianity and a local African society, and the process of (re-) conversion that transpired. As such, it explores the nature of revivalist and Pentecostal experience, but does so against the backdrop of local socio-political and economic developments, such as decolonisation and civil war, as well broader processes, such as modernisation and globalisation. In a recent survey of developments in African Christian Studies, the late Adrian Hastings called for further discussion as to how far the current Pentecostal wave differs from the earlier AIC movement, and the possible influence of global networks.[15] My research attempts to respond to this call by examining the relationship of the new churches with earlier local Christian initiatives and with global Pentecostalism.

---

[11] Terence Ranger, 'Religious Movements and Politics in Sub-Saharan Africa', *African Studies Review*, 29.2, June 1986, 1, 32, 37.

[12] Paul Gifford, *African Christianity. Its Public Role*, London: Hurst & Company, 1998, 333, 33.

[13] Ogbu U. Kalu, 'The Third Response: Pentecostalism and the Reconstruction of Christian Experience in Africa, 1970-1995', *Journal of African Christian Thought*, 1.2, 1998, 3.

[14] For example, Matthews A. Ojo, 'The Contextual Significance of the Charismatic Movements in Independent Nigeria', *Africa,* 58.2, 1988, 175-92; Ojo, *The End-Time Army. Charismatic Movements in Modern Nigeria*, Religion in Contemporary Africa Series, Trenton, NJ: African World Press, 2006.

[15] Hastings, 'African Christian Studies', 41-2.

Defining Revival and African Pentecostalism

At this stage, I introduce two important terms that recur throughout the book. In Africa, the term 'revival' has been employed rather loosely to describe prolonged evangelistic campaigns, renewal within mainline denominations and extensive church growth. In the academy, theological and sociological definitions differ over the role played by divine initiative, but beyond that there is a broad consensus. I propose the following working definition:

> A Christian revival is a communal event that assumes an element of decline, out of which believers are called to renewed heights of spiritual vitality, corporate worship and moral probity, issuing in efforts to spread the gospel in and beyond the local community, and resulting in a widespread sense of sorrow for sin, extensive conversion experiences, and altered religious and socio-cultural landscapes.

This definition distances itself from the modern use of the term, popular in Africa, to describe organised evangelistic campaigns. We need to discriminate between what Bebbington refers to as 'spontaneous popular revival, deeply rooted in the community, and meetings carefully designed to promote the work of the gospel'.[16] Because of this, some have preferred the expression 'renewal' when writing about African revival movements.[17] While this makes room for spontaneity, revitalisation and innovation within the Church, it takes insufficient account of the broader effects of the phenomenon in the wider community. This study uses the term 'revival' to describe the movement that began among the Igbos of Eastern Nigeria during the civil war and reached its climax in 1970/'71. It was also the expression generally used by participants to describe what happened, both at the time and retrospectively. Henceforth, I will refer to it as the Civil War Revival.

There has been an ongoing debate about the appropriateness of 'Pentecostalism' as an umbrella term for African movements and churches which stress the experience of the Spirit. Western definitions that focus on historical continuity with the US American Azusa Street Revival or adherence to a doctrine of 'initial evidence' have proved inadequate due to the great variety of movements elsewhere. Here I follow Hollenweger and

---

[16] David Bebbington, *Evangelicalism in Modern Britain. A History from the 1730s to the 1980s*, London: Unwin, 1989, 116.

[17] For example, J. Kwabena Asamoah-Gyadu, *African Charismatics. Current Developments within Independent Indigenous Pentecostalism in Ghana*, Leiden: E. J. Brill, 2005, 32.

Anderson by adopting a more inclusive definition. They use the term 'African Pentecostalism' to describe any African church or movement that stresses the experience of the Spirit and the practice of spiritual gifts.[18] In this sense, it includes older AICs, called 'prophet-healing churches' by Turner,[19] mission-related Pentecostal churches, and newer (post-1970) African-founded Pentecostal churches, fellowships and ministries. Members from each of these broad categories feature in the story of the Civil War Revival.

In Igboland, members of other churches usually refer to 'prophet-healing' AICs as prayer houses (*ụka ekpere*, Igbo), 'prayer-healing', Aladura (Yoruba: 'praying'), 'spiritual', 'white garment' or 'hand-clapping' churches, reflecting their interest in prayer, their stress on the Holy Spirit and belief in lesser spiritual beings, their preference for wearing white robes and their lively worship. I use the term 'prayer house' as this was the most common designation used by my informants, and to distinguish them from the various non-Christian 'spiritualist' groups which draw heavily upon traditional religious categories and popular 'occult' literature imported from abroad. Due to their diversity and dynamic nature, they are difficult to classify with any precision, though various typologies have been proposed which I discuss briefly in chapter 2.

Different terms are used to denote the newer (post-1970) locally generated movements, ministries and churches in Nigeria. In the literature, they are referred to variously as 'charismatic', 'Pentecostal', 'neo-Pentecostal', 'revivalist', 'born-again' and 'Evangelical-Pentecostal'. Members of other churches sometimes refer to those groups which have attained denominational status as 'new generation' churches, to distinguish them from the older mainline churches and AICs. 'Pentecostal' is the common term of self-designation, while 'charismatic' usually refers to renewal movements within the mainline mission churches.[20] Here I use the expression 'neo-Pentecostal' (or the abbreviation 'NPC') to denote the

---

[18] Walter J. Hollenweger, *The Pentecostals*, Minneapolis/London: SCM Press, 1972, 149; Allan H. Anderson, *Zion and Pentecost. The Spirituality and Experience of Pentecostal and Zionist/Apostolic Churches in South Africa*, Pretoria: University of South Africa Press, 2000, 26-7, 35-37.

[19] Harold W. Turner, 'A Typology of Modern African Religious Movements', *Journal of Religion and Religions*, 1.1, 1967, 23.

[20] Those who use the term 'charismatic' to denote these movements do so to distinguish them from the mission-related Pentecostal churches or the earlier wave of AICs. See Matthews A. Ojo, 'Charismatic Movements in Africa', in Christopher Fyfe and Andrew F. Walls (eds.), *Christianity in Africa in the 1990's*, University of Edinburgh: Centre of African Studies, 1996, 92-3; Rosalind I. J. Hackett, 'Charismatic/Pentecostal Appropriation of Media Technologies in Nigeria and Ghana', *JRA*, 28.3, 1998, 259.

Igbo-founded churches, to distinguish them from the mission-related Pentecostal churches. The term 'charismatic fellowship' is used to describe the inter-denominational groups that arose within the ranks of the mainline mission churches during the revival, often around a charismatic individual(s), and formed the basis for the new churches.

Exploring Issues of Cause and Effect

Most of the important questions about the revival are closely connected to explanations for its growth and decline. This study attempts to explain the growth of the revival, and the provenance and popularity of its Pentecostal progeny, by examining local and global influences, exploring the issue of religious motivation, and investigating the nature of revival and neo-Pentecostal experience. Although I am operating principally within the frameworks of history and anthropology rather than theology, my study privileges participant accounts which invariably explain the advent and decline of revival in terms of the descent and withdrawal of the Holy Spirit. The main thesis of this volume, however, is that the success of the revival and its Pentecostal progeny depended upon a balance between supply and demand. The revival itself provided a means for Igbos to resolve their collective identity crisis through their absorption into a dynamic missionary fellowship, whose ideology propelled those touched by the 'Spirit' into the margins of society where they were able to exploit the disorder, dislocation and disruption caused by the forces of modernisation, decolonisation and conflict. The formation of this band of itinerant preachers out of the furnace of the civil war crisis was principally responsible for the spread of the revival. But their efforts were successful because local conditions of socio-political and economic distress created new religious demands as Igbos looked for practical solutions to current dilemmas through the lens of existing religious categories. It was precisely because they bore the brunt of the suffering that Igbo response to the revival during the 1970s was so dramatic compared with their counterparts in Western Nigeria. Here the revival's willingness to take African cosmology seriously was crucial. Part of its success lay in its continuity and discontinuity with existing religious forms. The revival introduced new ideas to the Igbo religious repertoire and new means to obtain old objectives. Nevertheless, its form was influenced by traditional religious aspirations and its roots in mission church spirituality. The revival's Pentecostal progeny also benefited from this missionary impulse and the flexibility of Pentecostal spirituality which enabled participants to adapt their message and methodology to suit local contexts affected by global flows.

This brings me to the second question that has guided my study, the movement's cultural and socio-political significance. As well as exploring issues of causation, I examine the way it altered existing religious, cultural and socio-political landscapes. In doing so, I pay close attention to two processes in African Christian history. On the one hand was a desire to contextualise the gospel by accommodating to existing cultural, religious and social patterns; on the other, a tendency to challenge and resist elements of indigenous culture and religion deemed incompatible with Christianity's core values and beliefs. These processes may intensify during periods of revival. This was the case with the East African Revival which, according to Kevin Ward, was both a 'genuinely African expression of Christianity' and a critique of local cultural values.[21] However, as institutional forces set in, revival movements can lose their counter cultural potential, relax their ethical demands and move towards a state of low tension with their social environment. One of my aims will be to explore the way these processes operated within the revival and Pentecostal communities as the movement developed over time and space. Thus I will examine both the movement's capacity to contextualise the gospel for local consumption and its record as an agent of cultural, social and moral transformation.

The public role of African religious movements has been a subject of recent debate. Some commentators have noted their allegedly conservative political stance or the reluctance of participants to engage in the political process.[22] Pentecostals have been accused of an 'otherworldly' spirituality which withdraws from issues like politics and the struggle for justice. Others refer to the latent elements of political resistance and protest within African Pentecostal movements, expressed in symbolic practices, such as prayer and deliverance, and the creation of 'autonomous space' to contest dominant power monopolies and challenge gerontocratic structures.[23] This study will explore the evolution of the movement's vision and values from its roots in the Civil War Revival to the new millenium, and the way this has influenced the socio-political behaviour of its adherents.

---

[21] Kevin Ward, '"Tukutenderiza Yesu": The Balokole Revival in Uganda', in Z. Nthamburi (ed.), *From Mission to Church: A Handbook of Christianity in East Africa*, Nairobi: Uzima Press, 1999, 135-56.

[22] For example, Gifford, *African Christianity*, 111, 341-42.

[23] Kalu, 'Third Response', 13-14; Rijk van Dijk, 'Pentecostalism, Gerontocratic Rule and Democratization in Malawi: the Changing Position of the Young in Political Culture', in Jeff Haynes (ed.), *Religion, Globalization and Political Culture in the Third World*, New York: St. Martin's Press, 1999, 164-88; Ruth Marshall-Fratani, 'Power in the Name of Jesus: Social Transformation and Pentecostalism in Western Nigeria "Revisited"', in Terence O. Ranger and Olufemi Vaughan (eds.), *Legitimacy and the State in Twentieth-Century Africa*, London: Macmillans, 1993, 21.

Any discussion of the political significance of the Christian movement in Nigeria must include its encounter with Islam. Religious observers, such as Philip Jenkins and Alister McGrath, have identified the Christian/Muslim divide as the critical fault line in tomorrow's world and Nigeria as a nation where this issue is particularly acute.[24] Nigeria today is evenly divided between Christians and Muslims, though estimates of the exact balance vary. The situation is complicated by the geographical distribution of the two faiths. Of the three main ethnic groups, the Northern Hausa-Fulani are predominantly Muslim, the Eastern Igbo are predominantly Christian, and the Western Yoruba are divided between the two faiths. While both religions carry cultural baggage and have global missionary ambitions, Islam has a distinctive political agenda, the imposition of *Shari'a* religious law, which has created considerable regional tensions. Jenkins predicts that Nigeria could either become a Muslim state or it could fracture into several smaller entities depending upon the course of religious conflicts. The 'religious fate of Nigeria', according to Jenkins, 'could be a political factor of immense importance in the new century'.[25] This study will explore the progress of the Igbo initiated neo-Pentecostal movement as it encountered Muslim communities in Nigeria's Northern territories.

Globalisation, Modernisation and Local Identities

Explanations of contemporary Pentecostal expansion in Africa are usually linked to debates on globalisation, modernity and identity. Rijk Van Dijk's work on Malawi is a case in point. Van Dijk describes Pentecostalism as a 'religion of modernity' which draws its appeal in Africa from the ways in which it 'mediates, negotiates and mitigates modernity'. This is reflected in the Pentecostal fascination with modern styles of consumption, new technologies, and 'with achieving a dominant location in the modern sectors of everyday life'.[26] For Van Dijk, Pentecostalism's popularity lies in the opportunities it provides for the restructuring of identity by allowing people to free themselves from social ties and 'sinful' pasts that impede their progress and mobility. He focuses especially on the way the 'born-again identity', shaped by local and global influences, functions as a protest against gerontocracy for young Pentecostals in post-colonial Malawi. The

[24] Philip Jenkins, *The Next Christendom. The Coming of Global Christianity*, Oxford: Oxford University Press, 2002, 163-75; Alister E. McGrath, *The Future of Christianity*, Oxford: Blackwell, 2002, 80-1.

[25] Jenkins, *Next Christendom*, 174-75.

[26] Rijk van Dijk, 'Christian Fundamentalism in Sub-Saharan Africa: The Case of Pentecostalism', Occasional Paper, Centre of African Studies, University of Copenhagen, February 2000, 6.

introduction of Anglo-American Pentecostalism, according to Van Dijk, 'provided the extraneous source for new religious ideas, modes of organisation, dress, style and general identity by which the young can turn away from structures dominated by the elderly'.[27]

The resonance between Pentecostal spirituality and the modern preoccupation with rupture and autonomy is the focus of a number of other studies. Birgit Meyer, in her examination of religious conversion among the Ewe in Ghana, finds parallels between Pentecostal discourse in Ghana, with its call to make a clean break from the past, and modernity's notion of progress and continuous renewal. She argues that Pentecostals have an ambivalent attitude towards modernity. While they aspire to the ideal of the modern autonomous individual, they revisit their pasts through the ritual of deliverance which enables them to 'address the gap between aspirations and actual circumstances' and assert the practical relevance of their traditional roots.[28] Ruth Marshall-Fratani's work on Nigeria focuses on another aspect of the relationship between Pentecostalism and modernity. She refers to the way Pentecostalism, with its 'central theme of personal and social rebirth', creates 'autonomous spaces' of practice which enable participants to challenge 'current power monopolies' and develop 'new opportunities for survival'. This is especially appealing in a context like Nigeria, where the modern state resorts to 'authoritarian methods of social control' and fosters 'relationships of inequality'.[29]

Other studies draw on Bayart's notion of extraversion. Bayart suggests that external connections provide indispensable resources for African governments. Yet this does not imply passive dependence. African governments turn global links to their own advantage by exploiting the 'resources of a dependence which is . . . astutely fabricated as much as predetermined'.[30] Thus much recent writing on Pentecostalism in Africa focuses on the way participants utilise external resources to construct their identities and negotiate global flows to appropriate the 'goods' of

---

[27] Rijk van Dijk, 'Young Born-Again Preachers in Post-Independence Malawi: the Significance of an Extraneous Identity', in Paul Gifford (ed.), *New Dimensions in African Christianity*, Nairobi: AACC, 1992, 59, 77.

[28] Birgit Meyer, '"Make a Complete Break with the Past": Memory and Postcolonial Modernity in Ghanaian Pentecostal Discourse', in Richard Werbner (ed.), *Memory and the Postcolony. African Anthropology and the Critique of Power*, London/New York: Zed Books, 1998, 183, 203.

[29] Marshall, 'Power', 215.

[30] Jean Francois Bayart, *The State of Africa: The Politics of the Belly*, London: Longmans, 1993, 25-6.

modernity for local consumption.[31] More controversial is the so-called 'Americanisation thesis' which interprets contemporary African Pentecostalism as a US American import and a political tool of America's Religious Right.[32]

What these studies have in common is a preoccupation with the issue of identity, which has become a central concern of recent social scientific and historical research.[33] Among social scientists associated with the functionalist school, culture and identity are regarded as fixed and relatively unchanging, with little scope for human initiative and agency in identity construction. Culture and identity are viewed in essentialist terms. Culture - including religion as a cultural phenomenon - is bounded, with individual and collective identities shaped by processes of socialisation. Constructivist approaches, such as symbolic interactionism, have challenged this by suggesting that cultural reality is in a constant state of flux. Individuals and collectivities construct their identity through interaction and personal initiative. Constructivism, therefore, stresses individual agency and choice in identity construction.[34] The weakening of the impact of traditional and inherited conventions due to modernisation and globalisation has led to a shift away from the concept of fixed identities and essentialist notions of culture towards less stable concepts.

The rising concern with identity is partly a reflection of a growing awareness of the way that societies and individuals are affected by global flows. In the globalised setting, the boundaries of autonomous cultures are becoming increasingly subject to interpenetration and perforation. Cultures are becoming 'deterritorialised' through flows of information, images and people, such that individuals and communities are faced with a repertoire of cultural scripts with which to construct their identities. There has been considerable debate over the concept of globalisation both in terms of definition and impact. Early approaches by economists, political scientists and mass communication experts focused on homogeneity. Through the impact of flows of information, people and goods, cultural difference was

---

[31] For example, Gifford, *African Christianity*, 314, 321; Ruth Marshall-Fratani, 'Mediating the Global and Local in Nigerian Pentecostalism', *JRA*, 28.3, 1998, 278-315; Hackett, 'Charismatic/Pentecostal', 258-77.

[32] See Steve Brouwer, Paul Gifford and Susan D. Rose, *Exporting the American Gospel: Global Christian Fundamentalism*, London: Routledge, 1996.

[33] See Karen A. Cerulo, 'Identity Construction: New Issues, New Directions', *Annual Review of Sociology*, 23, 1997, 385; Jeremy Black and Donal M. MacRaid, *Studying History*, New York: Palgrave, 2000, 149.

[34] Anthony Giddens, *Sociology*, 4th ed., Cambridge: Polity, 2001, 30.

supposed to disappear, to be replaced by a uniform global culture.[35] Associated with this was the assumption that globalisation is westernisation and is driven by imperialistic ambitions. A common interpretation of globalisation was that the world was becoming increasingly uniform through technological, economic and cultural flows emanating from the West. However, the more recent entry of anthropologists into the debate has made this one-sided emphasis problematic. Meyer and Geschiere argue that the process of globalisation itself 'appears to lead to a hardening of cultural contrasts or even to engender new oppositions'. They suggest that the homogenising tendencies of globalisation imply continued or even reinforced cultural heterogeneity.[36] An example of this was the cultural revival in Africa during the 1970s associated with FESTAC '77 (Festival of Arts and Culture), an event designed to promote African cultural identity in a global age. The consensus among scholars is that globalisation implies an intensification of worldwide social relations such that societies and cultures have become closer together, resulting in a compression of time and space, and stimulating processes of homogenisation and differentiation.

The open-ended flows of information, people, images and commodities associated with globalisation have several consequences for identity construction, including religious identity. Firstly, different parts of the world are increasingly drawn into a global system so that local happenings are shaped by events occurring elsewhere. We see this in the way that fluctuations in the price of oil in the Middle East influence the global economy, and the political repercussions of the terrorist attacks on the New York twin towers, which sparked off the war against terror and contributed to the fall of dictatorial regimes in Afghanistan and Iraq. Another example is the recent violence against Christians in the Northern Nigerian cities of Maiduguri, Katsina and Bauchi perpetrated by Muslims reacting against the cartoons of the Prophet Muhammed in the Danish media.[37] Secondly, globalisation creates global awareness, a process that has accelerated under the influence of the technological revolution and the increasing accessibility of electronic media (especially satellite television and the internet). Related to this is the way that people with a global outlook look to sources other than the nation-state to construct their identity, be they ethnicity, colour, local community, global ideologies or religion. Within the Nigerian

---

[35] Birgit Meyer and Peter Geschiere, 'Globalization and Identity: Dialectics of Flow and Closure. Introduction', in Birgit Meyer and Peter Geschiere (eds.), *Globalization and Identity. Dialectics of Flow and Closure*, Oxford: Blackwell, 1999, 1-15.

[36] Meyer and Geschiere, 'Globalization and Identity', 2.

[37] During the Maiduguri crisis, Muslims destroyed 53 church premises, including large buildings belonging to Living Faith and Deeper Life Bible Church. There was also extensive loss of life.

context, this has been exacerbated by the failure of nationalism, following colonialism, to provide a stable niche for identity construction, resulting in what Marshall-Fratani refers to as an 'explosion' of multiple identities. Those identities shaped by transnational movements, such as Pentecostalism and Islam, pose a threat to national unity by challenging the state's monopoly of public space.[38] Finally, the complex interaction between globalising and localising tendencies (so-called 'glocalisation') can produce new cultural forms through a process of hybridisation or precipitate resistance resulting in the strengthening of local identities. Individuals within so-called 'receiving' cultures are not passive but active agents, making use of globalising forces for their own purposes and blending disparate cultural forms with their own traditions, resulting in 'hybrid' or 'creole' cultures.[39] This book will explore the implications of this for the Igbo people as they responded to global flows through Scripture Union, global Pentecostalism and Western economic capitalism.

Other consequences of globalisation for African identity construction are linked to its role as a carrier of modernity and modernisation. However, modernity is experienced differently in different contexts, such that there are multiple modernities. What has to be explored, as Meyer has argued, is how people dealt and still deal locally with 'globalising' and 'modernising' forces.[40] Various features of modernity and modernisation have flowed into Africa through global processes and have contributed to the African identity crisis. Firstly, the imposition of Western civilisation, education and culture associated with colonialists and missionaries has acted as an agent of secularisation and disenchantment. Yet the secularising influence of Western modernity has provoked a search for local expressions of Christianity which resonate more closely with indigenous worldviews. Until recently, secularisation theory dominated discussions about the relationship between religion and modernity worldwide. But contemporary global religious resurgence has prompted some observers to challenge it. So-called sacralisation theory focuses attention on religion gaining in strength in modern times. Thus Peter Berger, an early advocate of secularisation theory, now believes that while modernisation has had some secularising effects, it has also triggered 'powerful movements of counter-secularisation', particularly in Asia, sub-Saharan Africa and Latin

---

[38] Marshall-Fratani, 'Global', 281-82.

[39] Hannerz coined the term 'creolization' to refer to those processes in which cultural meanings and forms are shaped by the interaction between central and peripheral societies. Ulf Hannerz, *Cultural Complexity. Studies in the Social Organization of Meaning*, New York: Columbia University Press, 1992, 39.

[40] Birgit Meyer, *Translating the Devil. Religions and Modernity among the Ewe in Ghana*, Edinburgh: Edinburgh University Press, 1999, xxii.

America.[41] The Civil War Revival was one of a succession of such initiatives in Nigeria which helped to counter the secularising forces of modernity.

Individualism is a second feature of modernity exported to Africa through global processes. Friedman describes the modern individual as a 'miniature society unto himself,' whose sense of identity is disembodied from social relations. The separation of the subject from any fixed identity follows from this, resulting in an acute sense of alienation as the self is released from the constraints of extended kin and local community.[42] Various features of African revival movements suggest the influence of Western individualism, such as the stress on personal conversion, the quest for individual prosperity, the focus on the nuclear family and the rejection of traditional authorities. Yet the idea that globalisation and modernisation represent an onslaught on an otherwise African communal identity must be qualified. In the Igbo context, communalism and individualism were both important aspects of traditional society.[43]

Moral relativism is a third feature of modernity closely linked to individualism and the autonomy of the self. Modernising processes through global flows have contributed to a breakdown in morality in Africa by weakening traditional social restraints and promoting individual freedom. Globalisation has also exposed African societies to modern consumer culture through their incorporation into global economic processes. Meyer refers to the way early African Christian identity was influenced by the consumption of Western commodities, associated with colonialism and modernisation.[44] More recently, African Pentecostals have promoted economic individualism and an ethic of consumerism through their advocacy of prosperity teaching. For many, this has become a welcome addition to the repertoire of scripts available for local identity construction and resonates with the traditional correlation between wealth and status acquisition.

---

[41] Peter L. Berger, 'The Desecularization of the World: A Global Overview', in Peter L. Berger (ed.), *The Desecularization of the World. Resurgent Religion and World Politics, Washington: Ethics and Public Policy Center*, Grand Rapids, MI: Eerdmans, 1999, 3, 8.

[42] Jonathan Friedman, *Cultural Identity and Global Processes*, London: Sage, 1994, 194, 219.

[43] Cyril C. Okorocha, 'Religious Conversion in Africa: its Missiological Implications', *Mission Studies*, 9.2, 1992, 169; Victor C. Uchendu, *The Igbo of Southeast Nigeria,* New York: Holt, Rinehart and Winston, 1965, 34, 19.

[44] Birgit Meyer, 'Commodities and the Power of Prayer: Pentecostalist Attitudes Towards Consumption in Contemporary Ghana', in Meyer and Geschiere (eds.), *Globalization and Identity*, 152.

Globalisation contributed towards the Igbo crisis and stimulated a search for new forms of identity. The Civil War Revival and its Pentecostal progeny became a rich resource for reinforcing local identities against the corrosive impact of 'globalising' and 'modernising' forces. One of the intentions of this study is to show the way participants engaged in a bargaining process of accommodation and resistance. They embraced modern concerns for progress, socio-economic mobility and the use of modern technologies, but resisted secularisation, moral relativism and, at least in the movement's early stages, modern consumer culture.

Narratives of Conversion, Oral Histories and Local Theologies

The success of the Civil War Revival and its Pentecostal progeny depended partly upon their ability to trigger conversions. Current debates on religious conversion in Africa, particularly among social scientists, are closely linked to discussions about modernisation and identity. Here we return to Birgit Meyer's work on religious conversion in Ghana and the parallels she finds between the Pentecostal conception of conversion in terms of a 'rupture with the past' and the ideal of the modern autonomous individual. In Meyer's view, conversion to Pentecostalism is a kind of conversion to modernity, insofar as it assists believers to become progressive individuals by freeing themselves from social ties and 'traditions' associated with their pasts. The 'new identity of the Born-Again Christian', according to Meyer, 'emphasises not social ties but, rather, the independent, modern individual who does not need to find positive roots in "the past" in order to be guided on the way towards the future'.[45]

The debate on African conversion was initiated by Robin Horton, who, in his seminal 1971 article, argued that the response of traditional societies emerging into the wider world is for less attention to be paid to the lower tier of lesser spirits and more to the upper tier occupied by the Supreme Being. He put forward the controversial thesis that even if confronted with modernity without the presence of Islam or Christianity, traditional religions had the capacity to develop a monotheistic cosmology.[46] For all its limitations, Horton's intellectualist theory does draw attention to the way that changes in socio-cultural context can precipitate religious change and modernising influences can provide significant motivation for conversion. What remains problematic is Horton's assertion that 'lesser gods' lose their importance at the expense of the Supreme Being as traditional societies are

[45] Meyer, 'Break with the Past', 182-84, 202.

[46] Robin Horton, 'African Conversion', *Africa,* 41.2, 1971, 91-112; Robin Horton, 'On the Rationality of Conversion', Part 1, *Africa,* 45.3, 1975, 219-35.

exposed to an expanding universe. Meyer has shown, in contrast to Horton, that globalising and modernising forces may even stimulate an emphasis on the lower tier of lesser spirits. In the case of the Ewe in Ghana, by diabolising local gods and witchcraft Christians confirmed their existence and incorporated them into Christian belief as demons.[47] By the end of our study, we will be in a better position to assess whether the same was true of Igbo Christians as they encountered global flows through Scripture Union and Euro-American Pentecostalism.

One of the elements of evangelical culture exported to Africa was an emphasis on personal conversion. This was the defining feature of Scripture Union spirituality and one of the central components of global Pentecostalism. Crucial to the success of the Civil War Revival and its Pentecostal progeny was the idiom of new birth, which enabled Igbos to construct new identities for themselves and negotiate modernity's call to make a clean break with individual and collective pasts. Participants reinforced these new identities by composing and retelling their personal stories of conversion, and relating them to the grand narrative of the Bible.

The role of texts and narratives in identity construction is among the current interests of Africanist historians and social scientists.[48] This study makes narrative (written and oral) central to how it deals with the past. One of its aims is to tell the story of the Civil War Revival and its Pentecostal progeny from a participant point of view. This will involve relating local narratives of Christian conversion to the broader narratives of decolonisation, modernisation and globalisation. Secondly, it recognises how human subjects construct identities through the stories they listen to and the stories they tell. In her work on Nigerian Pentecostalism, Marshall-Fratani refers to the way that 'new identities are realised through narrative, whether this be the sacred text, authoritative discourses such as sermons, prophecies, or narrative of a more immediate, informal and personal nature, such as testimonies, prayers and songs'.[49] In the case of Igbo revivalists, identity reconstruction began when they were 'born-again' through their encounter with the gospel story and the testimonies of their peers. It developed as they read their Bibles, identified themselves with the missionary community of the early Church, and began to share their own stories of conversion and religious encounter. Finally, this study relies chiefly on narrative source material. Paul Jenkins stresses the need to 'go

---

[47] Meyer, *Translating the Devil*, xxiii.

[48] Maxwell, 'African Imagination', 3. For a recent treatment of narrative in the exploration of religious encounter in Nigeria, see J. D. Y. Peel, *Religious Encounter and the Making of the Yoruba*, Bloomington & Indianapolis: Indiana University Press, 2000.

[49] Marshall-Fratani, 'Global', 289.

to the people', rather than depend upon one-sided missionary accounts.[50] The only way to gain access to the stories of faith is by getting people to share their testimonies.

Yet evaluating conversion experiences on the basis of personal narratives is not straightforward. Converts are motivated by a wide variety of factors which change over time. As Peel notes, the interplay of motivations that produce conversion can only be apprehended through individual case histories. Peel further points out the difficulty of assessing the interiority of the experience, when there is little evidence about the inner states of the individuals concerned.[51] I was fortunate to have access to a relatively large number of oral and written accounts produced by the converts themselves, sometimes close to the time of their conversion experience. In these, they present themselves as both active and passive agents. The problem arises of how to access motives for conversion from retrospective accounts, inevitably influenced by the expectations and discourses of the group into which the person is converted. Motives are vulnerable to reformulation and redefinition through interaction over time. James Beckford argues from a sociological perspective that actors self-reported accounts of religious conversion cannot be taken as objective reports of experience, but are the creation of the convert and combine 'personal experience with the expectations, theology, and symbolism of the group which the person wants to join'.[52] Despite this caveat, I proceed on the assumption that conversion narratives, while vulnerable to reformulation and coloured by the group's 'universe of discourse', are valuable sources for evaluating religious change.

This study attempts to explore the symbolic dimension of religious belief and the way people from a different culture interpret and attach meaning to past religious experiences. Consequently, it privileges participant accounts by allowing informants to tell their stories in their own words and uses oral histories to gain access to the past.[53] This approach is particularly helpful for exploring the personal and private dimensions of religious belief, and the inner life of a movement, rather than to extract facts. However, in Africa oral sources are also important for constructing history as they are often the only ones available. Furthermore, oral history provides access to

---

[50] Paul Jenkins, 'The Roots of African Church History: Some Polemic Thoughts', *International Bulletin of Missionary Research*, 10, April 1985, 68-70.

[51] Peel, *Religious Encounter*, 226, 216.

[52] James Beckford, 'Accounting for Conversion', *British Journal of Sociology*, 19.2, June 1978, 149.

[53] For the use of oral history to examine the religious beliefs of historical actors, see Sarah Williams, 'The Problem of Belief: The Place of Oral History in the Study of Popular Religion', *Oral History*, Autumn 1996, 27-34.

'hidden histories', the 'stories of faith' often ignored by socio-religious commentators. This can help to counteract the bias that is often present in written sources and to challenge so-called 'official' histories. However, there are problems associated with the use of oral histories, related to the personal bias of interviewer and respondents, and the unreliability of memory.[54] Yet documentary sources are no less susceptible to bias and selectivity, and memory is more reliable than is often acknowledged. It is usually the most recent memories that are lost first, while early memories remain clear. I was surprised at the accuracy of my informants' memory of events that took place thirty years previously. I put this down to the depth and intensity of their involvement in what happened. Yet to counter these potential problems, I have augmented oral sources with a variety of written sources discovered during the research process. Discrepancies did occur between different testimonies, and between oral and written accounts. Sometimes this was a question of memory, but it was also due to differing interpretations of the past. Protagonists tended to present themselves as central figures in the movement and to marginalize others. An example occurred when I tried to interview a rather controversial Pentecostal figure. An Anglican leader, a former revivalist himself, advised me against this because in his opinion this man was only a peripheral figure. When we eventually met, I discovered he had an important story to tell. Of course, he too was probably distorting the past in his favour. But by viewing the past through multiple lenses one is able to move closer to a holistic version of what happened.[55]

Another way that African Christians have reconstructed and reinforced their identities in response to globalisation is through the production of local theologies. This was one of the recommendations of a recent conference of African ecumenical theologians, which encouraged churches to promote local identities in response to globalisation by developing 'local theologies, christologies, pneumatologies, and ecclesiologies'.[56] This study necessarily deals with aspects of theology as they impinge upon identity construction, patterns of growth and social influence. Post-colonial attempts to develop African theology have followed two broad routes. The first - African Christian theology - is concerned with cultural identity and

---

[54] For a discussion of problems associated with the use of oral history, see Alistair Thomson, Michael Frisch, Paula Hamilton, 'The Memory and History Debates: Some International Perspectives', *Oral History,* Autumn 1994, 33-43.

[55] The geographical development of the movement was also a factor. As we see later, the revival had several centres, and participants were often unaware of what was happening in other localities.

[56] AACC/CIRCLE/CATI/EATWOT/OAIC Joint Theological Conference, Mbagathi, Nairobi, 14-18 August 2000: 'The Church Making a Difference in the 21st Century', Resolution 12.

liberation from European cultural domination. Early African writers, mostly Western trained, engaged in a dispute with Western theology over the role of Africa's pre-Christian heritage and the foreignness of mission Christianity. At the heart of their method was the issue of identity as they sought to explore the continuities between African primal religions and Christianity. The second approach - Liberation theology - is concerned with socio-political and economic injustices, and concentrates on liberation from class domination and neo-colonialism through social change and praxis.[57] However, as Maxwell correctly observes, this Africanisation 'from above' often turns out to be as externally imposed as the early missionary enterprises themselves.[58] It reflects a tendency for African theologians to neglect the actual operation of the churches at the grassroots, and to deny any ontological reality to the old powers. But there is an alternative channel of Africanisation, one that emerges 'from below'. Increasingly, scholars are paying closer attention to 'actual life' theologies, those emerging from the experiences of local African Christian communities as they reflect upon the Scriptures and their own context.[59] Often buried in sermons, songs, prayers, testimonies and popular literature, these emerge as local churches seek to live out their faith.

As local Christian communities, AICs are now recognised as an important source for African theological reflection. Theirs is an enacted theology, in contrast to the more formalised written theology of the European mission churches. Recent attention has focused on contemporary African Pentecostalism as a form of Africanisation 'from below' with potential for identity construction.[60] This study adds to the repertoire of local theologies emerging from the African continent and pays close attention to the way ordinary Africans read their Bibles. In response to an ongoing context of crisis, the Civil War Revival generated an evolving theology 'from below' which contributed to its popularity. This functioned as an ideological construct which influenced the way participants interpreted events around them and motivated their actions. It helped them adapt to changing socio-political and economic realities, and refashion their identity in terms of a missionary community.

---

[57] Josiah Young III, *African Theology. A Critical Analysis and Annotated Bibliography*, Westport, Connecticut: Greenwood Press, 1993, 13-33.

[58] David Maxwell, *Christians and Chiefs in Zimbabwe. A Social History of the Hwesa People c.1870s-1990s*, Edinburgh: Edinburgh University Press, 1999, 4.

[59] This is a term coined by Kwame Bediako, 'Types of African Theology', in Fyfe and Walls (eds.), *Christianity in Africa*, 63.

[60] See Meyer, *Translating the Devil*, 134-35; Martin, *Pentecostalism*, 142.

Method

Most of the material for this study was collected during two periods of fieldwork in Nigeria. From April to June 1999, I was based in the city of Enugu where I participated in a conference, entitled 'Remembering the Seventies', jointly organised by Professor Ogbu Kalu (formerly of the University of Nigeria, Nsukka), Pentecostal pastor Amaechi Nwachukwu, and myself. Subsequently, I spent seven months (July 2001-January 2002) in the city of Jos as a part-time lecturer at the Theological College of Northern Nigeria (TCNN).[61] During both visits, I was able to interact with former revivalists and neo-Pentecostals. In March 2005, I returned to Jos as a full-time lecturer at TCNN. This has enabled me to engage in a variety of Pentecostal activities. Perhaps the most rewarding aspect from my point of view has been my regular participation in the life of a local branch of Redeemed People's Mission, one of the denominations with roots in the Civil War Revival.

My status as a European outsider presented potential problems related to gaining entry into the field and understanding the movement from a participant point of view. In this respect I benefited from methods drawn from two disciplines: the phenomenology of religion and anthropology. As a method employed in the study of religion, phenomenology is linked to the use empathy and *epoche* (suspension of belief) in an attempt to enter into the experiences and intentions of participants and elicit the meanings they attach to religious acts. I have followed Harold Turner's five principles for gaining an 'inside' view of a particular religious movement, employed in his study of the Church of the Lord (Aladura) in Nigeria during the 1960s: sympathy, participation, partnership (establishment of a joint enterprise), openness and listening.[62] Turner refers to the cultivation of friendship as 'the only door to an understanding of the inner reality of an African religious movement', and the way that this makes the research process to some extent 'a joint enterprise wherein both parties gain a deeper and a clear comprehension'.[63] This approach was particularly helpful as I sought to gain access to the research field. The Remembering the Seventies Conference enabled participants to share their memories in a group context.

---

[61] As we will see in chapter 4, from the early 1970s Igbo revivalists ventured beyond the borders of Igboland to urban areas in the North, preaching the gospel and planting churches. This marked a new phase in the movement's development, and Jos subsequently became an important centre of Igbo neo-Pentecostal activity.

[62] Harold W. Turner, *Religious Innovation in Africa. Collected Essays on New Religious Movements*, Boston, Mass.: G. K. Hall & Co., 1979, 24.

[63] *Ibid.*, 39.

From my point of view, it enabled me to establish relationships of partnership with potential informants and led to further opportunities to interview them on an individual basis. By first listening to them in this context I was able, I think, to gain their trust, and they were able to relate to me as sympathetic outsider. During this initial period of field research, I also stayed with the senior pastor of a large neo-Pentecostal church and attended their meetings, which were frequent. This too helped me to establish a relationship of partnership and friendship, which facilitated my entry into the field.

As local histories and theologies in Africa are rarely written down in a systematic fashion and are often expressed orally in sermons, songs, prayers and testimonies, I used methods drawn from ethnography to understand the perspectives, beliefs and cultural contexts of the people under study. Ethnography is usually associated with anthropology and sociology, but in recent years has become an acceptable method in historical research. My examination of the Civil War Revival and its Pentecostal progeny led to the production of a large number of oral texts, as well as the discovery of a variety of written materials. These are read as 'cultural texts' to illuminate the worldview and cultural traits of the historical actors. To ensure that the voices of the participants are adequately represented, I quote extensively from both oral and written texts. Participant observation is the primary ethnographical method of research. I adopted this approach in my study of Pentecostal churches linked to the revival. My membership of a similar faith community, albeit in the U.K., made it easier for me to become an active participant rather than a detached observer, and this helped me to experience the 'meanings and interactions of people from the role of an insider'.[64]

The methodological agnosticism (or neutrality) associated with the phenomenological method can encourage the assumption that observations are objective. I agree with Van Dijk and Pels that ethnographic dialogue involves 'power relationships' that condition and inhibit it.[65] The imbalance of power can hinder effective communication. For example, respondents may give answers they think the interviewer wants to hear. It can also generate bias as indifference to one's own beliefs during research is difficult to sustain. Jenkins refers to centres and peripheries in writing history in an African context, where the academic world is the 'centre' possessing power and influence through its relationship to publication and

[64] Danny L. Jorgansen, *Participant Observation: A Methodology for Human Studies*, London: Sage, 1989, 21.

[65] Rijk van Dijk and Peter Pels, 'Contested Authorities and the Politics of Perception: Deconstructing the Study of Religion in Africa', in Richard Werbner and Terence O. Ranger (eds.), *Postcolonial Identities in Africa*, London: Zed Books, 1996, 245.

teaching, and the local Christian community is the 'periphery'.[66] Despite the desire to enter into a partnership of dialogue with the subjects of my research and allow participants to speak for themselves, I recognise that my role as an academic outsider, with control over the research process and the production of the text, makes me the dominant partner. Bourdillon advises researchers to establish relationships that allow conversations between equals, rather than conversations controlled by the observer.[67] In this respect, I found it helpful to share my own beliefs with my informants and express a willingness to be challenged. This seems to run contrary to the phenomenological ideal of maintaining *epoche*. The value of the phenomenological method from my point of view lay in its instructions to listen rather than its prescription to suspend judgement. Gifford points out that attitudes of cultural superiority underlying much previous research, due to the link between social sciences and colonialism, have made Africanists sometimes reluctant to criticise the phenomena they study.[68] Following Gifford, this study attempts to describe the Civil War Revival and its Pentecostal progeny but also to judge their adequacy.

Oral sources consisted of four groups: expatriate missionaries, former revivalists who maintained their mission church affiliation, Pentecostal leaders and members, and mainline church leaders with no direct link to the revival. The majority of informants were former revivalists who became neo-Pentecostal pioneers. During fieldwork, I spoke with a large number of people using a combination of group discussions, individual interviews and informal conversations. During the Remembering the Seventies Conference, we invited participants to speak on a variety of topics related to the revival, and most talks were followed by group discussion. As well as being an efficient method for gathering information, it presented different perspectives on the past. In a group context, moreover, memories were triggered, facts verified and views challenged. As anticipated, this led to further opportunities to interview former revivalists and neo-Pentecostal pioneers on an individual basis. Where possible I used a narrative approach that allowed respondents to tell their stories with minimal intervention. My aim was to promote free-flowing conversations, in keeping with traditional Igbo methods for extracting information.[69] However, because I also wanted

---

[66] Jenkins, 'Roots', 68.

[67] M. F. C. Bourdillon, 'Anthropological Approaches to the Study of African Religion', in Jan Platvoet, James Cox and Jacob Olupona (eds.), *The Study of Religions in Africa, Past, Present and Prospects. Proceedings of the Regional Conference of the International Association for the History of Religions, Harare, 1992*, Zimbabwe, Cambridge: Roots and Branches, 1996, 140.

[68] Gifford, *African Christianity*, 53.

[69] Cyril C. Okorocha, *The Meaning of Religious Conversion in Africa. The Case of the Igbo of Nigeria*, Aldershot: Avebury, 1987, 285.

to extract information related to specific issues identified, I used a flexible interview schedule to maintain an element of control over the interview process. Because most informants were comfortable in English, I was able to conduct all interviews without an interpreter. These were normally tape recorded with the consent of the informants. After listening to the recordings, I then transcribed those relevant to the project.

To explore the historical and theological development of the neo-Pentecostal churches, I used a case study approach based on participant observation, interviews, documentary research and survey questionnaires. To gain an insight into the movement as a whole, with its different theological emphases and geographical centres, I visited as many churches as possible. My selection of churches depended largely upon access in the field. I only chose those that had direct links to the revival and reflected its different centres. I interviewed founders and leaders from twenty-six neo-Pentecostal denominations (all founded by former Igbo revivalists), attended meetings in twelve, and carried out case studies on eight with headquarters in seven different cities. Congregational sizes varied from several thousand in the cities to under fifty in the townships and villages. Ideally, I hoped to select members based on age, role in society and church, and gender, but this was often not possible. Most interviews and informal communications were with male neo-Pentecostal church leaders rather than lay members due to limitations of time and accessibility. A danger was that my study could end up as an analysis of the faith of the clerical élite. To counter this I visited churches as a participant observer and carried out more in-depth studies of three denominations in Jos using a questionnaire survey to gain access to membership at the grass-roots. One hundred and sixty-seven respondents from five separate congregations completed questionnaires, which were distributed equally between the Men's Fellowship, Women's Fellowship and Youth Fellowship. Due to time restraints and logistical problems, not all were returned and so sample sizes were small. Moreover, members were often reluctant to criticise their churches or their leaders. However, a general pattern did emerge which I used to supplement other data.

Interviews and surveys were not used in isolation. Historian Frans Verstraelen insists that African Christian historiography requires a methodology that combines the use of oral and written sources.[70] During research, I employed data triangulation to validate or challenge descriptions given through a process of cross-verification. Oral histories and life stories were used in conjunction with primary and secondary written sources. These included popular revival accounts, private correspondence,

---

[70] Frans J. Verstraelen, 'History of Christianity in Africa in the Context of African History – Four Recent Contributions Compared', *Exchange. Journal of Missiological and Ecumenical Research*, 31.2, April 2002, 175.

missionary reports, locally produced church documents and postgraduate theses written by Igbo scholars (housed in the library of the University of Nigeria, Nsukka).[71] Unfortunately, the havoc wreaked by the civil war has meant that relatively few written documents related to the revival have survived in Eastern Nigeria. However, I had access to a collection of private papers owned by the British Scripture Union travelling secretary Bill Roberts. Roberts was based in Biafra during the civil war, but left in 1969 due to illness and was unable to return. His collection includes conversion testimonies and letters written by Igbo revivalists, personal prayer letters composed for a British audience, and minutes of Scripture Union Nigeria committee meetings. Church documents collected during fieldwork included membership manuals, Bible study materials, magazines and newspapers, minutes of church meetings, and religious tracts and books produced by the movement's leaders. These proved a valuable resource to use alongside oral sources. All research material is used qualitatively and quantitatively in the text to arrive at 'tendencies and emphases' that reflect the general tenor of the movement.

I encountered some practical difficulties during my research. Repeated illness hindered my movements during my first period of fieldwork. Sometimes access to sources was restricted due to the reluctance of members and subordinate ministers to release information about their churches until I had met with the Founder or General Overseer. On occasions, people were understandably suspicious of a white outsider. It helped if my first contact with a church was through attendance at one of their meetings, though this was not always possible. The Jos religious riots in September 2001 posed a more serious difficulty. For ten days, we were confined to the college compound where I was working, and for weeks afterwards, there was considerable tension in the region. However, it did give me firsthand experience of how a crisis can affect a community and it was interesting how often conversations during that time dwelt on the Biafran conflict of thirty years previously.

[71] Popular accounts of the revival include: Bolton, *Glory*; Nnaji Godwin Chukwuka, *Looking Beyond the Night*, Enugu: SNAAP Press, 1997; W. B. Roberts, *Life and Death among the Ibos*, London: Scripture Union, 1970.

Chapter 2

The Nigerian Context: Sketching the Landscapes

> Iboland's confrontation with an alien culture, its conquest, and the experience of alien rule, created a spiritual and intellectual crisis - a phase of that history of thought in Africa which still awaits its historian. The missionary presence - and the success of British arms, with which they were inevitably associated - challenged the inherited certainties of traditional religion. . . . Angst and religious uncertainties were not necessarily resolved by adherence to a Christian denomination. Many concluded that in a time of change it was safest to keep to the traditions of the past. . . . The most common solution was perhaps that of eclecticism - a personal synthesis of elements of the old and new (Elizabeth Isichei).[1]

By the 1960s, most Igbos identified themselves as Christians.[2] Why did so many abandon their traditional religious heritage and embrace Christianity during the colonial era? What was the nature of this encounter, and what was the depth of Igbo conversion prior to the civil war? The answers to these questions, the focus of this chapter, will help us understand Igbo responses to the Civil War Revival and the subsequent popularity of neo-Pentecostal spirituality. Igboland 'confrontation with an alien culture', as pointed out by Isichei, created a spiritual and intellectual crisis, which facilitated the introduction of Christianity.

We begin by defining the contours of Igbo ethnic identity. The Igbo are one of the three major ethnic groups in present-day Nigeria and occupy a landmass of approximately 15,800 square miles, situated in the southeast. They have common boundaries with the Igala and Idoma to the north, the

---

[1] Elizabeth Isichei, *The Ibo People and the Europeans. The Genesis of a relationship - to 1906*, London: Faber and Faber, 1973, 180-81.

[2] Elizabeth Isichei, 'Seven Varieties of Ambiguity: Some Patterns of Igbo Response to Christian Missions', *JRA*, 3, 1970, 212.

Ijaw and Ogoni to the south, the Ibibio to the east, and the Bini and Warri to the west. Prior to independence, the writing of Igbo pre-colonial history was a neglected field compared to the state of research and knowledge of the Yoruba and Hausa-Fulani. Early studies were largely undertaken by British colonial scholars and missionaries. However, since the ending of the civil war, an increasing number of Igbo historians and anthropologists, influenced by nationalist currents, have become interested in their own cultural history. One of the impulses behind this is a desire to reinforce Igbo collective identity by showing that Igboland had a civilisation long before contact with Europeans. Yet the issue of Igbo origins and early history remains an area of much speculation, partly due to the lack of oral tradition and written records.[3] One of the problems, as Isichei points out, is that Igboland's decentralized and democratic political culture was not conducive to the preservation of knowledge about the past.[4] Yet drawing upon the available evidence (archaeological, linguistic, oral tradition and written observation), Isichei concludes that while the first human inhabitants probably came from areas further north, people have lived in Igboland for at least 5,000 years. This is supported by the exceptionally high population density, which suggests a long period of continuous occupation, and the fact that as an agricultural people they were tied to their land by strong traditions and taboos. The Igbo began to diverge from other related peoples belonging to the Kwa language group, such as Edo, Yoruba and Igala, perhaps 4,000 years ago.[5] However, oral traditions also suggest a degree of geographical mobility due to population pressures and land shortages, and later due to the slave trade. This has sometimes resulted in a blurring of ethnic distinctions at the periphery.

Since the amalgamation of the Northern and Southern Protectorates in 1914, which ushered in the modern Nigerian state, different sets of essentially artificial administrative boundaries have been imposed on Igboland. In 1951, the Macpherson constitution divided Nigeria into three regions, each dominated by a major ethnic group: the Eastern Region (predominantly Igbo and Christian), the Northern Region (predominantly

---

[3] For Igbo origins and precolonial history, see F. Chidozie Ogbalu and E. Nolue Emenanjo (eds.), *Igbo Language and Culture*, Ibadan: Oxford University Press, 1975; A. E. Afigbo, 'The Age of Innocence: the Igbo and their Neighbours in pre-Colonial Times', The 1981 Ahiajoku Lecture, 1981; John Nwachimereze Oriji, *Traditions of Igbo Origin. A Study of Pre-colonial Population Movements in Africa*, Frankfurt: Peter Lang, 1994; Don C. Ohadike, *Anioma. A Social History of the Western Igbo People*, Athens: Ohio University Press, 1994; Isichei, *Europeans*; Elizabeth Isichei, *A History of the Igbo people*, London: Macmillan Press, 1976.

[4] Isichei, *Europeans*, 19.

[5] *Ibid.*, 18-20.

Hausa-Fulani and Muslim), and the Western Region (predominantly Yoruba, and Christian or Muslim).[6] Later, the Mid-West Region (predominantly Edo) was created, carved out of the Western Region. This has had implications for Nigerian political culture ever since, which has been dominated by ethnic and religious politics. Nigeria obtained independence in 1960, and in 1967, the government created the first twelve states, with the bulk of Igboland occupying East Central State. This increased to nineteen states in 1975, thirty in 1991 and thirty-six in 1996. Present-day Igboland consists of five states: Abia, Imo, Anambra, Enugu and Ebonyi. There are also a number of peripheral Igbo-speaking groups west of the river Niger in Delta State, known as *ndị Anịọma* ('those who live on the good and prosperous land'), and further south in Rivers State. In addition, Igbo migratory and trading habits have generated large diasporic communities in some of the major Nigerian urban areas, such as Lagos in the southwest, Kano, Kaduna, Jos, Zaria in the North and Calabar in the southeast, which as we will see facilitated the growth of the Civil War Revival and its Pentecostal progeny.

Because of their political implications, census results in Nigeria are generally considered unreliable.[7] According to the contested 1963 census, Igbos numbered 9.3 million (16.6 per cent of the total population of 55.6 million), compared to Hausa-Fulani (29.5 per cent), and Yoruba (20.3 per cent). The 1952-1953 census, which put Igbos at 17.9 per cent, Yorubas at 16.6 per cent and Hausa-Fulani at 28.1 per cent, was probably a more accurate reflection of the demographic balance of peoples because the 1963 census was compiled in a more politically charged atmosphere, running up to the elections. The 1991 census put the population of Igbo states at 10.7 million out of 88.5 million, but this did not include Igbo communities outside Igboland. Based on projections from earlier censuses, the estimated Igbo population in 2000 was 19.9 million, compared to 20.3 million (Yoruba) and 35.3 million (Hausa-Fulani), out of 111.5 million.

Before direct European contact, the Igbo consisted of over two hundred independent village groups or towns, each composed of one or more villages. Villages commonly contained several hundred people, but in more densely populated areas some village-groups consisted of more than 5,000 members. Some scholars have suggested that Igbo ethnic identity

---

[6] Islam reached the North in the eleventh century, influencing the two Hausa states of Kano and Katsina. In the early nineteenth century, a reforming *jihad* by the Fulani cleric Uthman dan Fodio overthrew the Hausa kings and set up the Sokoto Caliphate, a federation of emirates covering most of the North. It aimed at the formation of an Islamic state based on *Shari'a* (Islamic) law.

[7] For a discussion, see S. A. Aluko, 'How many Nigerians? An Analysis of Nigeria's Census Problems, 1901-63', *Journal of Modern African Studies*, 3.3, October 1965, 371-92.

was a European 'invented tradition', applied during the slave trade and later by colonialists to facilitate administration by promoting linguistic and cultural divisions.[8] However, this implies too one-sided a process and overlooks local agency and initiative in identity construction. Benedict Anderson's concept of 'imagined communities' is more helpful. Anderson applies the term primarily to nationalities and examines their creation and global spread, but suggests that 'all communities larger than primordial villages of face-to-face contact . . . are imagined', because many members do not know each other.[9] Early documents and traditions from the core areas of Igbo settlement and migration in Nri-Awka and Orlu-Owerri axis suggest that while the primary sense of attachment was to the village group, a pan-Igbo identity existed prior to the arrival of European colonialists. This was reinforced when people left Igboland because of the slave trade, and when colonial conquest and missionary endeavour exposed the Igbo to global forces and an expanded universe. Under colonialism, a bounded Igbo ethnic identity replaced more fluid networks of interactions. The combination of migration to urban areas outside Igboland (mainly for trade purposes) and the Nigerian civil war further strengthened ethnic consciousness.

While there is considerable homogeneity in terms of language, religion, economics and politics, there is also cultural and genetic diversity due to cross-fertilisation with neighbouring ethnic groups. This has given rise to the culture area approach adopted by anthropologists and historians.[10] A culture area is a geographically delineated territory with common cultural traits. Early schemes divided Igboland into five major subcultural groups: the Northern or Onitsha Igbo (Nri-Awka, Enugu, Onitsha town); the Southern or Owerri Igbo (Isuama, Oratta-Ikwerre, Ohuhu-Ngwa, Isu-Item), the Western Igbo (Northern Ika, Southern Ika, and Riverain); the Eastern or Cross River Igbo (Ada, Abam-Ohafia, Aro); and the Northeastern Igbo (Ogu Uka, Abakalike and Afikpo groups).[11] Here I follow Kalu's scheme which divides Igboland into nine culture areas: Western, North-Western,

[8] For example, Daryll Forde and G. I. Jones, *The Ibo- and Ibibio-Speaking Peoples of South-Eastern Nigeria*, London: Oxford University Press for the International African Institute, 1950, 9; Isichei, *Igbo People*, 19-20.

[9] Benedict Anderson, *Imagined Communities: Reflections on the Origin and Spread of Nationalism*, London: Verso, 1991, 6.

[10] For discussions, see A. E. Afigbo, 'Igbo Cultural Sub-Areas: Their Rise and Development', in A. E. Afigbo (ed.), *Groundwork of Igbo History*, Lagos: Vista Books, 1991, 144-60; Ogbu U. Kalu, *The Embattled Gods: Christianization of Igboland 1841-1991*, Lagos/London: Minaj, 1996, 9-10; M. A. Onwuejeogwu, 'The Igbo Culture Area', in Ogbalu and Emenanjo (eds.), *Igbo*, 1-10.

[11] See Forde and Jones, *Ibo*, 10; Onwuejeogwu, 'Igbo', 1-2.

Northern, North-Eastern, Central, South-Western, Southern, Eastern, and Cross River.[12] I use it as a tool for navigating Igbo territory rather than to analyse cultural variations or differential responses to Christianity.

Political and Socio-Economic History, pre-2006

Colonialism and decolonisation have exposed African societies to severe forms of stress and have created individual and social crises, which in turn have acted as catalysts for religious change. Within Igbo religious history, there have been two major communal crises which have affected Igbo responses to Christianity. The first occurred with the 'invasion' of Igbo territory by British colonialists and Christian missionaries, beginning in the mid-nineteenth century; the second began with the granting of independence in 1960. Decolonisation, civil war, and subsequent political instability and economic decline created a series of crises comparable in their impact to the colonial conquest and precipitated further changes in the religious landscape.

Pre-Colonial Political and Socio-economic Cultures

In contrast to traditional political systems in Western and Northern Nigeria, the Igbos had few centralised states and resisted any form of autocracy.[13] This is reflected in the popular Igbo adage, *Igbo ọmạghi eze* (Igbos know no king). Exceptions were the monarchical state systems of Onitsha, Aboh, Oguta, Aguleri, Nri and Arochukwu, which attributed their origins to outside influences such as the Edo kingdom of Benin and the Igala state of Idah. But these are generally not considered representative of the rest of Igboland. Yet Igboland was not an acephalous society. It consisted of largely autonomous, middle-level political systems or mini-states and like other African societies was traditionally gerontocratic and hierarchical. Igbos lived in large patrilineal village democracies or *ụmụnna* (children of one father), each made up of *onụmara* (extended families). Igbo anthropologist M. A. Onwuejeogwu identifies the *ụmụnna* concept as a

---

[12] Kalu, *Embattled Gods*, 10.

[13] For Igbo traditional politics and economy, I have used the following sources: Afigbo (ed.), *Groundwork*; U. D. Anyanwu and J. C. U. Aguwa, (eds.), *The Igbo and the Tradition of Politics*, Enugu: Fourth Dimension, 1993; Toyin Falola, *The History of Nigeria*, Westport, Connecticut: Greenwood Press, 1999; Isichei, *Igbo People*; F. I. Nzimiro, *Studies in Ibo Political Structures. Chieftaincy and Politics in Four Nigerian States*, London: Frank Cass, 1972; Uchendu, *Igbo*.

central Igbo cultural theme, which determines membership of the patrilineage, individual rights and duties, economic behaviour and traditional political roles. Even where the concept of kingship was present, political organisation and power were located in the *ụmụnna* and title-system.[14] This meant that political power was diffused and democratic. Before making decisions, community members would gather together for discussion or consultation (*igba izu*) in order to arrive at a consensus.

The viability of Igbo political units depended upon their land-administering functions and the ability to maintain control through land allocation. Thus land (*ala*) stood at the centre of Igbo traditional life. It not only formed the basis of the economy, but, as the Igbo historian Adiele Afigbo has shown, it determined migration and settlement patterns and influenced socio-political evolution. Communities which were able to agree together concerning the use of the land on which they lived had the potential to become workable political units. Consequently, in most areas the village-group was the largest grouping.[15] Communities were generally ruled by the *ndị oha* (the council of elders), comprising the oldest members of specific families, assisted by age grades, kinship associations and religious specialists.[16] Leadership was by consensus and based on age, physical ability, good character, and the possession of oracular, ritual or magical powers. Igbos are prepared to give authority to their leaders but retain the right to withdraw that authority and give it to another. Moreover, traditional rulers were part of the community rather than externally imposed, and political institutions were designed to 'combine popular participation with weighting for experience and ability'.[17]

Religion was interwoven into the fabric of Igbo traditional political culture. Ritual agents, who mediated between the visible and invisible worlds, possessed considerable public authority, and in contrast to modern Western political systems, traditional Igbo political institutions looked to religious sources for legitimacy and validation. Especially important were the built in restraints and moral sanctions based on religious principles, which governed political action and authority, and the belief that spiritual entities can exert control over earthly affairs. Because of its pivotal role in agriculture, land figured prominently in Igbo religious politics. Ala (Earth goddess), the most important Igbo deity, was the guardian of Igbo morality and maintained social control through *omenala*, the traditional code of

---

[14] Onwuejeogwu, 'Igbo', 5-6.

[15] A. E. Afigbo, 'Prolegomena to the Study of the Culture History of the Igbo-Speaking Peoples of Nigeria', in Ogbalu and Emenanjo (eds.), *Igbo*, 41-2.

[16] In some Igbo communities, the council of elders are called *ndị-ichie* (Anambra area) or *amala* (Imo area).

[17] Isichei, *Igbo People*, 21

conduct. These laws, created in the name of Ala by the *ndị oha*, were regarded as sacred and their violation attracted severe punishments.

Oral tradition and archaeological studies suggest that agriculture and trade were the main Igbo economic activities from early times. Each community had a market located in its political and religious centre. Yam cultivation became the early economic basis of society and was given ritual and symbolic significance in Igbo traditional life. The cult of the yam deity, Njọkụ, became an important institution, and the annual Yam Festival a prominent event. Trade as a factor in Igbo economic culture arose partly in response to over exploitation of land, as locals were forced to look for alternative sources of revenue, and partly in response to the differential distribution of mineral resources. It included exchanges of natural products as well as locally produced textiles. Prior to the nineteenth century, Igbo society did not encourage the accumulation of wealth, except in the form of yams which were perishable. It consequently lacked the extremes of wealth and poverty prevalent today. Consumer goods were limited, and most Igbos preferred to exchange their assets for their community's esteem by purchasing a title to gain political influence or assisting poorer relations, thus facilitating the redistribution of wealth.[18]

The trans-Atlantic slave trade had its greatest impact on Igboland during the years 1730 to 1810, when it was dominated by the English. Most of the slaves were purchased from the Biafran hinterland, where the vast majority were of Igbo descent. Isichei has outlined the effects of the slave trade on Igbo society. Not only did it cause the loss of many of its strongest members and deprive it of their skills, it also had a brutalising and corrupting influence. Igbo communities grew used to collecting slaves, and disregard for human life became more pronounced. Human sacrifice, which existed before the slave trade, expanded and became a source of terror. Most slaves were kidnapped by fellow Igbos or were trophies of war. The slave trade also encouraged the conspicuous consumption of goods by introducing additional products into Igboland. This had socio-political effects as greater access to wealth enabled more men to purchase titles and acquire political influence.[19]

Colonial Legacies

One of the symptoms of globalisation, as we noted in chapter 1, is that people are increasingly drawn into the global system, so that local happenings are shaped by events occurring elsewhere. The experience of colonial encounters has shown that the history of Africa has been tied to the

[18] *Ibid.*, 34.
[19] *Ibid.*, 45-9; Isichei, *Europeans*, 55-7.

expansion of Europe. The colonial era introduced new elements and altered Nigerian socio-political and economic landscapes. It stimulated the emergence of the modern nation state and incorporated it into global economic processes. This created tensions that continue to be felt within post-colonial Igboland. In particular, it undermined the traditional democratic system of government and shifted the focus of the economy from Igbo to European interests and from subsistence farming to production of cash crops and export of raw materials.

To assist colonial control, a more formal political structure was adopted, based on indirect rule and designed to secure local cooperation. But in decentralised and fragmented societies like the Igbo, where a system of 'warrant chiefs' presiding over 'native authorities' was imposed, it alienated rulers from subjects and ignored local traditions of democracy. The warrant chief system was originally designed for communities of the Oil Rivers (Ijo and Efik), with a tradition of powerful chiefs. When Lugard took over after the amalgamation, he used a system evolved in the Fulani emirates. Problems arose in Igboland mainly because the warrant chiefs were not representative of village groups and often abused their powers. Colonial administrators preferred to deal with a few 'strong' chiefs, whose delegated authority often extended far beyond their own village communities. Following communal resistance, colonial authorities added a council of elders in 1933/1934 to narrow the gap between ruler and subjects. Later, territorial, district and local councils replaced native authorities. By the 1950s, a shift had occurred from age and integrity to wealth and education as the main qualifications for political leadership, with opportunities now available for younger men with education, prominent traders, businessmen, and professional people to play prominent roles in local government. However, the growing divergence between rulers and subjects continued, with authority weighted in favour of elders, and men of wealth and influence, who had become title-holders.[20]

The prominence of ethnicity and religion in Nigeria's post-colonial politics had its roots in the colonial era and the formation of the Nigerian state. The construction of artificial boundaries and the creation of the North-South divide, described by Osaghae as a 'structural flaw of colonial rule', led to increasing ethnic and religious rivalry that had 'grave consequences for post-independence politics'.[21] The British policy of indirect rule strengthened Muslim predominance in the North by permitting

---

[20] Falola, *History*, 70-2; Emma O. Inyama, 'Trends in Traditional Rulership in Igboland', in Anyanwu and Aguwa (eds.), *Igbo*, 218-20; A. I. Nwabughuogu, 'Economic Aspects of Igbo Political Evolution', in Anyanwu and Aguwa (eds.), *Igbo*, 165-68; Ottenberg, 'Ibo Receptivity', 131.

[21] Eghosa E. Osaghae, *Nigeria since Independence. Crippled Giant*, London: Hurst & Company, 1998, 6-7.

the application of a limited version of *Shari'a* law and excluding Christian missions from Muslim areas. Despite the 1914 amalgamation, the British reinforced the North-South divide by creating three regional governments in the 1940s and pursuing different regional policies for each of the three regions. By the 1950s, the mainly Christian South was more advanced in terms of Western political ideals and education due to greater access to Christian missionary schools.[22] Its leaders had also gained considerable political experience compared to their counterparts in the North due to their longstanding membership of the central legislative council and their participation in the various nationalist movements of the early twentieth century. This not only stirred up political rivalry between North and South, but, as Osaghae observes, it created competition for socioeconomic goods, employment in the public sector, and admission to government educational institutions. Because Northerners feared Southern domination following independence they threatened to pull out of the colonial union unless certain demands were granted. These included a 50 per cent allocation of seats in the House of Representatives (later increased to 52 per cent), the distribution of nationally collected revenue based on population, and regional autonomy. The granting of these demands paved the way for Northern domination, which became a major source of the nation's political problems after independence.[23] Regionalism also fostered ethnic divisions because one major group predominated in each region. When political parties emerged in 1949-50, they did so along regional lines and, as the Nigerian historian Toyin Falola has noted, attempts to build parties on the basis of ideology rather than ethnicity or religion were rare.[24]

But colonial rule and missionary education also introduced Enlightenment ideals resulting in a partial desacralisation of political space and a loosening of individual ties with traditional religion and culture. In their discussion of religious politics in sub-Saharan Africa, Ellis and ter Haar note the way that religion and politics, as two closely related systems of ordering power, have been separated into distinct spheres in modern

---

[22] Joseph Kenny, 'Sharia and Christianity in Nigeria: Islam and a "Secular" State', *JRA*, 26.4, 1996, 340; Matthews A. Ojo, 'The Church in the African State: The Charismatic/Pentecostal Experience in Nigeria', *Journal of African Christian Thought*, 1.2, December, 1998, 26. Most schools were established by Christian missions, and by 1950, there was only one Northern university graduate compared to hundreds in the South. Isichei notes that in 1952 there were only 23,000 people literate in English in the Northern city of Kano out of a population of 3.4 million, and half of these were southerners. Elizabeth Isichei, *A History of Nigeria*, London: Longman, 1983, 441.

[23] Osaghae, *Nigeria*, 5-6.

[24] Toyin Falola, *Violence in Nigeria. The Crisis of Religious Politics and Secular Ideologies*, Rochester: University of Rochester Press, 1998, 53-4.

Western tradition. Colonial governors and missionaries have then attempted to impose this distinction on African societies.[25] But in the case of Nigeria this has only met with partial success due to the resistance of Nigerian society to secularising influences. The quest for Western education had further consequences which contributed to the Igbo crisis, as the rise in expectations, accompanied by shrinking employment opportunities, led to an increase in crime and prostitution, particularly in urban areas.[26]

British colonialists laid the foundation of the modern Nigerian economy, which was based on the peasant production of cash crops (such as cotton and cocoa), mineral extraction and the export of raw materials chiefly for the European market. British interests were predominant as colonialists set about creating new markets for British industries and exploiting Nigeria's natural resources, to the detriment of local food production.[27] In Igboland, the major economic changes were the ending of the external slave trade and the expansion of palm oil exports. These developments had several socioeconomic consequences. To facilitate trade, colonialists provided basic infrastructures, mostly established in urban areas, to the neglect of rural areas where the majority of people lived and where most of the production of food and crops took place. This helped to increase the disparity in development within urban and rural areas. Related to this was the opportunity it offered for those with no land to earn a living through salaried employment, thus freeing them from traditional control exerted through land allocation, a development which Afigbo describes as the main economic innovation under colonialism.[28] Thirdly, the ending of the international export of slaves did not mean that the slave trade ceased in Igboland. Instead, slaves became a cheaper commodity and their number increased significantly. Isichei identifies this as a cause of social polarisation in Igboland as slaves were accumulated as status symbols. They were also used to collect palm oil or as farm labourers, thus further enhancing the economic status of their owners, who tended to value wealth largely as a source of prestige and political influence.[29] Finally, European trade affected the balance of power between Igbo states. Isichei contrasts the fortunes of Aboh and Onitsha. Aboh had attained a position of considerable wealth and power by the early nineteenth century due to its

---

[25] Stephen Ellis and Gerrie ter Haar, 'Religion and Politics in Sub-Saharan Africa', *Journal of Modern African Studies*, 36.2, 1998, 195.

[26] Isichei, *Igbo People*, 195-96.

[27] Bolanle Awe, 'Conflict and Divergence: Government and Society in Nigeria', *African Studies Review*, 42.3, 1999, 8-9.

[28] A. E. Afigbo, *Ropes of Sand. Studies in Igbo History and Culture*, New York: University Press, 1981, 347-48.

[29] Isichei, *Igbo People*, 95, 103; Isichei, *Europeans*, 63.

strategic position at the apex of the Niger Delta. But the reluctance of missionaries and European traders to endure the inconveniences caused by periodic flooding hastened its decline. Onitsha, with its inland site, was poor and underdeveloped in comparison. Yet the establishment of a new settlement on the waterside, and its selection as a missionary and trading centre, transformed it into a major economic and educational centre.[30]

Urbanisation was a direct outcome of colonialism and contributed towards the Igbo crisis. Here we must distinguish between traditional and European initiated cities. Most traditional cities were located in Western Nigeria and to a lesser degree in the North. In Igboland, urban centres developed through European initiative around existing towns (Onitsha, Umuahia) or new modern cities (Enugu, Aba, Port Harcourt). Most Igbos were not city dwellers, and prior to European contact, there were no major Igbo urban areas. However, by 1952, there were four - Enugu, Aba, Onitsha and Port Harcourt. Based on the 1963 Census, population figures were as follows: Port Harcourt (179,563), Aba (131,033), Enugu (138,457) and Onitsha (163,932). Other smaller urban communities included Owerri (26,017), Nsukka (26,206) and Umuahia (28,844).[31] Consequences of this trek to the urban centre in search of wage labour included social dislocation and isolation, a shortage of accommodation and amenities, moral decline due to a weakening of traditional social control mechanisms, and a loosening of ties to the traditional religious and social structures of the village.

The Post-Colonial State

Decolonisation brought about rapid social change within Nigeria. From being a society organised around the local community, Nigeria became a large-scale nation state. This was a direct result of the colonial project and created profound tensions within Igbo society that continued to be felt following independence. The legacy of colonialism left the newly independent state with severe constraints. Instead of the creation of a genuine African democracy and an economy firmly focussed on Nigerian interests, independence meant the Africanisation of colonial political and economic structures.

The process of decolonisation was rapid (1957-68) once it was realised that independence was inevitable. Gifford has noted that for those African countries that gained independence during the 1960s it was accompanied by an air of optimism due to a period of unprecedented global economic

[30] Isichei, *Europeans*, 40, 106.

[31] Ray Ofoegbu, 'Urbanisation and the Rise of Modern Igbo Enterprise', in Afigbo (ed.), *Groundwork*, 585.

growth (1945-75). The new governments subsequently set about modernising according to Western models of development.[32] Nigeria adopted a Western capitalist model inherited from its British colonial masters. During the First Republic (1960-66), Igbo hopes were raised due to the improving economy and the growth in secondary and tertiary educational institutions. Oil had taken over from agriculture as the mainstay of the economy, and by 1966, Nigeria, with an output of £N100 million about two-thirds of which was in the East, ranked thirteenth among the world's crude-oil producers.[33] Kalu describes them as 'heady days characterized by new opportunities, improved quality of life and an onslaught on traditional values'.[34]

However, optimism gave way to disillusionment due to pervasive corruption, the collapse of the parliamentary democratic system in 1963, the contested 1964/5 elections, and the growth of regional and ethnic antagonisms. The growing divergence between rulers and ruled continued as the new politicians took for granted the basic structures and assumptions of colonialism. In 1966, a military coup, followed by a counter-coup, left General Yakubu Gowon in charge. Meanwhile, a series of violent pogroms in the North, largely directed against easterners, resulted in a mass exodus of a million or so Igbos from all over Nigeria back to their crowded homeland. Especially shocking was the September/October 1966 pogrom, described by Isichei as the most traumatic experience in Igbo history up to that time. This was partly a reaction to the first military coup of January 1966, which to Northerners appeared an Igbo and Christian takeover. By the end, thousands had lost their lives and many more had been injured. Estimates of Igbos who died varied considerably from 10,000 to 30,000, but few disputed that it was a pogrom of genocidal proportions.[35] In May 1967, with secessionist currents running high among Igbo élites, Colonel Odumegwu Ojukwu, military governor of the Eastern region, declared the 'Republic of Biafra' an independent state. This was viewed differently from different perspectives. The Federal Government viewed it as rebellion, but most Biafrans believed they were forced out of the Federation.

The series of crises following independence reached their climax with the civil war (1967-70), described by Falola as 'Africa's first and most costly modern war', when an estimated three million Igbos died (over a

---

[32] Gifford, *African Christianity*, 4.

[33] E. Wayne Nafziger, 'The Economic Impact of the Nigerian Civil War', *Journal of Modern African Studies*, 10.2, July 1972, 233-34.

[34] Kalu, *Embattled Gods*, 268.

[35] Isichei, *Igbo People*, 245-46.

quarter of the population).[36] The combination of social dislocation, growing fatalities, lack of food and medical facilities, air raids and the threat of genocide created a series of individual and social crises that precipitated profound changes in the Igbo religious landscape. Many Igbos became refugees, resulting in intense feelings of insecurity as they became separated from family, kinship group and village. Abandoning one's village or town was also seen as a betrayal of one's ancestors. The refugee problem flowed from two sources: the Igbo exodus following the 1966 pogroms in the North and the war itself. By July 1968, over 650 refugee camps existed, and at the close of the war there were between three to six million displaced persons and refugees.[37] Biafrans saw the conflict as a war for survival. In Ojukwu's public speeches and Biafran propaganda, it was presented as 'genocide' and as a northern Islamic 'jihad'. Indeed, one of the reasons given for seceding was the inability of the Federal government to protect the Igbo people from destruction. Consequently, most Igbos believed that to lose the war was as suicidal as to fight on.[38]

The war had enormous consequences for the economy of Biafra, which was left in ruins with its infrastructure and utilities destroyed. There were also severe shortages of shelter, food, clothing and medicines, as well as extensive loss of material possessions. According to Nafziger, the Biafran economy was 'geared almost entirely towards mobilisation for the war and the production of bare necessities', and Biafra 'received virtually no civilian goods from abroad, except food and other essentials from relief organisations'. Inflation was rampant, and prices of basic food items and clothing escalated. Nafziger attributes the scarcity of food to war damage and lack of access to international trade.[39] Nigeria considered starvation (by economic blockade) a legitimate instrument of war and tried to prevent aid agencies from delivering relief to Biafra. In August 1968, Time

[36] Falola, *Violence*, 1. Some accounts of the civil war are fiercely partisan. For relatively balanced accounts, see Alexander A. Madiebo, *The Nigerian Revolution and Biafran War*, Enugu: Fourth Dimension, 1980; John de St. Jorre, *The Nigerian Civil War*, London: Hodder and Stoughton, 1972; A. H. M. Kirk-Greene, *Crisis and Conflict in Nigeria. A Documentary Sourcebook 1966-1970*, 2 Vols, Ibadan: Oxford University Press, 1971.

[37] Kalu, *Embattled Gods*, 269-70; Anthony Haden-Guest, 'Legacy of a War: Special Report from Biafra', *The Daily Telegraph Magazine*, 23 August 1968, 12; Osaghae, *Nigeria*, 69.

[38] Cyril C. Okorocha, 'Reconciliation: What Price? Some Biblical and Practical Reflections from Africa', in Barbara Butler (ed.), *Open Hands. Reconciliation, Justice and Peace Work around the World*, Bury St. Edmunds, Suffolk: Kevin Mayhew, 1998, 193.

[39] Nafziger, 'Economic Impact', 239-40.

Magazine described Ojukwu's Biafra as 'a land of physical ruin', with Biafrans starving to death at an estimated 1,000 a day.[40]

The tension within Igboland was exacerbated by a breakdown in traditional social morality and an escalation of corruption, bribery, sexual promiscuity, prostitution and armed robbery. Igbo political scientist O. B. C. Nwolise links this directly to the economic circumstances of the war. Food shortages, starvation and scarcity of other essential items generated a struggle for individual survival at the expense of traditional Igbo communal obligations and morality. The situation was exacerbated by imbalance in power relations and unequal access to guns. Corruption started within government agencies, moved to the army and judiciary, and then spread to the civilian population. Bribery and prostitution became common methods for obtaining relief food and fuel.[41] Some of my informants described how girls, raped during the war, no longer considered sexual immorality to be wrong, and married women in the absence of their husbands engaged in prostitution as a means of survival. More worrying was the escalation in armed robbery. Informants again attributed this to the war, as young men who had learnt to shoot in the army came out with their guns. To halt this moral decline the Biafran government established tribunals to try cases of fraud, robbery and corruption. In June 1969, it launched the 'Biafran Revolution', symbolised by the 'Ahiara Declaration', which condemned the moral breakdown in Igbo society and upheld the sanctity of life.[42] But these initiatives arrived too late, and by the end of the war, morality and morale were at their lowest ebb.

The main elements of post-war Nigerian politics, according to Osaghae, were political instability, a low level of national cohesion, and economic crisis. While paying lip service to ideology, politics tended to be organised around ethnic, regional and religious interests, which encouraged instability, rivalry and disunity. This is reflected in the high turnover of governments. Since 1970, there have been eight military coups, seven military regimes and three civilian governments.[43] For the Igbo, perhaps the most serious political consequence of the war was their marginalisation in post-war military regimes. For a long time, their demands for more states were ignored and they were under-represented in the armed forces. There has been no Igbo head of state since General Aguiyi-Ironsi in 1966.

---

[40] James Wilde, 'Nigeria's Civil War: Hate, Hunger and the Will to Survive', *Time Magazine*, 23 August 1968, 22.

[41] O. B. C. Nwolise, 'The Social Consequences of the Civil War in Biafra', in T. N. Tamuno (ed.), *Nigeria Since Independence, Vol.III, The Civil War Years*, Zaria: Nigeria Since Independence History Project, 1984, 37-8

[42] *Ibid.*, 38.

[43] Osaghae, *Nigeria*, 14-15

Government mismanagement and pervasive corruption resulted in economic decline, despite abundant natural resources and high-level manpower. Economic mismanagement and corruption was linked to prebendalism or neo-patrimonialism, a system of government dominated by patron-client relationships and the use of public office for private accumulation.[44] But Osaghae refers to the larger crisis of 'extraversion which resulted from the country's peripheral location in the global system'.[45] As a rentier state, Nigeria's revenues accrued from taxes or rents on production of minerals by multinational corporations rather than directly from productive activity. This left it vulnerable to fluctuations in the world market and made it economically unstable. Dependence on oil discouraged agricultural development (the mainstay of the rural economy) and the growth of non-state capitalism.[46]

Following the civil war, Gowon maintained national unity by promoting the 'three Rs' (Reconciliation, Rehabilitation and Reconstruction) and implementing a national cohesion project, which included the setting up of 'unity' schools (federal government colleges) and introduction of the National Youth Service Corps (NYSC) in 1973. Under the NYSC scheme, graduates of universities and polytechnics did a compulsory one year of national service outside their states of origin. From 1973, Nigeria also entered a period of economic boom due to substantial oil revenues. By 1974, these made up 80.8 per cent of Nigeria's total revenue and transformed Nigeria into the thirtieth wealthiest nation in the world.[47]

Yet it was still a period of crisis for the Igbo people as many had lost family members and possessions during the war, and while Federal troops were relatively well contained, atrocities continued to occur. There were episodes of looting, kidnapping of young girls and indiscriminate killing of civilians by Federal troops. Gratitude to Gowon for his magnanimity and restraint was tempered by local economic realities, and surviving the peace became almost as precarious as surviving the war. Schools and universities in the east did not resume immediately and jobs were scarce. Sometimes

---

44 *Ibid.*, 15, 29. The term patrimonialism was coined by Weber to describe a form of leadership based on the kind of authority a father has over his children; one which was held together by kinship ties. Gifford (*African Christianity*, 5) uses the term 'neo-patrimonialism' to describe the system in Africa where patrimonial authority operates within the machinery of a modern nation state and officials exercise their powers as a form of private property rather than public service and use money to buy support. Other scholars prefer the term 'prebendalism'.

45 Osaghae, *Nigeria*, 15-16.

46 *Ibid.*, 28-9. For Nigeria as a rentier state, see William D. Graf, *The Nigerian State*, London: James Currey, 1988, 219ff.

47 Osaghae, *Nigeria*, 78; Graf, *Nigerian State*, 219; Falola, *History*, 138.

government policies also hindered Igbo rehabilitation. As well as the freezing of Igbo bank accounts and the provision of only £20 each with which to reconstruct their lives, Igbo property abandoned during the war in the newly created Rivers State (and especially the predominantly Igbo city of Port Harcourt) was not restored to its owners. In 1974, the Gowon regime introduced the indigenisation programme, an attempt to wrest control of the Nigerian economy from foreigners and ensure that Nigerians were 'the main beneficiaries of the country's resources'.[48] Unfortunately, Igbos were often too poor to buy shares, and it was left to Yorubas in the West to take over most enterprises. Finally, the formation of new states in 1976 created an imbalance of political power and revenue allocation in favour of the Hausa-Fulani and Yoruba.

The Gowon regime eventually fell into disrepute, accused of corruption, mismanagement of the economy and reneging on its promises to return the nation to civilian rule. The consensus was that Gowon was too weak to curb abuses of power and control his corrupt lieutenants in a government dominated by patrimonialism and clientelism. In 1975, a military coup brought General Murtala Mohammed to power. He immediately embarked upon a campaign to 'cleanse' the public sector and society of corruption and instil a sense of responsibility and discipline. He replaced the existing state governors and retired or dismissed large numbers of civil servants. However, his assassination eight months later left General Olusegun Obasanjo in charge.

In 1979, Obasanjo successfully presided over the transition to civil rule, which ushered in the Second Republic, led by Shehu Shagari. Like its predecessor, it was a dismal failure, as corruption reached new heights and political office became a means for personal accumulation due to petro-naira resources and permissive political culture.[49] In fact, oil revenues had reached a peak in 1980, and by 1983, the economy was in serious decline due to the 1981 oil glut and the global economic recession. Oil revenues fell from $25 billion in 1980 to $6 billion in 1984.[50] Ihonvbere and Shaw refer to the massive scale of government plunder between 1979 and 1983, where the 'criteria of success escalated from Mercedez-Benz to personal

[48] Osaghae, *Nigeria*, 100.

[49] 'Petro-naira' refers to revenue from petroleum products (the basic unit of Nigerian currency being the naira). For the Second Republic, see Toyin Falola and Julius Ihonvbere, *The Rise and Fall of Nigeria's Second Republic, 1979-1983*, London: Zed Books, 1985; Graf, *Nigerian State*, 77-114; Richard J. Joseph, *Democracy and Prebendal Politics in Nigeria: the Rise and Fall of the Second Republic*, New York: Cambridge University Press, 1987.

[50] Pade Badru, *Imperialism and Ethnic Politics in Nigeria*, Trenton, NJ: Africa World Press, 1998, 92.

jets for "big men" and from stereos to VCR's for the middle class'.[51] Economic recession, austerity measures and gross government mismanagement led to severe problems of unemployment and inflation. While politicians continued to enrich themselves, the urban poor and rural peasants bore the brunt of economic neglect. This generated an upsurge in civil disobedience, which in turn led to political repression, human rights violations and press restrictions. Added to this was an escalation of religious violence between Christians and Muslims. All these factors - government corruption and mismanagement, economic recession, austerity measures, civil disobedience, repression and religious violence - have become recurring themes within Nigerian political and economic culture.

The collapse of the Republic in 1983 brought General Muhammad Buhari to power and ushered in an extended period of authoritarian rule and economic crisis under successive military regimes not previously experienced in Nigeria's post-colonial history. The main flaw of the Second Republic was its mismanagement of the economy, which was also the reason given by the military for their intervention. Initially the coup was widely welcomed due to popular disenchantment with politicians and their failure to reverse the economic recession, but soon it was reaping a harvest of discontent. Its harsh authoritarianism and 'War against Indiscipline' project were justified in terms of its economic recovery programme. But these austerity measures became increasingly unpopular mainly because there was no significant improvement in living conditions. As a Muslim, Buhari was also accused of favouring Northern interests.

The repressive regime's eventual overthrow in 1985 via a military coup led by General Babangida was greeted by most Nigerians with relief. The two main projects during Babangida's tenure (1985-93) were the IMF/World Bank Structural Adjustment Programme (SAP), and the transition to civilian rule, which coincided with Africa's 'second liberation', a period of widespread democratic change and economic reform.[52] Both were unsuccessful and both generated considerable civil disobedience. SAP was an expression of the globalisation of the world economy, an attempt to integrate peripheral nations like Nigeria into world capitalism. But it only succeeded in intensifying Nigeria's marginalisation and subordination. Though the World Bank presented her as an example of successful adjustment, economic recovery was far from impressive, with little improvement in general living standards. Osaghae refers to the 1991 World Bank Report, which ranked Nigeria as thirteenth poorest country in

---

[51] Julius Ihonvbere and Timothy Shaw, *Illusions of Power. Nigeria in Transition*, Trenton, NJ: Africa World Press, 1998, 106.

[52] For structural adjustment in Nigeria, see A. O. Olukoshi (ed.), *The Politics of Structural Adjustment in Nigeria*, London: James Curry, 1993; Ihonvbere and Shaw, *Illusions of Power*, 114-23.

the world, and the United Nations Development Programme's 1990 survey, which concluded that it had one of the worst records for human deprivation in the third world.[53] During the 1980s, civil associations organised anti-SAP strikes and demonstrations, and were at the centre of the struggle for democratisation, precipitated by Babangida's reluctance to complete the transition programme. Religion also attained a new level of political prominence, becoming increasingly an instrument for acquiring power, destabilizing government at local and national levels, reinforcing ethnic identities and precipitating violent conflicts. These developments had far-reaching consequences for Pentecostal political engagement, an issue we return to later.

The democratic transition process was fraught with difficulties and threatened by civil unrest. Against all odds, elections took place in 1993 and were won by Chief M. K. O. Abiola, a businessman and Yoruba-Muslim. Early in its administration, the Babangida regime had set a mandatory limit of two parties in an attempt to bring an end to ethnic politics. The two parties were the left-leaning Social Democratic Party (SDP) and the right-leaning National Republican Party (NRP). Abiola was the SDP candidate. Unfortunately, despite the relatively free and fair electoral process, the elections were annulled, ushering in a period of civil strife and political violence unprecedented in Nigeria's post-civil war history. Osaghae suggests a number of factors behind the annulment: the unwillingness of the North to relinquish political control, and the personal problems Abiola had with the military. But the main reason was Babangida's reluctance to relinquish power.[54] Following his eventual retirement, an Interim National Government (ING) headed by Chief Ernest Shonekan was formed, but from its inception it faced severe problems of legitimacy and was perceived as a continuation of the Babangida regime. Before his retirement, Babangida appointed his protégées to key positions and retained General Sani Abacha as defence minister. The country was plunged into near anarchy, thus playing into the hands of Abacha, who had long entertained presidential ambitions.

Abacha's accession to power, after Shonekan's 'resignation', ushered in an era of despotism that lasted until 1998. Abacha was brazenly corrupt and presided over a repressive government that saw living standards reach their lowest level since the beginning of the twentieth century.[55] Among other human-rights violations, he imprisoned Abiola for treason after he declared himself President, and Obasanjo for his involvement in an alleged coup plot. In his maiden speech, Abacha had announced a new transition programme, but then proceeded to obstruct democratic takeover at every

[53] Osaghae, *Nigeria*, 204.
[54] *Ibid.*, 254-55.
[55] Falola, *History*, 196.

turn. The combination of economic decline, human-rights violations, and the failure of the transition programme, resulted in an explosion of civil society and an escalation of riots, strikes and protests. This led to a corresponding crackdown on pro-democracy groups, labour unions and the popular press.

In June 1998, Abacha died suddenly, and the military installed General Abdulsalami Abubakar, who promptly announced his intention to prepare the country for civilian rule. He also released many political prisoners, including Obasanjo, by this time retired from the army, and promised to release Abiola, but the latter died while still in detention. Obasanjo won the 1999 elections. He also claimed a conversion to born-again Christianity while in prison, which made him popular with evangelicals and Pentecostals. Despite allegations of irregularities and corruption, the military accepted the result, and Obasanjo was sworn in as President. In 2003, Obasanjo was re-elected for a second four year term.

The Igbo Primal Religious Landscape, pre-1967

While political and economic distress provided a favourable environment for religious change, inherited religious beliefs actually determined the shape of Igbo Christian conversion. Here we are concerned with issues of continuity and discontinuity so prevalent in discussions of African appropriations of Christianity. Part of the appeal of the Civil War Revival and its Pentecostal progeny rested upon the willingness of participants to take African cosmology seriously and communicate the gospel in religious categories familiar to their audience. The Igbo primal worldview, and in particular their traditional concept of salvation, supplies us with an important hermeneutical key for understanding Igbo responses to revival and Pentecostal spirituality. My treatment here is primarily descriptive rather than analytical and does not take full account of the variation in belief systems among Igbo-speaking communities and their change over time. As an outsider, I am also relying heavily upon studies by Igbo scholars, supplemented by my own interactions with members of the Igbo community.[56]

---

[56] For much of what follows see Emefie Ikenga-Metuh, *God and Man in African Religion. A Case Study of the Igbo of Nigeria*, London: Geoffrey Chapman, 1981; Emefie Ikenga-Metuh, *African Religions in Western Conceptual Schemes. The Problem of Interpretation (Studies in Igbo Religion)*, Onitsha: Imico, 1985; Okorocha, *Religious Conversion*; Uchendu, *Igbo*; Edmund Ilogu, *Christianity and Ibo Culture*, Leiden: E. J. Brill, 1974; Kalu, *Embattled Gods*; Emmanuel Nlenanya Onwu, 'Uzo Ndu Na Eziokwu. Towards

One of the key elements of primal spirituality is the belief that an invisible world of benevolent and malevolent powers is constantly interacting with the visible material world. This is the final feature of Harold Turner's six-feature framework for understanding the primal worldview and the one that Ghanaian theologian Kwame Bediako considers the 'key to understanding the rest'. Turner refers to the conviction that humans live in a 'sacramental universe' with no clear demarcation between the physical and the spiritual, where ritual action and material objects, whether fetishes or magical charms, act as vehicles for spiritual power.[57] In the case of the Igbo, these two intersecting and interacting realms are called *ụwa* (the visible world) and *ala mmụọ* (the invisible land of the spirits). *Ala mmụọ* is filled with a variety of spiritual beings which influence the material universe. The Supreme Being is called Chukwu (the Great Chi) or Chineke (Chi the Creator). The meaning of *chi* is difficult to grasp. According to Ikenga-Metuh, it evokes three related concepts: the 'Supreme Being', the 'Guardian Spirit', and the idea of 'destiny' or 'fortune'. *Chi* is best understood as a personal spirit imparted to a person at the moment of conception or creation. It reflects the Igbo belief that each person's *chi* receives his destiny from Chukwu, the Great Chi.[58] Chukwu is not a remote being with little influence over human affairs, as has been suggested by scholars such as Uchendu and Nwogu, but he is transcendent and is sometimes approached indirectly through intermediaries.[59] These include *ndị mmụọ* (deities), such as Ala (Earth goddess) and Anyanwụ (Sun god), *nna-anyị ha* (ancestors) and *alụsị* (spirit-forces). The Igbo find no difficulty in accepting one Creator and many deities, believing that the number and power of the intermediaries enhances the prestige and importance of Chukwu. *Nna-anyị ha* (or *ndị-chie)* are regarded as the most benevolent intermediaries, responsible for the social-moral control of traditional life under the presidency of Ala. They occupy an important position and are often addressed in worship and prayer rituals, but if neglected may unleash destructive powers or withdraw their protection from extended family members. In contrast, the *alụsị*, of which there are

---

an Understanding of Igbo Traditional Religious Life and Philosophy', Ahiajoku Lecture Series: the 2002 Ahiajoku Lecture.

[57] Harold W. Turner, 'Primal Religions and Their Study', in Victor C. Hayes (ed.), *Australian Essays in World Religions*, Adelaide: Australian Association for the Study of Religions, 1977, 32; Kwame Bediako, *Christianity in Africa: The Renewal of a Non-Western Religion*, Edinburgh: Edinburgh University Press, 1995, 96.

[58] Ikenga-Metuh, *God and Man*, 22-24.

[59] Uchendu, *Igbo*, 94; D. I. Nwogu, *The Supreme God as Stranger in Igbo Religious Thought*, Owerri: Owerri Hawk Press, 1984. For a critique, see Ikenga-Metuh, *God and Man*, 119-35.

many, are generally feared because of their unpredictability, even though they may act for the good of the society. *Alụsị* are 'metaphysical forces', which belong to the clan and may inhabit material objects such as rivers, forests or hills. Sometimes they dispense blessings to their devotees, but often they are bearers of misfortune. While each village and town has many *alụsị*, there is usually one that has the allegiance of the whole community and is worshipped at a common shrine. This helps to strengthen communal ties and maintain collective cohesiveness. A final category of spiritual beings consists of a variety of evil spirits. Evil spirits of the dead are classified in three age groups: *ụmụ arọ* (evil spirits of dead children), *ọgbanuke* (evil spirits of young men who have died prematurely before they can fulfil their destiny), and *akalogeli* (adults who have died without offspring or wealth). They may also be ancestors who have not been properly buried or have lived wicked lives here on earth. One of the most feared afflictions is *ọgbanje* ('repeaters' or returning children). These are spirits of children who punish their parents by taking over or causing a pregnancy, only to die before adulthood. The process is repeated so that a woman infested with *ọgbanje* can give birth many times without the child (usually a girl) surviving beyond infancy. Sometimes an *ọgbanje* will escape premature death but in her teenage years will be afflicted with various misfortunes.[60] The Igbo consider evil spirits to be a major source of suffering, including such afflictions as barrenness, prolonged or frequent sickness, accidental death, psychiatric problems, family strife, agricultural infertility and economic hardship. They are evil because they bring misfortune, unlike the Christian conception of the Devil and his demons which are considered evil because they incite immoral behaviour.[61]

Together these lesser spirits, corresponding to Horton's lower tier, constitute the dominant feature of Igbo religion. However, there are two other important sources of power in Igbo cosmology: *ọgwụ* (medicines) and *amusu* (witchcraft). These are not spirit-forces but are completely within the control of human beings. As a generic term, *ọgwụ* includes simple curative herbs, modern medicines, charms and various protective or destructive potions. But these tangible objects must be charged with spiritual power by the *dibịa ọgwụ* or medicine-man. Whereas *ọgwụ* can be used for good or for evil, *amusu* is always used for harmful purposes. Igbos distinguish between witches and sorcerers. A witch is a person whose spirit (*mmụọ*) is able to leave her body (*arụ*) through the power of *eriri* and take the form of an animal in order to inflict injury on others or

[60] For a helpful discussion of *ogbanje*, see Misty L. Bastion, 'Married in the Water: Spirit Kin and Other Afflictions of Modernity in Southeastern Nigeria', *JRA*, 27.2, 1997, 116-23.

[61] Ikenga-Metuh, *God and Man*, 75-7.

even 'eat their souls'. A sorceror, on the other hand, is one who uses medicine *ọgwụ* or *nkọ nsị* for evil purposes.

The Igbo concept of salvation is crucial for understanding the appeal of revival and Pentecostal spirituality. Igbo theologian Cyril Okorocha has shown that the main goal of Igbo primal religion is the search for salvation in the form of *ezi-ndụ* (good life), and the most important factor that makes life worthwhile is the gift of children to extend life, along with material prosperity, physical health, and more abstract ideas such as justice and peace. *Ezi-ndụ* is either enhanced or diminished through the manipulation of spiritual forces, and religious rituals, moral provisions and social relations are channelled towards its preservation.[62] Thus salvation in Igbo traditional thought is understood primarily in terms of problem solving, protection from evil, the achievement of success, and the acquisition of the good things of this life until old age (*nka na nzere* or old age with dignity), thus ensuring the attainment of ancestorhood. Nwogu considers the concept of *nka na nzere* the primary focus of the Igbo traditional worldview. An Igbo man's goal is to reach a ripe old age, where he is given respect for what he has achieved in life through a combination of hard work, the favour of the gods, and the assistance of fellow human beings.[63]

Okorocha identifies four vital aspects of primal spirituality, linked to the Igbo concept of salvation, which have influenced conversion to Christianity.[64] Firstly, the Igbo holistic worldview means that religion permeates all aspects of life, and considerable effort is devoted to finding ways to manipulate spiritual forces for the benefit of the community. Secondly, Igbos are pragmatic and success-oriented. Any religious form that does not deliver the 'goods' (in terms of *ezi-ndụ*) is discarded in favour of a more effective alternative. This, together with their receptivity to change, helps to explain the eclectic nature of Igbo spirituality. Thirdly, Igbos have a keen sense of community and collective responsibility. A popular Igbo saying is *igwe bụ ike* (unity is power). Igbos are aware of their dependence on the kinship group (*ụmụnna*) and seldom become detached from it wherever they live. Group solidarity permeates every facet of Igbo social life, including religion, which is communally regulated and expressed in a community setting. The Igbo concept of salvation has a

---

[62] Okorocha, *Religious Conversion*, 69-72, 293.

[63] D. I. Nwogu, *Nka na Nzere: The Focus of Igbo Worldview*, Ahiajoku Lecture, Owerri: Owerri Culture Division, Ministry of Information, Culture, Youth and Sports, 1984.

[64] Okorocha, 'Conversion', 168-69; Okorocha, *Religious Conversion*. While I follow Okorocha's outline, I supplement it with the work of other Igbo scholars, especially Uchendu, *Igbo*; Kalu, *Embattled Gods*; Ikenga-Metuh, *African Religions*; Ilogu, *Christianity*.

communal dimension. Reciprocity and altruism are expressions of *ezi-ndụ*, and generosity towards others is an indication that one is an *ezi mmadụ*, a good or saved person. According to Bastion, productive persons are those who manifest 'goodness' (*mma*) by working hard, accumulating and redistributing wealth (through title-taking, credit associations and the establishment of patron-client relations), and successfully rearing children, thus reproducing potential for the community at large.[65] Group expectations influence Igbo morality, which is geared towards maintaining harmony within the 'community', made up of the living, the ancestors and the deities. The extended family, age grade associations and elders help to regulate morality and socialise young people. Thus, shame is a major deterrent to crime. There is an Igbo proverb which says that if one finger touches oil, the oil invariably spreads to other fingers. Igbos believe that the consequences of individual acts of evil in terms of divine retribution affect the whole community. Finally, Igbo traditional spirituality is power-oriented. Like other African societies, its goal is to appropriate power by establishing enduring covenants with a wide variety of deities and other spirits of the land. These covenants are initiated and sustained through ritual practices such as prayer, sacrifices and festivals of renewal. For example, in the Anambra State capital of Awka, the community's covenant with *Imo-ọka*, the chief *alụsị*, is renewed during an annual festival which attracts not only local church members but also many of the town's non-resident 'sons' and 'daughters'.

Igbos have a precarious vision of the universe and believe that powerful forces exist which may prevent people from enjoying *ezi-ndụ* and fulfilling their destiny. These fall into two categories. Afflictions can result from the activity of witches, sorcerers or evil spirits. The Supreme Being, deities, *alụsị* or ancestors can also inflict misfortune or withdraw protection as punishment for violations of the moral code (*omenala*). When this occurs it is believed to be for the ultimate good of the individual and community. The belief in punishment and rewards is strong. Chineke imparts power to enhance life only on those who live according to *ọfọ-na-ogu* (justice and fair play with innocence) and conduct their lives according to *omenala*. Thus, fear of sin's consequences is a dominant factor in traditional morality. Failure to comply with *omenala* incurs the wrath of the gods, the withdrawal of their protection, and a reduction in the workings of power. It is the experience of wrath and its consequences (in the form of affliction) which creates an awareness of sin and calls for cleansing rituals to be performed. To maintain the cosmological balance, ensure the ongoing

[65] Misty L. Bastion, '"Bloodhounds Who Have No Friends": Witchcraft and Locality in the Nigerian Popular Press', in Jean Comaroff and John Comaroff (eds.), *Modernity and its Malcontents. Ritual and Power in Postcolonial Africa*, Chicago: University of Chicago Press, 1993, 138.

experience of *ezi-ndụ* and realise one's destiny (*akara aka*), various preventive and purificatory rites are performed. These immunise potential victims against the attacks of evil spirits, witches or sorcerers. When a person actually experiences affliction, a *dibịa-afa* (diviner) is consulted to ascertain the cause and prescribe appropriate actions needed to restore *ezi-ndụ*. Sin pollutes the individual or community (and hence, the land) and must be cleansed to ward off the wrath of the gods. A person who commits sin is referred to as *onye aruru ala* (one who pollutes the land).

The eschatological aspect of *ezi-ndụ* is summed up in the term *ahamefula* (that my name may not be obliterated). This partly explains the value placed on children, and the efforts to live a good life to attain ancestorhood and eventually return to the world through reincarnation. Although there is no concept of a future day of judgement, there *is* a belief in posthumous moral redress. As Ikenga-Metuh observes, 'the good go to *ala mmụọ*, the spirit-land, where they continue to live a life similar to their earthly life and are allowed to reincarnate, while the bad are banished to *ama nri mmụọ na mmadụ*, the Igbo hell, and turn into frustrated wandering spirits'.[66]

The Christian Missionary Enterprise, 1857-1967

This was the religious culture that confronted European missionaries as they landed on the shores of the River Niger in the mid-nineteenth century and began to penetrate the Igbo interior. Inevitably, there were clashes between Igbo traditional religious beliefs and the evangelical culture exported from the missionary metropolitan centres.

The explorations on the River Niger (1830-57) laid the foundations for the Christianisation of Igboland. Their purpose was two-fold: to open up trade with the local population and to investigate their receptivity to religious and secular education. Strictly speaking, Christian mission in Igboland began in 1841 when Simon Jonas, a former Igbo slave and member of the 1841 Niger expedition, spent a few weeks preaching in Aboh. But it was not until the 1857 expedition that the Anglican Church Missionary Society (CMS) opened the first permanent missionary base at Onitsha, North-Western Igboland, and until 1885, it remained the only missionary organisation within Igboland.[67] An outstanding feature was the role of indigenous agents as the early missionaries were Africans from Sierra Leone, often of Igbo descent, who were later joined by local

---

[66] Ikenga-Metuh, *God and Man*, 138.

[67] The Church Missionary Society (CMS) is an Anglican missionary society, founded in 1799. In 1985, it changed to the Church Mission Society.

Christians. One of the pioneers of the Niger Mission, Reverend John C. Taylor, was himself a Sierra Leonean of Igbo extraction.[68]

The high imperial era (1880 to about 1920) saw a significant increase in European missionary recruitment due in part to the influence of evangelical revivalism and Keswick spirituality. Interdenominational rivalry was an important theme, a development which intensified missionary efforts, according to Igbo historian Felix Ekechi, and contributed to the growth of Christianity in Igboland.[69] Following the Berlin Conference (1884-85) and the subsequent scramble for Africa, missionary societies competed for territory. From 1892 until their reunion in 1931, there were two Anglican bodies, the CMS and the Niger Delta Pastorate (NDP). The NDP flourished in southern Igboland. Meanwhile, in 1905 the CMS established a base in Owerri, Central Igboland, from where it spread rapidly. Presbyterians opened their first Igbo station in 1888 and were largely responsible for the Christianisation of Cross River Igboland, the territory of the Eastern Igbo. But Presbyterian activity in Igboland did not really take off until the twentieth century and for the most part remained localised until the 1960s. Methodists entered Igboland in 1910 and established a chain of missions along the Port Harcourt to Enugu railway line, but their comparative failure to develop a 'native' agency hindered their progress. These were Primitive rather than Wesleyan Methodists, but the two groups amalgamated in 1932 to become the Methodist Mission. The first interdenominational faith mission to enter Igboland was the Qua Iboe Mission, which established a station at Oloko, Southern Igboland, in 1920. The French Holy Ghost Roman Catholic Missionary Society arrived in 1885 and opened a mission in Onitsha, which became the headquarters of Catholic mission in Eastern Nigeria. Later, they were replaced by the Irish Holy Ghost Fathers. Igboland soon became the centre of Catholic missionary activity in Nigeria, a development which Omenka attributes to

---

[68] For the history of mission Christianity in Igboland, see Kalu, *Embattled Gods*; Ogbu U. Kalu, 'Colour and Conversion: The White Missionary Factor in the Christianisation of Igboland, 1867-1967', *Missiology*, 18.1, January 1990, 61-74; Isichei, *Igbo People*; E. A. Udo, 'The Missionary Scramble for Spheres of Influence in South-Eastern Nigeria 1900-52', in Ogbu Kalu (ed.), *The History of Christianity in West Africa*, London: Longmans, 1980, 159-81; P. B. Clarke, 'The Methods and Ideology of the Holy Ghost Fathers in Eastern Nigeria 1885-1905', in Kalu (ed.), *History*, 36-75; Nicholas Ibeawuchi Omenka, *The School in the Service of Evangelization. The Catholic Educational Impact in Eastern Nigeria 1886-1959*, Leiden: E. J. Brill, 1989; F. K. Ekechi, *Missionary Enterprise and Rivalry in Igboland 1857-1914*, London: Frank Cass, 1972.

[69] F. K. Ekechi, 'Colonialism and Christianity in West Africa: The Igbo Case, 1900-1915', *Journal of African History*, 12, 1971, 107.

Igbo susceptibility to change, their propensity to seek external linkages and their predilection for Western education.[70]

Church historians acknowledge that a turning point occurred from 1906 with a mass movement to Christianity involving Protestants and Roman Catholics. Hastings includes this movement in his examination of five significant West African conversion movements during the early twentieth century. From 1906 to 1918, the Catholic community alone increased from under 5,000 to approximately 74,000.[71] The first fifty years of Christian mission in Igboland yielded about 1,000 baptised Igbo converts, but by 1910, Christians in Eastern Nigeria outnumbered those west of the Niger. The 1921 census claimed that 284,835 out of 3,927,419 Igbo were Christians.[72] This rapid expansion, described by Ekechi as a 'religious revolution', followed the British conquest of the Igbo interior.[73] The arrival of missionaries at Owerri in Central Igboland precipitated the mass movement. As Okorocha notes, rather than having to plead to be allowed to stay, the missionaries found that people were appealing to them to come and were even willing to pay for the schools which they wanted so desperately.[74] Missionaries were able to travel with relative security, and many Igbo communities were exposed to missionary influence. They saw the missions as allies against the violence of conquest, and interpreted their defeat and the white man's relative prosperity as evidence that their gods had failed and the new should be given a chance.[75] For Isichei, the key factor was the close association between mission and education. Nineteenth century Igbo communities had shown little interest in Western education because it seemed to offer few opportunities. This changed when Western education offered an escape from the tyranny of the Warrant Chief and opened new employment opportunities.[76] Education became the principal means of evangelisation, and different missions established schools in villages and towns in their efforts to expand. But it would be wrong to conclude from this that the primary motives for conversion were secular. As Okorocha argues, the quest for education, and the opportunities

---

[70] Omenka, *School*, 27-8.

[71] Adrian Hastings, *The Church in Africa 1450-1950*, Oxford: Clarendon Press, 1994, 443-53. See also Kalu, *Embattled Gods*, 13; Ekechi, *Missionary*, xiii; Isichei, *Igbo People*, 165.

[72] E. A. Ayandele, *The Missionary Impact on Modern Nigeria, 1842-1914. A Political and Social Analysis*, London: Longman, 1966, 343, 345; Isichei, *Igbo People*, 161.

[73] Ekechi, *Missionary*, 114, 149.

[74] Okorocha, *Religious Conversion*, 207-208.

[75] *Ibid.*, 223-25.

[76] Isichei, *Igbo People*, 166-67.

it offered in terms of enhanced status and prosperity, was a search for salvation in terms of *ezi-ndụ.*[77]

Protestant cooperation has been neglected as a theme in Nigerian nationalist historiography, which has tended to focus on missionary rivalry.[78] Despite disagreements, Protestant missions formed a united front against Roman Catholics and established comity agreements, resulting in the partition of Eastern Nigeria into five Protestant denominational districts: CMS, NDP, Presbyterian, Qua Iboe Mission and Methodist. They also embarked on a number of joint ventures, including Trinity Theological College and Queen Elizabeth II Hospital in Umuahia. While Roman Catholics refused to recognise these agreements, Protestants continued to contest mission boundaries until 1932 when they became fixed. Anglicans occupied Northern, North-Western, North-Eastern and Central Igboland, but were especially dominant in the cities of Onitsha and Owerri. Methodists occupied Southern Igboland, the Okigwe-Isuikwuato corner of Central Igboland, and established a strong base in Umuahia. Later, they penetrated North-Eastern Igboland and the urban districts of Enugu and Abakaliki. Presbyterians were initially restricted to Cross River Igboland, but during the 1960s spread to Port Harcourt, Aba, Mbawsi, Umuahia, Abakaliki and Enugu. The Qua Iboe Mission continued to work mainly in the Aba district of Southern Igboland. Meanwhile, Roman Catholics established churches and schools throughout Igboland. Later, Africans disputed these boundaries, and during the remainder of the colonial era, Protestant denominations spread beyond the territory allotted to them. But for a long period, religious pluralism was mainly confined to urban areas.

Catholic and Protestant missions in Africa experienced contrasting fortunes during the inter-war years. Catholic missions prospered as personnel moved increasingly into education and used the school as an instrument of evangelisation. In contrast, Protestant missions and the CMS in particular experienced a steady decline in missionary recruitment, effectively reversing their dominance in Igboland. Hastings cites economic and intellectual reasons for this development. Financial trouble resulted in a drop in recruitment levels, except among conservative evangelicals. However, the main factor was a theological shift from fundamentalism to liberalism, which shattered Western evangelical unity during the 1920s.[79] This affected the CMS and the Student Christian Movement, and had repercussions in Nigeria. The formation of the Ruanda Mission in 1926 as

---

[77] Okorocha, *Religious Conversion*, 234-35.

[78] For example, Ekechi, *Missionary*; Udo, 'Scramble', 159-60. One Igbo historian who has redressed the balance is Ogbu U. Kalu. See his *Divided People of God. Church Union Movement in Nigeria: 1867-1966*, London/New York: NOK, 1978.

[79] Hastings, *Church*, 551.

an independent wing of the CMS meant that East Africa tended to attract conservative evangelical CMS recruits, and West Africa, liberals.[80]

During the 1950s, the 'paternalistic benevolence' of the inter-war years gradually gave way to a more self-critical awareness and recognition of the validity of African experience. This was partly due to the influence of CMS Secretary Max Warren, the principal Protestant mission strategist, whom Hastings describes as a man of 'considerable historical and cultural sensitivity'.[81] This intellectual vitality was more apparent within Protestantism than Roman Catholicism, which would have to wait until the effects of the Second Vatican Council (1962-65) had filtered down before any significant reform could take place. Mission churches continued to increase at a prodigious rate, and the quality of church institutions (schools and medical facilities) improved. According to the 1953 census, 64 per cent of Owerri Province, 28 per cent of Enugu Province and 26 per cent of Onitsha were classified as Christian.[82] Mainline churches in Nigeria obtained a degree of autonomy, with first the Presbyterians and then the Methodists gaining independent status in 1960 and 1962 respectively. Anglicans and Catholics did not obtain the same degree of independence, though the Anglican Province of West Africa was formerly established in 1951 and the Catholic Church hierarchies were set up in British West Africa in 1950. By the 1960s, the mainline churches represented the dominant brand of Christianity in Igboland. This is reflected in the 1963 Census figures, which show that there were 103,250 Anglicans and 723,568 Catholics in Owerri Province, and 101,356 Anglicans and 548,106 Catholics in Onitsha Province.[83] As we see in the next chapter, most civil war revivalists were drawn from the ranks of the four largest mainline denominations: Anglican, Methodist, Presbyterian and Roman Catholic.

From the 1950s, there was also a growing conservative evangelical presence in Igboland. The Sudan Interior Mission (SIM), part of the Faith Missions movement, was influenced by the US American Holiness movement through its founder Rowland Bingham. Bingham entered

---

[80] Stanley, 'Revival', 7; Kevin Ward, '"Taking Stock": The Church Missionary Society and its Historians', in Kevin Ward and Brian Stanley (eds.), *The Church Missionary Society and World Christianity 1799-1999*, Grand Rapids, MI: Eerdmanns, 2000, 35.

[81] Hastings, *Church*, 567.

[82] Cited in C. V. Ifeka-Moller, 'White Power: Social-Structural Factors in Conversion to Christianity, Eastern Nigeria, 1921-26', *Canadian Journal of African Studies*, 8.1, 1974, 62-3.

[83] Cited in Kalu, *Embattled Gods*, 178.

Nigeria in 1901 and established his first mission station at Patigi in 1902.[84] SIM's goal was to reach Muslims and due to comity agreements agreed to concentrate on the North. Its early opposition to the 'school approach' to evangelism hindered its progress, but after it opened its first school in 1930 it expanded rapidly and by 1940 had planted sixty-two mission stations. SIM was committed to indigenous church principles, and in 1954, its Nigerian churches became an autonomous body called the Evangelical Churches of West Africa (ECWA), with headquarters in the Northern city of Jos.

The spread of SIM/ECWA to Igboland occurred gradually through indigenous and missionary initiative. During the 1950s, Igbos converted in the North through ECWA requested SIM to extend their work to the East. SIM responded by working through its media ministries (African Challenge magazine and Radio ELWA). In 1957, it appointed field representatives in Aba and Enugu, and during the 1960s opened bookshops in Enugu and Port Harcourt. Meanwhile, some Igbo ECWA members had returned to the East to engage in evangelistic activity and plant churches. During the 1966 pogroms in the North, many more Igbos returned to the East, including ECWA pastors and members, and this added momentum to the work. By 1967, ECWA had planted a small number of churches in rural areas and major cities (such as Enugu, Umuahia, Aba and Onitsha), which later attracted young people associated with Scripture Union and the Civil War Revival. ECWA's growing popularity in Igboland was a reaction to the low spiritual condition of some of the mainline churches.

Scripture Union (SU) was another significant conservative evangelical presence. In an address given to the 1999 SU Nigeria Summit Meeting, National Chairman Dr Augustus Mbanaso described it as the 'foremost Evangelical Movement' in Nigeria during the twentieth century.[85] Scripture Union was started in England in 1867 when Joseph Spiers began to hold special meetings for children neglected in the churches. Later, it introduced a scheme for encouraging children to read their Bibles on a regular basis using SU cards and notes. SU's growth in Nigeria was closely linked to Western liberal-modernist controversies. It was this issue that prompted the Cambridge Inter-Collegiate Christian Union (CICCU) to break away from the Student Christian Movement (SCM) in 1910. SCM was originally established as an evangelical mission-orientated organisation in British and American universities, but as direct missionary work declined, it began to focus on theological and socio-political issues. To

---

[84] I have relied on oral and written sources for SIM/ECWA history in Nigeria. Especially helpful is Yusufu Turaki, *An Introduction to the History of SIM/ECWA in Nigeria, 1893-1993*, Jos: Challenge Press, 1993.

[85] Augustus Mbanaso, 'Keynote Address by the National Chairman', First Scripture Union (Nigeria) Summit, Camp of Faith Okigwe, 16 October 1999, 5.

make the gospel more relevant to a new scientific generation, it became committed to liberal Christianity and a critical approach to the Bible.[86] CICCU was a branch of SCM, but its members were mainly conservative evangelicals opposed to the liberalism of SCM. This led to the formation of the Inter-Varsity Fellowship (IVF) in 1920 and the Inter-Varsity Fellowship of Evangelical Students (IFES) in 1947. Since then, a clear distinction has existed between SCM and the more conservative evangelical IVF or Evangelical Christian Unions (ECU), as its member branches were known.[87] This had implications for the work of SU Nigeria.

Igbo Presbyterian Francis Akanu Ibiam introduced SCM into Igboland after his return to Nigeria in 1935 following medical training in Scotland, but for some years it remained outside the educational institutions. In 1944, SCM work in Eastern and Western Nigeria was amalgamated and in 1948 was introduced into the University of Ibadan, where British expatriate teachers reinforced its status. Until the mid-1960s, it remained the only interdenominational student organisation in the universities of Ibadan, Ife, Lagos and Nsukka. By the end of the decade, however, it was in decline, largely due to the increasing influence of SU and the ECUs, introduced into universities by British lecturers as an alternative evangelical witness.

Despite pressure from liberalism, SU maintained its strong conservative evangelical stance, partly due to its links with the IVF and British Christian Unions. SU work in Nigeria was directed towards young people rather than children, an innovation that Ojo attributes to the Nigerian context. SU required a literate environment, and this was found in the secondary schools and colleges.[88] Its work in Nigeria actually began in the late nineteenth century, long before the introduction of SCM and the ECUs, but was initially limited to the circulation of Bible reading notes. It was introduced by CMS missionaries in 1884, and by 1892, a SU group had started to meet at Onitsha. It almost disappeared in the 1940s, but was resurrected by British expatriate teachers who introduced it into secondary schools. Most were former members of the British IVF, and later a close relationship developed between SU and the ECUs. In the early 1950s, SU flourished in

---

[86] For the history of SCM and SU and their introduction into Nigeria, see Nigel Sylvester, *God's Word in a Young World. The Story of Scripture Union*, London: Scripture Union, 1984; Matthews A. Ojo, 'The Growth of Campus Christianity and Charismatic Movements in Western Nigeria', Ph.D. thesis, University of London, 1987; Ojo, *Army*, 23-31.

[87] For details of the split from someone sympathetic to the evangelical viewpoint, see Douglas Johnson, *Contending for the Faith: A History of the Evangelical Movement in the Universities and Colleges*, Leicester: IVP, 1979, 66-83.

[88] Ojo, 'Campus Christianity, 70.

Figure 1. Scripture Union Boys' Camp, Umuahia, 1955.

Nigeria as more expatriate Christian teachers and government workers arrived, and by 1960, there were twenty-two SU groups in Western Nigeria, eleven in the East, and thirty-eight in the North. John Dean, a missionary with the Sudan United Mission, became the first SU travelling secretary in Nigeria. The groups in the North belonged to the autonomous Fellowship of Christian Students (FCS), formed in Northern Nigeria in 1957, with first John Dean, then Reuben Ariko and Emmanuel Oladipo as successive general secretaries. As it was thoroughly evangelical, it was felt unnecessary to form separate SU groups in the North. The same year, students at the universities of Ibadan, Lagos and Nsukka met to read SU literature as a supplement to their SCM activities, and in 1961, the Ibadan Varsity Christian Union (IVCU) was formed out of an existing SU group. Later, IVCU became an early focal point of Nigerian neo-Pentecostal activity.

The first SU school groups in Igboland were established at Umuahia in 1955 and Enugu in 1957, and by 1966, the number of groups in the East had grown to approximately thirty. SU groups existed in some of the more prestigious Protestant mission schools in the East, such as Hope Waddell Training Institute (Calabar), Dennis Memorial Grammar School (Onitsha), Methodist College (Uzuakoli), and the Government Colleges at Umuahia, Owerri, Afikpo and Enugu. Some of these later became centres of revivalist and Pentecostal activity. In 1966, a young British missionary called Bill Roberts was appointed the first SU travelling secretary in the

East. As we will see in chapter 3, he was to become a key figure during the Civil War Revival and its main expatriate influence.[89] In the early 1960s, a SU group was started at the newly opened University of Nigeria at Nsukka (UNN), Northern Igboland. Following the 1966 pogroms, Igbo students from Ibadan and other Western Nigerian universities relocated to UNN. This was an important factor in the growth of SU in the East as the influx of ECU members helped to revive the small SU group at UNN, which was soon re-organised and renamed the Christian Union following the model of IVCU, Ibadan. After the closure of UNN (due to the war) some of these ECU members joined Roberts and shared leadership of SU Umuahia, which became the focal point of early revivalist activity.

There were several reasons for SU's growth and popularity. Firstly, the Nigerian educational system was expanding rapidly, and SU was welcomed into schools as most were still run by Christian missions. Its conservative evangelical stance proved an attractive alternative to the more liberal SCM and the dominant brand of mission church spirituality. Secondly, large numbers of Christian expatriates arrived to work in Nigeria, and they were responsible for starting SU groups in Nigerian educational institutions. There was also an element of prestige attached to the presence of a white travelling secretary, and this encouraged cooperation from British mission churches. Thirdly, SU's interdenominational stance meant that members could participate fully while still maintaining their church affiliation. In fact, SU was arguably more successful at promoting unity and cross-denominational fertilisation than the church union movement discussed below. Other important factors included SU's policy of promoting indigenous leadership, and its attempt to contextualise the gospel and relate the Bible to contemporary life. The introduction of adult Pilgrim's Groups and the publication of the Nigerian version of SU daily Bible-reading notes in 1963 contributed to this. Yet SU continued to use English as the main language of worship and study, and like ECWA/SIM adopted an anti-Pentecostal stance which limited its appeal.[90]

To return to the theme of Protestant interdenominational cooperation, the roots of the Nigerian church union movement, a major ecumenical initiative, go back to the early missionary enterprise in the East when mission field exigencies encouraged 'cooperation and comity' among

---

[89] Roberts grew up in the Anglican Church and was converted in 1954. After a brief spell in Nigeria during his National Service, he became a student at the University of Cambridge where, like members of the Ruanda Mission a generation earlier, he was involved with CICCU.

[90] Ojo, 'Campus Christianity', 80; Sylvester, *God's Word*, 211, 223-25, 244-45.

different Protestant groups.[91] They found they shared a common goal (the propagation of the gospel) and a common enemy (the Roman Catholic Church). An early catalyst was the 1910 Edinburgh World Missionary Conference, where church unity as an essential element of effective mission was a major theme.[92] A year later, an interdenominational conference in Calabar passed a resolution accepting the principle of organic unity. Though the initial impulse for unity came from missionaries, Africans later took up the vision. The influence of the World Council of Churches (WCC), the example of the South India scheme which resulted in the formation of the Church of South India in 1947, the Lambeth Conference of 1958, the advent of political independence, and theological reflection on the nature of the church, all added impetus to the project.

The impulse for church union was stronger in the East than in Western Nigeria, and the 1947 Onitsha Conference involving Anglicans, Presbyterians, Methodists, Qua Iboe Mission and the Sudan United Mission (SUM) defined the contours of the proposed union. The Baptists and SIM refused to participate, and later QIM and SUM withdrew when they realised that the goal went further than federalism. Significantly, none of the African initiated churches (AICs) or mission-related Pentecostal churches were invited to participate. So negotiations continued between the three largest mission churches in Igboland (Anglican, Methodist and Presbyterian). The new united church (set to be launched on 11th December 1965) would have been by far the largest Protestant church in black Africa, but at the last moment the scheme collapsed, not over doctrinal differences or the issue of episcopacy, but over property rights, personality clashes, inter-ethnic and interdenominational rivalries. However, deeper issues lay beneath the surface. Kalu refers to disagreements over what kind of united church was envisioned (whether a truly indigenous church or one 'imprisoned within a foreign structure'), and to an emphasis on organisational issues rather than mission and worship.[93]

---

[91] For the church union movement in Nigeria, see Kalu, *Divided People*; O. U. Kalu, 'The Shattered Cross: the Church Union Movement in Nigeria 1905-66', in Kalu (ed.), *History*, 340-64; G. E. Igwe, *Church Union in Nigeria*, Umuahia: Ark, 2000; Adrian Hastings, *A History of African Christianity 1950-1975*, Cambridge: Cambridge University Press, 1979, 162-63.

[92] Timothy Yates, *Christian Mission in the Twentieth Century*, Cambridge: Cambridge University Press, 1994, 29.

[93] Kalu, *Divided People*, 74.

Missionary Ideologies from the Metropolitan Centre

Writing in 1980, Kalu warned of a tendency for some historians to focus on the activities in the mission fields to the neglect of the home base. By doing so, they failed to recognise the influence of missionary ideology on the pattern of Christian mission and religious encounter in Africa.[94] Since then, the balance has been redressed with increasing attention given to the cultural processes that have shaped missionary thinking and praxis on the field.[95] Several interweaving strands of missionary ideology are of interest to us here. Together they helped to shape the religious context in which the Civil War Revival and its Pentecostal progeny flourished.

The first was a belief in the benefits of civilisation and specifically the superiority of Western civilisation, which resonated with the Enlightenment ideal of progress. Hastings refers to the 'nineteenth-century missionary fixation with civilization'. As people of their age, they absorbed the 'assumptions of its ideology', adopting the catchphrase 'Civilisation and Christianity' along with everyone else implicated in the colonial project.[96] The Saro missionaries from Sierra Leone, known collectively as 'Black Europeans', were also influenced by this ideology. According to Kalu, J. C. Taylor, pioneer of the Niger Mission, believed that his task was to civilize through religious instruction and trade.[97] For most missionaries, however, civilisation was not the primary goal. They considered it a necessary condition for the gospel to prosper with any permanence. They also remained committed to the priority of Christianity over civilisation. The gospel as the only means of social, moral and cultural transformation was, according to Stanley, the majority missionary opinion in the English evangelical tradition from the late eighteenth to the mid-twentieth centuries.[98] Yet the perception of Africa as a 'dark' continent and its inhabitants as 'heathens', awaiting emancipation from the clutches of the devil through the civilising impulses of the gospel, sometimes fostered a hostile view of other cultures, which had unfortunate consequences for the missionary enterprise. That this helped to shape their conception of the missionary task is hinted at in these words of Taylor's, written in the late

---

[94] Ogbu U. Kalu, 'The Task', in Kalu (ed.), *History*, 3.

[95] For example, Brian Stanley, *The Bible and the Flag. Protestant missions and British imperialism in the nineteenth and twentieth centuries*, Leicester: Apollos, 1990; Peel, *Religious Encounter*.

[96] Hastings, *Church*, 284-85.

[97] Kalu, *Embattled Gods*, 83-5.

[98] Brian Stanley, 'Christian Missions and the Enlightenment: A Reevaluation', in Brian Stanley (ed.), *Christian Missions and the Enlightenment*, Grand Rapids, MI: Eerdmans, 2001, 177.

1850s: 'May many come willingly to labour in pulling down the strongholds of Satan's kingdom, for the whole of the Ibo district is his citadel'.[99]

The popularity of the 'civilisation' model among early nineteenth century Protestant missionaries is attributed rather tentatively by Hastings to a lack of a viable missionary theology over and above an 'enthusiasm for world evangelism'. But when they acquired one, they began to recognise the dangers attached to the civilising project.[100] The indigenous church concept and the 'three self' policy, articulated most clearly by CMS Secretary Henry Venn (1841-72), challenged the missionary preoccupation with 'civilization'. This represents the second strand of missionary ideology. Venn's accession to the office of CMS Secretary happened to coincide with the 1841 Niger Expedition. Consequently, his thinking influenced early Protestant missionaries in Igboland. Venn anticipated the formation of self-governing, self-supporting and self-propagating indigenous churches, and hoped to shift the focus from a civilising mission, promoting European ways, to the adoption of African ones and the promotion of local agency.[101] This vision was based on his belief in the fundamental equality of humankind and his confidence in the 'native' capacity to rule in secular as well as ecclesiastical positions. Two key ideas emerged, according to Williams, which it was hoped would shape missionary work in Africa. The first was the development of 'native' pastors under European supervision as a preparation for leaving the work entirely in their hands. The second was a direct consequence of this: the so-called 'euthanasia' of missions.[102]

During the high imperial period, there was a partial reversal of this approach in Igboland, as European missionaries, influenced by Keswick holiness spirituality, gradually replaced local leaders. Ironically, those at the forefront of the reforming party were opposed to the 'Christianity and Civilization' model but accepted the new imperialist currents represented by the Royal Niger Company of Sir George Goldie. The purge of the Niger Mission and the humiliation of its head Bishop Samuel Ajayi Crowther precipitated the first wave of Nigerian independency, as 'African' or 'Ethiopian' churches were founded in Western Nigeria as a response to white discrimination of African agents.[103] In the East, Anglican congregations of the Niger Delta became an independent self-supporting

---

[99] Samuel Crowther and J. C. Taylor, *The Gospel on the Banks of the Niger*, London: Seeley, Jackson & Co., 1859, 325.

[100] Hastings, *Church*, 290.

[101] *Ibid.*

[102] Peter Williams, '"Not Transplanting": Henry Venn's Strategic Vision', in Ward and Stanley (eds.), *Church Missionary Society*, 147-72.

[103] For a brief overview of the 1890 Niger purge, see Hastings, *Church*, 388.

Pastorate within the Anglican Church, and by 1921, there were 29,225 Christians attached to the African churches of Lagos and an almost equal number attached to churches of local origins, though most were located outside Igboland.[104]

Africanisation was even slower within the Roman Catholic Mission. In his assessment of the methods and ideology of the Holy Ghost Fathers in Igboland, Peter Clarke refers to the 'changing missionary attitudes towards the African, discernible in the 1890s', when RCM missionaries showed little confidence in lay evangelists, preferring to rely upon European and 'native' clergy. Furthermore, commitment to a sacramental approach to evangelisation (a ministerial function) and focus on the school made them reluctant to use African catechists.[105] Despite a shift from 'paternalism' and the notion of white superiority during the early twentieth century, due to the increasing use of the school system of evangelisation, this attitude persisted, and it was not until 1930 that the first Igbo priest, John Anyogu, was ordained. Nevertheless it was Igbo agents who were largely responsible for evangelisation and pastoral care during the mass movement to Catholicism after 1906. Significantly, between 1906 and 1918 the number of Catholic missionaries in Igboland remained at around 30, while the number of Igbo catechists increased from 33 to 552.[106]

During the inter-war years, the Protestant missionary enterprise was influenced by J. H. Oldham, Secretary of the Edinburgh Conference and later the International Missionary Council (IMC). Oldham was a firm advocate of the civilising potential of Christianity and the 'benefits' of imperialism. The new generation of missionaries believed in the enduring quality of the colonial order, insisted on the retention of control, and felt that the achievement of an indigenous church could safely be left on hold. Little attention was given to the formation of African clergy, and by 1950, no African Anglican diocesan bishop had been appointed since the death of Crowther. However, at local church level, pastoral care and evangelism remained largely in the hands of local catechists and the small number of ordained Africans.[107] The situation was similar within the Roman Catholic Mission.[108]

During the 1950s, with independence looming and missionary recruitment levels low following World War II, there was growing awareness of the need to increase the number of ordained Africans and improve their level of training. Yet despite the granting of a level of

[104] James B. Webster, *The African Churches among the Yoruba 1888-1922*, Oxford, 1964, 95-6; Kalu, *Embattled Gods*, 170; Isichei, *Igbo People*, 181.

[105] Clarke, 'Methods', 49-50.

[106] Hastings, *Church*, 450-51.

[107] *Ibid.*, 550-55.

[108] Hastings, *African Christianity*, 60-1.

autonomy to Anglican and Catholic communities, there was only a limited transfer of ecclesiastical authority. By 1960, there were Nigerian Anglican diocesan bishops in Lagos, Ibadan, Ondo-Benin and the Niger Delta, but Igboland remained under the authority of the British Archbishop C. J. Patterson in Onitsha. The situation was slightly more promising in the Roman Catholic Mission. Although there was still a reluctance to appoint African priests to the episcopate, by 1960 there were Igbo bishops over the dioceses of Umuahia, Port Harcourt and Enugu, and in 1967, Frances Arinze was appointed the first Igbo Archbishop. Yet in Onitsha Archdiocese, with approximately 380,890 Catholics, there were still only 15 Igbo priests in 1960 (compared to 112 expatriate clergy).[109] While there was a steady increase in the number of ordained African clergy, especially within Catholic ranks, the training of catechists for lower, localised ministries was neglected. Prodigious church growth meant that the burden of congregational responsibility rested largely with these catechists and increasingly with lay members. But clericalism and hierarchical structures remained dominant features of mainline churches in the 1960s, and there was reluctance on the part of missionaries to relinquish control.

Kalu has argued that the missionary response to decolonisation was to maintain control by adopting a policy of 'passive revolution', a term coined by Gramsci to refer to the way a dominant socio-political group may have to change its way of wielding power if it wants to maintain its hegemony. Yet this was hindered on two fronts: from the centre by the moratorium debate, and from the fringes by various forms of independency, especially during the 1970s.[110] We return to the subject of independency and local initiative later. Moratorium became an issue during the 1958 International Missionary Council meeting in Ghana, following an appeal by Walter Freytag for fewer missionaries. This call was to become more strident in the 1970s and reflected African dissatisfaction with the missionary version of indigenisation. Meanwhile, during the 1960s, while older missions were trying to diminish their presence, new missionaries were arriving from other more 'theologically conservative' groups such as SIM, which by 1966 had 648 missionaries in Nigeria.[111]

---

[109] Hastings, *African Christianity*, 112-13; Kalu, *Divided People*, 68-9; Omenka, *School*, 277; V. A. Nwosu, 'The Era of Archbishop Charles Heerey 1931-1967', in V. A. Nwosu (ed.), *The Catholic Church in Onitsha. People, Places and Events (1885-1985)*, Onitsha: Etukokwu Press, 1985, 62.

[110] Ogbu U. Kalu, 'Passive Revolution and its Saboteurs: African Christian Initiative in the Era of Decolonization', in Brian Stanley (ed.), *Missions, Nationalism, & the End of the Empire*, Grand Rapids, MI: Eerdmans, 2003, 250-51, 268-70.

[111] Hastings, *African Christianity*, 165.

Scripture Union was more successful at devolving power and developing an indigenisation strategy in Nigeria. It did this by what Ojo refers to as a process of 'Nigerianisation', involving leadership training courses, one-to-one discipleship and the placement of Nigerians in key leadership positions.[112] The appointment of Mike Oye as the first Nigerian travelling secretary in 1966 was an important landmark. Born in Ghana of Nigerian parentage, Oye came to Nigeria in 1962 to study at the University of Ibadan, where he joined IVCU and became its President in 1965. After his graduation, he worked for SU from 1966 to 1972 and was a key figure during the Civil War Revival. The establishment of Pilgrims groups in 1967 to cater for school leavers also encouraged the development of Igbo Christian leadership. They were originally the idea of Bill Roberts and his Igbo colleague Augustus Mbanaso, later to become a senior figure in SU Nigeria. SU adopted a policy of national autonomy in Africa aimed at fostering financial and governmental independence, and in 1966, SU Nigeria became an autonomous body.

The third strand of missionary ideology which influenced the shape of the Igbo religious landscape was Enlightenment scientific rationality. As a 'child' of the evangelical and pietist movements, the modern missionary movement spawned a generation of missionaries committed to a dualistic conception of God and the devil, and a confidence in the message of the cross as the sole agent of individual and social transformation.[113] But mission historians, such as Andrew Walls and Brian Stanley, have also recognised the influence of Enlightenment assumptions, not only in its concern with education and health care, and its confidence in science, but especially in its emphasis on the all-sufficiency of reason.[114] As missionaries preached the gospel, they also promoted an Enlightenment worldview. Enlightenment thinkers constructed a 'frontier' between the empirical and spiritual worlds. Empiricists and rationalists insisted that we can know nothing about the spiritual world or went further by denying its existence altogether. According to Walls, the Christian Enlightenment 'accepted the frontier between the worlds, but asserted that there were identifiable crossing places: the incarnation, the resurrection, revelation, prayer, perhaps miracles'. Theology's task was to police these frontiers and adapt Christianity to modern rational thinking. During the eighteenth and nineteenth centuries, some Western theologians responded to the Enlightenment by developing liberal theology, which explained the

---

[112] Ojo, 'Campus Christianity', 85-7. See also Sylvester, *God's Word*, 211.

[113] Meyer, *Translating the Devil*, 40-3; Stanley, *Bible*, 62.

[114] A. F. Walls, 'Missionary Vocation and the Ministry: the First Generation', in Kalu (ed.), *History*, 22-35; A. F. Walls, 'Christian Scholarship in Africa in the Twenty-first Century', *Transformation. An International Dialogue on Mission and Ethics*, 19.4, October 2002, 223; Stanley, *Bible*.

miracles of the Bible scientifically and discarded belief in the devil and demons. Others accepted that some features of the New Testament, such as prophecy and healing, were 'frontier crossings formerly in use but no longer available'.[115] While many pastors were inspired by the Enlightenment and adopted liberal theology, Pietists and Puritans still endorsed traditional diabology and soteriology. Protestant revivalism, reacting against Enlightenment assumptions, attacked liberal theology and promoted belief in the devil, heaven and hell, and the need to evangelise the 'heathen'. Nevertheless, the Enlightenment left its mark on Protestant missionary thinking.

It was within this framework that the gospel came to Igboland and was appropriated by local communities. Early CMS missionaries were evangelical, and their goal was to preach the gospel, promote individual conversion and plant local churches. Initially they concentrated on evangelism. Because of their belief in human depravity and their focus on the cross, they conceived their task in terms of a 'crusade' against idolatry. Consequently, they demonised traditional religion and opposed local cultural practices, declaring 'war on *omenala* Igbo, on the moral and religious fabric of Igbo existence'.[116] Evangelism and civilisation, the Bible and the plough, became the twin goals of early missionary endeavour in Igboland. Nevertheless, early missionaries and Igbo communities had one point in common - they accepted the ontological reality of demons.

However, gradually many missionaries and local church leaders came to regard traditional spirits and witchcraft as figments of the imagination. Following the Berlin Conference (1884), the school system took over as the principal missionary strategy. Missionary education, which promoted Enlightenment assumptions and attacked local worldviews, became a secularising and modernising influence. This precipitated a spiritual crisis, a 'dislocation of identity', which Sierra Leonean missiologist Jehu Hanciles attributes to the fact that 'vital dimensions of the African spiritual universe – to which *power* is crucially applied - remained outside the scope of the Christian faith and, by implication, outside the cognisance of the Christian God'.[117] The gap between received theology and inherited worldview proved harmful, especially in moments of crisis when churches were often unable to solve problems associated with witchcraft and evil spirits. Even

---

[115] Walls, 'Christian Scholarship in Africa', 223-24.

[116] Charles Chkezie Agu, *Secularization in Igboland. Socio-religious Change and its Challenges to the Church Among the Igbo*, Frankfurt: Peter Lang, 1989, 260.

[117] Jehu Hanciles, 'Conversion and Social Change: A Review of the "Unfinished Task" in West Africa', in Donald M. Lewis (ed.), *Christianity Reborn. The Global Expansion of Evangelicalism in the Twentieth Century*, Grand Rapids, MI: Eerdmans, 2004, 168.

with the ideological sea change during the early twentieth century, when the need to recognise positive elements within receptor cultures was appreciated, missionaries still regarded traditional religious values and thought patterns with suspicion. Adaptation was usually limited to local customs, rather than issues of more fundamental concern to the Igbo such as healing and protection from evil. This was a consequence of what Isichei refers to as the antithesis between Igbo traditional religion and missionary Christianity, the different assumptions about the ends which religion is supposed to serve. Igbo religion was directed towards long life and temporal blessings; missionary Christianity towards the eschatological dangers of hell and joys of heaven.[118]

This provoked a variety of responses from Igbo communities during the colonial era.[119] First were the traditionalists who resisted Christianity and intensified their commitment to primal religion as a means of preserving the traditions of their fathers against the corrosive power of the gospel. Second were those who embraced mission Christianity wholeheartedly, rejected all external forms of the old religion and showed little concern for inculturation. This response occurred chiefly among first generation converts. Sometimes second generation Christians chose to combine elements from the old and new, a form of dual allegiance, reflecting the eclectic and pragmatic nature of Igbo spirituality. At moments of crisis, they were prone to revert to old ways of problem solving. Robert Schreiter, in his study of local theologies, refers to this as the problem of dual systems, when people follow the religious practices of two distinct systems, especially in times of distress.[120] Other second generation Christians, exposed to Western education and urbanisation, became increasingly detached from their religious heritage.

None of these responses proved satisfactory. There were persistent conflicts between converts who rejected primal religion, traditionalists and those with dual allegiance. The negative attitude of Western missionaries to Igbo traditional culture left what Okorocha has called a legacy of 'two faiths in one mind' and encouraged the persistence of primal religious beliefs and practices after conversion. Despite adopting the outward symbols of mission Christianity, Igbo converts continued to 'view religion

---

[118] Isichei, 'Igbo Response', 216.

[119] For helpful discussions, see Isichei, 'Igbo Response'; Okorocha, *Religious Conversion*, 261-83; Christopher I. Ejizu, 'Endurance of Conviction: The Persistence of the Traditional World-view in Igbo Christian Converts', *Neue Zeitschrift fur Missionswissenschaft*, 43.2, 1987, 125-35.

[120] Robert Schreiter, *Constructing Local Theologies*, Maryknoll: Orbis, 1985, 145, 148.

in terms of power, and salvation to include *ezi-ndụ*'.[121] Some scholars suggest that traditional religion still ruled the minds of most Igbo Christians during the colonial era.[122] While this is an overstatement, the old covenants proved far more resilient than expected and were often inadequately challenged by mission Christianity.

Local Initiatives from the Margins, 1914-1967

The failure of Western missions to fully implement programmes of indigenisation and adaptation precipitated a series of local initiatives which generated new denominations. As indigenous movements with an emphasis on the Spirit, they mobilised neglected forces in the Christian community, especially youth and women, and responded more effectively to consumer demands. They also prepared the ground for Pentecostal infiltration into mainline mission churches and influenced many who later became participants in the Civil War Revival.

Typologies

New religious movements, of which AICs are a part, have captured the imagination of scholars from different disciplines. Since Bengt Sundkler's regional study *Bantu Prophets in South Africa*, published in 1948, there has been a vast and complex array of literature both from within and outside the movement.[123] The diversity and dynamic nature of these movements makes classification difficult. Andrew Walls reminds us that 'motion is of the essence of movements' and sometimes they develop 'toward a classical type of Christian affirmation, sometimes away from it'.[124] Rigid typologies run the risk of being too complex or simply misleading, due to a tendency for making sweeping generalisations not sufficiently grounded in empirical data, or importing European categories not always familiar to the churches

---

[121] Okorocha, *Religious Conversion*, 271, 295. The persistence of Igbo traditional religious values and practices after conversion is a theme of a number of studies. See for example, Ejizu, 'Endurance'; C. N. Ubah, 'Religious Change among the Igbo during the Colonial Period', *JRA,* 18, February 1988, 71-91; Frank A. Salamone, 'Continuity of Igbo Values after Conversion: A Study in Purity and Prestige', *Missiology,* 3.1, 1975, 33-43.

[122] Ubah, 'Religious Change', 87-8; Salamone, 'Continuity', 34.

[123] Bengt Sundkler, *Bantu Prophets in South Africa*, London: Oxford University Press, 1961.

[124] Andrew F. Walls, *The Missionary Movement in Christian History. Studies in the Transmission of Faith*, Maryknoll: Orbis, 113.

themselves. Hence, Harold Turner advises us to think of a typology of 'tendencies and emphases', rather than of individual religious movements.[125]

Various typologies have been attempted since Sundkler's two-fold classification: Ethiopian and Zionist.[126] In the West African context, Turner has followed Sundkler's distinction but has preferred 'prophet-healing' to Zionist.[127] I use a simple typology to navigate the territory, recognising that such categorisation does not do justice to their diversity. Social historians and anthropologists have shown the degree to which African religious movements are responsive to local forces and should not be considered apart from popular culture.[128] Hence, I draw upon typologies derived from data collected in Nigeria and particularly those devised by Rosalind Hackett and Ogbu Kalu.[129]

Two related criteria for analysis are used. The first is sociological and focuses on the extent to which a group or movement is influenced by local or global forces and draws upon indigenous as opposed to imported sources. This is one of Hackett's criteria for classification. For Hackett, an African new religious movement is 'an indigenously created religious organization stemming from social and religious encounter, and selecting and combining local and exogenous elements in diverse and dynamic ways'.[130] All the movements I examine were locally instituted and to varying degrees made use of global resources, but some forged formal links with overseas organisations. Thus I distinguish between mission-related movements/churches and prayer houses. The second is theological and focuses on relationship to the Bible and Christology. Here I am responding to Kalu's call for a return to theological and biblical analysis of new religious movements in Africa, in order to identify those groups which are a proper concern of church historiography and missiology. Hence I follow

---

[125] Turner, *Religious Innovation*, 80.

[126] Sundkler, *Bantu Prophets*, 53.

[127] For a discussion, see Turner, *Religious Innovation*, 97-101.

[128] Terence O. Ranger and I. Kimambo, *The Historical Study of African Religion*, Berkeley: University of Calfornia Press, 1972; Ranger, 'Religious Movements'; Johannes Fabian, 'Six Theses Regarding the Anthropology of African Religious Movements', *Religion*, 11, 1996, 116-24.

[129] Hackett's data is drawn mainly from her research among the Efik-Ibibio, southeastern Nigeria. See Rosalind I. J. Hackett, 'Enigma Variations: the New Religious Movements in Nigeria today', in Andrew F. Walls and Wilbert R. Schenk (eds.), *Exploring New Religious Movements. Essays in Honour of Harold W. Turner*, Elkhart, Indiana: Mission Focus, 1990, 131-42. Kalu draws primarily upon empirical research within Igboland (Kalu, *Embattled Gods*, 289-304).

[130] Hackett, 'Enigma Variations', 140.

Kalu's scheme by dividing prayer houses into two broad categories: evangelical and Zionist. Kalu identifies the 'affirmation of Jesus Christ as Lord' as the crucial factor that distinguishes Christian from non-Christian groups or movements. Evangelical- and Zionist-type prayer houses are designated Christian. Others (messianic, revivalistic, vitalistic and nativistic) are non-Christian.[131] Evangelical-type groups are Bible oriented, Christocentric, and opposed to traditional religious practices and 'occult' activity. Zionist-type groups tend to lack a clear Christological focus and are more likely to incorporate rituals and symbols derived from inherited or imported sources other than the Bible. These indices are important because in revivalist and neo-Pentecostal rhetoric prayer houses were often demonised for misuse of the Bible, failure to preach the gospel, and incorporating traditional and/or imported 'occult' symbols and practices.

Revival Movements and Pentecostal Churches

Local initiatives divide broadly into two periods. From 1914 to 1939, a series of revivals with Pentecostal overtones swept through Igboland, coinciding with similar movements in Western Nigeria and the continent as a whole. Several themes recur in these initiatives which are characteristic of revivals generally. Firstly, there were elements of continuity and discontinuity with previous movements. Each new wave brought renewal to existing churches, often generating new theological emphases, and left traces of its influence once its charismatic impulses had subsided. Each movement contributed to the contextualisation of the gospel and the resacralisation of the religious landscape. Secondly, they generally appealed to the margins of the church but were rejected by the centre, resulting in schisms, new denominations and increased plurality. Finally, each movement was influenced by local and global forces.

The first wave of revival was associated with Garrick Sokari Braide, a member of the Anglican Niger Delta Pastorate. Although it had no links with global Pentecostalism, Turner describes it as the first Pentecostal movement in Nigeria because of the prominence of healings and prophecies.[132] Local response was spectacular, mainly due to Braide's healing gifts and crusade against idolatry, 'a radical departure from the conversion by catechism approach of the established church'.[133] His ministry appealed to the margins of the church but was rejected by the centre. Anglican Bishop Johnson initially approved but later objected to Braide's faith-healing practices, mass baptisms and the use of the title

[131] Kalu, *Embattled Gods*, 289.
[132] Turner, *Religious Innovation*, 2.
[133] Hanciles, 'Conversion', 169.

'prophet' by his followers. His ministry also posed a threat to white missionary control of the NDP, and some of his prophecies were interpreted as politically subversive. In 1916, Braide and his followers broke with the Anglican Church, and the same year he was arrested and imprisoned by the colonial authorities. He died two years later during the 1918 influenza epidemic. Though it was never Braide's intention to start a new church, some of his followers formed the Christ Army Church. Between 1918 and 1921, they numbered approximately 43,000, though these were split between three main factions: the Niger Delta Native Church, the Christ Army Church and the Christ Army Church - Garrick Braide Connexion. In 1916, some of Braide's co-workers carried the movement into southern Igboland, an area already influenced by mission churches, and Christ Army Church became Igboland's first prayer house, a precursor of modern Igbo Pentecostalism. The movement produced many converts, especially in the Owerri area, but by the late 1920s it was a spent force and a decade later only a few Christ Army Church congregations survived in Igboland, partly due to competition from other missions.[134]

Faith Tabernacle was the other precursor of modern Pentecostalism in Igboland, despite its anti-Pentecostal stance. While it was a local initiative with no Western missionary involvement, its early progress in Nigeria shows the importance of external links. The denomination's origins were in the US American Holiness Movement and its subsequent spread to Nigeria occurred through literature and correspondence rather than missionary agents. Links were established independently with individuals in Western Nigeria and Eastern Nigeria. Key actors in the East were E. T. Epelle, an Anglican NDP minister influenced by the Braide movement, and Elijah Obimba, an Igbo member of the NDP based near Aba. The critical year was 1925, when Epelle joined Obimba to oversee the work of Faith Tabernacle in Igboland. Though it remained a relatively small denomination in the East, Faith Tabernacle is important because it helped to introduce the 'faith alone' concept to the church in Eastern Nigeria. It also had close connections with two mission-related churches that trace their origins in Igboland to the 1930s: the Apostolic Church and the Assemblies of God, both important Pentecostal influences during the Civil War Revival.[135]

---

[134] Kalu, *Embattled Gods*, 144-54; G. O. M. Tasie, 'Christian Awakening in West Africa 1914-1918. A Study in the Significance of Native Agency', *West African Religion*, 16.2, 1975, 32-42; Frieder Ludwig, 'Elijah II. Radicalisation and Consolidation of the Garrick Braide Movement 1915-1918', *JRA*, 23, 1993, 296-317; Lamin Sanneh, *West African Christianity: The Religious Impact*, London: Hurst & Co., 1983, 182-84.

[135] Ogbu U. Kalu, 'Doing Mission through the Post Office: Naked Faith People of Igboland, 1920-1960', unpublished paper, University of Nigeria,

The Apostolic Church was the first denomination with global Pentecostal links to enter Igboland. Not only was it one of the largest Pentecostal churches prior to the civil war, it also experienced a number of secessions which facilitated the spread of Pentecostal spirituality throughout Igboland. Apostolic Church origins in the British Pentecostal movement are well documented, as is its entry into Western Nigeria in 1931 through links established with the Nigerian Faith Tabernacle Church.[136] Its spread to Igboland was an indigenous venture, though British Apostolic missionaries played an active role. The church entered Igboland through local agents (possibly Efik traders) in 1931, but was properly established in 1932 when Pastor Albert Emetanjo was sent from Calabar to Aba in order to gather up existing assemblies and form them into districts. In November 1932, British Apostolic missionaries Idris Vaughan and George Perfect visited Calabar and southern Igboland, following invitations from Faith Tabernacle leaders. Revival added impetus to Apostolic Church growth in Eastern Nigeria. A return visit to Calabar by Vaughan in 1933 coincided with a period of stress in the area caused by a witchcraft scare. Vaughan's acceptance of the reality of witchcraft, in contrast to some mission church leaders, and his proclamation of Christ's power, appealed to local demands and resulted in the formation of new churches. By 1938, the Apostolic Church in Igboland had grown to thirteen districts with over 120 assemblies, and in 1940 Vaughan arrived as their first Missionary Superintendent.

Two schisms in the late 1930s affected Apostolic Church progress in Igboland, both reactions against the dominance of non-Igbo leaders over local churches. In 1937, J. W. Wankey left to form the Christ Apostolic Church Gospel Mission (or Apostolic Church of God), and in 1939, the first Igbo apostle, J. Anyahuru, formed the True Apostolic Church, taking with him seventy-five assemblies. Subsequently, the two groups merged to become the Apostolic Christian Church Mission. In 1941, a more serious schism in Western Nigeria over the use of medicine led to the formation of the Christ Apostolic Church and the subsequent shift in focus of Nigerian Apostolic Church work to the East. Its initial reluctance to open schools

---

Nsukka, n.d; Hastings, *Church*, 514-15; Sanneh, *West African Christianity*, 184-85.

[136] See James E. Worsfold, *The Origins of the Apostolic Church in Great Britain, with a Breviate of its Early Missionary Endeavours*, Wellington, New Zealand: Julian Literature Trust, 1991, 71-2, 258-75; T. N. Turnbull, *What God Hath Wrought. A Short History of the Apostolic Church*, Bradford, 1959, 71-2; I. J. Vaughan, *Nigeria. The Origins of Apostolic Church Pentecostalism, with Particular Reference to the Years 1931-52 together with some Personal Reminences of I. J. Vaughan*, n.publ., 1991; J. D. Y. Peel, *Aladura: A Religious Movement among the Yorubas*, London: Oxford University Press, 1968.

also hindered its progress in Igboland, but by 1964, Apostolic Church membership had grown to around 15,000, though it remained a relatively minor presence compared to the mainline churches. The Igbo field of the Apostolic Church continued under the supervision of British missionaries until 1980, except during the civil war when the incumbent Superintendent, G. S. Selby, was forced to leave. In Selby's absence, Apostle Anyachor was appointed Superintendent of the Igbo field until 1972. He was reappointed in 1980 when Selby retired from the field.[137] The Apostolic Church in Igboland has retained the Faith Tabernacle emphasis on Biblicism, conversionism and faith healing, but has added to this the Apostolic teaching on Holy Spirit baptism and the five-fold ministries of apostles, prophets, evangelists, pastors and teachers.

British Apostolic missionary S. G. Elton served as a link between the two major strands of intensive revivalist and Pentecostal activity in Nigeria (1914-1939 and 1967-1975). He began his missionary career in 1937, based in Ilesha, Western Nigeria. In 1953, he invited a team from the US American Latter Rain movement to conduct evangelistic campaigns in Southern Nigeria.[138] The delegation arrived via Ghana, and their visit precipitated a fresh wave of Nigerian Pentecostal activity, though it remained relatively localised. Large healing crusades were held in Lagos, Ibadan, Ilesha, and other towns in Western Nigeria. Three members of the Latter Rain team also visited Igboland where they conducted an evangelistic campaign at Nbawsi, hosted by the Apostolic Church. British Apostolic leaders were unhappy with Elton's initiative and recalled him. Subsequently, he returned to Nigeria as an independent missionary representing American Pentecostal organisations and supported initially by the Latter Rain movement. This released him to work more widely across Nigeria and placed him in a position where he could later influence leaders of the Civil War Revival.[139]

---

[137] Vaughan, *Nigeria*, 39-50, 91, 94; A. O. Iwuagu, 'The "Spiritual" Churches in the Eastern States of Nigeria', Ph.D. thesis, University of Ibadan, 1971; Monday Mboko Anyachor, *History of the Apostolic Church in Igboland*, Owerri: Ihem Davis Press, 1998, 12-15, 72; Monday Mboko Anyachor, 'Welcome to Igbo Field of the Apostolic Church, Nigeria', May 1998, 1-3; Sanneh, *West African Christianity*, 194-95; G. S. Selby, Letter to the author, 14 April 2001.

[138] The Latter Rain movement originated in Canada during the late 1940s, and was linked to the US American 'Healing Revival' associated with William Branham, T. L. Osborn and Gordon Lindsay. For its history, see R. Riss, 'The Latter Rain Movement of 1948', *Pneuma*, 4.1, Spring 1982, 32-45.

[139] Kalu, 'Naked Faith', 14; Anyachor, *Apostolic Church*, 80-1; G. S. Selby, Letter to author, 14 April 2001; Ojo, *Army*, 38.

The Assemblies of God (AG) Nigeria was another major Pentecostal influence during the Civil War Revival. Its origins and subsequent growth again show elements of continuity and rupture with previous movements, as well as the importance of local and extraneous influences. AG was the first Igbo-founded Pentecostal church and like the Apostolic Church traces its origins in Igboland to the 1930s. It was a local initiative with roots in a revival that occurred in the southern Igbo townships of Umuahia and Port Harcourt, but later it established links with the US American Assemblies of God. As with other movements of renewal and revival, it was embraced by the margins but rejected by the centre. Early protagonists were lay members of Faith Tabernacle who eventually left to form the Church of Jesus Christ, following opposition from their denominational leaders. Faith Tabernacle teaching on salvation, faith healing and holiness appealed to the young revivalists, but their exposure to US American Pentecostal literature stimulated a quest for Holy Spirit baptism, which resulted in their rejection and resignation in August 1934. Within a month of their separation from Faith Tabernacle, they experienced 'an outpouring of the Holy Spirit', which precipitated a fresh wave of evangelistic activity, resulting in rapid growth. By December 1934, there were six Church of Jesus Christ (CJC) congregations, and in 1935, two more were planted in Enugu (the present location of AG Nigeria headquarters). By the late 1930s, CJC had moved beyond Igboland and planted churches in the Benin Province of Western Nigeria (1937), and the Northern cities of Kafanchan, Kaduna, Zaria and Kano (1938/39). Meanwhile, its leaders were actively pursuing links with overseas organisations and in 1939 they affiliated with the US American Assemblies of God. Subsequently, it became one of the strongest indigenous churches in AG's foreign missions programme.[140]

From the outset, AG Nigeria pursued a policy of indigenisation, but prior to the Civil War Revival expanded slowly compared to other denominations due in part to an early reluctance to engage in social welfare projects and use the schools approach to evangelism. Church growth is difficult to determine. According to the *World Churches Handbook*, by 1961 AG Nigeria had approximately 130 congregations with a membership

---

[140] For AG Nigeria, see G. M. Alioha, *The Grain of Mustard Seed (The History of Assemblies of God, Nigeria)*, Aba: Assemblies of God Press, 1975; R. I. Ebuade *et al.*, *The Growth of Assemblies of God in Nigeria*, Aba: Assemblies of God Press, 1989; C. S. Ndubuisi, 'Fifty Years of Assemblies of God Mission in Igboland, 1930-80', Ph.D. thesis, University of Nigeria, Nsukka, 1992; Gary B. McGee, *This Gospel shall be Preached. A History and Theology of Assemblies of God Foreign Missions to 1959*, Springfield, Missouri: Gospel Publishing House, 1986, 146.

of 23,000. This had increased to 256 churches by 1965.[141] Igbo church historian C. S. Ndubuisi suggests that by 1964, there were 148 congregations in Igboland alone. Churches also existed in the Western Nigerian cities of Ibadan (1948) and Lagos (1962/3), and the Northern townships of Jos (1943), Lafia, Sokoto, Gusau, Maiduguri and Gyom.[142] In 1961, Matthew Ezeigbo became the first indigenous National Superintendent, and in 1964, the Nigerian District of the Assemblies of God became an autonomous body.

Prayer Houses

A further wave of Pentecostal activity began in the 1940s and consisted of smaller groups, often associated with charismatic figures possessing healing and visionary gifts, and bearing a close resemblance to the Garrick Braide movement in terms of their focus on 'prophetism' and symbolic ritual, and their lack of formal global connections. Some were imported from Western or southeastern Nigeria. Others grew directly out of Igbo soil. Again there were elements of continuity and discontinuity with previous movements and influences from local and global forces. But as they lacked any formal Western links, they generally took on more local colour in their quest to relate their indigenous heritage to the symbols and message of Christianity. Many civil war revivalists and neo-Pentecostal pioneers patronised them during the 1960s, when dual allegiance to mission church and prayer house was relatively common.[143]

In contrast to Western and southeastern Nigeria, prayer houses were of relatively minor importance in Igboland prior to the 1960s and the civil war. This was partly due to Igbo loyalty to mission churches and the relative strength of Anglican and Roman Catholic churches. It was only when they had failed to meet consumer demands and nationalist fervour had removed the constraints to patronising alternatives that prayer houses flourished. Mission church members tended to disparage them, regarding them as superstitious and unsophisticated, especially those imported from Western Nigeria. This is reflected in the Igbo saying, *adị eji anya dị mma eje ụka ekpere* (no sane or clear-minded person goes to prayer houses).[144]

---

[141] Peter Brierley (ed.), *World Churches Handbook*, London: Christian Research, 1997, 630. But Turner (*Religious Innovation*, 127) estimates the membership in 1961 at closer to 60,000.

[142] Ndubuisi, 'Assemblies of God'.

[143] For prayer houses I am relying on oral sources, personal observation, local church documents and academic works.

[144] Elizabeth Isichei, *A History of Christianity in Africa. From Antiquity to the Present*, Grand Rapids, MI: Eerdmans, 1995, 290-91; Kalu, *Embattled*

Table 2.1 Prayer Houses in Igboland, pre-1967
(Note: year of origin in parentheses)

Abosso Apostolic Faith Church (1941)
Cherubim and Seraphim Society (1944)
Christ Apostolic Church (1953)
Christ Apostolic Church Gospel Mission (1937)
Christ Apostle Church - *Onu Uzo Ndu* (1953)
Christ Army Church (? 1916)
Christ Disciple Church (1958)
Christ Healing Church (1936)
Christ Healing Sabbath Mission (1956)
Christ Holy Church (1947)
Christian Fellowship Group (1967)
Church of the Lord (Aladura) (1956)
Holy Chapel of Israel Church
Holy Church of God (1966)
Holy Sabbath Christ the King (1965)
St. Joseph's Chosen Church of God (1947)
True Apostolic Church (1938)
True Church of God (1953)
United Church of Christ (1964)

I begin with Igbo-founded prayer houses. During the late 1930s and 1940s, most were associated with the Apostolic Church movement rather than Assemblies of God, possibly because of the latter's Igbo roots, its relative freedom from missionary control and its promotion of indigenous church principles, which made secession less likely. I have mentioned the two schisms in the late 1930s which resulted in the formation of the Christ Apostolic Church Gospel Mission (1937) and True Apostolic Church (1938). During the 1940s, there were at least two further secessions: Abosso Apostolic Faith Church, founded in 1941 by Daniel Ejeofor, and St. Joseph's Chosen Church of God (formerly Apostolic Chosen Church of God), founded by Apostle Joseph Ikechukwu in 1947.[145]

Christ Holy Church, founded in 1947 by Agnes Okoh, also had links with the Apostolic Church movement. It is currently one of the largest

---

Gods, 269, 321; Kalu, 'Color and Conversion', 70. Turner mentions at least 140 distinct prayer houses active in Eastern Nigeria during the 1960s, though many were small 'healing homes' and located in the southeast rather than Igboland (Harold W. Turner, *African Independent Church, Vol.1*, Oxford: Clarendon Press, 1967, 8).

[145] Iwuagu, 'Churches'; chapters 12-15; Anyachor, *Apostolic Church*, 69.

Figure 2. St. Joseph's Chosen Church of God, near Umuahia, with containers of 'holy water' (left), and a photograph of Apostle Joseph Ilechukwu (on the wall).

Igbo-founded prayer houses and a member of the Organisation of African Instituted Churches (OAIC), with an estimated 720 branches across Nigeria in 2001.[146] It was a local initiative, but during its early history was influenced by external sources. Agnes Okoh (later the Holy Prophetess *Odozi-Obodo*) claimed a call to ministry through divine revelation after being healed from a long-standing illness. In 1947, she opened a prayer house in Onitsha and gained a large following due to her healing and prophetic gifts.[147] After a visit from a group attached to the Christ Apostolic Church, Western Nigeria, she named her prayer house Christ Apostolic Church *Odozi Obodo* (as opposed to Christ Apostolic Church Babalola), and in the early 1970s it was registered as Christ Holy Church. It fits the profile of Kalu's evangelical-type prayer house due to its strong Christological and evangelistic emphasis. Christ Holy Church describes

[146] *Glad News*, 2001, 1.

[147] Her predictions concerning the Nigerian civil war have become part of the church's official history. Apparently she predicted both its advent and ending.

itself as a Pentecostal, spiritual, and evangelical church, upholds the Bible as the word of God, and in its mission statement claims to 'worship the triune God in holiness . . . and spread the good news of our Lord Jesus across borders, race and cultures urgently . . . till Jesus Christ returns again'.[148] Though it has undergone changes, including the introduction of modern musical instruments, the church still uses 'holy water' for healing, and ministers wear white garments.

During the 1950s, other Igbo-founded prayer houses emerged. The most popular was Ufuma Practical Prayer Band (UPPB), which had important links to the Civil War Revival.[149] Established in 1958 as a fellowship affiliated to the Anglican Church, UPPB developed around the ministry of prophetess Madame Nwokolo. Its popularity rested upon her healing ministry and the group's strong interdenominational emphasis, which meant that initially it was endorsed by the Anglican Church and received official approval from Archbishop Patterson. Madame Nwokolo and her husband were active members of Holy Trinity Anglican Church (Ufuma), but UPPB attracted both Protestants and Roman Catholics, and by 1972, had established approximately thirty branches. Since the 1970s, it has become an independent body with branches throughout Nigeria. UPPB fits the profile of Kalu's zionist-type prayer house due to the ritual nature of its liturgy (which includes fasting, the use of candles, 'holy water' and oil for healing), its lack of a clear Christological focus, and its reluctance to engage in evangelistic activity.

During the 1950s, we also see the emergence of the first of many Igbo-founded sabbatharian groups, the Christ Healing Sabbath Mission, founded in 1956 by Mark Onuabichi.[150] These prayer houses vary considerably, ranging from those that incorporate traditional practices, such as ancestor worship and animal sacrifices, to those with a more Christological focus. Their roots in Igboland go back to Dede Ekeke Lolo, who was briefly associated with the Garrick Braide movement and later became Onuabichi's mentor. During the 1960s, they multiplied and diversified, attracting clientele from mainline churches, including some who later became participants in the Civil War Revival.

---

[148] *Glad News*, 4.

[149] For UPPB's history, I have relied on oral sources and the following written accounts: G. C. Ikeobi, 'Catholic Response to the Challenge of "Prayer Houses" - Origins of the "Tuesday Prayer" in Onitsha', in Nwosu (ed.), *Catholic Church*, 266-67; David C. Okeke, 'Report: Ufuma Praying Band', n.publ., 1972; V. A. Nwosu, *Prayer Houses and Faith Healing*, n.publ., 1971.

[150] For sabbatharian prayer houses in Igboland, see J. O. Anyaegbu, 'Sabbatharianism in Igboland 1916-1990', Ph.D thesis, University of Nigeria, Nsukka, 1993; Kalu, *Embattled Gods*, 298-303.

Prayer houses from Western Nigeria arrived in the 1940s, but did not become popular until the 1960s. Initially they attracted non-indigenes, but later were patronised by Igbos dissatisfied with mission church spirituality. Yoruba immigrants or Igbos who had lived in the West introduced them, and they were more successful in urban areas such as Aba and Owerri, where there were large migrant populations. Rural areas were usually more resistant to innovations. The first to arrive was the Cherubim and Seraphim Society, introduced in 1944 by a Yoruba woman called Deborah Phillips. The Christ Apostolic Church followed in 1953, brought over by an Igbo pastor called O. N. Godwin who later left to start Christ Ascension Church, a large Pentecostal denomination with headquarters in Enugu.[151] Church of the Lord (Aladura) arrived in 1956. According to Turner, it was started in Aba by an Igbo pastor and two Yorubas, who had belonged to the church in Western Nigeria.[152] Like other prayer houses, their initial unpopularity was due to Igbo loyalty to mission churches. But it was also due to their roots in Yoruba culture and domination by non-indigenes. Their centralised, authoritarian leadership styles, which corresponded with Yoruba traditional society, conflicted with Igbo democratic culture.[153]

Protest Movements or Mission Churches?

These local initiatives mobilised neglected forces by providing space for women and young people to participate in ministry. They also alleviated the dilemma of dual allegiance to church and traditional cult by responding more effectively to consumer demands. Significantly, they were more successful than Western mission churches at implementing Venn's 'three-self' policy, even if they were not conscious of doing so. They could also be said to be self-theologising, though theirs was an enacted theology 'from below', one that was acted out in rituals and experiences rather than worked out systematically and philosophically. To the extent that they challenged the Enlightenment assumptions and rationalist theologies of mission churches, they were religious protest movements.[154] But by focussing

[151] Kalu, *Embattled Gods*, 104, 170, 291; C. O. Nwanunobi, 'Sects as an Urban Phenomenon in Contemporary Eastern Nigeria', *Anthropos*, 75, 1980, 120-22, 125.

[152] Turner, *African Independent Church*, 82-7.

[153] *Ibid.*, 87-8.

[154] Protest or resistance theories dominated early literature on African religious innovation. Some scholars argued that AICs were responding to socio-political oppression associated with colonialism; others that they were movements of religious protest and in particular a reaction to mission church spirituality. For helpful discussions, see Marthinus L. Daneel, 'African

solely on reaction to the limitations of foreign missions, we fail to appreciate the innovations and creativity of local agents whose primary motivation was to respond to the gospel and engage in mission activity during moments of individual and collective crisis in ways appropriate to local culture. Many of these initiatives were 'missionary churches' rather than 'protest movements', as Daneel has noted of Shona AICs in Zimbabwe.[155] Their distinctive spirituality developed as participants read their Bibles through cultural lenses and responded to consumer demands in a situation of rapid social change and an atmosphere of heightened spiritual and evangelistic fervour. During the period 1914 to 1939 in particular, Igbo initiatives were primarily movements of conversion rather than secession, and were attempts to 'reproduce missionary Christianity rather than to reject it'.[156] Thus they not only mobilised neglected forces, they effectively enculturated the gospel in Igbo soil and prepared the ground for Pentecostal infiltration of mainline churches in the 1970s by their presentation of charismatic experiences, such as healing, dreams, and visions, as a normal feature of corporate church life. André Droogers refers to this as the 'normalisation of religious experience', the 'acceptance of views and practices initially considered abnormal as normal' and their inclusion as a regular feature of religious activity.[157]

In many cases, these groups continued the iconoclastic strategy and maintained the strong ethical stance of the early missionaries. This was especially so with evangelical mission-oriented movements such as the Braidists, Apostolic Church and Assemblies of God, though prayer houses like Christ Holy Church and St. Joseph's Chosen Church of God adopted a similar posture. However, in Igbo evangelical parlance other prayer houses were less discriminating in their approach to traditional allegiances and popular culture, creating hybrid forms of spirituality that bore little resemblance to biblical Christianity. Harold Turner refers to the 'pagan' features of some Nigerian independent churches, which included a 'subordinate cult of angels' and employment of 'mystic words of power'.[158] Rituals practiced in some Igbo prayer houses included the use of candles,

---

Initiated Churches in Southern Africa: Protest Movements or Mission Churches?', in Lewis (ed.), *Christianity Reborn*, 190-94; Allan H. Anderson, *African Reformation. African Initiated Christianity in the 20th Century*, Trenton, NJ: Africa World Press, 2001, 33-4.

155 Daneel, 'African Initiated Churches', 201.

156 Hastings, *Church*, 531.

157 André Droogers, 'The Normalisation of Religious Experience: Healing, Prophecy, Dreams, and Visions', in Karla Poewe (ed.), *Charismatic Christianity as a Global Culture*, Columbia, SC: University of South Carolina, 1994, 33.

158 Turner, *Religious Innovation*, 170.

incense, incantations and purification rites, such as animal sacrifices and ritual washing, which had their origins in traditional piety and extraneous 'occult' literature imported from Europe and Asia. This was one reason why many Igbo Christians deserted zionist-type prayer houses in the 1970s as they encountered the Civil War Revival.

Religious Culture in the 1960s

By the 1960s, the charismatic impulses of early Igbo revival movements had waned and the churches they generated had declined in Pentecostal vigour, resulting in a loss of democratic potential and missionary fervour. Both the Apostolic Church and Assemblies of God were a relatively minor presence compared to the mainline churches. In contrast, prayer houses expanded rapidly, initially as an urban phenomenon. The stresses associated with urbanisation and unemployment stimulated a quest for practical solutions to current dilemmas, making the problem solving approach of the prayer houses appealing. And sometimes founding a 'church' solved the problem of unemployment. Yet for some prayer houses, this pragmatic emphasis was also part of their undoing as clientele were dominated by those motivated by a search for practical solutions rather than a commitment to membership. Dual allegiance to mission church and prayer house was never a satisfactory state of affairs. Resistance to globalising and modernising influences also detracted from their appeal, especially among educated upwardly-mobile youth in post-colonial Nigeria.

However, two prayer houses, started during the 1960s, later had important links to the Civil War Revival and consequently attracted a large membership. Both founders, Victor Onuigbo and Godson Ogbansiegbe, were former mission church members but stood firmly in the tradition of other Igbo prophetic figures. Their churches fit the profile of Kalu's evangelical-type prayer house. Brought up in an Anglican family, Onuigbo's call to ministry occurred through a series of visionary and auditory experiences, and in 1966 he started the Holy Church of God in Enugu, a 'white garment' church with an emphasis on prophecy and healing. Subsequently he became caught up in the revival, and his church underwent a metamorphosis. Today, it bears the name Victory Christian Mission and resembles other Pentecostal churches in Igboland. A former Methodist, Ogbansiegbe founded the Christian Fellowship Group in 1967.

Figure 3. Godson C. D. Ogbansiegbe, Aba, n.d.

His life story describes his call to start a new church through an audible voice and after a long illness. Subsequently, his ministry as an itinerant evangelist took him all over Nigeria and he became a popular preacher during the Civil War Revival. For a while, Christian Fellowship Group was one of the largest churches in Aba.[159]

The extent to which Igbos had abandoned traditional religion and embraced Christianity by the 1960s is difficult to determine due to a lack of consistent church records following the civil war, when many documents were destroyed. Missionary historiography and local scholarship sometimes paint a picture of the triumphant conquest of Igboland by Christian agents and the defeat of Igbo gods, especially during the period 1901 to 1961.[160] Popular literature and oral evidence provide a more nuanced account. Despite the effects of distorted lenses, novelists are often sensitive observers of society. A major interest of Igbo writers has been the clash between Christianity and Igbo culture. Thus Chinua Achebe, in his novel *No Longer at Ease*, identifies three distinct groups during the 1950s:

---

[159] Godson C. D. Ogbansiegbe, *The Manual of the Christian Fellowship Group*, n.publ., n.d.

[160] See Ubah, 'Religious Change', 85.

traditionalists who had rejected Christianity; those who had become Christians; and those in urban settings who appeared indifferent to religion and spirituality.[161] Okorocha's oral material also suggests the continuing presence of Igbo traditionalists, the strong influence of *dibịa-afa*, and the persistence of traditional religious practices and values among Igbo Christians.[162] My own research concurs with this, though few of my informants defined themselves as traditionalists without any church affiliation prior to their contact with the Civil War Revival. Most were brought up in Christian households and regularly attended church, though some resorted to traditional practitioners in moments of crisis. *Dibịa-afa* continued to operate mainly in villages, and Igbos patronised them to achieve certain ends, such as protection from enemies, the achievement of success, healing and the acquisition of children. Rural communities continued to make covenants with a variety of deities. One member of Scripture Union recalled that each New Year members of his village participated in a traditional 'swearing ceremony' to renew their covenant with the local deity.[163] Another was the grandson of the local chief priest and regularly participated in traditional practices prior to becoming born-again. He told me that members of his village used to worship an *alụsị*, which lived in a large tree, and each year they would offer a human sacrifice to secure its favour. There was also a widespread belief in witchcraft and evil spirits, including *ọgbanje* and 'mami-wata' spirits, both important sources of misfortune in Igbo cosmology. 'Mami-wata' is a water spirit, which, according to Bastion, 'afflicts her victims in a most "modern" way: promising them riches (like fine automobiles, wristwatches and even computers) but usually giving them disease and death when they transgress one of her prohibitions'.[164]

Another popular strand of Igbo spirituality during the 1960s drew heavily upon a tradition of secret knowledge and mysticism contained in popular literature imported from overseas, such as the *Sixth and Seventh Books of Moses*, a collection of 'spells' and incantations intended to conjure up spirits.[165] We have already identified this as a significant influence upon some of the prayer houses that littered the Igbo religious landscape. But there were also non-Christian groups, labelled 'spiritual science movements' by Hackett, whose spirituality was drawn from a variety of heterogeneous sources - 'occultism', metaphysics, mysticism and psychic

[161] Chinua Achebe, *No Longer at Ease*, London: Heinemann, 1980.

[162] Okorocha, *Religious Conversion*, 133-40, 154, 274.

[163] Uchenna Emezue, 'New Year's Victory', written testimony, 1969.

[164] Bastion, 'Married in the Water', 123-24.

[165] I came across this book in the 'Spiritual Bookshop' in Enugu, which had an assortment of 'occult' literature, incense and 'medicines' on display.

sciences - but who possessed certain common characteristics: 'a quest for higher states of consciousness, increased spiritual power and knowledge and direct experience of the divine, as well as the use of procedures, techniques, and practices which draw on hidden or concealed forces to manipulate the empirical course of existence'.[166] They were a reflection of 'the widening religious, social, and cultural horizons of many Nigerians'.[167] Groups that were popular in Igboland during the 1960s included the Rosicrucians (AMORC), Freemasons and the Grail Movement, all imported from overseas, and the Ogboni Fraternity from Western Nigeria. There were also a growing number of indigenous spiritual science movements, whose founders were invariably former members of imported groups. Like the prayer houses, their spirituality was rooted in Igbo traditional pragmatism and the search for power to enhance life (*ezi-ndụ*).

The narrative accounts of former revivalists paint a vivid picture of their perception of prevailing Christian culture immediately prior to the war. The impression we are left with is of a community dominated by nominal Christians and liberal clerics, whose focus was on religious rituals such as baptism and communion rather than gospel preaching; of large numbers of Igbos flocking into mainline churches every Sunday, but in moments of crisis resorting to traditional practitioners, secret societies or prayer houses. While these accounts represent typical revivalist and evangelical critiques of nominal Christianity and should be treated with caution, they also represent valid perspectives which need to be respected and understood. They describe a church community so shaped by Western Christianity and Enlightenment assumptions that it was unable to respond satisfactorily to consumer demands and bore little resemblance to the pragmatic brand of religious problem-solving mechanisms familiar to the Igbo.

Conclusion

Within Igbo history, periods of socio-political distress have created favourable contexts for religious innovation and initiative. However, this chapter has argued that Igbo Christian conversion is essentially a religious transaction determined by the traditional search for power to enhance life, with sociological factors as catalysts. Due to the influence of Enlightenment values, the colonial encounter between Igbo primal religion and mission Christianity precipitated a crisis of identity and left a legacy of 'two faiths in one mind' which encouraged dual allegiance among Igbo converts. This identity crisis was exacerbated by the reluctance of mission

---

[166] Hackett, 'Enigma Variations', 135.

[167] *Ibid.*, 139.

church authorities (both white missionary and black African) to devolve power and provide space for ministry at the grassroots.

To an extent, the various local initiatives and innovations that burst upon the scene from 1914 alleviated these dilemmas by counteracting the secularising influences of mission Christianity, mobilising neglected forces, and responding more effectively to consumer demands. By the 1960s, however, neither the mission-related Pentecostal churches nor the prayer houses posed a significant threat to the hegemony of mainline churches. It was within Scripture Union ranks that a new wave of revival would arise at a critical moment in Igbo history. To this we now turn.

Chapter 3

The Civil War Revival, 1967-73

In September 1966, James Ukaegbu, an Igbo pastor living in the Northern city of Jos, heard rumours of an impending attack by Muslim Hausa-Fulani on the immigrant Igbo population. Two days later, some young men arrived at his compound armed with bows, arrows and machetes. Left with only his Bible and a little money, he took refuge in a nearby theological college and from there was flown to Enugu, the capital of Igbo territory (Eastern Nigeria). Unbeknown to Ukaegbu, similar events were occurring all across the Northern states in what appeared to be a well-orchestrated operation. So began the September-October pogroms intended to drive the Igbo Diaspora out of the North. As noted in chapter 2, they precipitated a mass exodus of over a million Igbos back to their crowded homeland. Afterwards, the demand for Igbo secession became overwhelming and in May 1967, Eastern Nigeria declared its independence from the Nigerian Federation, renaming itself the Republic of Biafra. Tensions reached a climax two months later with the advent of the Nigerian civil war (1967-70).

By this time, Ukaegbu had moved to Umuahia Township in Southern Igboland where he joined the local Scripture Union group. This group was to become the mainspring of the Civil War Revival, responsible for transforming the local religious landscape and generating a fresh wave of indigenous Pentecostalism which eventually spread beyond the borders of Igboland. This chapter discusses why the revival flourished where and when it did, and reflects upon the nature of the revival experience and its influence upon existing religious and socio-cultural landscapes. The revival's success rested on a balance between supply and demand. The combined effects of decolonisation, modernisation and conflict created new religious demands. But the primary reason for growth lay in the revival's missionary impulse and the formation of a band of itinerant preachers out of the furnace of the civil war. Other features examined here, such as extensive conversion experiences, radical holiness ethic, the erosion of boundaries and the stress on divine healing, flowed from this missionary impulse.

I begin by considering the effects of the war on existing religious forms. This is important because the revival's success rested partly on the loss of efficacy of other religious options. I then give an overview of the revival based on participant accounts. The main focus will be a detailed analysis of the movement, using a multi-disciplinary approach to arrive at tentative answers to the above stated questions. Again I take note of elements of continuity in change, local and global influences, and opposing currents of accommodation and challenge.

Expanding Religious Markets

If we recall from chapter 2, religious pluralism and an expanding religious marketplace were features of Igbo society during the 1960s. Western education and urbanisation loosened ties with traditional control structures and increased the level of individual autonomy and choice. But the various religious options available experienced different fortunes during the civil war.

One consequence of the war was an increasing demand for traditional religion, especially those aspects concerned with 'explanation, prediction, and control' such as divination and magic. To solve their pressing problems and ward off danger, many Igbos reverted to the old ways as a means of gaining access to the power inherent in their indigenous piety. One Biafran ex-soldier told me that he regularly consulted 'witchdoctors' and prepared charms to protect himself during the war even though he was a Roman Catholic at the time. The use of protective charms was relatively common among Igbo combatants from all religious shades, and those who consulted traditional priests did so for protection or for 'power' to overcome enemy soldiers. As well as the individual use of protective charms, Igbo communities employed communal rituals to acquire protection. One was the guardian shrine (*egbo*), located along village entrance pathways or at the access points to family compounds, and intended to protect the community from evil of any kind, whether intruders or evil spirits.[1] Another was the institution of *ịgba-ndụ* (covenants), the strongest assertion of the rule of *ọfọ-na-ogu* (social justice) in Igbo society.[2] During the war, soldiers and politicians made covenants with one another to reinforce their relationships in the face of a common enemy. *Igba-ndụ* was also used to protect local communities from the constant threat of saboteurs. In this case, community members demonstrated their loyalty to the Biafran cause by swearing on the *ọfọ*, the Igbo symbol of authority.[3] One informant recalled an occasion during the war when all adult members

---

[1] Simon Ottenberg, 'Statement and Reality; The Renewal of an Igbo Protective Shrine', *International Archives of Ethnography*, 51, Amsterdam, 1968, 143-44.

[2] Okorocha, *Religious Conversion*, 116.

[3] Okorocha, 'Reconciliation', 192; Chukwuemeka Ike, *Sunset at Dawn*, Glasgow: Williams Collins & Co., 1976, 61.

of his village were required to gather at the local shrine to swear their innocence on the *ọfọ*. Christians were given the alternative option of swearing on the Bible at the Catholic Church, but first had to join others at the traditional shrine.

At the end of the war there was an urge to reassert traditional standards of morality and purify the land of pollution (*alụ*). In Igbo traditional culture, *alụ* is caused by any breach of *nsọ Ala* (prohibitions of the Earth deity, Ala), and is believed to result in supernatural sanctions, especially land and human infertility. Igbos distinguish between major pollutions (or abominations) and minor pollutions. Major pollutions upset the cosmic and social order, and include moral offences such as homicide, adultery, incest, suicide, wilful abortion and stealing of yams, as well as abnormal or unnatural behaviour such as giving birth to twins or a person dying without anyone in attendance.[4] In chapter 2, I referred to the escalation of corruption and armed robbery brought about by the struggle for survival in the aftermath of the war. Post-war poverty also forced many Igbo women into prostitution with Hausa-Fulani soldiers and traders, sometimes in traditional shrines or churches. In Igbo popular imagination, these moral offences polluted the land, threatened the ontological order and called for purification rituals. In many Igbo towns after the war, elders and church leaders hired traditional priests to help renew the force of *omenala* (the moral code) in society.[5]

But despite evidence for increased traditional religious activity, several factors associated with the war militated against it. The refugee problem uprooted people from their local communities, loosening their ties with ancestors and local shrines. A second factor was the relief operation, closely associated with Christian organisations. Caritas, the Roman Catholic relief agency, was especially apt to use the offer of relief as a means of proselytism. Finally, the war helped to desacralise Igbo traditional religion. Charles Agu alludes to this in his study of secularisation in Igboland. In the course of fighting, young people sought refuge in the 'Evil Forest', the reserved areas of the deities, and in the traditional shrines. 'They literally trampled underfoot traditional religious objects and places - and they did not die!'[6] In the aftermath of the war, many Igbos became disillusioned with their old gods and ancestors who had failed to protect them and give them victory.

Prayer houses were another religious option available to those looking for protection and practical solutions. As noted in chapter 2, they had not been a significant presence before the war due to the strength of the mission

---

[4] Ikenga-Metuh, *African Religions*, 90-2; Okorocha, *Religious Conversion*, 101.

[5] *Ibid.*, 127, 116.

[6] Agu, *Secularization*, 325, 327.

churches. But the Biafran crisis exposed the frailties of mission church spirituality and the inflexibility of their organisational structures. In their quest for quick solutions to their problems, an increasing number of Igbos began to patronise prayer houses, often located near refugee and army camps. Their popularity rested on their close affinity to Igbo traditional piety, their pragmatic approach to religion, and their promises of protection and security. Accounts by former Biafrans suggest that large numbers of army commanders, soldiers and refugees patronised prayer houses during the war.[7] Many revivalists also became members prior to their conversion to 'born-again' Christianity. These included Scripture Union members and neo-Pentecostal church pioneers.[8] Out of seventy-nine contacted, at least nineteen attended prayer houses during or immediately after the war, while maintaining their mission church affiliation. In the aftermath of the war, some prayer houses became a target of revivalist critique and evangelistic ventures, and consequently lost many of their members.

Several factors contributed to a decline in mission Christianity during the war. Firstly, many Igbos found the brand of Christianity represented by the mainline churches lacked the power to help them cope with the stresses engendered by the war. In this they were influenced by their traditional religious heritage, which associated spiritual power with piety. If we recall, Igbos expect power to emanate from religious forms and for Christianity to achieve what their primal religion was fulfilling for them.[9] During the war, they looked for religious support to protect them from death and render them successful in battle. When they failed to find this in the mainline churches, many resorted to alternative means by appealing to traditional ritual agents or attending a prayer house. A second factor was the departure of expatriate missionaries and the flight of local church clerics in the face of Nigeria's advancing army, which left congregations short of leaders. The rigidity of their hierarchical structures, and their dependence on ordained ministry, made it difficult for them to adapt to new situations. Ojo states that most Protestant church activities collapsed during the war.[10] Oral accounts suggest otherwise. Church meetings, albeit on a limited scale, continued in urban areas until overrun by federal troops. The conduct of the British government also caused some Igbos influenced by socialist ideologies to react against mission Christianity. From their perspective, so-

---

[7] For written accounts, see N. U. Akpan, *The Struggle for Secession 1966-1970*, London: Frank Cass, 1976, 196; Madiebo, *Nigerian Revolution*, 357-58; Ben Gbulie, *The Fall of Biafra*, Enugu: Fourth Dimension, 1989, 108.

[8] See Stephen Okafor, Raphael Okafor and Arthur Oruizu, Letter to SU Executive Committee, 1970, quoted in Bolton, *Glory,* 17; Minutes of the 4th East Central State Subcommittee of Scripture Union held on 4 December 1970.

[9] Okorocha, 'Conversion', 169.

[10] Ojo, 'Campus Christianity', 100.

called 'Christian Britain' supported genocide in Biafra, and they attacked the mission churches as agents of imperialism and neo-colonialism.[11] This negative attitude was reinforced by the relief operation, a responsibility shared by the mission churches. Unfortunately the behaviour of some of their relief personnel exposed them to severe criticism. There were accusations of corruption and uneven distribution of supplies. When they finally lost the war, many Igbos felt disappointed in God and disillusioned with mission Christianity. In accordance with their traditional religious heritage, which associates divine blessing with social justice, they had believed the Biafran cause to be a just one. It was this passion for social justice, according to Okorocha, which was the decisive factor in Igbo secession prior to the war, rather than the desire for oil revenues or Ojukwu's personal ambition. The Igbo considered the pogroms of 1966 gross injustices against them as a people and were convinced of the justness of their cause and the support of Chineke.[12] Consequently, defeat shattered their confidence in Chineke's justice and providential control.

The effect of the war on mission-related Pentecostal churches is difficult to determine. The Apostolic Church expressed disappointment over the Home Mission's apparent indifference to their plight, and suffered the effects of dislocation caused by the refugee problem. The Assemblies of God seemingly benefited as displaced members planted new churches in their villages, a strategy encouraged by the mission's indigenisation policy. Neither group received a significant influx of members from mainline churches, probably due to the latter's anti-Pentecostal stance. After the war, however, both experienced rapid growth as members became caught up in the revival. To this we now turn.

The Story of the Revival

The Civil War Revival followed the contours of Igbo history and proceeded in several distinct stages.[13] The first occurred soon after the outbreak of war. Following the closure of educational institutions, many young people began to congregate at Scripture Union headquarters in Umuahia which had

---

[11] Kalu, *Embattled Gods*, 272; Andrew F. Walls, 'Religion and the Press in "the Enclave" in the Nigerian Civil War', in Edward W. Fasholé-Luke *et al.* (eds.), *Christianity in Independant Africa*, London: Rex Collings, 1978, 210-11.

[12] Okorocha, *Religious Conversion,* 116.

[13] For the history of the revival I have drawn on material from oral interviews with former revivalists, letters and testimonies written by participants, postgraduate theses by Igbo scholars, and the following published sources: Roberts, *Life and Death*; Bolton, *Glory*; Kalu, *Embattled Gods*.

become the capital of Biafra after the fall of Enugu in September 1967. At the time Bill Roberts was the British SU representative in the East. His decision to remain made a great impression upon the youth, particularly as Britain had come out in support of the federal government of Nigeria. Yet Roberts was by no means the only Western missionary in Biafra. If we recall, Igboland was a focus of Roman Catholic missionary activity, and up to one hundred priests and nuns from the Irish Catholic Order of the Holy Ghost stayed behind.[14] In contrast, most Protestant missionaries left before or during the war. Those who remained included a small number from CMS and other missionary societies, mostly medical personnel and those engaged in the relief programme. All Assemblies of God and Apostolic Church missionaries left on the advice of their respective home missions.[15]

As the war escalated, refugees poured into Umuahia, and many secondary school students sought refuge at SU headquarters, where they were gradually forged into an interdenominational community. Most were Anglicans and Methodists, the main denominations in the area. At this stage, the impetus for their coming together was social; they were forced together by the circumstances of the war. Some of the older, more senior members of SU Umuahia were Scripture Union leaders from Enugu. Others were former Evangelical Christian Union (ECU) leaders who had come to Umuahia following the closure of the University of Nigeria (UNN) at the beginning of the war. One was John Onuora, currently a university lecturer and member of the Anglican Church. His story shows the repercussions of political events in post-independence Nigeria upon the lives of its Igbo citizens. Onuora was born in 1944 and brought up a Presbyterian in Cross River Igboland. Later he attended the prestigious Hope Waddell Secondary School in Calabar, where he was introduced to Scripture Union. In 1965, Onuora proceeded to the University of Ibadan, where he became an active member of the Christian Union (IVCU). In July 1966, a second military coup brought General Gowon to power and precipitated a wave of violent pogroms directed against Igbos. This occurred while Onuora was on vacation in the East and forced him and his fellow Igbo students to relocate to UNN (Nsukka) where they reorganised the small Scripture Union group along the lines of IVCU, Ibadan. Onuora became the first President of the new Christian Union. Following the outbreak of war and closure of UNN, he joined SU Umuahia. After the

---

[14] St. Jorre, *Nigerian Civil War*, 251.

[15] Ralph L. Cimino, *Linking Hands to Plant the Church. A Compilation of the Profiles of the Assemblies of God Missionaries in Nigeria*, n.publ., 1999. The Apostolic Church missionary G. S. Selby worked for a SIM relief agency during the war but was based in Port Harcourt outside the Biafran enclave.

Figure 4. Mission Hill Chapel, where SU Umuahia held meetings during the civil war, 1999.

war, Onuora became a Scripture Union travelling secretary, and in October 1970 resumed his studies at UNN where he was re-elected President of the Christian Union.

The second stage of the revival was a period of mobilisation. As Igbo urban centres were overrun by federal troops, revivalists migrated to rural areas where they reported a favourable response to their message. The fall of Umuahia in April 1969 was a critical event and provided the main impetus for this second phase. SU members later referred to it as the 'dispersion of Umuahia'. In his account, Roberts describes their evacuation along with 100,000 other refugees as enemy shells bombarded the outskirts of Umuahia. SU headquarters subsequently moved to a remote village in Mbano, Central Igboland, and during the next six months the number of SU groups in Biafra increased from twenty-five to eight-five, most started by young people nurtured within the ranks of SU Umuahia. Because of Scripture Union's organisational flexibility groups were able to meet in a variety of locations, and by the end of the war many villages had become centres of renewal.[16] For example, in the Obizi area there were SU groups

[16] Roberts, *Life and Death*, 78-9; Daphne Beauchamp, 'First-hand News from Biafra', *Life of Faith*, January 10, 1970; Roberts, SU Prayer Letter No.17, 7 October 1969.

at the Biafran army convalescent camp, the WCC relief store (Obizi), St. Andrew's Anglican Church (Obizi), St. Peter's Anglican Church (Obizi), Avutu Refugee Camp, the Engineers Camp (Aforogbe) and the Methodist Church (Umunwanwa).[17]

Figure 5. SU meeting at a Biafran convalescent camp during the civil war.

The following war-time testimonies show how Igbo revivalists interpreted the events of April 1969 in the light of their twin beliefs in God's providential control and the efficacy of prayer, and their conception of the missionary task. Ben Onwochei, a member of SU Umuahia's leadership team, worked as a medical orderly at Queen Elizabeth Hospital. After the town's evacuation, he followed Roberts to Mbano and was subsequently appointed SU representative at a hospital for wounded soldiers.

> I remember praying very hard that Umuahia should not be disturbed. But it was! But remarkably the Nigerian troops entered Umuahia on 22nd April, and on 23rd April, just the very next day, the Lord gave us back Owerri. Moreover, with the evacuation the Lord dispersed the Christians

[17] List of SU Groups in Biafra, 1969.

> in Umuahia, whom He had been training for a purpose. Wherever these Christians went, they carried with them the light of Christ which they spread as they went. This later resulted in the springing up of many more S.U. groups in Biafra, bringing the number of S.U. groups therefore to about seventy. This has given many more people the opportunity to hear the good news, and to turn to Jesus.[18]

Nnenna Okoye, another member of SU Umuahia's leadership team, was converted in 1964 at a Scripture Union conference. She was a graduate of the University of Ibadan and one of the few married members of SU during the war.

> In April, Umuahia, which is only ten miles from my home, Uzuakoli, was threatened and the Nigerians were advancing from the Uzuakoli end. You can imagine my fear and anxiety. I prayed the Lord for a whole week not to let Umuahia fall or let my home be affected in any way. I found out that the more I prayed in this vein the more my anxiety mounted. It was not until I asked the Lord to let anything that would bring glory to His name happen, but let Him provide, that I had complete peace and calm. Uzuakoli fell first with my parents, my two youngest sisters and other relatives behind the enemy line. They are still there now. Later Umuahia fell and we were forced out. The population moved out into Mbano, Okigwe, Mbaise and Orlu areas. The word of God was taken to these areas which had been athirst for it. It is spreading like wild fire and people are coming to a personal knowledge of our Lord. One can look back now and thank the Lord for allowing Umuahia to fall.[19]

It is possible to detect echoes of an earlier Christian dispersion in these accounts, the story of the Jerusalem Church's dispersal throughout Judea and Samaria in Acts: 'On that day a great persecution broke out against the church at Jerusalem, and all except the apostles were scattered throughout Judea and Samaria. . . . Those who had been scattered preached the word wherever they went' (Acts 8:1, 4). By narrating their experiences in these terms, revivalists were reinforcing their identity as Christian missionaries and their belief in God's providential control over adverse circumstances.

The climax of the revival occurred in the aftermath of the war. Prior to this, access to cities had been severely restricted because they were the main focus of the conflict, but now the movement was able to penetrate the major urban areas of Onitsha, Enugu and Aba. As revivalists migrated to

---

[18] Ben Onwochei, written testimony, 1969.

[19] Nnenna Okoye, 'Do not despise the Lord's discipline or be weary of his reproof', written testimony, 1969.

these metropolitan centres in search of employment or to reclaim homes, they carried the revival message with them. It was still a period of crisis. Many had lost family members as well as possessions. Educational institutions in the East did not resume immediately and jobs were scarce, so there were many young aspiring evangelists with time on their hands. Preaching the gospel became their full-time occupation. A new wave of revival swept through Igboland, again centred on Scripture Union.

Soon after the war, young people reactivated Scripture Union township groups in all the major Igbo urban areas. By this time, SU Pilgrims groups, intended to cater for school leavers, had replaced the school groups as the focus of Scripture Union in the East. One reason for this was that most schools were run by mission church authorities, who objected to the radical behaviour of SU members and consequently closed the groups down. But it was also an example of the indigenisation of global flows as SU Nigeria adapted its ministry to include young adults. The government takeover of schools, however, made it possible for SU to re-enter secondary schools in 1971, and by January 1971, 75 out of 275 secondary schools in East Central State had SU groups.[20]

In Onitsha, North-Western Igboland, a Scripture Union group was started early in 1970 by Emmanuel Ekpunobi, a former associate of Bill Roberts. Ekpunobi was brought up in Onitsha where he lived with his grandfather, an Anglican priest. He was 'born-again' in 1963 while attending the CMS Dennis Memorial Grammar School (Onitsha), but only began to 'grow as a Christian' after joining SU Umuahia in 1967 following the outbreak of war. In 1970, Ekpunobi returned to Onitsha to resume his secondary school studies. After a season of prayer and house-to-house evangelism, he started a SU group as a means of nurturing his converts, and this grew rapidly as increasing numbers of young people joined its ranks. Members included semi-literate traders and artisans, as well as secondary school students, some of whom later became Pentecostal pioneers responsible for starting autonomous charismatic fellowship groups and neo-Pentecostal churches (NPCs).[21]

In Enugu, North-Eastern Igboland, a Scripture Union group started in the home of Justin Ogugua. Ogugua was a member of SU Enugu before the war but left when Enugu was overrun by Federal troops. In 1969, he paid a brief visit to SU Umuahia and later testified to the effect this had upon his life: 'The type of Christian fellowship I witnessed there started reviving me

---

[20] Sam C. Nnamuah, Letter to Roberts, 21 January 1971. The government of East Central State took over sole responsibility for public education in 1970. A. E. Afigbo, 'The Missions, the State and Education in South-Eastern Nigeria, 1956-71', in Fasholé-Luke *et al.*, *Christianity*, 176.

[21] Emma Ekpunobi, written testimony, 1969; interview, 24 October 2001, Awka.

right from the time I arrived there'.[22] In 1970, Enugu replaced Umuahia as the capital of East Central State, and many school leavers, and unemployed or displaced civil servants, descended on the city in search of jobs. Consequently, the SU offices and Bible study centres became a refuge for migrant jobseekers. The SU township group grew rapidly once its Sunday afternoon meeting had become an evangelistic guest service, and in May 1970, it moved first to the ECWA/SIM church premises and a month later to St Andrew's Presbyterian Church to accommodate its members. Fortunately, Mike Bonomi and James Ukaegbu, pastors of ECWA and the Presbyterian Church respectively, were both sympathetic to the revival, in contrast to most other mission church leaders in Enugu, and this facilitated its growth. SU members became aggressive evangelists. Apart from holding evangelistic 'guest services', which by September 1970 were attracting up to seven hundred people, they embarked on a programme of house-to-house visitation to gain territorial control of the city. By 1971, SU township group in Enugu had become the largest in Nigeria with members responsible for starting other groups in surrounding schools.[23]

Similar developments occurred in urban centres further south. SU Umuahia restarted after former leaders Peter Nwangwu and Raymond Nwosu returned to the SU headquarters soon after the war. One SU member wrote in June 1970: 'The SU House here in Umuahia has become a very busy Youth centre. Enthusiastic youths turn up in vast numbers from the town and its environs, especially for the guest services'.[24] According to Felix Obiorah, the first post-war President of SU Umuahia, these monthly meetings were soon attracting over 1,000 young people. SU groups in Aba and Owerri also resumed soon after the war. Both benefited from the patronage of established church leaders such as Evangelist Godson Ogbansiegbe (Christian Fellowship Group), ECWA pastors W. O. Madubuka and R. O. Onokola, and Anglican Bishop of Owerri Benjamin Nwankiti. SU Aba quickly became one of the largest in Nigeria and was responsible for producing several neo-Pentecostal pioneers from among its members, including John Ugah, General Superintendent of Jesus the Way Mission, Kenneth Eboh, Assistant General Overseer of Holiness Evangelical Church, and Emmanuel Okorie, founder of Living Word Ministries.

---

[22] Justin Ogugua, written testimony, 1969.

[23] Monica Chigozie Ezenwa, Letter to Roberts, 14 September 1970; S. C. A. Chukwuka, 'The Pilgrims Ministry: Its Developmental Stages', *Plumbline (The Journal of the Pilgrims Ministry, S.U. Nigeria)*, 1992 Maiden Edition, 7.

[24] Sam Okoli, Letter to Roberts, 7 June 1970.

Other local Scripture Union groups sprang up in churches and schools within close proximity to these cities. Meanwhile, SU work expanded

Figure 6. SU leaders, University of Nigeria, Nsukka, 1971. From left: Raymond Nwosu, Chris Onuoha, Grace Iwuora, (-), Chibozo Iwuora, John Onuora, Benjamin Onwochei.

rapidly as schools reopened and dispersed members started new groups in towns and villages throughout Igboland. By January 1971, there were 173 SU groups in schools and churches across East Central State, compared to 160 in Western State, 48 in Mid-Western State, and 30 in South-Eastern State.[25]

Igbo-founded charismatic fellowship groups were among the earliest to emerge in Africa, and in contrast to Western Nigeria, where they arose mainly on university campuses, it was the SU township groups which

[25] Sam C. Nnamuah, Letter to Roberts, 21 January 1971; Scripture Union Nigeria, News/Prayer Letter, January - March 1971. At the time there were a total of 422 SU groups in Nigeria, distributed as follows: Lagos (33), Ijebu-Ode (33), Ibadan (24), Akure (70), Mid-Western State (48), East Central State (173, including 95 Church groups), South Eastern State (30), and Rivers State (11).

provided the foundation for their emergence in Igboland.[26] Consequently, they initially attracted a broader cross-section of society than their counterparts in the West. Here I disagree with those scholars who suggest that the Nigerian charismatic movement had its deepest roots and found most of its early leaders within the university campuses and among the educated élite.[27] In the East, most founders of charismatic fellowships did not attend university. Out of sixteen informants who founded Igbo charismatic fellowships during the 1970s five had primary level education only, eight secondary and three tertiary. By 1973, there were at least thirteen Igbo-founded charismatic fellowships, most started by young men without tertiary education. None had any formal links with university campus activities in the early 1970s. Yet the founders of these groups were often highly intelligent and motivated. What they lacked was opportunity to further their education, due to post-war conditions.

Table 3.1 *Igbo-initiated Charismatic Fellowship Groups, 1969-73*
(Note: headquarters in parentheses)

Bethel Fellowship Group (near Umuahia)
Calvary Evangelistic Mission (Umuahia)
Canaan Gospel Centre (Umuahia)
Central Christian Fellowship Association (Nnewi)
Christian Revivalist Missionary Team (Aba)
Holiness Evangelistic Association (Owerri)
Hour of Deliverance Ministry (Otuocha)
Hour of Freedom Evangelistic Association (Onitsha)
Last Days Messengers (Okigwe)
Master's Vessel Group (Umuahia)
Redeeming Time Pilgrims Mission (Owerri)
Riches of Christ Evangelistic Association (Onitsha)
Save the Lost Programme (Nnewi)

The most important charismatic fellowship group for the progress of the revival was the Hour of Freedom Evangelistic Association (popularly known as Hour of Freedom), based in North-Western Igboland. In 1969, three young men were converted from a prayer house background. Their names were Stephen Okafor, Raphael Okafor (not related) and Arthur

---

[26] For Western Nigeria, see Matthews A. Ojo, 'Deeper Christian Life Ministry: A Case Study of the Charismatic movements in Western Nigeria', *JRA*, 18.2, 1988, 141-62; Ojo, 'Contextual', 175-92; Ojo, *Army*.

[27] The studies I have in mind include Ojo, 'Contextual', 175; Peel, *Religious Encounter*, 314; Kalu, 'Third Response', 7.

Oruizu, members of Ufuma Practical Prayer Band (UPPB). Hour of Freedom, the platform for their ministry, was started towards the end of 1969 while the war was still in progress and soon became the main vehicle for the spread of the revival. Stephen Okafor, a trader from the village of Ojoto, was the leader of Hour of Freedom. Brought up a Roman Catholic, he became a member of UPPB in 1963 where he occupied a position of influence and claimed a close association with the prophetess, Madame Nwokolo. In 1969, a friend introduced him to the SU group at Mbano, and later that year he was 'born-again' while listening to a sermon preached by Bill Roberts. Immediately he returned to Ufuma hoping to convert his fellow members, and was joined by Raphael Okafor and Oruizu, both Anglicans and former members of the Cherubim and Seraphim Society. It was not long before all three were expelled from UPPB because of their overt preaching activities. They then became itinerant evangelists and founded Hour of Freedom. In a letter written in early 1970, Stephen Okafor describes his expulsion from Ufuma and early gospel ministry:

> Ufuma has been shaken to its foundation and many souls from there have come to my Saviour. In marketplace, in the road, in houses, in chapels, in halls, in fields, in university campuses, in secondary schools I have pleaded with sinners. To capitalists and poor I have told about the love of Jesus and His hatred of sins.[28]

Hour of Freedom had its headquarters at Ojoto, but Stephen Okafor recognised the strategic importance of Onitsha and soon established a base at 22 Amobi Street.[29] Initially, Hour of Freedom encountered opposition from SU Onitsha because of its Pentecostal emphasis and aggressive evangelistic style. Yet it was not long before SU members joined its ranks, resulting in its rapid expansion. As the revival spread, interdenominational fellowship groups affiliated to Hour of Freedom were started all over Igboland, including Enugu, Aba and Owerri. Like Scripture Union, Hour of Freedom did not believe in starting new churches. Later, however, these fellowship groups became the basis for the formation of many neo-Pentecostal churches.

Soon after the formation of Hour of Freedom, two events occurred which acted as catalysts for the new wave of revival and helped to introduce Pentecostal spirituality into Scripture Union in the East. Both were indirectly related to the civil war. Firstly, Mike Oye and Muyiwa Olamijulo, Yoruba SU travelling secretaries from Western Nigeria, came to

---

[28] Stephen Okafor, Letter to Roberts, early 1970.

[29] Among Igbo revivalists in Onitsha this location attained a similar position of prestige to Azusa Street during the US American Pentecostal revival.

Biafra to engage in relief work. Oye and Olamijulo were Pentecostals from the Apostolic Faith Church and products of the relationship between Scripture Union and the growing Christian Union (IVCU) at the University of Ibadan, a centre of charismatic renewal in Western Nigeria.[30] Their arrival in Igboland sparked off a new wave of revivalist activity and helped to unite the revival in Eastern and Western Nigeria.

Another important milestone was the arrival from Western Nigeria of the Igbo evangelist J. M. J. Emesim, described by Anyaegbu as the 'apostle of Pentecostalism in North-Western Igboland'.[31] A former Anglican, Emesim had migrated to Lagos in 1961 where he was converted in 1964 and introduced to Pentecostal doctrine by an indigenous church called Souls of Christ Crusade Ministry. Later, he joined Light Apostolic Church in Lagos, who sheltered him during the civil war until tensions eased in 1968. Emesim formed the Hour of Deliverance Ministry as a vehicle for training workers for the evangelisation and rehabilitation of Igboland. When the war ended he resigned from his job and returned to the East. In August 1970, Stephen Okafor invited him to be the guest speaker at an evangelistic campaign in Awka-Etiti, near Onitsha, and in Ogbu Kalu's words, 'he simply set the whole area ablaze'.[32] This event introduced many revivalists to Pentecostal spirituality. Emesim called on his audience to repent from their sins, accept Jesus as their personal saviour and receive Holy Spirit baptism. Subsequently, he set up a Bible school in Igboland, which became the training ground for many future Igbo NPC pioneers.

In Central Igboland, the Holiness Evangelistic Association in Owerri was the first charismatic fellowship group to emerge from the revival. Accounts differ as to its early history. Here we encounter one of the problems associated with oral sources where the tendency is for participants to present themselves as central figures while marginalising others. According to one version, it was started by Alexander Ekewuba in 1970

---

[30] The Apostolic Faith Church (AFC) traces its roots to the US American Azusa Street Revival. The Nigerian branch was started in 1944 in Lagos by Timothy Oshokoya, a former Apostolic Church member, and later an evangelist with Christ Apostolic Church. In 1987, AFC membership in Nigeria was 20,000, compared to a global membership of 54,000. See Gordon J. Melton, *The Encyclopaedia of American Religions*, Tarrytown, NY: Triumph Books, 1991, 351; Benjamin Steward, *Historical Background of Churches in Nigeria*, Lagos: Interwale Press, 1984, 27-8.

[31] The main source used for Emesim is J. O. Anyaegbu, 'The Growth and Development of Pentecostal/Evangelical Movements in Igboland: A Case Study of North-West Igboland, 1965-1990', M.A. thesis, University of Nigeria, Nsukka, 1991, 201-210.

[32] Kalu, *Embattled Gods*, 277.

and subsequently handed over to his half-brother, Chima Amadi, a motor mechanic. Ekewuba initially used Scripture Union as the platform for his evangelistic activities and for a time was leader of Hour of Freedom in Owerri. Another account suggests that Amadi started Holiness Evangelistic Association in 1971 after he had linked up with a group of Scripture Union

Figure 7. Former revivalists J. M. J. Emesim (right) and Augustine Nwodika, Enugu, 1999.

secondary school students, eager to evangelise their communities. Either way, it followed the pattern of other charismatic fellowship groups, with members continuing to attend different churches until it too eventually became a church.

Meanwhile in Umuahia developments were underway which would culminate in the formation of Master's Vessel Group, the third major Igbo charismatic group formed after the war. Following a call to full-time ministry, Felix Obiorah, President of SU Umuahia, approached the Anglican Church for ordination. When they turned him down, he joined his friend Joshua Uhiara, another Anglican and fellow SU leader, to pray and engage in evangelistic activities. In November 1971, they formed the

Master's Vessel Group. Their vision - based on the Bible text 2 Tim 2:21 - was to recruit 'vessels' for the evangelisation of Igboland.[33] A letter written in September 1971 shows the tensions that existed within Scripture Union after the war and how this contributed to the formation of charismatic fellowships such as Master's Vessel Group:

> In your last letter you mentioned something about Felix Obiora [*sic*] and his group. His Group is called 'Masters Vessel's Group (M.V.G).' It is non-denominational but evangelical. It was formed in 1971. I AM NOT A MEMBER! But I want to testify that God is using the Group to reach the hungry masses with the Word. In Umuahia today, the M.V.G is doing the evangelical work, which S.U. did during the war. The S.U. Groups in the schools are almost back to the pre-war standard. In some schools it's a mere society. Since the war converts left school there has been big compromises in the S.U. school Groups. And it seems the S.U. Big Men in Enugu and Ibadan love it so. This may sound strange to you but it is true. This is why groups spring up here and there. . . . Most of the members used to be keen S.U. members but backed out as a result of S.U. Nig.'s gradual and steady drive on the road to compromise. In my home group we have resolved to be S.U. and no other thing but we can't restrict our members from joining or fellowshipping with any other sound Christian fellowship group.[34]

In Aba, Emmanuel Okorie founded the Christian Revivalist Missionary Team as a platform for his evangelistic ministry. Okorie was one of Roberts's protégées in Umuahia, and after the war, while still in secondary school, helped to reactivate the SU township group in Aba. For a while he operated under the umbrella of the Qua Iboe Church, a large denomination in the area, but also held evangelistic campaigns in the southeast and North. A branch of Hour of Freedom also existed in Aba, later absorbed into Riches of Christ Mission, the first major neo-Pentecostal church formed after the war. Eventually each of these charismatic fellowships underwent a transition to denominational status, a subject I return to in chapter 4.

---

[33] 2 Tim 2: 21 - 'Therefore, if a man cleanses himself from these things, he will be a vessel for honor, sanctified, useful to the Master, prepared for every good work' (NASB).

[34] Uchenna Emezue, Letter to Roberts, 28 September 1971.

Global Flows and Local Identities

I turn now to an analysis of the revival and a discussion of growth factors in terms of an economic model of supply and demand. Here I draw upon insights from rational choice theory (RCT), associated with sociologists Rodney Stark, William Bainbridge, Roger Finke and the economist Larry Iannaccone.[35] RCT proceeds on the assumption that religious demand remains constant and competitive pluralism increases religious vitality and participation. It assumes the possibility of choice and argues that religion flourishes especially in unregulated contexts. In this competitive environment, religious providers necessarily adapt their products to suit consumers. While I disagree with RCT over its tendency to shape the world to fit the explanation, and its contention that religious demand remains constant, the economic market model is a helpful tool for interpreting current religious trends in Nigeria where freedom of religion is constitutionally guaranteed and people tend to discard impotent religious forms in favour of more effective ones. Its value lies in its presentation of churches as competing firms in a free marketplace, and its focus on suppliers *and* consumers of religious commodities. I use it here as a metaphor for examining issues of cause and effect rather than as a general theory of religious change. As noted, the revival's success depended largely upon the maintenance of a balance between supply and demand. Socio-economic and political pressures created demands for alternative religious producers able to respond more efficiently to changing consumer requirements. The revival's missionary impulse provided competition for the mission churches and broke their monopoly in a way that earlier initiatives failed to do.

I also reflect upon the nature of revival experience and its effects upon existing landscapes. Themes characteristic of earlier waves of revival and Pentecostal activity were present during the revival. As we will see, there were elements of continuity and rupture with existing religious forms, strong currents of accommodation and challenge, and significant influences

---

35 See for example, Rodney Stark and Laurence R. Iannacone, 'A Supply-side Reinterpretation of the Secularization of Europe', *Journal for the Scientific Study of Religion*, 33, 1994, 230-52. For critiques of RCT, see N. J. Demerath, III, 'Rational Paradigms, A-Rational Religion, and the Debate over Secularization', *Journal for the Scientific Study of Religion*, 34.1, 1995, 105-12; Steve Bruce, 'Religion and Rational Choice: A Critique of Economic Explanations of Religious Behavior', *Sociology of Religion*, 54, 1993, 193-205. For a recent application of the economic model to the Nigerian religious context, see Asonzeh F.-K. Ukah, 'Advertising God: Nigerian Christian Video-Films and the Power of Consumer Culture', *JRA*, 33.2, 2003, 203-31.

from local and external forces. I begin by examining the influence of two carriers of global religious culture.

Scripture Union

The primary reason for the revival's success lay in its missionary impulse, which was kindled within the Scripture Union fellowship groups during the war. Most revivalists were mission church members and attended Scripture Union activities. Out of seventy-nine informants who participated in the revival, thirty-four were Anglicans, nine were Methodists, three were Presbyterians, five were members of Qua Iboe Church, three were members of ECWA/SIM, five were members of Assemblies of God, seven were Roman Catholics, and four belonged to prayer houses.[36] The rest were members of other Protestant denominations or from unknown church backgrounds, and all belonged to Scripture Union.

As a transnational organisation, Scripture Union acted as a globalising force and a bearer of evangelical religious culture. However, as we noted in chapter 1, global flows can strengthen local identities and precipitate resistance and heterogeneity. SU supplied participants with a new repertoire of images and narratives for identity construction. In particular, it expanded their world by providing access to an 'imagined community' with global dimensions and missionary ambitions. But these images and narratives underwent transformations as revivalists appropriated them for local consumption. An important objective is to examine the way participants negotiated the local and the global in their search for new forms of individual and collective identity. During the revival, local distinctiveness and global generality occurred simultaneously, in interconnected ways.

Scripture Union's evangelical and ecumenical religious culture was a suitable medium for the expression of revival Christianity. Members were critical of the mainline churches for promoting a liberal and nominal form of Christianity. The mission-related Pentecostal churches offered an alternative option, but had declined in Pentecostal vigour due to the combined effects of bureaucratisation and ageing, and were regarded with suspicion by mainline churches. The Civil War Revival was a radical response to perceived deficiencies within existing Christian communities, and SU provided a safe environment for these sentiments to be expressed. As an evangelical movement, SU stressed personal conversion, devotion to

[36] In the case of prayer houses, I only include those participants who did not adopt dual allegiance to mission church and prayer house. The four revivalists were members of either Christ Holy Church or St. Joseph's Chosen Church of God.

the Bible, a life of active service and an emphasis on the cross. Along with its commitment to ecumenical principles, its relative freedom from missionary control, and its focus on youth, this made it an ideal vehicle for the revival. Aside from its Pentecostal emphasis, most of the features that were present during the revival were already in place within SU, albeit on a smaller scale. Yet despite its commitment to evangelical and ecumenical ideals (which emanated from its Western metropolitan centres), SU set in motion certain trends that hastened the fragmentation of the movement as autonomous charismatic fellowships emerged from its ranks.

Biblical Texts in Critical Contexts

> My little pocket Bible has been of immense value to me in this art of witnessing. Even when I am alone, I continue reading it and picking out some helpful verses for witnessing. I bought this pocket Bible before the war broke out but I had never known what treasure I have until the war broke out. So many people have been requesting for Bibles through the Scripture Union Group, and we feel that this is very necessary if they must get on in the Lord. I cannot imagine a Christian remaining for one day without the Bible, and yet many have none now, having got out of disturbed areas without theirs. It was such a great blessing to us when we received some dozens of New Testaments from the Scripture Union Headquarters. These sort of became Scripture Union badges to many members who kept moving about with the New Testament.[37]

Among other labels, revivalists were referred to as 'Bible carriers' due to their habit of carrying their Bibles as a form of symbolic identity marker, signifying their membership of the global 'born-again' community. One informant said you could identify 'born-again' Christians during the early 1970s by their clothes, their speech and their fondness for publicly displaying their Bibles. Another revivalist described the way his conversion in September 1967 changed his relationship to the Bible:

> I could on that first night, at home, and then on, open my Bible (the reading of which had been very seldom, in fact a Sunday - Sunday affair) and read without feeling the surprised eyes of my family members on me nor feeling their comments on the change showing in me. I could now carry my Bible without shame to church.[38]

---

[37] Justin O. Ogugua, written testimony, 1969.

[38] Ume Kalu, 'What God has done for me', written testimony, 1969.

But the Bible was more than a mark of identity. It became an important source for the reconstruction of Igbo Christian identity and the production of an African theology 'from below' that appealed to consumer demands.

While its role as the universal Christian text has acted as a homogenising and restraining influence upon global Christianity, the Bible has also precipitated local initiative and difference, and stimulated hybrid forms of spirituality. In Africa, re-readings of the Bible have sometimes sparked off local revivalist activity and generated new religious movements.[39] During the Nigerian civil war, many young people, exposed to the influence of SU, began to devote themselves to the study of the Bible and to regard it as one of their most prized possessions. One revivalist described it as his 'best companion' and the 'most important factor' behind his Christian growth. Another referred to it as his 'only priceless property', his 'source of comfort in time of sorrow', his 'chief adviser in time of temptation', and the source of his knowledge of God's will.[40]

Anthony O. Nkwoka shows how the combination of waning missionary control, cultural nationalism and the Biafran crisis led to a greater degree of Bible reading autonomy among the Igbo. The translation of the Bible into the Igbo language by the Anglican Archdeacon T. J. Dennis between 1913 and 1917 made the Bible more accessible, but responsibility for interpretation remained largely in the hands of mission-trained church pastors. However, SU (Nigeria)'s achievement of national autonomy in 1966, and the introduction of adult Pilgrim Groups, provided a favourable environment for individual and collective Bible study, relatively free from missionary and clerical control. This coincided with the rise in cultural nationalism (following independence) and the advent of civil war.[41] One 'benefit' of the war, according to SU travelling secretary Muyiwa Olamijulo, was the re-emergence of Bible-based Christianity and a return to New Testament belief and ethics in the East.[42] This Bible reading culture was reinforced by SU policy, which encouraged its members to read the Bible systematically, ask questions, and apply it to their lives, and the publication of daily reading notes in English (Daily Power and Daily

[39] Maxwell, 'African Imagination', 14; David B. Barrett, 'Interdisciplinary Theories of Religion and African Independency', in David B. Barrett (ed.), *African Initiatives in Religion*, Nairobi: East African Publishing House, 1971, 152-53.

[40] Written testimonies, Emma Ekpunobi, Chioma Amalu, 1969.

[41] Anthony O. Nkwoka, 'The Role of the Bible in the Igbo Christianity of Nigeria', in G. O. West and Musa W. Dube (eds.), *The Bible in Africa. Transactions, Trajectories and Trends*, Leiden: E. J. Brill, 2000, 328.

[42] Muyiwa Olamijulo, 'Report of visit to the East Central State', 15 June-30 September, 1970.

Guide) and Igbo (*Inye Aka*) during the 1960s.[43] These were crucial factors in the recovery of an evangelical spirituality and sparked off a new wave of intense evangelistic activity, which became the dominant feature of the revival. As the 'pre-eminent African text',[44] the Bible played a significant role in shaping the lives of Igbo revivalists and stimulated an unprecedented outbreak of revivalist activity.

Soon after the beginning of the war, Roberts started a Sunday afternoon Bible study meeting for local youth at Mission Hill (SU Umuahia headquarters), which continued until their evacuation in April 1969. By the end of 1968, the full Scripture Union programme consisted of Sunday afternoon Bible study (with Guest Service on last Sunday of the month), Tuesday afternoon meeting with nurses and wounded soldiers in the local hospital, Wednesday afternoon fellowship meeting for Bible study, talks and prayer, and Friday afternoon Bible study. Subsequently, Bible study groups in towns and villages throughout Igboland became the launching pads for significant mission initiatives. Most autonomous charismatic fellowships began as Bible study groups associated with Scripture Union.

The Bible was a means of adapting to new and often critical contexts, and a basis for challenging existing religious options and lifestyles. The pragmatic nature of Igbo indigenous spirituality meant that Scripture Union's emphasis on the Bible's life-changing potential proved popular among young people looking for practical help during a time of severe stress. As they read their Bibles, they found it resonated with their own experiences of crisis. For example, one revivalist identified his suffering with Jesus' teaching about the escalation of conflicts during the last days:

> The present war has brought untold hardship. You no longer see your loved ones for they are either killed or missing. You no longer feed as before. There is unrest within and without. But for all these the Lord Jesus has the answer for each. In Matt 24.6-13 he told us about the war and all that would happen; but that if anyone endures to the end he would be saved.[45]

Revival testimonies show that Bible texts were a source of comfort and guidance, and played a critical role in conversion experiences, problem-solving and ethical renewal. Revivalists regarded the Bible as a means of enlightenment and a source of knowledge, exposing personal sin and giving

[43] Andrew Olu Igenoza, 'Contextual Balancing of Scripture with Scripture: Scripture Union in Nigeria and Ghana', in West and Dube (eds.), *Bible in Africa*, 293-94.

[44] Maxwell, 'African Imagination', 13.

[45] Felix Okafor, written testimony, 1969.

fresh revelation of Christ's love and God's plan of salvation. And once incorporated into the Christian community, personal and corporate study became an important means of applying the Bible to contemporary life. The case of Ume Kalu illustrates this well. Kalu was brought up in the Presbyterian Church where he underwent infant baptism and confirmation, and attended Sunday school. His testimony describes his introduction to born-again Christianity through SU Umuahia in September 1967 and his early Christian experience. He refers to having his 'eyes opened more and more' to his 'sinfulness and helplessness' and need for salvation as he attended SU meetings, listened to lectures on 'sin, man and sin, Christ the Only Saviour', and studied the Bible for himself. After his conversion, Kalu continued to study 'the Book' and memorise 'helpful verses' as a means of personal guidance and problem-solving: 'I have through its study come to know God's commands and what he feels about Marriage, Money, Wealth, Sex, and many other difficult problems in society'. He concludes by describing the ongoing effects of Scripture Union's Bible reading culture: 'The constant prayer meetings, Bible studies, Bible Discussions have been a great help in my growing faith and Christian growth'.[46]

The revival enabled the youth to read the Bible through fresh lenses and cast a critical eye over existing religious forms. Many concluded that the mainline churches were dominated by compromise with the 'world' and mixed with traditional religious practices. This new appreciation of the Bible's authority caused them to reject other religious options, resulting in an exodus from the prayer houses and a repudiation of 'traditional' cultural beliefs and practices after the war. Later, it contributed to the emergence of charismatic fellowships as revivalists became dissatisfied with mainline church spirituality and its inability to meet the new demands thrown up by the civil war crisis.

The demonisation of prayer houses became a popular theme in post-war revivalist discourse. In written participant accounts, they are referred to variously as 'satanic Prayer bands', 'occult groups' and 'prayer cults'. Their origins are traced to the influence of malignant spirits, and members are assumed to be in bondage to the devil and deceived by false prophets.[47] Revivalists criticised the prayer houses for incorporating elements of indigenous religion and 'occultism' into their belief systems and rituals (including the use of animal sacrifices, candles and incantations), for failing to preach the gospel, and for the magical use of the Bible.[48] One informant

---

[46] Ume Kalu, 'What God has done for me', 1969.

[47] See for example, Okafor, Okafor and Oruizu, Letter to SU Executive Committee, 1970; Rosebud Okorocha, Letter to Roberts, 31 May 1971; Nnamdi Okagbue, Letter to Roberts, 3 February 1971.

[48] See Bolton, *Glory*, 8-10; Okafor, Okafor and Oruizu, Letter to SU Executive Committee, 1970.

commented that members 'read the Bible to acquire power and perform their miracles, to fight their enemies, but not to change their lives'.[49] Their visionary practices were also deemed demonic, and further suspicion was generated by the alleged immoral lifestyles of some of the leaders. However, the issue of typology is important here. If we recall, prayer houses like Christ Holy Church and St. Joseph's Chosen Church of God strongly opposed both traditional religious practices and 'occult' activity. Other groups were less discerning, however, and became the target of revivalist critique.

The Bible fuelled the Igbo imagination and provided a rich source for new ideas and new means to attain old objectives. War-time testimonies show the way that revivalist written discourse was filled with biblical references, language and imagery.. Often direct quotations are blended into these narratives to make a point or bolster an argument. Consider this excerpt from a testimony written by Benjamin Onwochei:

> After my conversion I lacked lively fellowship. The instrument God used soon left for further studies. We were left like sheep without a shepherd, my friend and I. So I gradually went to sleep for three years. I began to compromise on quite a number of things which might have appeared to be minor but were quite serious. No wonder the word of God says, 'But exhort one another everyday . . . that none of you may be hardened by the deceitfulness of sin'. . . . After three years the Lord brought me into contact with a Scripture Union group at S.U. House, Umuahia, where I was awakened out of my deep slumber. . . . I now know that no temptation comes to me which has never come to anybody else, and that our faithful God and Father will not let me be tempted beyond my strength, but with the temptation will also provide a way of escape. 1 Cor 10: 13. Through the Bible I am daily taught to lead a holy life, to 'walk in newness of life', and to walk after the Spirit and not gratify the desires of the flesh. Though I have often fallen, I am continually being taught to persevere and not to faint; to 'run with perseverance the race that is set before me'.[50]

Of course, Scripture Union was not wholly responsible for inculcating a biblical worldview into the lives of Igbo revivalists. In his testimony, Onwochei describes how he was 'brought up in the fear of the Lord' (in a family where Christianity was taken seriously) and 'tried to put into practice the good Christian ethics' he was taught. Like many of his contemporaries, he attended Sunday school and listened to Bible-based

[49] Interview, Eliezer Okoye, 13 May 2000, Onitsha.

[50] Ben Onwochei, written testimony, 1969.

sermons at his local Anglican church. But Onwochei's family had eclectic tastes and sometimes resorted to traditional means of problem-solving. 'My people were interested in my security, and so just before I entered secondary school I was taken to two different witch-doctors, one after the other, for some protective potions'. Ironically, it was at this mission school that he encountered evangelical teaching. Onwochei describes what happened when he and a friend paid a visit to a Christian teacher: 'There he opened the word of God to us, and we saw how that the Lord was inviting us to come to Him. We knelt and, amidst tears, openly confessed our sin to the Lord, trusting Him to be able to save us'.

Revival hermeneutics was context sensitive, communally regulated and pragmatic. Like liberation theology, participants sought to understand local contexts in the light of Scripture, but they did so by retaining a literalist approach to biblical interpretation which was dependent upon the Spirit and accountable to the community of faith. They looked for correspondences between their own life situations and the Bible, and expected Biblical texts to have practical relevance and problem-solving potential. Thus one war-time participant wrote, 'Sometimes one just finds the happenings of that day similar to the Bible passage read'.[51] This dynamic is evident in Ume Kalu's narrative referred to earlier. Here the Spirit gives understanding of 'God's commands' in the Bible as they relate to contemporary 'problems in society' and provides practical guidance on how to apply them. 'When I have decisions to take I pray about it, read what God says about [it], gather advice from brethren and I have found that in this way the Holy Spirit has all the time led me to take the right decisions'.[52]

Because they believed the Bible possessed authority as God's Word, revivalists allowed it to challenge and shape their personal lifestyles. This contributed to the revival's emphasis on holiness and Christian unity. For instance, one revivalist described the way his habit of memorising Bible verses helped him to overcome the Devil's temptations to sin.[53] Another referred to the powerful influence of Bible texts such as I John 3:15 and James 1:26, which encourage love for the 'brethren' and control of the tongue.[54] Sometimes portions of Scripture resonated with the traditional search for power in Igbo piety. As they read their Bibles, revivalists found within its pages stories of God's empowering presence transforming individuals and communities, and this initiated personal quests for spiritual power. Eddi Onugha's revival narrative illustrates this well. It shows the

---

[51] Raymond Nwosu, written testimony, 1969.

[52] Ume Kalu, 'What God has done for me', 1969.

[53] John Nwangwu, written testimony, 1969.

[54] Augustine Nwodika, 'The Relationship of the Movement with the Churches in the Seventies', Remembering the Seventies Conference, audiocassette, 29 April 2000, Enugu.

dialectical relationship that existed between Christian experience and Scripture, and the way that literal readings of the Bible generated faith and precipitated quests for providential interventions.

> The revival made people to realise that some of the things that are written in the Scriptures were not just stories, but were things that happened and could still in our time. That some of the miracles that were performed in times of old were not just stories, but they were actually events that took place; they were actually manifestations and demonstrations of the power of God; they were actually events that showed that God was interested in the things that were happening in this world, and that he could intervene in certain situations to upset natural laws in order to show his supremacy as the sovereign Lord.[55]

Thus the Bible was more than a collection of stories of historical interest. It was a repository of promises to be received by faith and a representation of life (*ezi-ndụ*) as it ought to be lived. Ume Kalu's testimony shows how this hermeneutic operated. It describes the effects of the economic blockade on family life during the war, and the way that Bible texts stimulated prayer and generated faith for providential provision.

> The war has made life very difficult in Biafra especially with the Blockade still effective. Clothing and Food have to be brought at high prices. Problems from this were pronounced in my family where there is no well-to-do bread winner. The High Prices would soon choke up my mother's petty-trading which maintained us. As the three senior members of the family who should have found war-time jobs had not got employed one would have expected a total crisis in the family caused by want. But God has ever supplied us all even till now and the more as we learned to commit all to Him in prayer and thank Him for previous days blessings. Just near difficult times of lack, after praying, we would start to get gifts from many angles (both expected and unexpected) in kind and cash, and in this way God has blessed us till today always fulfilling his promises in 1 Peter 5.v.7 and Phil 4.v.6-7, as I and my family learned to cast away all anxiety about anything but casting every burden on Him.[56]

The Bible played a critical role in the formation of missionary communities by providing an ideological basis for evangelistic activity and ingredients for evangelistic discourse. The use of badges and stickers with

---

[55] Eddi Onugha, personal reminiscence, May 2000.
[56] Ume Kalu, 'What God has done for me', 1969.

Scripture texts was a novel approach to evangelism, and participants sometimes had texts actually sown into their clothes, such was the urge to expose others to God's Word. Revivalists also combined oral communication with the distribution of Scripture tracts, an approach which was instrumental in winning many new converts. Out of forty-seven informants 'born-again' during the revival (1967-73), six said that a Christian tract played a significant role in their conversion experience. Protagonists believed that the Word itself, not just the messenger, was replete with spiritual potency. However, in contrast to prayer houses, where the Bible was sometimes used in a magical fashion, revivalists assumed a literate audience and expected the words they proclaimed, displayed, and distributed to bring enlightenment and 'new life' through the agency of the Spirit.

Paths to Conversion

I now consider the issue of conversion, a key feature of revivals generally, and reflect upon religious motivation and consumer demands during the revival. Three fundamental issues have dominated research on religious conversion.[57] The first is the nature of the experience. Conversion as radical change is one theme that pervades the literature, whether theological or social scientific, and dates back to the Biblical use of the term.[58] But there is disagreement about the precise nature of the change involved and how much change is enough to constitute conversion. The second issue is the analytical status of converts' accounts, which we considered in chapter 1. While they are vulnerable to reformulation and coloured by the group's 'universe of discourse', conversion narratives are valuable sources for evaluating religious change, especially if written close to the time of conversion.

Most research on conversion has focused on identifying causes. My analysis will employ a holistic model which draws upon insights from the disciplines of anthropology, sociology, psychology and religious studies. Explanations of conversion must explore the interpenetration of cultural,

---

[57] For helpful surveys of research on religious conversion, see David A. Snow & Richard Machalek, 'The Sociology of Conversion', *Annual Review of Sociology*, 10, 1984, 178-84; Lewis R. Rambo, 'Current Research on Religious Conversion', *Religious Studies Review*, 8.2, April 1982, 146-58.

[58] A. D. Nock, *Conversion, the Old and the New in Religion from Alexander the Great to Augustine of Hippo*, Oxford: Clarendon Press, 1933, 7; Stephen Neill, *The Unfinished Task*, London: Lutterworth Press, 1953, 44, 46; 169-70; Lewis R. Rambo, *Understanding Religious Conversion*, New Haven and London: Yale University Press, 1993, 2.

socio-political, psychological and religious factors. As Rambo notes, conversion experiences take place in specific contexts and are shaped by external socio-cultural milieu, and internal motivations, experiences and aspirations.[59] In the case of the Civil War Revival, the combination of urbanisation and Western education associated with modernisation, and social dislocation caused by the civil war, contributed to increasing religious pluralism and an expanding religious marketplace as existing traditional social and religious ties were loosened. This facilitated the process of autonomy of the individual, including religious choices, and created an environment favourable to religious conversion. Rambo also argues that some form of crisis (be it social, political, cultural, or religious) normally precedes conversion.[60] War-time and post-war conditions confronted Igbos with a variety of individual and collective crises which created tensions and precipitated multiple conversions as they encountered revival Christianity.

However, a more complete understanding of conversion processes should start from the internal religious convictions of participants and then proceed from there to prevailing social processes. During the revival, strong theological beliefs and powerful religious experiences energised the conversion process. Furthermore, Igbo converts appropriated the gospel via inherited religious categories. It was the existing religious matrix - its ideas, images, and metaphors - that gave shape to the conversion experience. Without an adequate exploration of these themes, our analysis would be incomplete.

My study draws upon Rambo's model of religious conversion, adapted from the work of sociologists Lofland and Stark, and the missiological model of Alan Tippett.[61] Rambo's model involves seven sequential stages: context, crisis, quest, encounter, interaction, commitment and consequences.[62] Conversion during the Civil War Revival was situated in a variety of critical settings, which precipitated individual and collective quests for religious renewal. Along the way, prospective converts encountered advocates, with stirring stories of personal conversion, eager to share the gospel. For those who responded, group interaction and participation in a variety of evangelical rituals helped to consolidate the

---

[59] Rambo, *Religious Conversion*, 17.

[60] *Ibid.*, 46.

[61] J. Lofland and R. Stark, 'Becoming a World-Saver: A Theory of Conversion to a Deviant Perspective', *American Sociological Review*, 30, 1965, 862-75; Alan R. Tippett, 'Conversion as a Dynamic Process in Christian Mission', *Missiology*, 2, 1977, 203-21. Tippett's model conceives conversion as a process involving a period of *awareness*, a point of *realization*, a period of *decision-making*, a point of *encounter*, and a period of *incorporation*.

[62] Rambo, *Religious Conversion*, 44-55.

conversion process. They then became gospel carriers themselves and the process was repeated. This unleashed powerful forces that reshaped the Igbo religious and social landscapes.

Born-again Conversion

The stress on personal conversion, an element of SU spirituality, points to the influence of Western individualism spread through global flows. As one informant recalled, 'the coming of the revival emphasised the need to have a personal experience with the God of Christianity . . . to give up traditional Christianity and really seek for a personal relationship'.[63] In revivalist discourse, 'traditional Christianity' meant a form of Christian affiliation based on a process of socialisation through family, school or church, but where a personal relationship with God through faith in Christ is absent. Some revival narratives follow a standard format: a description of growing up in a (nominally) Christian family, infant baptism, regular church attendance, and an outwardly respectable lifestyle, followed by an encounter with the gospel in a variety of settings, a realisation of personal sin and a commitment to Christ. Thus Ume Kalu's testimony begins with a personal reminiscence of life before conversion, characterized by membership of a Christian family, church attendance, infant baptism and confirmation, and mission school education. Yet despite outward and public respectability, Kalu admits that at home he was stubborn, disobedient and proud. He contrasts his former lifestyle with 'real Christianity', which he began to understand after engaging in discussions with a friend about 'new life' and new birth, and attending SU talks and Bible studies.[64]

In revivalist discourse, conversion was usually understood as a process culminating in the crisis experience of being 'born-again' through repentance and faith in Christ. So definite and vivid was this experience that sometimes revival converts could recall the exact date it occurred. Uchenna Emezue is a case in point. In a written testimony, he recalls his conversion through SU Umuahia two years earlier: 'But God being a loving father sought and found me by 4 p.m., Thursday 31st August 1967, when I surrendered to Him from my sinful hide-out . . . just exactly 4 p.m. that evening of Thursday 31st August 1967 I got up from my knees a new man'.[65] And in a letter written soon after the war: 'It is three years today since I made peace with God through the blood of Jesus. . . . Today is my

[63] Eddi Onugha, personal reminiscence, May 2000.
[64] Ume Kalu, 'What God has done for me', 1969.
[65] Uchenna Emezue, 'My Journey into Life', written testimony, 1969.

real birthday'.[66] The prominence of 'born-again' terminology in revivalist conversion narratives is an indication of the widespread dissemination of evangelical culture during the revival, largely through the agency of Scripture Union. The idiom of new birth was an important element in SU travelling secretary Bill Roberts's teaching, and Bible studies on the necessity of personal salvation were a regular feature of SU activity in Umuahia during the war.[67] SU converts talked about 'being saved', 'receiving Jesus as personal Saviour', 'surrendering to Christ' and being 'born-again'.

The impression sometimes given in war-time revival narratives is of Scripture Union standing out as an evangelical beacon in an otherwise liberal landscape. Thus one SU member from a Methodist background wrote, 'My little village Ossah is about a mile away from Umuahia township and dominated by non-evangelicals. The church is dead. The gospel of Christ suffered and made very few friends'.[68] However, there were mission church pastors within the Biafran enclave who maintained a strong conservative evangelical stance. These included the ECWA pastors in Umuahia and Aba, the Anglican Bishop of Owerri diocese, and some of the students and staff of Trinity Theological College, the training centre for Anglicans, Methodists and Presbyterians on the outskirts of Umuahia. Pastors from Assemblies of God and Apostolic Church were also strong proponents of evangelical Christianity. The metaphor of new birth captured the Igbo imagination at an unprecedented moment of crisis in their history and provided the basis for the construction of new forms of identity.

A Variety of Converts

Rambo's insightful treatment of religious conversion provides us with a helpful framework for understanding religious change during the revival. He identifies a range of conversion processes. Three are especially relevant: *intensification,* the revitalised commitment to a faith which the convert has had previous, if nominal, affiliation; *institutional transition*, the change of an individual or groups from one community to another within a major tradition; and *tradition transition*, the movement from one major religious tradition to another.[69] Igbo conversion to Christianity was a dynamic process of transformation in response to fresh challenges and changing contexts. For those who encountered the revival, conversion sometimes involved a transition from traditional religion to Christianity, but

[66] Uchenna Emezue, Letter to Roberts, 31 August 1970.
[67] Roberts, Letter to SU Groups Area Representatives, 20 November 1969.
[68] Emezue, 'New Year's Victory', 1969.
[69] Rambo, *Religious Conversion*, 13-14.

more often a movement from a nominal form of Christianity to a revitalised 'born-again' faith commitment. A third category included members of mainline churches who later converted to Pentecostalism. For many, conversion involved a combination of these processes, sometimes taking place over a prolonged period. As such, the revival resacralised the landscape in Christian terms by precipitating multiple conversions and intensifying existing religious commitments.

It is not possible to determine precisely how many were converted. Roberts refers to a 'gentle flow' of SU converts in Umuahia and to a significant increase in the rate of conversion during the war. Attendance at SU Umuahia's monthly evangelistic services sometimes reached as high as 300, but no mention is made of how many responded to the gospel.[70] Other accounts refer to large numbers of people converted in villages, refugee centres and army camps, especially after the dispersion of Umuahia in April 1969. One participant mentions a SU meeting in Uzuakoli during the war where 'hundreds of young boys and girls, old men and women confessed their sins and accepted Christ'.[71] After the war, there was a rapid escalation in the rate of conversion as the revival spread to other urban and rural areas, and teams from SU township groups and charismatic fellowships organised frequent evangelistic 'crusades' in their home towns and villages. Bolton's eyewitness account and Raphael Okafor's journal provide estimates of numbers who responded at postwar evangelistic events. These vary enormously from several hundred at some meetings to under ten. For example, during the week-long Hour of Freedom Unwana Afikpo crusade in August 1971, Bolton claims that thousands 'received Jesus', including the town's Chief.[72] Estimates at other events were more modest. Raphael Okafor describes a gathering in Agulu Grammar School, where over 400 people 'accepted the Lord'. And at meetings during Hour of Freedom's Onitsha evangelistic campaign (4th – 15th April 1971) converts ranged from five to one hundred, with an average daily attendance of 200. During a three day crusade in the town of Oba (12th – 14th March 1971) approximately 450 people responded to gospel. Journal entries suggest that these were conservative estimates. Thus the entry for 6th April 1971: 'Evans Ogbansiegbe also preached today. A brother from Oba testified and sister Nkechi led the choruses with exhortations at intervals as usual. . . . About sixty souls accepted the Lord. I have not been sure of my estimates

---

[70] Roberts, Scripture Union Prayer Letter, No.13, 17 June 1968; 'Bill Roberts of the Scripture Union tells of Outstanding response to the Gospel in Biafra', Interview with Bill Roberts, *Church of England Newspaper*, No. 3961, January 9 1970; Roberts, *Life and Death*, 40.

[71] Chioma Amalu, written testimony, 1969.

[72] Bolton, *Glory*, 128.

and I try to underestimate'.[73] But this only tells part of the story. The quality of converts was as important as the quantity, if not more so. I interviewed twenty-two former revivalists responsible for founding charismatic fellowship groups and Pentecostal denominations during the 1970s and 1980s. Of these, eighteen were converted during the revival (1967-1973). I also interviewed twelve other revival converts who currently occupy senior leadership positions within these organisations.

The conversion of traditionalists was not especially common. One reason was the revival's status as a youth movement in a gerontocratic society. Most traditionalists were older and disinclined to heed the radical message of the young revivalists, especially if delivered in English with little sensitivity to local social structures, which was often the case. This does not mean that older men and women were immune to the effects of the revival. I have mentioned the case of the SU meeting in Uzuakoli when a significant number of 'old men and women' were converted.[74] Another revivalist refers to the conversion of his father (a traditionalist) at a SU meeting in Umuahia during the war, two years before his death:

> My father died on 20th May 1970 at the Methodist Hospital Amachara. He showed remarkable faith before his death. I am certain that he is resting in Jesus. I was beside him, reading out the Lord's promises to him with challenges. At last he said 'Amen'. Two hours after this his relations came to suggest to him to allow them go and see a witchdoctor. He refused entirely. He told them, 'If I'll die, I die; do not worry my children and do not see any juju'. . . . He made a final break with Satan. He died four hours after this incident. But before this time he had committed his life during one of our S.U. Guest Services in my village – 25th Dec. 1968 but he was not growing. But immediately after the war, he saw Jesus in a real and special way.[75]

This episode shows the pressure that can be exerted by relatives upon those from a traditionalist background even after conversion, and the way this is interpreted in revivalist discourse as a tussle between Jesus and Satan. Marshall-Fratani describes these family members and friends who are not born-again as 'dangerous strangers', because the power of 'blood and amity' threatens the 'new life in Christ'.[76]

Another reason for the failure of the revival to attract more traditionalists was Scripture Union's initial reluctance to carry the gospel across church

---

[73] Quoted in Bolton, *Glory*, 113.
[74] Chioma Amalu, written testimony, 1969.
[75] Uchenna Emezue, Letter to Roberts, 31 August 1970.
[76] Marshall-Fratani, 'Global', 285-86.

boundaries into the streets and marketplaces. Later, we see the erosion of these boundaries and the revival encountering traditionalists in their own environment. For instance, a letter written in 1971 describes the exploits of a team from SU Umuahia: 'From Jan. 2, a team led by Emmanuel Okorie "invaded" an interior village at Nsukka . . . They received the good news joyfully and willingly brought out their shrines for destruction'.[77] It was Hour of Freedom which popularised open-air evangelistic campaigns and broadened the revival's appeal. However, while many traditionalists attended these events, relatively few became Christians. Usually, those who did convert had some prior contact with Christianity, perhaps through attending a mission school. I interviewed six former revivalists converted from a traditionalist background during the revival, but all had been previously exposed to Christian influences. Five of them were introduced to Christianity when they entered mission schools. Most revival converts were mission church members, often with dual allegiance to one of the prayer houses or 'occult' societies.

In Raphael Okafor's journal, an account of Hour of Freedom activities, there are several references to members of secret or 'occult' societies converted during the revival. One entry mentions the conversion of an 'occultist' called Ben Ifediba of Ezinifite, who brought out 'six different rings and amulets and his Hindu outfit' for destruction. Another refers to the conversion of thirty people, including one 'occultist'.[78] Bolton's account recalls the conversion of a businessman called Michaelson, a 'Free Mason and an occultist', who had 'read many books on witchcraft, magic and the occult and had spent many nights at burial grounds to acquire spiritual power'.[79] But the fact that these converts are singled out for special mention suggests that they were relatively rare.

The Quest for Power: the Key to Igbo Conversion

During the revival, why did so many Igbos reject existing religious options in favour of born-again Christianity? Maxwell notes that the success of new forms of African popular Christianity 'lay in both their continuity and discontinuity with what had gone before'.[80] If we recall, Igbo converts appropriate the gospel via existing religious categories. Despite the variety of motivational factors involved, I agree with Okorocha that the quest for power to enhance life (*ezi-ndụ*) is the hermeneutical key to understanding

[77] Uchenna Emezue, Letter to Roberts, 24 May 1971.

[78] Raphael Okafor, Journal, 19 & 27 March 1971, quoted in Bolton, *Glory*, 105.

[79] Bolton, *Glory*, 97-8.

[80] Maxwell, 'African Imagination', 7.

Igbo conversion during the revival. While the focus of Okorocha's research is religious encounter among the Igbo during the colonial era, he maintains that the search for power continued as a factor in Igbo conversion in later contexts, and in the rise of new religious movements, including new forms of Christianity.[81] It was a pervasive theme in Igbo society which took prospective converts along a variety of paths prior to the actual moment of conversion and was often intensified during periods of personal stress. As noted in chapter 2, *ezi-ndụ* embraces physical health, material prosperity, fertility, individual success, communal satisfaction and practical guidance - all fruits of power looked for in Christianity.

However, 'rupture' was also an important element in Igbo Christian conversion as new contexts created new demands and exposed the deficiencies of existing religious options. The revival introduced new ideas to the Igbo religious repertoire, and new means to attain old objectives. And sometimes these objectives themselves were transformed in the process of conversion. Here Peel's concept of transvaluation is helpful. He suggests that in the Yoruba context, missionary preaching challenged the ends of indigenous piety by making out 'that the most important human objectives lay beyond earthly existence, not within it'.[82]

For some Igbos, the search for salvation was initiated by a quest for healing or deliverance, though this was not common among informants and clashed with 'official' Scripture Union theology. For one informant, the conversion process began with a quest for healing from barrenness, in accord with Igbo traditional aspirations for children to extend life and perpetuate the family name. Another described his conversion after becoming seriously ill during the war. Despite seeking assistance from *dibịa* and medical doctors, and attending a prayer house, his condition failed to improve. Finally, in 1971, a friend persuaded him to visit Stephen Okafor at Hour of Freedom headquarters, where he received healing after prayer. In revivalist discourse, the experience of healing did not guarantee conversion. In this case, my informant was persuaded to 'make a conscious confession of Jesus Christ as Lord and Saviour'. Here is an example of what Lofland and Skonovd refer to as 'experimental' conversion involving the active exploration of religious options, a consumerist approach characteristic of an expanding religious marketplace.[83] It supports the economic market model proposed by rational choice theorists where religion is expected to flourish in a competitive environment. Entries in Raphael Okafor's journal suggest that a quest for healing was sometimes a motive for attending Hour of Freedom events. For example, the entry of 1

[81] Okorocha, *Religious Conversion*, 206, 278; Okorocha, 'Conversion', 171.

[82] Peel, *Religious Encounter*, 165.

[83] John Lofland and Norman Skonovd, 'Conversion Motifs', *Journal for the Scientific Study of Religion*, 20, 1981, 373-85.

May 1971: 'Divine healing from Exodus 14.13-16 preached by brother Stephen. People flocked to the altar call for deliverance. . . . It was at Nnewi that the greatest number of miraculous healings was recorded'.[84] Yet prayers for healing at these events were normally accompanied by a call for repentance and an invitation to receive Christ.

Christian conversion was also linked to wartime insecurity and post-war deprivation. Note the following extract from an oral testimony:

> The war generated spiritual hunger because of security needs. So people naturally sought for God. . . . Because you can't predict whether you will survive or not, so naturally people wanted to know God more. So lots of people repented in refugee camps, army camps and so on. When the war ended they all came back, still desperate, because there was no money, no houses to live in, people were in trouble. So naturally we resorted to prayers, seeking God, and that was the beginning of a great revival after the war.[85]

In Chukwuemeka Ike's historical novel *Sunset at Dawn*, wartime conditions in Biafra are compared with those in Nigeria, where schools and universities continued to function, the economy suffered little disruption, and for the average Nigerian 'the noise of war was too distant to give him sleepless nights'. But the situation in Biafra was very different. 'The war raged on Biafran soil. Every inch of Biafra had become a war front and every child in Biafra felt the full impact of the war. It was Biafra that absorbed all the material losses'.[86] One reason Igbo response to the revival was so dramatic compared with their counterparts in the West was that it was they who bore the brunt of the suffering. This is born out by SU Travelling Secretary Muyiwa Olamijulo, who experienced the revival in Eastern and Western Nigeria. He told me that the spiritual hunger he encountered amongst the Igbo was the most intense he had witnessed in forty years of Christian ministry.[87]

For some revivalists, born-again conversion was a direct consequence of their war experience and was again linked to the pursuit of spiritual power and abundant life. Out of forty-three informants born-again during the revival, eleven said that the civil war contributed to their conversion. This supports Rambo's assertion that some form of crisis can act as an initiator of conversion processes by stimulating activity to relieve discomfort and

---

[84] Quoted in Bolton, *Glory*, 119.
[85] Interview, Don Odunze, Enugu, 22 October 2001.
[86] Ike, *Sunset at Dawn*, 243.
[87] Interview, Ikot Enwang, 17 January 2002.

remove the sense of tension.[88] Sometimes feelings of insecurity and anxiety for the future made Igbos more receptive to the gospel and intensified their religious quest, resulting in the rejection of other religious options in favour of revival Christianity as they sought for power to counteract evil and acquire protection. Fear of not surviving the war was one reason given for conversion to 'born-again' conversion. If we recall, the goal of Igbo traditional life is old age with dignity (*nka na nzere*), thus ensuring the attainment of ancestorhood. Consequently many Igbos are fearful of dying prematurely before they have had a chance to fulfil their destiny. The following Igbo traditional prayer shows the importance of long life (and the consequent fear of premature death):

Nnaa hụ lee	Our beloved Fathers,
Biko nyenu anyị ndụ O.	Please give us life.
Ezi ndụ, Ogologo ndụ	Viable life, long live.
Na ahụ ike n'ọdịnma	Good health and wellbeing.
Ọnwu Egbuchulanyị!	May we not die before our time![89]

The fear of death was a prominent theme in Nnenna Chukwuma's conversion narrative. Brought up in a Christian household, Chukwuma regularly attended the local Methodist church, but her parents also consulted 'witchdoctors' to protect the family from the activity of 'evil spirits' and 'witches'. 'My father took us to church every Sunday. But I didn't know the Lord personally and was always afraid of witches, afraid of dying. Especially during the war, I didn't have answers to the death I was seeing around me, and I was afraid that one day I might die and I wouldn't know what would happen to me'. It was this fear of dying, intensified by her experience of air raids, which contributed to Chukwuma's conversion: 'I was afraid of dying, because we woke up one morning and we saw the planes coming, scattering bullets and killing people. And you ask yourself, where are these people going after? We knew there was something like hell. What if it happened to me?' Eventually, she was converted at a meeting organised by SU Umuahia in 1967 after listening to a testimony by one of her peers and a sermon preached by Bill Roberts.[90] For those who accepted the revival message, its promise of protection from enemies (human and spiritual), and its emphasis on the imminent return of Christ and the hope of physical resurrection, enabled them to break free from their fear of death and fix their eyes on heaven.

War trauma and deprivation also intensified religious commitments by dealing a severe blow to materialistic lifestyles and future ambitions, and

---

[88] Rambo, *Religious Conversion*, 44, 54-6.
[89] Quoted in Okorocha, *Religious Conversion*, 70.
[90] Interview, 26 May 2000, Enugu.

creating a crisis of identity. The Igbos, as we have noted, are an achievement-orientated society where success and status, linked to material prosperity, are prevailing cultural themes.[91] While the pragmatic search for *ezi-ndụ* was the main basis for embracing revival Christianity, in some cases non-instrumentalist factors, such as a search for meaning, also contributed to the conversion process. In his study of religious encounter among the Yoruba during the colonial era, Peel refers to the metaphysical attraction of the world religions and 'the superior answers they were felt to give to questions of meaning posed by the experiences of the Age of Confusion' in Western Nigeria.[92] For Igbos in post-colonial Nigeria, the civil war was also a period of intense confusion and triggered similar quests for meaning. It precipitated a dialogue in Igbo hearts and minds as they searched for new meanings to explain present dilemmas and new means to reconstruct shattered identities. Felix Obiorah, President of SU Umuahia in the early 1970s, explained it in this way:

> I think there were a lot of resources in the country in those days, and every person was just thinking how much you can get, especially in this part of the country. . . . But the war disenchanted everybody and impoverished everybody. People who were millionaires, at the end of the war they were given £20 period. It levelled everybody. . . . So they had to find some meaning somewhere. Life didn't mean much anymore. People lost dear ones during the war. And then people were famished with hunger and that kind of thing. You just begin to think that there has to be meaning somewhere.[93]

The example of Frances Lawjua Bolton (née Egwu) is a case in point. In her narrative, she describes her privileged Anglican upbringing in Onitsha and her membership of the élite Iweka clan. Her father, John Egwu, was a leading Igbo pharmacist and businessman, and a prominent member of the NCNC (the party that led the country to independence); her mother was the first Igbo female pharmacist; and her uncle was Sir Francis Akanu Ibiam, the first governor of Eastern Nigeria. But her family lost everything during the war and were forced to become refugees. As a direct result of war-related stress, Frances also developed psychosomatic quadriplegia. These circumstances initiated a search for salvation and a quest for meaning, which culminated in her conversion through contact with Scripture Union

[91] Uchendu, *Igbo*, 16, 92; Okorocha, *Religious Conversion*, 193.

[92] Peel, *Religious Encounter*, 230.

[93] Interview, 6 October 2001, Umuahia.

in 1970.[94] Another informant described the crisis he experienced after the war when he found himself unable to continue his education and with no employment prospects. His religious quest was precipitated by the example of a friend who 'was going through the same situation, the same hunger, the same deprivation, but he had attached a different meaning to life than I had'.[95] Sometimes conversion narratives contained contrasts between losses incurred during the war and gains from the experience of 'new life in Christ'. One SU member wrote, 'Though I might have lost dear ones in the war and lost some years of education yet my gain is greater for I gained the greatest and the best which is my salvation'.[96] In each of these cases, born-again Christianity offered compensations to those suffering forms of deprivation and loss associated with the war. Here the revival represented a rupture with traditional thought and challenged the Igbo concept of 'life' with its focus on this-worldly blessings. It emphasized the future enjoyment of 'heaven' as compensation for present sufferings and injected purpose and meaning into the experience of adversity by stressing its redemptive qualities. But in line with traditional thought patterns, Igbo revivalists expected compensations in this world as well as the next.

For many informants, the quest for ethical renewal was a prominent feature of their conversion narratives. Invariably the actual moment of 'new birth' was preceded by a period of 'conviction of sin' either alone or in a communal setting, and on occasions a desire for moral transformation actually initiated a religious quest. Ume Kalu's conversion narrative is a rich source for understanding the internal state of prospective converts. It contains a description of his growing awareness of sin as he encountered a variety of evangelical influences and read the Bible for himself. While this is a retrospective account and is coloured by SU's 'universe of discourse', it was written close enough to the time of his conversion (two years earlier) for him to have recalled his feelings with reasonable accuracy. Kalu describes the tension he felt as he continued in his 'careless life without Christ' after first becoming aware of his 'sinfulness and helplessness' and need for salvation. As he attended SU events, his sin 'weighed heavily' on him and he became 'less and less happy and more anxious about life'. Finally, in September 1967, after one particular meeting, he returned home and confessed his sins before God. 'My heart then knew joy and peace in Christ, peace and joy I had never before experienced. I became happy. My anxiety left as I came to trust all God's promises to me'.[97]

---

[94] This account is based on Bolton's written account (*Glory*, 47-52) and an oral interview (23 May 1999, London).

[95] Meshak Ilobi, personal reminiscence, May 2000.

[96] Elizabeth Onukwue, Letter to Roberts, 23 May 1971.

[97] Ume Kalu, 'What God has done for me', 1969.

Uchenna Emezue's conversion narrative follows a slightly different pattern. He describes his quest for renewal over a period of four years from 1963, when he entered secondary school, until August 1967, when he was born-again. 'I thought that the secondary school discipline would transform my life and make me a new person but I was disappointed'. He then refers to his first communion and confirmation, which he also expected to have 'transforming power': 'Confirmation and communion made no difference in my life. I was still the same old person'. Emezue goes on to describe the internal conflict he experienced at school as he continued to engage in worldly activities with his peers, such as dancing, smoking, drinking and 'chasing girls'. 'There was a battle in my heart; I wanted a change; I wanted a new life; I had no real peace. I was so restless and unhappy that on many occasions, I sobbed and was mad at people without cause'. This is clearly building up to a climax. In mid-1967, he began to attend SU meetings where he listened to talks and Bible studies on such topics as 'man and sin' and 'new birth', and heard people 'testifying their sins forgiven'. This precipitated a period of self-examination: 'As the full shame and guilt of all this burnt into my soul I wondered how I could ever get rid of the past or how I could get a real start in living a new and better life'. Emezue's 'journey into life' ends with him confessing his sins and being born-again: 'I knelt down and poured out my heart in confession to Jesus. And just exactly 4 p.m. that evening of Thursday 31st August 1967 I got up from my knees a new man'. The imagery of new birth and new beginnings dominates this narrative and seems to resonate with the ideas of 'rupture from the past' and 'autonomy of the self' so prevalent in discussions on modernity. Yet in Emezue's case, the motive for pursuing this goal was primarily ethical rather than social. It was a response to a growing disillusionment with a way of life governed by deceit, selfish ambition and pride, rather than a desire to free himself from social ties impeding his progress and mobility. And it was through an experience of God's forgiveness that he was able to break from his sinful past and submit to Christ as 'living Lord and Saviour'.[98]

An important theme in revival narratives was the way people were sometimes overwhelmed with a sense of sorrow for sin, usually in response to preaching and orchestrated by the Holy Spirit. The revival provided a safe setting for such sentiments to be expressed. Raphael Okafor, co-founder of Hour of Freedom, told me that during their evangelistic events people would sometimes spontaneously fall down and weep as they confessed their sins. And Bolton's eyewitness account describes scenes of mass emotional outbursts as people came under 'conviction of sin' in response to gospel preaching. After public confession of sin, feelings of

[98] Emezue, 'My Journey into Life', 1969.

joy replaced feelings of sorrow.[99] Of course, one must take care when assessing such anecdotal evidence. Revivals are communal events which expose individuals to powerful social pressure to emulate the behaviour of the group.

Why was there this urge for radical change, and what did it represent? Here we return to issues of continuity and rupture in religious conversion. Most revival converts would have said it was due to the influence of the Spirit, their response to the Bible and evangelical preaching, their exposure to the testimonies and lifestyles of revivalists, and their fear of imminent judgment (hell). However, it was also consistent with 'moral' explanations for misfortune and the search for power in traditional piety. If we recall, Igbos traditionally associate moral rectitude (*ogu*) with the acquisition of power and divine blessings (*ogu bu ike* or 'moral probity is the source of genuine power'). Thus the pursuit of a moral lifestyle is closely linked to a quest for power to enhance life (*ezi-ndụ*), both now and in the hereafter.[100]

For some Igbos, the catastrophic conditions induced by the Biafran crisis precipitated a quest for ethical renewal. This was more so towards the end of the war when a good deal of heart-searching went on and some began to wonder whether personal and corporate evil within the enclave was prolonging the war. For instance, one revivalist wrote in 1969:

> We are praying that God may bring an end to this war. God searches our hearts for repentance. Just as He heard the Israelites when they repented and called on Him, so would He also hear us. There is evil everywhere in Biafra and we must fight against it. Do you think that it is impossible for God to stop this war now? It is not. But we are prolonging the war by our evil ways.[101]

While these are sentiments expressed by a member of SU, it reflected a more general concern among some sectors of Igbo society as conditions deteriorated in the enclave. Okorocha refers to the hunger among church leaders and traditionalists at the end of the war for a return to 'that morality which always insisted that those who desire salvation or *ezi-ndụ* must live according to *ọfọ-na-ogu*'.[102]

---

[99] Bolton, *Glory*, 126-28.

[100] Okorocha, *Religious Conversion*, 117-18, 278; Salamone, 'Continuity', 34-5.

[101] Simon Ugwuoke, written testimony, 1969. Others asked different questions. For instance, one informant told me that he often read from the book of Habakkuk, which poses the question, why does God allow the wicked to 'swallow up those more righteous than they?' Hab 1:13 (NASB).

[102] Okorocha, *Religious Conversion*, 127.

Part of the appeal of revival Christianity rested in its promise of power for moral and social transformation. In their testimonies, converts refer to the impotence of existing religious options in this respect. Igbo traditional religion expects its adherents to secure salvation through moral rectitude, and while there are rituals for cleansing 'sin' and warding off the wrath of the gods, 'no lasting remedy is provided for man's guilt'.[103] In revivalist narratives, similar sentiments are expressed of mainline mission churches and prayer houses. Converts refer to the 'hypocritical' and immoral lifestyles of members and leaders, and the stress on religious ritual and outward behaviour rather than new birth. In mainline churches, baptism, communion, and church attendance were the primary marks of Christian identity. And in revivalist discourse neither the mission churches nor the prayer houses provided access to the kind of power that would enable them to live holy lives. The revival reintroduced the evangelical doctrines of sin and hell, judgment and grace into the Igbo religious repertoire. The evangelical concept of sin as an intrinsic disposition, and salvation as transformation, conflicted with Igbo notions of *mmehie* (wrongdoing or moral fault) and the ability of individuals to save themselves through personal effort and religious ritual.[104]

Igbos traditionally understand 'sin' in terms of specific moral and social acts rather than feelings of internal sinfulness, and the focus is on consequences (affliction) rather than agency. Moral offences are thought to endanger the 'ontological equilibrium' of the community.[105] But revival Christianity insisted that inner 'heart sins' such as pride, jealousy, covetousness and anger, also rendered the individual guilty before God, and it created an awareness of sin irrespective of the experience of affliction. Thus one revival convert described his old way of life as follows: 'I was stubborn, disobedient, proud, selfish, told lies, hated my brothers and sisters, bore grudges, committed little thefts in the family. Most of my obedience at School was in pretence, for fear of punishment made me behave. . . . The meaning of real Christianity had not dawned on me as yet'.[106] Another revivalist used a series of contrasts as a rhetorical device to draw the reader's attention to the problem of internal sinfulness.

---

[103] *Ibid.*, 293.

[104] Igbos distinguish between *mmehie* and *ajo ihe*, a generic term denoting anything they consider evil, whether physical, moral, social, or religious, including hostile spiritual forces. Emefie Ikenga-Metuh, *Comparative Studies of African Traditional Religions*, 2nd ed., Onitsha: Imico, 1992, 239.

[105] Ikenga-Metuh, *God and Man*, 4, 109; Okorocha, *Religious Conversion*, 293-94; Austin Echema, *Corporate Personality in Traditional Igbo Society and the Sacrament of Reconciliation*, Frankfurt: Peter Lang, 1995, 52.

[106] Ume Kalu, 'What God has done for me', 1969.

> My parents exerted strict discipline on me that when I entered secondary school all my teachers were pointing at me as the best behaved student. They were seeing the outside. I need not enumerate how jealousy, covetousness, strife, anger, pride and many other deadly sins had eaten deep in me. 'Man looks on the outward appearance, but the Lord looks on the heart' (1 Sam. 16:7). During a series of lectures arranged by our chaplain . . . one of the lecturers, outlining the characteristics of God, said God is everywhere. God is seeing everything even those done in secret. I was arrested by a set of steady looking eyes that had been seeing all my cheatings in the dining hall, all my false pretences and all the gossips, slanders and lies told against my fellow students.[107]

Notice the way the writer contrasts his outwardly respectable behaviour with his inner sinfulness; the impotence of his parents externally imposed discipline with the power of the Christian lecturer's words; and the human inability to see beneath the surface with God's penetrating gaze. With its focus on 'new life in Christ', the revival offered the promise of redemption and transformation, and appealed to those looking for power to break from past associations with traditional religious practices, leave behind old habits and live a consecrated life. The message of groups like Hour of Freedom was liberating because it presented a new way of receiving as opposed to achieving *ezi-ndụ*.

The Conversion Ritual

In revivalist discourse, the actual moment of 'new birth' was often presented as a power encounter between competing religious options. Sometimes this was dramatic, especially in the case of traditionalists or those involved in some form of 'occult' activity. In these instances, conversion was invariably accompanied by a demonstration of power, a miraculous healing for example, or a visual display of Christ's power over malign spirits. SU travelling secretary Muyiwa Olamijulo records the case of a traditionalist in North-Eastern Igboland, converted during the early 1970s after his child was apparently raised from the dead following prayer.[108] And Samson Onwubiko, General Overseer of Calvary Evangelistic Mission, describes two separate encounters with traditionalists during campaigns conducted in the 1970s. In each case, the critical moment came with a visual 'power encounter' between two rival factions,

---

107 Emmanuel Ekpunobi, written testimony, 1969.

108 Muyiwa Olamijulo, SU Travelling Secretary, Eastern Newsletter No.6, January 1973.

resulting in a drift in the direction of power. In the first incident, Onwubiko and his team visit a community where members have the power to bring down rain, and previous attempts to evangelise have been frustrated by heavy downpours. For three nights he preaches, and each day it rains. The final day is dry, and the team show a film entitled 'The Burning Hell'. Then Onwubiko begins to preach.

> Within about five minutes of my preaching . . . rain came down in torrents. And as the rain was coming down, the whole community were all coming out, under the rain. I couldn't understand what was happening. I said to my interpreter, 'What have I said tonight. Why are they coming out under the rain? . . . . My interpreter said, 'Look behind you'. And I looked. There was literal fire coming down on the community. But it was not burning anybody anyway. . . . I just began to preach under the anointing I never knew before. And at the altar call, they all come down, knelt under the flood, crying. They gave their lives to Christ.

Onwibiko's other encounter occurred during an evangelistic campaign in Eket, south-eastern Nigeria, referred to in his narrative as the 'headquarters of witches and wizards in West Africa'. Here the metaphor of war is employed to describe the struggle for territorial control, and conversion is presented as a spiritual conflict between good and evil. 'Witches and wizards' and traditional religionists are portrayed as enemies of Christ, disrupting the gospel's progress. Again the critical contest is between competing claims to control the rain, but in this instance there is also a visible demonstration of healing.

> Well, we started, and I came to preach that night. The weather was so wonderfully great. But within 15 minutes of my preaching, thunderstorm came. There were more than 5,000 people from all over the place there on that field. . . . they began to leave, saying they had won the battle. Something happened to me, I said, 'God, in the name of Jesus, heavens close right now'. And the rain ceased immediately, and there was a warm wind. They all came back. Then I preached the gospel. God healed many. I gave two altar calls, that all who were witches and wizards come to my left; those who are coming for Christ come to my right. The witches, they all came out, many of them. . . . Today, in Eket the witches and wizards have no place in that land again.[109]

[109] Interview, 10 October 2001, Umuahia.

Most conversion experiences, however, were described in less dramatic terms, as a personal encounter with Jesus Christ and a relief from guilt resulting in inner peace. Through the experience of being 'born-again', participants constructed new identities for themselves. As a Christian rite of passage, enacted in a context of crisis, it marked the transition from one stage of life to another and involved symbolic performances, deconstructive and reconstructive rituals. Iconoclasm, altar calls, public confession of sin and water baptism were the most visible conversion rituals, and participants believed each to be infused with spiritual significance. Sociologist Virginia Hine refers to such commitment rituals as 'bridge-burning events'. They help to consolidate the conversion process by publicly dramatising change and providing the person with powerful subjective experiences.[110] They are especially important in contexts where religion is a public and social affair played out before Christians and non-Christians, as was the case in Igboland. Spontaneous public confession of sin was another way the revival departed from traditional practice.[111] In traditional culture, individuals are sometimes required to confess their sins to community elders or priests as part of the cleansing ritual, but usually after the actual discovery of an offence or an experience of affliction. In addition, some Igbo communities have annual rituals of public confession and cleansing held in local shrines, where adult males confess sins such as adultery, stealing, lying, witchcraft, bribery and the use of charms. But spontaneous confession in a public setting was rare.[112]

Marshall notes that stories of conversion to born-again Christianity in Nigeria contrast helplessness and sinfulness with 'empowerment that new life in Christ brings . . .'.[113] Revivalist conversion narratives were full of such contrasts. One revivalist compared his old life as a 'camouflaged bad boy' with the 'new man' he became after his conversion.[114] Born-again conversion provided opportunities for Igbos to make a clean break from their individual and collective pasts, and forge new identities, especially appealing following the traumatic events of the war.

---

[110] Virginia H. Hine, 'Bridge Burners: Commitment and Participation in a Religious Movement', *Sociological Analysis*, 31, 1970, 61-6.

[111] Public confession of sin was relatively common, though it never became institutionalised as it did during the East African Revival.

[112] See Okorocha, *Religious Conversion*, 139, 144; Ikenga-Metuh, *God and Man*, 113.

[113] Marshall, 'Power', 223

[114] Emezue, 'My Journey into Life', 1969.

Competing for Control of the Moral Landscape

I now move from motives to consequences and consider the effects of the revival on local landscapes. Revival Christianity presented Igbo society with a moral challenge at a time when traditional controls were breaking down due to urban migration and social dislocation. During the war, one of the arenas where participants competed for control of the moral landscape was the relief operation, an area riddled by corruption. It was here that they found an opportunity to mark out their difference from the 'world' and reinforce their identity as a separated community. In a personal testimony, Sammy Onwitalu describes how the behaviour of SU members checked the rate of corruption in the WCC relief store where they worked:

> It is tempting in that we work in the midst of corrupt people, who are out to plunder these things, sell and accumulate wealth – while thousands are being starved to death. I am tempted to let them have their way or to take part in the deal. But with God's help and assurance in 1 Corinthians 10:13, all the temptations are thwarted. Thanks to Him. By His grace, we are able to minimize the rate of corruption here and in no time to stamp it out. We the S.U. members have this as our task, as well as the task of witnessing to the people around.[115]

The Biafran crisis weakened existing moral boundaries, and after the war behaviour that was previously unacceptable now became commonplace. There was an escalation of corruption, sexual promiscuity and armed robbery. Participant accounts show the revival acting as a moral restraint by creating an ethical awareness and instilling a Biblical perspective, particularly among young people. Former revivalist and Anglican priest Chinedu Nebo contrasts the chaotic moral field in post-war Igboland with the counter force of the revival: 'The revival suspended what would have been massive moral depravity in our country. The war made beasts out of people. After the war, people were now like animals. . . . It [the revival] changed the orientation of young people a lot. I know people today who would have been criminals if not for the revival'. Symptoms of moral decay identified by Nebo and challenged by the revival included deviant sexual behaviour, prostitution, abortion, crime, corruption, and cultural practices that discriminate and divide (in this case, the *osu* caste system).[116]

---

[115] Sammy Onwitalu, written testimony, October 1969.

[116] Interview, 4 May 2000, Enugu. *Osu* were slaves dedicated to the service of traditional Igbo cults. Originally they commanded respect, but as their numbers increased they became outcasts. In 1955, the Eastern Nigerian Regional House of Assembly passed a Bill abolishing the *osu* caste system, but

The main arenas for competing moral agendas in post-war Igboland were the village, the school and college campus, and the urban workplace.

As the key component of revival spirituality, the experience of new birth enabled participants to relinquish 'worldly' behaviour, cultivate counter cultural lifestyles and resist the powerful influence of traditional religion. Corten and Marshall-Fratani argue that 'getting born-again is an event of rupture, with the self as it was, but also with the world as it is', and the mode of realising this rupture in early expressions of Pentecostalism was 'retreat from the world and sectarian behaviour'.[117] The Civil War revival developed around a doctrine of radical anti-materialism and strict personal ethics closely linked to the message of the cross and a belief in the imminent return of Christ. 'Take the whole world, but leave me Jesus' was a line from a popular revival song, and 'repentance' and 'holiness' were consistent themes in revivalist discourse and revival sermons. We see this in Raphael Okafor's journal entry for 30th July 1971: '3 Day Christian gathering at Onitsha. I spoke for about one hour 40 minutes on "Purity for Power and Christian Discipline" combined together in my theme "Go back to the Cross." Reading Ephesians 4:17-32'.

Moral transformation as a central motif of the conversion ritual is supported by revival testimonies. One participant described those she listened to during a SU leaders training conference: 'More often than not the testimonies I heard were of how people had been doing what was wrong, then after knowing Christ and accepting Him as their Saviour, they changed'.[118] In revivalist discourse, authentic conversion always involved transformation. The case of Ume Kalu captures this well. Kalu's conversion, related in a written testimony, affected him in a number of ways. There were psychological changes. He reported a new sense of peace, contentment and lack of anxiety. His religious behaviour changed, and he gained a new sense of mission. Christian meetings and fellowship took on new meaning, and he no longer felt ashamed of his faith. 'I could stand for Christ before friends without feeling their reproach'. He describes changes in his ethical behaviour, both on a personal and social level. He no longer compromised with the 'world', and became more obedient and less proud. In revivalist rhetoric, the concept 'world' is used to describe a way of life dominated by selfishness and alienation from God. Kalu began to

---

it continued to influence Igbo society after independence. For more on the *osu* caste system and its continuing social influence, see Okorocha, *Religious Conversion*, 147-50, 275-77.

[117] André Corten and Ruth Marshall-Fratani, 'Introduction', André Corten and Ruth Marshall-Fratani (eds.), *Between Babel and Pentecost. Transnational Pentecostalism in Africa and Latin America*, London: Hurst & Company, 2001, 7.

[118] Jessie Ilonuba, written testimony, 1969.

love his family and friends in a new way. Finally, there were changes in his relationship with God. He became more devoted to Bible study and prayer. God was no longer an abstract concept, but a living reality. He reported a new openness to the Holy Spirit. Though he refers to changes that began when he confessed his sins and gave his life to God, he anticipates an ongoing process of transformation. Kalu concludes his conversion narrative with these words: 'In fact my life became changed and is still being changed till now. . . . I have turned a new leaf in my life and things are really changed – 2 Cor. 5.v.17. All my careless life I have thrown away for Christ'.[119]

Why was there this urge for ethical renewal after conversion? According to revivalist accounts, it was created by the action of the Holy Spirit, their exposure to the Bible and Christian instruction, their ambition to be effective missionary agents, their belief in the imminent return of Christ, and their feelings of insecurity during the war. Excerpts from Ben Onwochei's testimony show the prominent ethical role played by the Holy Spirit and the Bible in revivalist imagination. After ascribing his conversion to the 'gracious work of the Holy Spirit' and his exposure to the 'word of God', he goes on to describe his ongoing relationship with God and his experience of 'sanctification', a term used to denote the actual experience of moral transformation. The 'Holy Spirit' and the 'Holy Bible' (the Spirit and the Word) are the twin agents of sanctification in Onwochei's account. The Spirit energises worship (sometimes leading him into 'moments of exhilaration'), instils a desire to pursue God's righteousness, and provides the stimulus for taking a stand on moral issues, in this case 'friendship between boys and girls'. The Bible, which he has 'learnt to value above all other literature', convicts of sin and gives daily instruction on how to live a holy life. Onwochei ends by linking the 'process of sanctification' with perseverance in the 'work of the Lord'.[120]

Bible teaching along Keswick lines was an important early influence. Roberts and other Protestant missionaries in Igboland sometimes attended the annual Keswick Bible conventions when home on furlough.[121] Keswick taught three steps to spiritual power: full surrender of one's self to Christ; being filled with the Spirit; and power for service. Thus a close link is made between a consecrated lifestyle and effective service. As Fiedler observes, the Spirit-filled, or sanctified, life is marked by power over sin and expresses itself in service to others.[122] At Scripture Union meetings in

---

[119] Ume Kalu, 'What God has done for me', 1969.

[120] Ben Onwochei, written testimony, 1969.

[121] For more on the relationship between Keswick and the modern missionary movement, see Klaus Fiedler, *The Story of Faith Missions*, Carlisle: Paternoster, 1994, 210-46.

[122] *Ibid.*, 215.

Umuahia, Bible talks were given on Keswick themes such as 'Absolute Surrender' and 'Brokenness', and members read books on holiness and victorious Christian living. The language of Keswick is also evident in revivalist written discourse, where there are references to 'total surrender', 'forsaking self', the 'victorious life', and 'brokenness'. In the following testimony the experience of surrender is linked to ethical renewal and Christian service:

> It was not until Dec. 1968 that, after hearing a series of talks on 'Absolute Surrender' of one's life to God that I went home and wept bitterly for having been so ignorant for all these years! The feelings I had that night is inexpressible with words. . . . I wanted to give up myself immediately to God! I wanted Him to change me that very moment. I wanted to serve Him all my life. I wanted Him to use me as an instrument for His glory.[123]

There are affinities here with the East African Revival, where Brian Stanley has argued that the Keswick tradition, with its emphasis on holiness and victorious Christian living, proved attractive to Africans discouraged about the shallow experience of Christianity within their community and the continuing commitment of many church members to traditional beliefs and practices.[124]

Sometimes adventist beliefs inspired the pursuit of a rigorous Christian life. This was a recurring theme in revivalist narratives. The imminent return of Christ was a crucial component in the revival's message, alongside its call to repentance and faith in Christ. Participants were encouraged to prepare for the rapture by shunning unnecessary material and carnal pleasures, and maintaining a life free from sin. There are elements, here, of continuity and rupture with traditional beliefs. If we recall, traditionally the Igbos *do* have a belief in posthumous moral redress, but this does not include the concept of a future 'day of judgment' or a promise of a 'new heaven and earth' as a reward for good conduct. The main incentive for moral probity in traditional thought was to obtain blessings in this life, which would then reverberate in the afterlife through reincarnation.

However, the continued association of moral probity with divine favour and acquisition of power in revivalist discourse does suggest the enduring influence of indigenous values, as does the stress on the moral conditions of effective prayer, which corresponded with Igbo traditional piety. Here

[123] Chioma Amalu, 'Some experiences I have had during this war', 1969.
[124] Stanley, 'Revival', 13.

worshippers protest their innocence before Chineke in their quest for life. Note the following excerpt from an Igbo traditional prayer:

Ọdịgh Onye m'nechere	I have no evil thoughts
Ihe Ọjọọ	against any one.
Akam abụọ dị ọcha	My two hands are clean.
Onye necherem Ọnwụ	The one who wishes me dead
Ya buru Kwam ụzọ jema	May he pass on before me.
Ejikwam Ọfọ n'Ogu	I always act justly and in
	fairness to all.
Chemanụ anyị	Please protect us.
Ogologo ndụ, ahu ike, ọdịmma	Long life, health and
	wellbeing.[125]

Yet there are important differences between traditional piety and revival spirituality. In revivalist narratives, the urge to live a life of moral purity was linked to a desire to respond to God's love as 'father' and become an effective channel of his power to others. In contrast, as Okorocha points out, Igbo traditionalists do not offer prayers to Chineke as Father, but to 'our fathers (the Ancestors)'.[126]

Finally, war-time insecurities sometimes intensified Christian commitments and precipitated quests for ethical renewal, reflecting the close association between moral probity and divine protection in indigenous piety. In the following testimony, Dennis Okafor describes his experience of enemy air raids while collecting supplies flown into Uli airport in his capacity as a Scripture Union relief worker:

> To me, the raids have made me to be more consecrated to God. Whenever the plane is in the air, many around me, who have not met the Lord, and who have no hope, panic a lot because they think they can save themselves. But to me as a Christian, during that moment, I try to satisfy the human conscience as much as I can. . . . Before I go to the airstrip every evening, I try as much as possible to reconcile with God in everyway in which I had wronged Him. I try as much as possible to confess every bit of sin in me, so as to make my body wholly His.[127]

How then did the actual process of sanctification take place in revivalist imagination? Important clues are found in two inter-related theological discourses, both prominent in participant accounts and drawn from biblical

---

[125] Quoted in Okorocha, *Religious Conversion*, 68.
[126] *Ibid.*, 89.
[127] Dennis Okafor, 'My Testimony', 1969.

motifs which resonated with contemporary culture and context. Firstly, the discourse of spiritual warfare and the image of God/Christ as victorious king, subduing his enemies. Here the believer is an actor in a cosmic drama, part of an 'invading army', resisting the temptations of the devil, fighting the forces of 'heathendom', and rejecting the enticements of the 'world' through the power of the Holy Spirit and the redemptive work of Christ. Thus one former revivalist writes, 'The devil may try his best, but we are confident that our God is always on the throne. Temptations will always come but we are more than conquerors through Him who died for us. Sin has no more dominion over us'.[128] In Uchenna Emezue's 'New Year's Victory', an account of SU exploits in his home village of Ossah, Christian commitment is presented as a 'clash with the world', represented by 'heathen practices', traditional priests, community elders, and even parents. 'The Christian life starts by being tired of the world and ends in being at war with it. No energy or power of our own is required in the battle. Christ is the Captain and Strength and He fights it by His Spirit'.[129] In this discourse, protagonists become active agents in the sanctification process by resisting temptations to compromise with the 'world', but they do so by drawing upon divine resources through prayer. As relief workers, they resist temptations to steal; they refuse to cheat in school exams or use 'look and crook' (bribery) to gain employment; they abstain from sexual immorality and resist communal pressure to participate in traditional religious practices.[130] The image of the Devil figures prominently in this drama, but as a defeated foe, and surprisingly, no explicit link is made between exorcism and sanctification.

The discourse of family, and the image of God as benevolent 'father' nurturing and disciplining his children, is also prominent in revivalist narratives. Here the focus is on personal relationship (fellowship), ongoing obedience, maturity through suffering and mutual support. One revivalist explained how a rereading of the Bible text Heb 12:5-6 helped her to come to terms with her own experience of suffering: 'My eyes opened there and then. My mind went through all I had passed through, and I realized they had happened because the Lord was breaking me for my own good because of His love for me'.[131] Peel refers to the way narratives of being tested

[128] Raymond Nwosu, Letter to Roberts, 22 September 1970.

[129] Emezue, 'New Year's Victory', 1969.

[130] 'Expo' (exposing question papers before the exam) became a widespread problem after the war as Igbo youth endeavoured to make up for lost years of education. Good exam results were important for gaining employment, and jobs were scarce, so many resorted to bribery.

[131] Nnenna Okoye, 'Do not despise the Lord's discipline', written testimony, 1969. Heb 12:5-6: 'My son, do not regard lightly the discipline of the Lord. . . . For those whom the Lord loves He disciplines' (NASB).

through suffering are used to redeem feelings of failure.[132] Another revivalist, reflecting on his war experiences, wrote, 'We could so easily harden our hearts or even blame God for injustice, indulge in self-pity, or despair, or live in a state of apathy, and in all not learn the lesson that our loving Father would have us learn from the recent tribulation'.[133] In this model, sanctification occurs through intimate fellowship with the 'Father' and following the way of the cross. Along the way, encouragement is provided by God's providential control over life circumstances and fellowship with Christian 'brethren'.[134] This discourse represents a rupture with traditional piety which has no notion of God as loving father or the redemptive possibilities of suffering.[135]

The influences of Keswick are apparent in both discourses. For example, one revivalist wrote, 'From the Bible I have also been taught that I can only live a victorious life as long as I TRUST, not TRY; as long as I "abide in the Vine", and keep looking unto Jesus, depending completely on Him'.[136] Another commented that 'if I was to have full enjoyment in the Lord, I had to forsake self, I had to be broken, I had to be pounded like foo-foo. . . . If we must enjoy real fellowship . . . we must be broken at the foot of the cross'.[137] The link between brokenness (through suffering) and sanctification was a common theme in participant accounts. Out of their experiences of crisis, revivalists developed a theology of suffering 'from below', drawn from Biblical motifs and Christian tradition, which embraced the cross as a crucial element in the sanctification process. The main components of this theology were a confidence in God's providential control and paternal love, a call to follow in the steps of Jesus and a conviction of the redemptive qualities of suffering. Allied to this was a belief in the inevitability of suffering because we live in a fallen world characterised by enmity and opposition to the gospel. The revival injected purpose into the experience of pain and stressed the future enjoyment of 'heaven' as compensation for present sufferings. But the redemptive possibilities of suffering were conditional upon the believer's response of faith and reliance upon God's grace. Here the popular image of God as a

---

[132] Peel, *Religious Encounter*, 17.

[133] Sam Okoli, Letter to Roberts, 7 June 1970.

[134] For example, Ume Kalu, 'What God has done for me', 1969. Rom 8:28 was a popular text: 'And we know that God causes all things to work together for good to those who love God, to those who are called according to His purpose' (NASB).

[135] Okorocha, *Religious Conversion*, 89; T. Uzodinma Nwala, *Igbo Philosophy*, Ikeja-Lagos: Lantern Books, 1985, 160.

[136] Benjamin C. Onwochei, written testimony, 1969.

[137] Nnenna Okoye, 'Do not despise the Lord's discipline', 1969. Okoye mentions the interrelated terms 'broken' and 'break(ing)' twelve times.

loving father disciplining his children enabled participants to come to terms with their adverse circumstances and maintain an outlook of hope. But this did not necessarily lead to a fatalistic approach to suffering. During the war, victims of sickness, poverty and enemy air raids often resorted to prayers of petition, and revival testimonies record episodes of God's healing power, provision and protection.

Strict moral codes of behaviour became ways of expressing 'born-again' identity and maintaining community boundaries as participants erected barriers between themselves and the world. Informants said one could clearly identify revivalists by their quality of life, their radical stance on ethical issues and their outward behaviour. Boundary markers were sometimes spatial (the SU fellowship group, for example), sometimes dress codes (long gowns and head coverings for women), but more often abstention. Revivalists abstained from immorality, marriage to non-Christians, corruption and stealing in the workplace, cheating in exams, smoking, alcohol consumption and dancing. Gladys Ekwo, founder of Scripture Union's Women's Fellowship, recalled her own experience of the revival's moral imperative:

> We were taught again how to relate with our brothers. We just regarded them as our biological brothers. I remember 1 Timothy 5:2 was our focus .... In fact we didn't feel that we were opposite sex like that. And thank God it so helped us. We were working together like that. I remember again that we were taught that there is a difference between a worldly girl and a Christian girl, the mode of her dressing and everything, according to the Scripture. We believed in modesty as a matter of fact.[138]

Barriers were also erected through abstinence from traditional rituals and participation in Christian alternatives. Crossing these boundaries was dangerous and carried the risk of backsliding, so they were reinforced through participation in prayer vigils, Bible studies and fellowship meetings.

But these barriers were permeable. Revivalists hoped that widespread conversions and individual transformations would provoke ethical renewal and cultural reformation within their communities. Emezue's 'New Year's Victory' describes how this dynamic operated in his home village where a group of young people, recently revitalised through contact with Scripture Union, held regular 'Revival Services' and challenged 'evil and heathen

---

[138] Gladys Ekwo, 'The Role of Women in the Seventies', Conference, audiocassette, 29 April 2000, Enugu. Several informants referred to 1 Tim 5:2 as an important text during the revival: 'Treat younger men as brothers . . . and younger women as sisters, with absolute purity' (NASB).

practices' in church and community. References in Emezue's narrative hint at revivalist expectations: the steady trickle of converts as a result of the group's witness; the visibility of the young people's transformed lifestyles; the public stand taken during the annual New Year's traditional 'swearing ceremony', when their refusal to participate and their prayers stopped it taking place.[139] In a letter written four years later, Emezue reflects on the group's ongoing influence:

> Parents have started joining us for Bible Studies. Many young men and women who used to persecute us are now on fire for Jesus. The Group has made a big impact on the whole village. Parents have come to see the usefulness of the teachings because they see the difference Jesus makes in the life of the youths who fellowship with us.[140]

We see a similar process operating in a different context soon after the war, this time the University of Nigeria (Nsukka), where some members of SU Umuahia had transferred to resume their studies. Raymond Nwosu's narrative presents the university Christian Union as a safe haven in a 'wilderness of sin where values are turned upside down', and shows how revivalists expected community transformation to take place. Nwosu describes what happened at the university's newly opened Enugu campus following the transfer of a small band of CU members from Nsukka campus. Prior to their arrival, life at Enugu Campus was 'notorious and very debased'. As the group engaged in prayer and Bible study, other students joined their ranks, resulting in its rapid expansion. Gradually, their influence was felt among rival Christian groups on campus, such as the more theologically liberal Student Christian Movement and the Roman Catholics, until it spread beyond Christian boundaries and affected the wider student community. Nwosu ends with this assessment of the group's religious and moral impact: 'The S.C.M. has become more spiritual with Bible studies and prayer meetings forming the major theme of their gatherings. . . . Even unbelievers or agnostics acclaim what is happening and fear to do many things that in the past they proudly could do'.[141]

Contesting Boundaries and Reconstructing Collective Identities

Revival spirituality reflected local community aspirations, and it was the Scripture Union and charismatic fellowship groups which became prime

---

139 Emezue, 'New Year's Victory', 1969.

140 Uchenna Emezue, Letter to Roberts, 28 September 1973.

141 Raymond Nwosu, Letter to Roberts, 12 April 1971.

venues for revivalist communal activity. The historian Richard Carwardine has noted the potential of revivals for creating and sustaining a sense of community, both locally and more widely. Though revival conversions are the 'ultimate expression of Protestant individualism', revivals themselves are only possible because 'geographically and psychologically displaced men and women corporately yearned for a shelter in which to "belong"'.[142] One reason the Civil War Revival flourished was that it allowed access to a caring egalitarian community at a time of collective identity crisis, when existing social and economic relationships were disintegrating due to the combined effects of modernisation and conflict; a community not based on territorial lines, but on a shared set of meanings, which allowed members to identify and interact with others. The revival enabled participants to construct new identities based on their mutual membership of a dynamic missionary fellowship which crossed denominational and ethnic lines. There are similarities here with the East African Revival which, according to Ward, has been conceived as a 'protest against the increasing individualism and functionalism of life, a re-assertion of traditional face-to-face values and human relationships'.[143]

As the refugee problem escalated, a growing number of Igbos became separated from kinship networks. Scripture Union, with its stress on Christian fellowship, offered the possibility of an alternative family based on a common spiritual experience and provided individuals with new opportunities for survival. Ties with Christian 'brethren' replaced those with kin. Respondents spoke of the strong bond of intimacy which was part of the revival experience during the early 1970s. The revival community crossed existing lines of demarcation and challenged denominational, ethnic and social boundaries. Victor Turner's concept of liminality is helpful here. He suggests that the liminal or middle phase of the ritual process can precipitate intense feelings of fellowship as ritualists are released from structure into *communitas*. When applied to revivals, periods of religious ecstasy can trigger conditions of 'spontaneous *communitas*' where for awhile participants inhabit a space freed from societal norms. Boundaries are contested, new bonds of intimacy created, and collective identities restructured and reconstructed.[144]

---

[142] Richard Carwardine, 'The Second Great Awakening in Comparative Perspective: Revival and Culture in the United States and Britain', in Edith L. Blumhofer and Randall Balmer (eds.), *Modern Christian Revivals*, Urbana and Chicago: University of Illinois Press, 1993, 94.

[143] Ward, 'Balokole', 136.

[144] Victor Turner, *The Ritual Process. Structure and Anti-Structure*, Ithaca, NY: Cornell University Press, 1974, 128-29; Victor Turner, 'Betwixt and Between: the Liminal Period in *Rites de Passage*', in William A. Lessa and Evon Z. Vogt (eds.), *Reader in Comparative Religion: an Anthropological*

Eroding Denominational and Ethnic Boundaries

The Civil War Revival eroded denominational boundaries. This was particularly significant in the light of the failure of the Church Union project discussed in chapter 2. However, the revival community was no ecumenical scheme produced by ecclesiastical mergers. It brought together people, divided by denomination and creed, on the basis of their mutual membership of Scripture Union and their common experience of being 'born-again'. This was partly a response to the civil war. In Igbo townships, shared feelings of insecurity and deprivation reinforced existing religious bonds and eroded denominational barriers. In refugee camps, Christians worshipped together regardless of denominational allegiances. Eating, sleeping and praying in communal settings became potent symbols for the expression of revivalist Christianity during and after the war. Though this reflected cultural models of commensality and fulfilled the social functions of local kinship groups, revivalists interpreted it as a work of the Spirit and a consequence of the new birth.

Despite its ecumenical stance, Scripture Union was partly responsible for loosening the ties of its members with existing churches and precipitating the rise of autonomous charismatic fellowship groups. In the immediate post-war period, the SU group which met on Sunday afternoon became the focus of fellowship for an increasing number of young people in Igbo urban areas, and members maintained only a loose attachment to their churches, often migrating from one to another or attending several different ones. For example, one member of SU Enugu told me that most Sundays he would attend Anglican, ECWA and Apostolic Faith churches. And an Anglican member of SU Onitsha said that he sometimes 'fraternised' with Assemblies of God, ECWA and Foursquare Gospel churches. SU contributed to trans-denominational mobility because it brought members of different churches into close contact and fostered a sense of unity based on a common experience rather than along organised denominational lines.

The revival also eroded ethnic consciousness, heightened by the war, and contributed towards reconciliation and restoration of peace.[145] Yoruba

---

Approach, New York: Harper Collins, 1979, 234-43. A number of scholars have applied Turner's concepts of ritual liminality and *communitas* to religious revival and Pentecostal activity. See for example, George A. Rawlyk, 'Writing about Canadian Religious Revivals', in Blumhofer and Balmer, (eds.), *Modern Christian Revivals*, 1993, 213-14; Daniel E. Albrecht, 'Pentecostal Spirituality: Looking Through the Lens of Ritual', *Pneuma*, 14.2, Fall 1992, 121-25.

[145] Of course the revival was not the only means of reconciliation. Other Christian communities in Western and Northern Nigeria, not directly influenced by the revival, welcomed Igbo Christians back into the Federation.

Christians from Western Nigeria were important here. During the war, they sometimes provided shelter for Igbo Christians, and afterwards SU groups in the West warmly welcomed their Igbo brethren.[146] Ojo mentions the conciliatory role of the World Action Team for Christ (WATC), a Yoruba-founded charismatic ministry which organised national congresses in Igbo cities during the early 1970s.[147] But it was the close relationship between Igbo revivalists and Yoruba SU travelling secretaries Mike Oye and Muyiwa Olamijulo which epitomised the erosion of ethic consciousness within the revival community. In 1969, Oye and Olamijulo migrated to the East to engage in relief work under the auspices of Scripture Union and formed a close alliance with their Igbo counterparts. Subsequently, Oye opened his home in Akure as a place of refuge and rehabilitation for young Igbo Christians suffering the traumatic effects of the war. He also teamed up with Igbo revivalist Cyril Okorocha to carry the revival message into schools and colleges in the West. Meanwhile, Olamijulo remained in the East until 1976 in his capacity as SU travelling secretary.

The traditional Igbo response to injustice is to demand for revenge.[148] According to participants, the revival challenged this, as we see from the following testimony:

> You are my brother if you are born-again in Christ; you are my brother, whether you are Yoruba or Hausa. . . . The Lord used it [the revival] to heal many hurts. For there were many Igbos who had sworn to remain in perpetual enmity with everyone else who had been involved in killing, in starving us to death. But the Lord removed the bitterness, removed the sore, and caused us to come together.[149]

Okorocha believes this was one factor that brought healing to the nation.[150] A remarkable phenomenon was the migration of Igbos to the North so soon after the war, and only a few years after the 1966 pogroms when many of

---

The Federal Government's policy of 'No Victor, no vanquished' and its implementation of the three 'Rs' also facilitated Igbo recovery, though some of my informants insisted that these policies remained at the level of discourse and propaganda.

[146] For example, Christians in Western Nigeria sheltered the Igbo revivalist J. M. J. Emesim and SU General Secretary Daniel Onwukwe (an Igbo) during the war.

[147] WATC held congresses in Owerri (1971) and Port Harcourt (1973). See Ojo, 'Contextual', 180.

[148] Okorocha, 'Reconciliation', 197.

[149] Meschak Ilobi, personal reminiscence, May 2000.

[150] Okorocha, 'Reconciliation', 197.

their people had been slaughtered. Mostly they migrated for trade purposes, to reclaim properties, or as part of their National Youth Corps service, but some did so with the express purpose of preaching the gospel and planting churches.

Challenging Gerontocratic Structures and Gender Boundaries

Like other African initiatives which have emerged as movements of renewal within existing denominations, the revival appealed especially to youth and women. This was partly because it offered access to a space relatively free from the control of elder males. But by doing so, it awakened old tensions as 'born-again' youth felt free to challenge traditional gerontocratic authority in church and community. Early Igbo revivalists were predominantly young people situated on the fringes of the church and nurtured within Scripture Union ranks. Though the revival eroded existing denominational barriers, later fresh ones were erected, partly precipitated by generational struggles.

If we recall, despite its decentralised political structures and fragmented communities, Igbo society was traditionally gerontocratic and hierarchical. By the 1960s, this was clearly reflected in mission church structures which were dominated by elders and clergy. Scripture Union had a democratising influence, creating ministry opportunities for young people disillusioned by the established church and bored with the routine of life. But it went further by equipping the youth with tools to challenge gerontocratic authority. This was an important factor behind the emergence of autonomous charismatic fellowships. Community elders, traditional priests and church leaders constantly challenged and opposed the young protagonists over their overt evangelistic activities and radical ethics. The experience of being born-again functioned as a protest against gerontocratic authority and created 'free' individuals able to embrace modernity's call for a 'break with the past'. Unfortunately, it also helped to weaken the tradition of obedience and respect for parents and elders, a process already set in motion by other modernising forces, such as Western education and urbanisation, as well as the civil war. One informant told me that young people conscripted into the army suddenly found themselves in command of older 'fathers', which disrupted Igbo society. Another reflected on the effects of revival spirituality on inter-generational relationships and church authority structures: 'As young ones we don't want to know what anyone was saying. Whether you are my father or mother, we don't care. . . . Whether you are bishop, we don't care'.[151]

---

[151] Nwodika, 'Churches in the Seventies'.

Here we return to Emezue's account of revivalist activity in Ossah village during the war and his description of the clash between SU young people, traditional priests, and community elders on the occasion of the New Year 'swearing ceremony'.

> On January 1, 1969, the Lord allowed an occasion for us to stand and glorify His Holy Name. In the morning of the new year, the juju 'priests' in our village announced that every (breathing) human being in the village should gather at the square for a swearing ceremony - a sort of covenant with the village god; one of many heathenic practices common in the village, even practiced by many of the so-called church members. My own father was even one of the chairmen of the occasion and as such brought pressure to bear on me. Since the Bible clearly condemns these heathenic practices - Matt 5.34-35, James 5.12, all the S.U. members backed out. The juju 'priests' viewed it seriously because this was the first time a person or group of people refused to obey the village juju or 'god'. They were so grieved by our defiance of their authority that they swore that not only would they punish us but that the village juju would do more. Parents were warned in their own interest to advise their children to take part in the ceremony. Most parents were so frightened that they came begging their children to attend for their sake. All was in vain because the answer was always, 'for the Lords Sake I would not attend'. When the priests and elders saw that their threats and intimidation failed, they made a direct appeal to me as the group leader to reconsider our stand. They even purposed allowing us to swear with the Bible as we 'claimed to be more religious than others', but we made them to understand that we were not even allowed to swear with the Lord's name. We went on our knees and prayed for more power to stand and all of a sudden we burst into joy, our fears were transformed into power and we started thanking God for counting us worthy to suffer for the Name even though it was painful. Our souls were filled with joy for obeying God, that we all stood, moved out in groups, and witnessed for the Lord. One of the sick people we prayed for that day was healed instantly. The day ended with thanks. We were happy and contented that even though we disobeyed our parents and elders we obeyed our Heavenly Father.[152]

In this instance, 'born-again' conversion enabled the young protagonists to challenge their elders in an unprecedented way and express in public that they had made a complete break with their former traditions and with unconverted friends and family. In one sense, the born-again experience is

[152] Emezue, 'New Year's Victory', 1969.

a 'conversion to modernity'.[153] But Marshall-Fratani is correct when she states that though conversion is a choice, it does not imply the creation of the 'autonomous secular subject of "modernity"'. The convert is freed from the past, but is consecrated to a higher power and incorporated into a new community.[154] This is important in our context because, as the above example demonstrates, Igbo revivalists constantly appealed to a higher authority - either the Christian God or the Bible - as justification for confronting their elders. And freed from the restrictions of traditional commensality, they found themselves accountable to an alternative 'born-again' community. The challenge to gerontocratic authority in this case proceeded from the revival's missionary imperative rather than a desire to break free from the control of elder males.

The revival also challenged gender boundaries. The traditional role of Igbo women is ambiguous.[155] While Igbo society is patriarchal, with women occupying a subordinate role in family and political life, male domination was discouraged in Igbo indigenous politics.[156] Judith van Allen maintains that women had a prominent role in traditional political life. But the introduction of 'native administration' under colonial rule, and the influence of missionaries and mission schools, weakened Igbo women's traditional autonomy and capacity to participate in local politics. According to van Allen, British colonialists failed to understand the political institutions of Igbo women, and missionaries made no attempt to protect Igbo women's political role because they believed their aim was to cultivate Christian wives and mothers rather than female political leaders. Igbo women also had less access to mission education, considered essential for political leadership.[157]

In the traditional religious arena, Igbo women enjoyed relative freedom, sometimes fulfilling a prophetic role, though the priesthood remained largely a male preserve.[158] But the missionary movement reinforced the

---

153 See Peter van der Meer, *Conversion to Modernities: the Globalization of Christianity*, London: Routledge, 1996; Meyer, 'Break with the Past', 182-84.

154 Marshall-Fratani, 'Global', 286.

155 For the role of women in Igbo traditional life, see Joseph Therese Agbasiere, *Women in Igbo Life and Thought*, London and New York: Routledge, 2000.

156 U. D. Anyanwu, 'Gender Question in Igbo Politics', in Anyanwu and Aguwa (eds.), *Igbo*, 119.

157 Judith van Allen, '"Sitting on a Man": Colonialism and the Lost Political Institutions of Igbo Women', in Roy Richard Grinker and Christopher B. Steiner (eds.), *Perspectives on Africa. A Reader in Culture, History and Representation*, Oxford: Blackwell, 1997, 536, 542-48.

158 Udobata Onunwe, *Studies in Igbo Traditional Religion*, Obosi, Anambra: Pacific Publishers, 1990, 65; Ikenga-Metuh, *Comparative Studies*, 206.

assumption that their proper role was as Christian helpmates rather than leaders.[159] Thus women frequently occupied marginal positions in mission church structures, even though they usually outnumbered men. Clergy were predominantly male, and there was little opportunity for women to acquire leadership positions. It was in the prayer houses that women found space for ministry, even though they were usually barred from the highest echelons of authority. As Hackett observes, these churches provided the structure whereby women could 'acquire and exercise responsibility'. A prophetess or senior lady member might command the respect of the church, even if this was in an indirect way through divine revelation, or through being the wife of the pastor.[160] Those women who actually founded prayer houses usually continued in leadership, but often in a subordinate role to other male leaders. In the case of Christ Holy Church, for example, the late prophetess Agnes Okoh is revered as founder, but it was her son, Marius Okoh, who became the first General Superintendent. It is a large denomination with over 700 branches, yet has no female pastors, though women do fulfil a prophetic role as 'visioners'.[161]

Scripture Union empowered women and gave them opportunities for leadership and ministry. Two young women, Grace Iwuora and Nnenna Okoye, were members of SU Umuahia's core leadership team during the war, and others occupied key leadership positions in SU township groups during the early 1970s. The revival enabled women to occupy positions alongside men as gospel carriers, and it was within SU ranks that they honed their evangelistic skills. This is reflected in Gladys Ekwo's revival narrative, which contrasts the status of women in the 'world' with their position in the 'born-again' community. According to Ekwo, the revival 'liberated' women to serve God on equal terms with men and gave them a voice to proclaim the gospel. Though they encountered opposition from those who objected to women preachers on biblical grounds, God vindicated them by giving them success. During the revival, Ekwo recalls, women 'brought many men into the fold, and they are great men today in the Lord'.[162]

The role of young women is captured in Raphael Okafor's journal. Entries show their active involvement, even though men continued to fulfil most official preaching engagements and retained overall leadership of the movement. Thus Lawjua Egwu, an eighteen-year-old secondary school student, worked alongside Raphael Okafor, supporting him in prayer, leading worship, counselling new converts and occasionally giving talks.

---

[159] Van Allen, 'Igbo Women', 547-48.

[160] Rosalind I. J. Hackett, 'Power and Authority in Nigeria's Independent Churches', *West African Religion*, 21.2, 1983, 47.

[161] *Glad News*, 2001, 1.

[162] Ekwo, 'Role of Women'.

Rhoda Morah founded a charismatic ministry called Aguata for Christ, which subsequently became the National Evangelical Mission, currently one of the largest Igbo-founded neo-Pentecostal churches. Eunice Eboh was another important figure. She was leader of the SU group at the Anglican Girls Secondary School, which helped to open up SU Onitsha to the ministry of Hour of Freedom. Those who followed these young girls into Hour of Freedom included future neo-Pentecostal church pioneers. The patronage of older women was also important. One was Agunyenwa Egwu, Lawjua's mother, who for a time allowed SU Onitsha to meet in her home. Another was her friend Dinah Erinne who as Principal of the Anglican Girls Secondary School invited Stephen Okafor and Muyiwa Olamijulo to hold a retreat for her students in 1970. When the local Anglican Church closed its doors to Hour of Freedom, Erinne allowed the group access to the school premises. She also helped to negotiate peace between Hour of Freedom leaders and the Anglican Bishop in Onitsha. These two older women were among the first members of SU Onitsha to participate in Hour of Freedom activities.

Through their membership of Scripture Union and participation in the revival, youth and women challenged gerontocratic structures and male dominance within the church, and helped facilitate the emergence and sustenance of autonomous charismatic fellowship groups.

Challenging Missionary and Clerical Control

The revival also challenged colour boundaries, missionary hegemony and clerical control. The relationship between white missionaries and African Christians is best summed up in the example of Bill Roberts, the SU travelling secretary, described by one of his African colleagues as a 'black man at heart' because he ate their food, shared his clothes with them, slept in the same room and used his salary to feed them. Again there are affinities with East Africa where the revival made it possible for missionaries and Africans to have fellowship on equal terms.[163] It was Roberts's willingness to remain in Biafra and open his home to Igbo young people which initially endeared him to them.

The revival also contributed to the development of an indigenous Christian community. The church historian Daniel Bays suggests that revivalism is an 'effective means for indigenous Christian leaders to break free of domination by missions'.[164] The Civil War Revival, as we suggested in chapter 2, 'sabotaged' missionary attempts to retain control of

[163] See Stanley, 'Revival', 16.

[164] Daniel H. Bays, 'Christian Revival in China 1900-1937', in Blumhofer and Balmer (eds.), *Modern Christian Revivals*, 175.

the church following independence and became a vehicle for African indigenous initiative. Prior to 1967, Scripture Union work in the East consisted of school visitation, SU camps and rallies, and literature distribution. These activities aimed at conversion and discipleship, and exposed young people to the Bible. Although the war adversely affected SU work in Nigeria, it had a positive effect on Roberts's activities. Schools in the East closed for the duration of the war and travel was severely restricted. This meant that there were no more school visitations, no camps and no books imported for literary ministry (due to the economic blockade).[165] But because SU activities were initially restricted to Umuahia, it allowed a community of committed lay young people to develop around Roberts and his co-workers. This group later became the mainspring of the revival during its civil war phase.

If we recall from chapter 2, a key factor in SU growth within Nigeria was its policy of national autonomy and its promotion of indigenous leadership and financial independence. Historians have acknowledged the contribution of both white missionaries and African agents to the introduction and expansion of Christianity in Igboland.[166] Though the Civil War Revival was primarily an African initiative, many informants paid tribute to the role played by Roberts, at least in its initial stages when Umuahia was the centre of revivalist activity. Early in his ministry, Roberts recognised the need to train indigenous leaders and this became an urgent priority when the war situation made his own future uncertain. Initially, he worked with some of the more senior SU members, and early in 1968 formed a planning committee to help organise SU activities. A significant step in the process of indigenisation took place when Roberts went on leave in mid-1968. In his absence, Igbo lay Christians took sole responsibility for SU work in the East. When he departed finally, towards the end of 1969, SU work in the East was left entirely in Nigerian hands.

SU Umuahia influenced many post-war revival leaders during their formative years. Two members of its leadership team, Chris Onuoha and John Onuora, became acting SU travelling secretaries in East Central State prior to resuming their university education, and most of those responsible for reactivating SU township groups were closely associated with SU Umuahia during the war. These fellowship groups soon became centres of intense evangelistic activity and the platform for significant mission initiatives as a host of evangelists emerged from their midst. The revival was a rediscovery of lay ministry and an avenue for the recruitment of a new generation of Igbo indigenous leaders. As such, it challenged clerical and missionary control, and facilitated the rise of independent charismatic ministries. Most founders and leaders of Igbo-founded charismatic

[165] Ojo, 'Campus Christianity', 98.
[166] Kalu, 'Color and Conversion', 61-74.

fellowships in the early 1970s were nurtured within SU ranks during the revival, and many were actually introduced to born-again Christianity through contact with existing members or attendance at SU events. I interviewed twelve men who founded nine different ministries between 1969 and 1973. All were members of SU, and seven were SU converts. At least five were influenced by Roberts in their formative years. I also interviewed thirteen others who belonged to these groups during the early 1970s. Again all were SU members and eight were SU converts. Invariably, founders of charismatic fellowship groups used SU as a platform prior to forming independent ministries.

Missionary Impulses

Attention so far has focussed on consumer demands and social consequences. But the supply-side of the revival was crucial. Normally conversion involved some form of interaction with individual and/or group advocates. Out of forty-three informants converted during the revival, twenty-seven said that individual advocates played a significant role in their conversion experience, either through personal witness (lifestyle and verbal) or invitations to group meetings where they encountered the gospel. In fact, personal invitation was a common means of attracting people to revival meetings during and after the war. Invariably these advocates were members of Scripture Union, and a common setting for the ritual of conversion was the SU Guest service. For at least twenty of my informants this was the occasion of their conversion to born-again Christianity. After the war, evangelistic campaigns organised by charismatic ministries like Hour of Freedom Evangelistic Association and Master's Vessel Group became venues for extensive conversions.

The Civil War Revival provided a means for Igbos to resolve their collective identity crisis through their absorption into a dynamic missionary fellowship, whose ideology was shaped by a conversionist stance, an adventist belief system, and a dualistic worldview, a conviction that souls were in the grip of the Devil and perishing without Christ. This ideology awakened a 'passion for the kingdom' which propelled those touched by the 'Spirit' into the margins of Igbo society and beyond. The formation of this band of itinerant preachers out of the furnace of the civil war was principally responsible for the spread of the revival. Though initially restricted to the Biafran enclave, the Civil War Revival fuelled significant mission initiatives that eventually reached beyond the borders of Igboland. All informants agreed that evangelism was *the* major feature of the revival. As Hastings observed of earlier 'prophet' movements, civil war revivalists were 'taking on the missionary's task because it seemed so important'.[167] Again there were elements of continuity in change, and influences from local and global forces. The revivalists adapted their message and strategies to cater for consumer demands, but also challenged existing religious institutions with their aggressive and innovative evangelistic style. The content of their message and method of transmission were shaped by their distinctive understanding of the Bible, their religious heritage, their local context, and forces from outside.

'Repent or Perish': the Revival Message

The revival message was Christological in flavour and aimed at conversion, reflecting its evangelical roots in Scripture Union. The person of Christ, the cross, repentance, the new birth and the 'Second Coming' were prominent themes in revival sermons and songs. Sermon topics and texts at Hour of Freedom events included the following: 'Go back to the cross', 'What think ye of Christ' (Matt 22:41-2), 'The peace of God' (Col 3:15-17), 'Repentance' (Ezekiel 18:30-32), 'The second coming of Christ', and 'Jesus is the same yesterday, today and forever'.[168] And Raphael Okafor's journal includes this entry for the 14th March 1971:

> Brother Stephen preached a powerful sermon in St. Stephen's Church from John 3:3. After the series he finished up the message with Matthew 11:28 and called the congregation to repentance. . . . In the evening at St. Paul's Oba, I spoke to the whole congregation from Luke 19:10 and challenged them about their salvation. About 300 people raised up their hands and prayed through.[169]

The content of revival songs also reflected the evangelical culture of Scripture Union, though they were often adapted for local consumption and sometimes sung in the vernacular. One former revivalist recalled, 'In those days the songs, the choruses were Christ-centred, Heaven-centred. You know we will say, "Take the world, and give me Jesus. I will not turn back. Should no one follow, still I will follow"'. If we recall, this was a reference to a popular revival song, often quoted in revival narratives. Other

---

[167] Hastings, *Church*, 531.

[168] Raphael Okafor, Journal, March-December 1971, cited in Bolton, *Glory*, 106-36.

[169] Raphael Okafor, Journal, 14 March 1971, quoted Bolton, *Glory*, 108. John 3:3: 'Truly, truly, I say to you, unless one is born again, he cannot see the kingdom of God' (NASB).

choruses regularly sung at revival meetings included 'Jesus is coming, is coming, is coming', *Lee ịhụnanya Jesus* (Lo, Behold the love of Jesus), and *Ijikerewo* (Are you ready, the Saviour is coming).

'Repent or perish' was a common refrain as revivalists exhorted their audience to be 'born-again' in preparation for Christ's imminent return. This phrase, based on Luke 13:3, was so vivid in revivalist imagination that it was often repeated in oral interviews and written texts to describe the revival's core message.[170] Note the following statement from an article in a neo-Pentecostal magazine, adapted from a Sunday morning sermon: 'In the early 70's, when I gave my life to Christ, the Christian message was simple. Repent or perish! It was a powerful tool of evangelism then and is still the same today. . . . Our primary text will be Luke 13:1-9'.[171] The revival's target audience included those within the mainline churches and the prayer houses. The focus on the imminent return of Christ and the realities of heaven and hell in revivalist discourse and gospel presentation conflicted with traditional religious beliefs and was often absent from mainline church and prayer house sermons.

I have noted the strong ethical content of revivalist preaching. According to informants, the revival message departed from 'orthodox' (mainline church) and prayer house preaching at precisely this point. Revivalists presented the new birth and gift of the Spirit, rather than human effort or religious ritual, as the source of ethical renewal, and emphasis was on grace rather than law. One revival convert recalled that despite regularly attending church, engaging in periods of prayer and fasting at a prayer house, and maintaining 'good conduct', he only found 'salvation' when he understood God's 'saving grace' and received Christ through the advocacy of revival evangelist Teddy Igbokwe.[172] And Hour of Freedom evangelist Stephen Okafor said that a major thrust of their message was 'freedom' from the legalistic and ritualistic demands of prayer houses like Ufuma Practical Prayer Band.[173] Another revivalist wrote that many mission church members first encountered teaching on the 'new birth' when they attended SU Bible study meetings during the war. 'We were always told to be good but new birth was never mentioned, instead emphasis was laid on baptism and paying of dues. . . . New birth . . . was an experience completely foreign to us. We were taught that joining a church and living respectably was all that God required'.[174] Later, as we will see, revivalists

---

[170] Luke 13:3: 'I tell you, no, but, unless you repent, you will also likewise perish' (NASB).

[171] Amaechi Nwachukwu, 'Repent or Perish', *Livingspring*, 1998, 16.

[172] Felix Okafor, written testimony, 23 October 1969.

[173] Interview, 16 December 1998, London.

[174] Emezue, 'New Year's Victory', 1969.

added the Pentecostal doctrine of Holy Spirit baptism to their religious repertoire.

Seizing the Landscape: Revival Strategies

Aggressive evangelism was a hallmark of the revival during its early stages. This grew in intensity and scope as protagonists embraced the Pentecostal experience and recruited increasing numbers of young people into their ranks. Lines from a popular revival song show how they conceived their mission:

> We are able to go up and seize the country,
> To possess the land from Jordan to the sea.
> Though the giants may be on our way to hinder,
> God will surely give us the victory.
> And so move on to the righteous side,
> Move on to the righteous side with Jesus.[175]

Using a variety of strategies, revivalists seized hold of the landscape (to use Ranger's phrase), but had to compete with other religious groups for territorial control. Rival groups included Protestant and Roman Catholic mission churches, SCM groups, prayer houses, Jehovah's Witnesses, and traditional religionists. The metaphor of battle captured the revivalist imagination and enabled them to refashion their identity in terms of an all-conquering army invading enemy territory, particularly poignant in the light of their civil war experiences.

Evangelism was already an integral part of Scripture Union ministry before the war, but during the revival it intensified. One advantage SU had over the churches was its informal organisation. With no building and no rigid ecclesiastical structure, SU Umuahia was able to continue holding meetings. Weekday camp-like activities were one example of the way revivalists adapted their evangelistic strategies to suit new and challenging contexts. The first day (13 September 1967) twenty came. Soon numbers increased until they were getting over 100, and activities continued until the evacuation of Umuahia in 1969. SU offered young people, separated from kinship groups and friends, the possibility of an alternative network of relationships. Talks, discussion groups, chorus singing, communal meals, and games, proved attractive to young people, bored, isolated, and hungry. Later, SU provided plots of land for farming, a strategy in keeping with the

---

[175] Quoted in Bolton, *Glory*, 140. This was sung during the Remembering the Seventies Conference in Enugu as an example of songs from the revival. It is not of indigenous origin, but Igbos adapted it to suit local styles.

Biafran government's 'war on hunger' policy which encouraged people to grow their own food.[176] Some who came simply for food and fraternity were later converted.

A turning point occurred in October 1967 when Roberts observed a new interest in the gospel and decided to organise evangelistic 'guest services'. These continued on a monthly basis until the evacuation of Umuahia 18 months later and became a focal point for Scripture Union's evangelistic activity. Many young people were converted, and attendance sometimes reached as high as three hundred. Apart from one occasion when Roberts spoke, all the preachers at SU guest services were Nigerian. Popular speakers included Presbyterian pastor James Ukaegbu, Godson Ogbansiegbe (founder of Christian Fellowship Group, Aba), and George Onugha (Principal of the Assemblies of God Bible School, Umuahia). These men provided a link with earlier movements and influenced the shape of the revival. If we recall, Ukaegbu was based in Jos before the war, where he worked as an ECWA pastor and itinerant evangelist with New Life for All, a popular evangelistic programme associated with the Sudan Interior Mission (SIM). During the 1966 pogroms, he returned to Umuahia and opened a branch of ECWA, which attracted many SU members due to its conservative evangelical stance. In 1968, he left ECWA to train for the Presbyterian ministry.[177] Ogbansiegbe was credited with introducing the term 'revival' and the practice of 'altar calls' to the group at Umuahia. Guest services were referred to as 'revivals' and people were encouraged to come forward and 'give their lives to Christ'. This was a more aggressive form of evangelism than previously employed by Roberts and his co-workers. As members of SU Umuahia dispersed throughout Biafra, they started new groups, and by the end of the war were holding guest services in ten different centres instead of one. Roberts believed they were an effective means of 'bringing many into a saving knowledge of the Lord Jesus Christ', but was uncomfortable with the excessive emotionalism and long appeals for salvation that were sometimes present.[178]

The influence of SU Umuahia is captured well in Justin Ogugua's narrative. A visit in January 1969 left him with a new eagerness to share the gospel. He 'witnessed for Christ' on the bus home, to his work colleagues, in market stalls and in the local hospital. Within a month a

---

[176] Roberts, SU Prayer Letter No.11, 13 September 1967; Roberts, Pilgrims of the Scripture Union, Newsletter No.3, 26 March 1968; Roberts, *Life and Death*, 33-4, 36.

[177] New Life for All was initiated in Nigeria's Middle Belt by SIM missionary Gerald Swank in 1964. For more on New Life for All, see Eileen Lagaar, *New Life for All*, London: Oliphants, 1969.

[178] Roberts, SU Prayer Letter no.17, 7 October 1969; Roberts, Letter to SU Groups Area Representatives, November 1969.

local SU group started which became the base for further evangelistic initiatives. Their 'gospel message' received a mixed reception, but gradually people began 'to understand the difference between being religious and being a Christian'. In revivalist rhetoric, the term 'religious' had negative connotations, implying a nominal form of Christianity that stressed outward ritual rather than personal faith in Christ. Ogugua equates this with the Roman Catholic Mission, the main denomination in the area, which had built a hospital, three secondary schools, a seminary and a large church in the town.[179]

Innovative use of music was another way revivalists adapted their strategies to attract prospective converts. Songs were a feature of SU activities during the war and proved popular within a culture where music is an important element of indigenous piety. Initially they sang mainly Western gospel songs rather than ones produced locally, but later new songs were composed in English and the vernacular. Biafran soldiers used to march to battle singing motivational songs, and post-war revivalists adopted this approach as they trekked from place to place to spread the gospel. Singing choruses was both an act of worship, a means of reinforcing their identity as gospel carriers, a conscious effort to attract people to listen to their message, and a channel through which the message was conveyed.

Members of SU Umuahia became aggressive evangelists, visiting homes, market stores, army camps, refugee camps, and hospitals to preach and pray for the sick and wounded. With the close of the war and removal of restrictions, there was a significant increase in evangelistic activities, particularly in urban areas. Enthusiastic young Christians, stirred by vivid conversion experiences, carried the gospel onto the streets and organised extensive evangelistic campaigns where they not only called on people to repent, but offered prayers for healing and deliverance. This approach was generally absent in existing religious institutions and created tensions between revivalists and their elders in church and community.[180]

Hour of Freedom popularised 'crusade' evangelism during the revival. Here global influences came into play. Stephen Okafor was impressed by the emphasis on mass evangelism in the writings of American Pentecostal evangelist, T. L. Osborn, readily available in Nigeria during the early 1970s. In one of his books, Osborn wrote: 'For years I have stood on crude open-air platforms before multitudes of underprivileged people, interspersed with lepers, demoniacs, witchdoctors, and hopelessly diseased

---

[179] Justin Ogugua, 'Testimony on war-time experiences', written testimony, 1969.

[180] Exceptions included Assemblies of God and evangelical-type prayer houses such as Christ Holy Church and St. Joseph's Chosen Church of God, who all engaged in open-air evangelism.

victims. I have preached Christ to these masses when it was all I could do to hold back tears of human sympathy'. Osborn refers to two types of evangelism practiced by the early Christians in the book of Acts: mass evangelism and personal evangelism.[181] It was the image of the mass evangelist, liberated from the confines of the church building, which inspired Stephen Okafor and changed the shape of the movement. This approach clashed with official SU policy and created tensions between leaders and members. Okafor and his co-workers carried the gospel beyond church boundaries, often trekking long distances to do so, and encouraged new recruits to organise 'crusades' in their hometowns or villages. On one occasion, members of Hour of Freedom walked from Awka-Etiti (near Onitsha) to Umuahia, a distance of about 175 miles, singing songs and preaching the gospel along the way. This later became known as the 'Great Trek'. A typical Hour of Freedom meeting lasted from 1.00 pm to 8.00 pm and consisted of worship and preaching, interspersed with prayers and testimonies. Choruses, sung in English or the vernacular, were often of local origin. The sermon was the focus of the meeting, usually delivered in English by a male leader of Hour of Freedom or a visiting evangelist, with Igbo interpretation. The 'altar call' was an important ritual and provided an opportunity for people to receive prayer for salvation, healing, Holy Spirit baptism and occasionally deliverance. Counselling and follow-up of new converts took place after the meeting.[182]

Iconoclasm, as we have noted, was another strategy employed during the revival. This was reminiscent of early mission initiatives in Igbo land, but had declined among second-generation converts. Revivalists, themselves chiefly third-generation Christians, preached a message that was equally intolerant of traditional and 'occult' practices. They required those involved in 'traditional' and 'occult' activity to demonstrate their commitment to 'born-again' Christianity by burning their shrines, idols and other traditional or 'occult' paraphernalia. This was the strategy adopted by Hour of Freedom. The destruction of previous objects of worship and 'occult' material was considered a mark of repentance, but was also part of a power encounter motif, a demonstration of the superior power of Christ over alternative sources of power, whether Igbo gods or other malign forces. A former revivalist described the occasion when he destroyed the idols in his family compound: 'One day when I had returned on holidays,

---

[181] T. L. Osborn, *Soulwinning out where the Sinners are*, 7th ed., Tulsa: Osborn Foundation, 1966, 49. I came across this book in an Igbo Christian bookshop. It had been reprinted by former Igbo revivalist and neo-Pentecostal pioneer Jonathan Ikegwuonu, co-founder of Save the Lost Mission and founder of Life Care Ministry International.

[182] See Raphael Okafor, Journal, quoted in Bolton, *Glory*, 106-36; Bolton, *Glory*, 156-57.

being filled with the power of the Holy Ghost, I was anxious to see that idol worship would not continue in my father's compound. By God's power in me, I destroyed all I could see of the idols and graven images'.[183]

Central to this power encounter motif was an emphasis on healing which partly arose in response to the civil war crisis and socio-economic climate and preceded the introduction of Pentecostal doctrine. Prayer-healing rituals evolved in the early stages of the revival but became more sophisticated and popular after the war. Scripture Union members in Umuahia and other Igbo towns would regularly visit Biafran hospitals to pray for the sick or wounded. Note this episode recorded in Justin Ogugua's war-time testimony:

> There was the case of a lady patient in the hospital. . . . When I was beside her bed, she told me that she had been operated upon three times and the doctor presently caring for her did not seem hopeful of helping her. She was really frustrated. Because I was in a hurry I promised to introduce another Doctor to her who will cure her with immediate effect by that afternoon. I later went back and gave her the gospel message. She received it with joy after which I told her of Christ's healing power. We then prayed for her to be healed of her illness. She left the hospital a few days later, fully healed. When I saw her some weeks later, she told me how the Lord healed her.[184]

But it was in rural areas, where access to medical facilities was restricted, that healing practices were more commonplace. One informant told me he began to pray for the sick in 1968 when he became cut off behind enemy lines. 'There was no hospital, there was nowhere to go, the whole place was sealed off, and I just prayed, people got well'.[185] The Bible and American Pentecostal literature also acted as stimulants for revivalist healing rituals, especially after the war, and by 1971, healing prayers had become a regular feature of evangelistic events organised by Hour of Freedom and other charismatic ministries. Yet it was not until 1973 that this practice became a dominant feature of the movement.

Raphael Okafor's journal entries are filled with references to healing prayers, usually in the context of Hour of Freedom evangelistic campaigns. For example, the entry for the 4 April 1971: 'Brother Stephen preached concentrating on "Come to me all ye who labour and are heavy laden and I will give you rest". The altar call was great with at least 60-70 people.

---

183 Simon Ugwuoke, 'Testimonies of my Christian life', written testimony, 1969.

184 Justin O. Ogugua, 'Testimony on war-time experiences', 1969.

185 Interview, Cyril Okorocha, 8 February 1999, Woking.

After this special prayers were said for the sick people and many raised up their hands testifying to instantaneous healing'.[186] And Bolton records the healing of three blind people during the Unwana crusade of August 1971.[187] Revivalists also claimed to have witnessed instances of resuscitations.[188] Emmanuel Okorie (founder of Living Word Ministries, Aba) recalled the case of a woman called Patience Abongowe, apparently raised from the dead through his prayers during an evangelistic campaign in the early 1970s, an event that boosted his reputation as an evangelist and raised his profile in Eastern Nigeria. Its prominence in later LWM publications suggests that it was often retold and circulated among members as a means of legitimising his ministry.[189] Healing rituals became popular because they resonated with biblical and traditional worldviews, and appealed to those affected by the civil war crisis.

Deliverance prayer sometimes occurred during the Civil War Revival, usually in an evangelistic setting, but was not a common theme in revivalist narratives. Raphael Okafor's journal records occasions when prayers for deliverance were offered during Hour of Freedom evangelistic campaigns. For example, the entry for the 5 April 1971: 'He [Godson Ogbansiegbe] spoke from "The Son of Man has come to save that which is lost" and expounded Revelation 21:8. Bigger altar call today, about 100. Then we prayed for their healing and deliverance'.[190] Several former revivalists said they were involved in 'deliverance ministry' during the early 1970s, and one informant recalled his personal experience of deliverance from 'evil spirits' in 1971, following prayer by Stephen Okafor. Those who underwent deliverance normally had some previous contact with prayer houses, 'occult' groups or traditional religion.

Why was there this sense of urgency to preach the gospel, and where did the youthful evangelists acquire the courage to confront their elders in church and community? Here we return to Emezue's narrative account of evangelism in Ossah village and the discourse of spiritual warfare. If we recall, the identity of being born-again equipped revivalists with tools to challenge gerontocratic authority. In this case, the young protagonists imagined themselves caught up in a cosmic battle and confronted by hostile forces. Their new identity, forged from personal experience and biblical motifs, enabled them to preach the gospel to parents, community elders and traditional religious practitioners without fear or shame. The Bible not only

---

[186] Quoted in Bolton, *Glory* 114-13.

[187] Bolton, *Glory*, 123.

[188] On two occasions, Hour of Freedom evangelists prayed for people who were apparently raised from the dead. See Bolton, *Glory*, 41-2.

[189] Interview, Emmanuel Okorie, 17 January 2002, Aba. The story appears on the church's 2002 calender and in one of their magazines (*Forum*, 2001).

[190] Quoted in Bolton, *Glory*, 113.

formed an authoritative base from which to challenge their community, it shaped their conception of the missionary task itself. Preaching the gospel was an act of obedience and an urgent priority, because 'souls were passing to eternity without Jesus'. As an army engaged in combat they anticipated opposition and welcomed suffering as an opportunity to 'glorify His Holy Name'. But Christ, their 'Captain and Strength', was ready to fight for them. In keeping with traditional thought, they believed that prayer went straight to the divine source of power. 'We went on our knees and prayed for more power. . . . Our fears were transformed into power and we started thanking God for counting us worthy to suffer for the Name'. And they discovered, as they 'moved out in groups', that they could draw strength from one another. So the combined effects of their 'born-again' experience, exposure to the Bible, communal prayer, and Christian fellowship were sufficient to sustain them when God granted 'an occasion to stand for Him'.[191]

In revivalist discourse, adventist beliefs also added urgency to evangelism. Protagonists were motivated by an expectation of Christ's imminent return and saw themselves as God's end time messengers. There are echoes here of early US American Pentecostal missionary fervour, which was characterised by a similar eschatological urgency.[192] In the case of Igbo revivalists, this conviction was derived from the Bible and Christian literature, but was strengthened by the war situation. Similar beliefs continued to influence their gospel presentation after the war. As one post-war participant stated, an expectancy of Christ's imminent return was behind everything they did and said, including evangelism.

It was this urge to engage in aggressive evangelism which led to tensions within Scripture Union and directly contributed to the formation of autonomous charismatic fellowships. The latter's commitment to mission was reflected in the names they adopted, such as Hour of Freedom Evangelistic Association, Holiness Evangelistic Association, Save the Lost Programme, Last Days Messengers, and National Evangelistic Association. As an organisation SU was also committed to evangelism, but wished to restrict evangelistic activities to its own groups and was reluctant to move beyond these boundaries. When, for example, Hour of Freedom first carried the gospel onto the streets of Onitsha and engaged in 'mass evangelism', they encountered opposition from SU leaders. It was similar in other Igbo urban areas. In Umuahia, Obiorah and Uhiara started Master's Vessel Group as an independent evangelistic ministry because they felt constrained by SU policy. Tensions also occurred in Enugu

---

[191] Emezue, 'New Year's Victory', 1969.

[192] L. Grant McClung, Jr., 'Pentecostal/Charismatic Perspectives on a Missiology for the Twenty-First Century', *Pneuma*, 16.1, Spring 1994, 14.

township group when members began to engage in house to house evangelism and organise open-air crusades.

Other revivalists channelled their evangelistic urges into forming indigenous cross-cultural missionary organisations. Calvary Ministries (CAPRO), founded in the predominantly Muslim city of Zaria (Northern Nigeria) in 1975 by young people associated with the National Youth Service Corps (NYSC), was the first non-denominational indigenous mission agency in Nigeria. Two of the principal actors, Bayo Famunore and Peter Ozodo, were influenced by the revival in Eastern and Western Nigeria. Famunore, a Yoruba from Western Nigeria, was 'born-again' in 1967 through Scripture Union and mentored by Mike Oye. He was briefly involved in the charismatic renewal west of the Niger before proceeding to the University of Nigeria (Nsukka) in 1971, where he became ECU President and came into contact with the revival in Igboland. In 1974, he left Nsukka to embark on his NYSC programme in Zaria. Peter Ozodo, an Igbo from the Midwestern region, was 'born-again' through the witness of a Baptist missionary and attended the University of Ife (now Obafemi Awolowo University) from 1969 to 1973, where he too became ECU President and came under the influence of S. G. Elton. Although he was from the predominantly Igbo town of Asaba, his admission to the University of Ife exposed him to the revival in Western Nigeria. In 1973, he too moved to Zaria for his NYSC programme. Initially, CAPRO concentrated on unreached people groups in Northern Nigeria, but by 1980 it had several missionaries working in the Gambia and Niger. It describes itself as 'an indigenous cross-cultural missionary movement taking the gospel to the remaining unevangelized parts of the world starting from Northern Nigeria and West Africa sub-region'.[193] Another leading indigenous missionary society, Christian Missionary Foundation, was founded in 1982 by Reuben Ezemadu, a Biafran army veteran and a convert of the Civil War Revival. After his conversion in 1970, he worked with the Assemblies of God in Igboland before attending the University of Ibadan from 1974 to 1978. CMF sent its first missionary, Philomena Chinwe Onochie, to Cote d'Ivoire in 1982, and by 1984, it was working in eight African countries.[194]

---

[193] *Occupy*, Vol.16, Nos.3 & 4, 1997, 2.

[194] For more on Nigerian indigenous mission agencies, see Matthews A. Ojo, 'The Dynamics of Indigenous Charismatic Missionary Enterprises in West Africa', *Missionalia*, 25.4, December 1997, 537-61; Wale Banks & Wale Olaniyan, *Nigerian Indigenous Missions: Pioneers Behind the Scene*, Ibadan: Alliance Research Network International, 2005.

Pentecostal Infiltration

Holy Spirit baptism also equipped protagonists with tools to challenge their communities and engage in aggressive evangelism. There has been a tendency among scholars of contemporary African Christianity to blur the distinction between 'born-again' and neo-Pentecostal identity.[195] One reason for this is the use of the term 'born-again' to signify the neo-Pentecostal community by African Christians themselves, both inside and outside the movement.[196] Igbo neo-Pentecostalism emerged from the womb of the Civil War Revival. Yet in revivalist discourse, a clear distinction is made between new birth and Holy Spirit baptism. A definite 'born-again' identity existed prior to the introduction of Pentecostal doctrines.

During the revival, why did so many members of mainline churches embrace the Pentecostal experience, and how did this process take place? To answer these questions, we return to the issue of conversion and take note of elements of continuity and rupture, as well as local and external influences. Revival narratives suggest that Pentecostal appropriation was consistent with the quest for power to enhance life and was stimulated by local contingencies and external forces. Yet in contrast to new birth, Pentecostal conversion was primarily associated with power for *service*. In its early civil war phase, the revival had no close links with Pentecostal denominations. The Assemblies of God (AG) did have a strong base in Umuahia, but most early protagonists were Anglicans and Methodists. As the movement progressed, a growing desire developed among members of SU Umuahia for a deeper experience of the Spirit, for revival to break out in the land, and for increased effectiveness in witness.[197] Gradually two distinct but inter-related strands of discourse on the Holy Spirit emerged, both drawing upon biblical motifs and Western theological traditions.

As noted above, Keswick teaching was an important early influence. This branch of the Holiness Movement regarded 'full surrender' as the decisive crisis experience after conversion, enabling the individual to

---

[195] The studies I have in mind include Marshall-Fratani, 'Global', 285; Hackett, 'Charismatic/Pentecostal'; Kalu, 'Third Response', 8; Rijk van Dijk, 'Young Puritan Preachers in Post Independence Malawi', *Africa*, 62.2, 1992, 159-80.

[196] For the Igbo context, see Amaechi Nwachukwu, 'How Born Again are the Born-agains?', *Livingspring*, May/June 1997, 3-7; Amaechi Nwachukwu, *How Born-again are the Born-agains?*, Enugu: Livingspring Communications, 2002.

[197] Roberts, SU Prayer Letter No.15, 7/8 November, 1968; Roberts, *Life and Death*, 69.

receive the infilling of the Spirit by faith.[198] The later Keswick tradition, reacting against the divisive nature of the Pentecostal doctrine of initial evidence, taught that the fullness of the Spirit is obtained through growth in sanctification rather than a second experience involving empowering for service.[199] Early revival narratives contain both versions. For example, a member of SU Umuahia wrote, 'I accepted Christ as my personal saviour on Sunday 15th November 1967 . . . but was not separate from the world. Not until 13th February 1968 I decided and surrendered my life absolutely to Him'.[200] Rather than using the term 'baptism of the Holy Spirit', early revivalists talked about 'being surrendered to Jesus' or 'being set on fire for Christ'. Sometimes this fire motif was associated with a religious experience whereby individuals felt a burning sensation on their bodies and saw flames of fire while praying. It was interpreted as the work of the Spirit purifying them from sin and giving renewed zeal for evangelism. Roberts himself was heartened by this new interest in the Holy Spirit, but taught that the fullness of the Spirit was a 'continual, day by day, process' of yielding in obedience to God.[201]

The gradual infiltration of Pentecostal doctrine occurred from the movement's inception, initially through Assemblies of God members attached to SU Umuahia, keen to promote Spirit baptism and 'tongues' as initial evidence (at least three AG members were attending SU Umuahia meetings as early as October 1967). But its introduction was contested. Here the global evangelical culture exported by Scripture Union's British headquarters clashed with local aspirations. The following is a statement on the doctrine of the Spirit written by Tony Wilmot (a British expatriate worker and SU leader) and adopted by SU Nigeria Council in May 1970. It was an attempt to curtail excesses and discourage behaviour which might interfere with SU's interdenominational stance and 'responsible church policy', intended to encourage members to remain in their churches and bring renewal from within.

> The Scripture Union recognises that the Scriptures teach both the baptism of the Spirit and the gifts of the Spirit. We hold the person and work of the Holy Spirit to be subjects of great preciousness to the believer and we notice with regret that these subjects, which call for great reverence, have in recent times become increasingly matters of contention. It is our united resolution that preaching likely to stimulate contention about gifts

[198] Fiedler, *Faith Missions*, 215.

[199] Richard F. Lovelace, *Dynamics of Spiritual Life: An Evangelical Theology of Renewal*, Exeter: Paternoster, 1979, 121-22.

[200] John Nwangwu, written testimony, 1969.

[201] Roberts, *Life and Death*, 69.

> such as 'tongues' or healing or miracles shall not be given at Scripture Union meetings or in association with the name of the Scripture Union. We counsel all staff workers, voluntary helpers and speakers at Scripture Union meetings to exercise restraint in this matter. Let everything be done decently and in order: make love your aim. The fruit of the Spirit is self-control.[202]

Roberts and senior SU members resisted Pentecostal doctrine and practice because they felt it was divisive and threatened the unity of the fellowship. They also believed that focusing on signs, such as tongues and healing miracles, could distract people from seeking after the infilling of the Holy Spirit. Towards the end of the war, the SU committee in Biafra expressed concern over the infiltration of certain Pentecostal doctrines and practices over the previous eighteen months. These included tongues as initial evidence of Holy Spirit baptism, healing without the use of medicine, an overemphasis on fasting and excessive emotionalism.[203] Yet as SU groups were established further afield, exposure to Pentecostal influences increased. More members came from Pentecostal churches, and Assemblies of God pastors became regular speakers at evangelistic guest services. Thus there were clear elements of continuity between the Civil War Revival and earlier movements of Pentecostal activity. Towards the end of the war, SU members began to leave the mainline churches to join AG and other Pentecostal churches, a development opposed by Roberts and some senior SU leaders.

After the war, there was a significant shift away from the Keswick emphasis on 'full surrender' towards a full-blown theology of Holy Spirit baptism. This gradually came to dominate the revival and provided the foundation for other features such as tongues, healing miracles, holiness and prophecy. Sixty-seven out of seventy-nine participants interviewed claimed to have received the experience. Out of thirty-three revivalists who told me the timing of their 'baptism', five received before the war (two were AG members at the time), two during the war, twenty between 1970 and 1973, four between 1974 and 1979, and two between 1980 and 1989. The experience sometimes occurred spontaneously in private or communal settings, particularly in the early post-war phase, but also at special meetings set aside for Christians to 'pray through'. For instance, out of twenty informants who received the 'baptism' between 1970 and 1973, six received on their own; four during communal prayer meetings (with no

---

[202] SU (Nigeria), Minutes of the 6th Meeting of Council, 2 May 1970, Ibadan, 3.

[203] Roberts, SU Prayer Letter No.18, 29 December 1969.

advocate); three through the laying on of hands; one while preaching; and six in an unknown context.

Pentecostal infiltration after the war was facilitated by local contingencies, exposure to the Bible and American Pentecostal literature, and human agency. The departure of Roberts towards the end of 1969 was a significant event, as was the spread of the revival to other urban areas where protagonists encountered a variety of Pentecostal influences. In the Onitsha area, for example, SU members became more receptive when Hour of Freedom evangelist Stephen Okafor started to promote Spirit baptism after working alongside Pentecostal SU travelling secretaries Oye and Olamijulo in early 1970. The arrival of J. M. J. Emesim and the presence of Pentecostal speakers at SU Onitsha events were also significant developments.[204] In other Igbo urban centres, the attitude of SU members changed as they read American Pentecostal literature and mixed freely with Pentecostals from Assemblies of God and other groups. There was also a snowballing effect as revivalists observed the impact of Spirit baptism upon their friends. Sometimes Pentecostal manifestations occurred without any apparent external influences, as in the case of one SU group in Umuahia who experienced a spontaneous 'outpouring of the Holy Spirit', accompanied by the gift of tongues, after a period of prayer and fasting in early 1970. Subsequently, Pentecostalism spread throughout the work of Scripture Union in the East.

Pentecostal appropriation was closely associated with the significant increase in evangelistic activity after the war and the search for power to enhance life. New challenges require new responses. If we recall, power encounter was an important mission strategy and revivalists wished to demonstrate Christ's superiority over alternative power brokers. Hour of Freedom evangelist Raphael Okafor told me, 'People are suffering and they needed a demonstration of power. . . . The occult people are there, the native doctors are there; we must demonstrate the power of the Holy Spirit'.[205] The Pentecostal message was attractive because of its close correspondence to traditional religious piety and biblical motifs. It emphasised the power of the Spirit, accepted the reality of the old deities (while demonising them), and provided alternative means for healing and protection from evil. As such, it represented a form of Africanisation 'from below' which differed from that proposed by African theologians.

If we move from motives to consequences, the consensus among informants was that Spirit baptism empowered them for more effective service, giving increased 'boldness' to witness and ability to exercise

---

[204] These included Godson Ogbansiegbe (Christian Fellowship Group), J. M. J. Emesim (Hour of Deliverance Ministry), British Pentecostal missionary S. G. Elton, and various Assemblies of God pastors.

[205] Interview, 8 May 2000, Enugu.

spiritual gifts, especially healing. In nearly every case, informants knew they had received when they spoke in tongues. Cox believes that tongues-speaking as ecstatic utterance is an example of Pentecostalism's 'power to tap into a deep substratum of human religiosity'.[206] It was especially appealing in the Igbo context where ecstatic states are traditionally associated with spiritual empowerment, divination and prophecy.[207] Moreover, as a form of cathartic expression it allowed Igbos to express their sense of injustice and loss following the war.

Prophecy was a feature of the revival, though not a major emphasis, and sometimes took place in evangelistic settings during prayer meetings. Here I use the term 'prophecy' in a broad sense to include visions and dreams which are not necessarily expressed in oracular speech. In revivalist discourse, they were often lumped together, as we see in this letter extract: 'Many went as far as forming S.U. prayer bands in the school, where S.U. members see vision, prophesy and dream dreams'.[208] Prophetic revelations were not always associated with Spirit baptism. Occasionally they were features of conversion narratives and calls to ministry as this dream narrated by former Hour of Freedom evangelist Augustine Nwodika shows:

> I just saw myself in a very big field, and there were thousands and thousands of people. So I walked straight to the platform there, and then the men sitting down there, one of them got up, and gave me the Bible and said, 'you are the preacher'. . . . I started preaching, and I was preaching repentance and the coming of Jesus. So people were crying, something I have never in my life experienced. I started crying too. Then I woke up; the whole thing was dream. I went on my knees and started to cry, 'Lord, save me, change me, come into my life, change me'. . . . I woke up in the morning, I started preaching. I was just running around like a mad man, preaching everywhere, crying, begging people to repent, that the Lord was coming. . . . Finally I left what I was doing at Calabar and came back home. So when I came back, I met some people that had got an experience of new birth; so we met up together and started preaching. From there '71 I came out fulltime.[209]

---

[206] Cox, *Fire*, 91.

[207] Okorocha, *Religious Conversion*, 141-2; Udobata Onunwa, *Studies in Igbo Traditional Religion*, Obosi/Anambra: Pacific, 1990, 58-93.

[208] Chuma G. Obijiofor, Letter to Roberts, 24 August 1972.

[209] Interview, 8 May 2000, Enugu.

In African religious movements dreams are sometimes useful for validating a person's faith or legitimizing the message of charismatic figures.[210] While they were not common among my informants, Nwodika's functioned as a mnemonic device for recalling his core message (repentance and the imminent return of Christ) and reinforcing his identity as a born-again member of the revival community. Occasionally prophecies contained predictions. One informant said that he received a 'revelation' in 1969 that the civil war would soon end. Another told me of an occasion in 1972 when Hour of Freedom evangelist Stephen Okafor predicted that his wife who was barren would have a child. But prophecies were normally in the form of exhortation rather than prediction and closely aligned with Scripture.[211] After the war, they usually contained words of consolation, but were sometimes directed towards exposing sin or warning against imminent dangers. We see this in the following entry from Raphael Okafor's journal, quoted in Bolton's revival account: 'During my morning prayers this morning I fell into a sort of trance. I was given a message to sister Kate Okafor. Serious message of danger to sister Regina Okafor'. The sequel to this prophecy is in a subsequent journal entry: 'An interesting letter of testimony from Uzuakoli . . . . Regina left their meeting and came down with a serious complaint of head trouble. We prayed together. She was almost unconscious'.[212] In her narrative, Bolton juxtaposes these episodes to show the way that predictive prophecy combined with prayer could sometimes alleviate potentially dangerous situations.

Igbo culture has a strong prophetic tradition running right up to the civil war period. Prophets or seers (*Ndị Ọhụ* or *Onye-Ọhụ*) are believed to consult the ancestors or receive revelations from the deities of impending danger or future events and often emerge at times of imminent crisis. Sometimes they also denounce the sins and social ills of their communities. For example, Madam Nwaekwe, who prophesied during the late 1890s, apparently predicted the coming of white colonialists to her district, and Mazị Uzokwe, a prophet of the Igbo deity *Idemmili*, foretold the influenza epidemic of 1917/18, the Women's Riot of 1929 and the advent of the Nigerian civil war.[213] Charismatic figures with strong prophetic gifts were also responsible for starting some of the many prayer houses that littered the Igbo religious landscape. Given this background and its location in a

---

[210] M. L. Daneel, *The God of the Matopo Hills*, The Hague: Mouton and Company, 1970; Richard T. Curley, 'Dreams of Power: Social Process in a West African Religious Movement', *Africa*, 53, 1983, 20-37.

[211] Bolton, *Glory,* 130.

[212] Raphael Okafor, Journal, 19 & 25 October 1971, quoted in Bolton, *Glory*, 150-51.

[213] Nwala, *Igbo Philosophy*, 125; Onunwa, *Igbo Traditional Religion*, 61, 66-72.

context of crisis, it is surprising that prophecy was relatively rare during the revival.[214] Reasons given by informants included the revival's strong Christological and Biblical focus, which rendered prophecy redundant, and reaction against the excessive use of visions in the prayer houses.

Pentecostal infiltration exacerbated tensions within Scripture Union and contributed towards the emergence of autonomous charismatic fellowships as some members claimed authority to challenge the authority structures in church and community. The flexible structures of SU facilitated the introduction of Pentecostal spirituality into its ranks as members from mission churches mixed freely with those from Pentecostal churches and gradually assimilated their doctrine of Spirit baptism and their experience of charismatic gifts. The insistence on tongues as initial evidence of Holy Spirit baptism aggravated tensions within SU and aroused the hostility of mainline church authorities.

Conclusion

The Biafran crisis exposed the deficiencies of existing religious options and created a favourable environment for a revival which was evangelical in its origins due to its Scripture Union roots, but quickly acquired a Pentecostal spirituality. The revival flourished because it adapted successively to new and challenging contexts. It resacralised the landscape in Christian terms by bringing renewal to existing churches, generating new theological emphases 'from below', and precipitating fresh mission initiatives. Many Igbos found the dominant brand of Christianity, represented by mainline churches, lacked the power to help them fulfil their deep-seated aspirations, cope with the stresses engendered by the war, and engage effectively in mission. Hence their attraction to 'born-again' Christianity with its potential for transformation, and to Pentecostalism with its reliance on direct experience of the divine, its affirmation of lesser spiritual entities, and its promise of power for healing and deliverance. The revival was a response to the crisis generated by decolonisation and civil war, but

[214] Various scholars have noted the connection between prophets/prophecies and local/large-scale crises. For a discussion, see Douglas M. Johnson and David M. Anderson, 'Revealing Prophets', in Douglas M. Johnson and David M. Anderson (eds.), *Revealing Prophets; Prophesy in Eastern African History*, London: James Currey, 1-26; Misty L. Bastion, 'A Tale of Two Visionaries: Father Edeh, Sister Kate and Visions of the Everyday in Southeastern Nigeria', unpublished paper presented at the symposium 'Prophets, Visionaries and their Publics in the Afro-Atlantic World', University of Maryland-College Park, October 9 and 10, 1998, 4.

received significant impulses from outside and was part of a larger global movement.

It also challenged the moral economy and contested existing denominational, social, and ethnic boundaries. As a lay movement, it provided new opportunities for neglected forces and contributed to the development of an indigenous Christian community free from missionary and clerical control. More importantly, perhaps, it provided a means for Igbos to resolve their collective identity crisis through their absorption into a dynamic missionary fellowship. And it was the formation of this band of itinerant preachers which was principally responsible for its success.

Despite its ecumenical and evangelical ideals, Scripture Union set in motion certain trends that hastened the fragmentation of the movement as autonomous charismatic fellowship groups emerged from its ranks. By opening up space for young people to assume leadership roles and acquire ministerial skills, SU sowed seeds of dissent within gerontocratic and male-dominated structures of society as members responded to modernity's call to make a clean break from the past. Born-again conversion and Holy Spirit baptism supplied revivalists with tools to challenge gerontocracy and reposition themselves with respect to existing religious and social relations. But this challenge proceeded from the revival's missionary impulse rather than a desire to break free from control of elder males or construct identities modelled on the autonomous secular subject of modernity. No longer content to remain on the margins, their aggressive evangelistic style, radical stance on moral issues, and adoption of Pentecostal spirituality created tensions within SU and alienated the young revivalists from elders in church and community. As the SU fellowship became the source of spiritual sustenance for a growing number of young people, links with existing denominations became increasingly fragile, facilitating the emergence of autonomous charismatic fellowships. Yet it is uncertain whether these would have evolved into fully-fledged churches if several other conditions had not been in place. This will be the focus of chapter 4.

Chapter 4

Neo-Pentecostal Church Origins, 1970-83

This chapter explores factors behind the transition of autonomous charismatic fellowship groups to denominational status.[1] Compared to Western Nigeria, this transition was relatively swift and was partly precipitated by local contingencies. It led to significant mission initiatives but ultimately resulted in the movement's fragmentation as institutional forces overtook charismatic impulses and leaders struggled for control. In his study of the Aladura movement among the Yoruba, Peel refers to the crucial importance of exploring the origins of African churches, and in particular the social factors that caused them to emerge, if one is to understand their nature.[2] While there is a considerable body of literature on the origins and growth of early African initiated churches, there is comparatively little on African neo-Pentecostal churches. Although the two groups arose in different settings, both emerged during periods of rapid social change and in contexts dominated by mainline churches. Hence, I will draw upon material relating to AICs and new religious movements in Africa.

I also use insights from the sociology of religion and in particular the church-sect typology derived from Weber and Troeltsch.[3] In sociological discourse, a church is a large well-established religious institution like the Anglican or Catholic Church. Sects are voluntary associations, with membership based on certain qualifications (a conversion experience, for example), and existing in a state of tension with their social environment and established churches. They tend to encourage the cultivation of counter cultural lifestyles and regard themselves as 'protest movements'. The church-sect typology has been further developed to include the denomination. A denomination is a sect that has lost its radical edge and become institutionalised.[4] For sociologists Rodney Stark and William

[1] I have chosen 1983 as a cut off point because by this time most of the early secessions from mission churches had taken place. It also marked the end of Nigeria's Second Republic.

[2] Peel, *Aladura*, 13.

[3] For example, Ernst Troeltsch, *The Social Teaching of the Christian Churches*, New York: Macmillan, 1931.

[4] Niebuhr was the first to note the tendency for sects to become denominations. See H. R. Niebuhr, *The Social Sources of Denominationalism*, New York: World Publishing, 1957.

Bainbridge, the key criteria of sects are deviance and breakaway from established religious organisations.[5] Another important distinction is between church-like tendencies of compromise with the world and the sectarian orientation of hostility towards the world.

Bryan Wilson picks up this theme of orientation towards the world in his typology of religious sects. Instead of classifying them theologically in terms of doctrine or sociologically by the degree of institutionalisation achieved, he analyses them in terms of their dominant social orientation or 'response to the world'. Wilson applies this model to movements outside western Christendom, including the Aladura churches in Nigeria, and examines ideal-types of sectarian response to the world and their transformations as they attain denominational status.[6] Of particular relevance are Wilson's conversionist sects, associated with evangelical Protestantism, revivalism and global Pentecostalism, which emphasise individual change as the appropriate response to a corrupt world. Members of conversionist sects initially gather around the ministry of the revivalist whose activity led to their conversion.[7] More recently, Wilson has distinguished between world-denying, world-indifferent and world-enhancing sectarian responses. World-denying sects emphasise the evil of the world; world-indifferent sects tolerate the world but encourage members to pursue puritan lifestyles; world-enhancing sects encourage members to enjoy life in the world.[8]

There is some disagreement as to the appropriateness of using the church-sect typology as a descriptive model for analysing African religious movements. Those who use the term 'sect' to describe AICs usually do so in a loose sense to distinguish them from the mainline churches, but sometimes pejoratively to connote deviancy or separatist tendencies, or to reinforce the allegation that they recruit members from existing denominations. Objections to the use of the church-sect typology in an African context focus on its Western orientation and its tendency to present local movements as sectarian responses rather than indigenous initiatives with different cultural and historical roots from those of existing

---

[5] Rodney Stark and William Sims Bainbridge, 'Of Churches, Sects, and Cults: Preliminary Concepts for a Theory of Religious Movements', *Journal for the Scientific Study of Religion*, 18.2, 1979, 125.

[6] Bryan Wilson, *Magic and Millenniun. A Sociological Study of Religious Movements of Protest among Tribal and Third-World Peoples*, London: Heinemann, 1973, 18-9, 22-6.

[7] Bryan Wilson, *Religious Sects. A Sociological Study*, London: World University Library, 1970, 41-2, 51.

[8] Bryan Wilson, *Religion in Sociological Perspective*, Oxford: Oxford University Press, 1982, 111-12.

denominations.[9] However, despite its origins in Western culture, it is useful for analysing the tension between revivalism and institutionalisation, and the dialectic between sectarian and church-like orientation to the world. As Hackett notes, most Nigerian AIC leaders were raised in mission churches and aspired to a structured 'Western-type' church.[10] Here I use it in a neutral sense as an analytical device for exploring the changes which occurred as Igbo initiated charismatic fellowships evolved into denominations and as the new churches themselves underwent transformations. Igbo charismatic fellowships and early neo-Pentecostal churches fitted the profile of Wilson's 'world-denying' and conversionist sects, and bore a close resemblance to Marshall's 'holiness' churches referred to in her study of Nigerian Pentecostalism.[11] Later, as they became increasingly institutionalised and modified their message to include an emphasis on prosperity, they moved closer to Wilson's world-enhancing sects and to Marshall's 'pentecostal' churches.

A History of Neo-Pentecostal Beginnings[12]

The institution of Sunday services and the employment of full-time workers heralded the transition of charismatic fellowship groups to denominational status. In Western Nigeria, this phase began in the early 1980s. Two of the earliest Yoruba initiated NPCs were William Kumuyi's Deeper Life Bible Church and David Oyedepo's Living Faith Church, which became denominations in 1982 and 1985 respectively. Deeper Christian Life Ministry began as a Bible study group in the University of Lagos in 1973. The Ilorin-based Faith Liberation Hour Ministries, founded by Oyedepo in 1983, moved to Kaduna two years later where it became known as Living

---

[9] Turner, *Religious Innovation*, 58; Bennetta W. Jules-Rosette, 'Tradition and Continuity in African Religions. The Case of New Religious Movements', in Jacob K. Olupona (ed.), *African Traditional Religions in Contemporary Society*, New York: Paragon House, 1991, 152-53.

[10] Rosalind I. J. Hackett, 'Thirty Years of Growth and Change in a West African Independent Church: A Sociological Perspective', in Rosalind I. J. Hackett (ed.), *New Religious Movements in Nigeria*, New York: Edwin Mellen Press, 1987, 161-77.

[11] Marshall, 'Power', 216-17.

[12] For Igbo NPC history I have relied on oral sources and the following written sources: Kalu, *Embattled Gods*; Anyaegbu, 'Pentecostal/Evangelical'; Peter A. Okoroafor, *William Okoye: Called To Serve*, Abuja: The Whole Gospel Publications, 1996; Chukwuka, *Beyond the Night*.

Faith Church.[13] In Igboland, the transition occurred significantly earlier. By 1980, there were at least twenty-six neo-Pentecostal denominations scattered across the Igbo landscape, all with direct links to the Civil War Revival.

Table 4.1 Igbo-initiated Neo-Pentecostal Churches, 1970-83
(Note: year of origin in parentheses)

All Believers Fellowship Group (1978)
All Christians Fellowship Mission (1976)
Ambassadors for Christ Mission (1975)
Bethel Gospel Mission (1972)
Bible Faith Mission (1979)
Body of Christ Mission (1982)
Canaan Gospel Centre (1977)
Calvary Evangelistic Mission (1973)
Central Christian Fellowship Mission (1974)
Christ for All Mission (1974)
Christian Pentecostal Mission (1977)
Fullness of Christ Mission (1976)
Gospel Crusaders Mission (1974)
Gospel Mission (1974)
Grace of God Mission (1978)
Holiness Evangelical Church (1976)
Holy Ghost Ministry (1979)
Hour of Deliverance Ministry (1970)
Jesus the Way Mission (1976)
Last Days Messengers (1972)
Life Care Ministries (1981)
Master's Vessel Church (1976)
National Evangelical Mission (1975)
Redeeming Time Pilgrims (1973)
Redeemed People's Mission (1977)
Revival Time Ministries (1980)
Riches of Christ Mission (1973)
Salvation for All Mission (1980)
Save the Lost Mission (1974)

---

[13] Ojo, 'Charismatic Movements, 98, 101; Ojo, 'Deeper Christian Life Ministry', 150, Ojo, *Army*, 164-67. Arguably, the earliest Nigerian NPC of significance was the late Benson Idahosa's Church of God Mission with its headquarters in Benin City, Mid-Western Nigeria. It started as a Bible study group in 1970 and became a church in 1972.

Revivalists founded two important churches in Central Igboland during the 1970s: Last Days Messengers in Okigwe and Holiness Evangelistic Mission (now Holiness Evangelical Church) in Owerri. During the September 1966 pogroms, a young Methodist called Gabriel Nwokoro left the Northern city of Kaduna and returned to the East, where he joined SU Umuahia and became an itinerant evangelist. After the war he was briefly associated with Master's Vessel Group before starting his own church, Last Days Messengers, in 1972. In 1976, Holiness Evangelistic Mission, formed out of the Holiness Evangelistic Association and with links to Hour of Freedom, became the first major neo-Pentecostal denomination in Owerri. It has since spread beyond Igboland and has branches in the North.

Several new denominations started in Southern Igboland. Master's Vessel Group became a church in 1976 (Master's Vessel Church), though it began to exhibit denominational tendencies as early as 1974. It has grown slowly, partly because its co-founder Felix Obiorah left Nigeria in 1974 to study in the USA. Most of its branches are in Igboland, but it has also planted churches in the state capitals of Lagos, Kano, Kaduna, Port Harcourt and Uyo. Several other NPCs started in the vicinity of Umuahia during the 1970s, but all have remained relatively small. These include Bethel Gospel Mission (1972), Calvary Evangelistic Mission (1973), Canaan Gospel Centre (1977) and Believers Gospel Mission. In 1974, Gospel Crusaders Mission started in Aba as a breakaway from Godson Ogbansiegbe's Christian Fellowship Group, but it too has remained relatively localised.

In North-Western Igboland, the first neo-Pentecostal church was J. M. J. Emesim's Hour of Deliverance Ministry, which functioned as a church as early as 1970. Most early NPCs, however, were founded by former members of Hour of Freedom Evangelistic Association. Particularly important was Riches of Christ Mission, started in 1973 by five young men: Edozie Mba, Paul Nweke, Augustine Nwodika, Emeka Eze and Charles Nwafor.[14] Within two years, it had sixty-six congregations, formed from the original Hour of Freedom fellowship groups with major branches in the cities of Onitsha, Enugu and Aba.[15] Although a relatively small denomination today, Riches of Christ Mission is important because former members started other denominations. These include Grace of God Mission (1978), All Believers Fellowship Group (1978), All Christians Fellowship Mission (1979), Bible Faith Mission (1979), Living Faith (1985), Bread of Life Mission (1988), Higher Dimensions Ministries

---

[14] Before becoming neo-Pentecostal church pastors, Mba was a secondary school student and Biafran army veteran, Nweke was a businessman/trader, and Nwodika a cobbler and a pastor with Gospel Faith Mission, a Lagos-based Pentecostal denomination.

[15] Anyaegbu, 'Sabbatharianism', 187.

(1988), Overcomer's Bible Church (1991) and Throne of Grace Church (2000).

In 1974, three other important churches started in North-Western Igboland: Christ for All Mission (Onitsha), Save the Lost Mission (Nnewi), and Central Christian Fellowship Mission (Nnewi). Christ for All Mission was founded by former Anglican Benson Ezeokeke, a primary school teacher and one-time President of SU Onitsha, who received his Pentecostal credentials from Emesim's Hour of Deliverance Bible School at Aguleri. The principal catalyst behind the emergence of Save the Lost Mission was Tony Okeke, a former Roman Catholic and Biafran army veteran. He was the leader of SU Nnewi and attended Hour of Freedom activities before founding his own ministry, Save the Lost Programme in 1972. Influenced by British Pentecostal missionary S. G. Elton and Benson Idahosa, Okeke started Save the Lost Mission with two Anglican colleagues, John Okafor and Jonathan Ikegwonu. By 1976, they had established approximately thirteen branches. Central Christian Fellowship Mission was founded by another former Roman Catholic called Peter Maduako, a trader from Nnewi. Following his ejection from the Roman Catholic Church, Maduako joined the Assemblies of God and started an evangelistic ministry called the Christian Fellowship Association. This became a church in 1974, which has subsequently spread to other parts of North-Western Igboland.

There were elements of continuity between neo-Pentecostal churches and earlier waves of Nigerian Pentecostal and prayer house activity. At least eighteen neo-Pentecostal church pioneers (including eleven founders) had contact with prayer houses prior to the revival. For example, Benson Ezeokeke (Christ for All Mission) briefly attended Ufuma Practical Prayer Band; Tony Okeke (Save the Lost Mission) attended a sabbath prayer house; J. M. J. Emesim joined Light Apostolic Church in Lagos; and Dominic Onuigwe (National Evangelical Mission) was a member of Saviour Apostolic Church. Several attained positions of leadership in these organisations. Mike Okoye (All Christians Fellowship Mission) and Leo Anorue (Redeemed People's Mission) were ordained ministers in the Cherubim and Seraphim Society and St. Joseph's Chosen Church of God respectively. A number worked with the Free Gospel Society (FGS), a Lagos-based prayer house with a strong evangelistic emphasis founded in 1956 by Pastor J. O. Martins. Others were former members of mission related Pentecostal churches. Edozie Mba of Riches of Christ was introduced to Pentecostal experience at an Assemblies of God crusade in Lagos in 1972 and attended Foursquare Gospel Church where he was baptised by Wilson Badejo, the present General Overseer. Later, he became a member of Assemblies of God in Enugu.[16] Victor Onuigbo,

[16] *Ibid.*, 181-82.

founder of Victory Christian Mission, was a former member of Assemblies of God and Christ Apostolic Church.

By the mid-1970s, the ecumenical impulses of the revival which were still influencing emerging churches had begun to give way to schismatic tendencies. The need for institutional norms resulted in conflicts as leaders struggled for ascendancy. Problems began to emerge among leaders of Riches of Christ in 1975, and the following year Nweke and Nwodika left to form Jesus the Way Ministry after allegations of sexual misdemeanour and authoritarianism against Mba, the General Overseer.[17] Over the next year and a half, Jesus the Way grew rapidly as many Riches of Christ congregations joined them and other churches were planted. Conflicts also arose among the leadership of Save the Lost and for a time Okeke left to pursue an independent evangelistic ministry.

In 1978, a number of NPCs in the Onitsha area of North-Western Igboland came together to form Grace of God Mission, a development later referred to as the 'New Move'. This had a significant impact upon the neo-Pentecostal landscape.[18] Here we encounter problems associated with historical sources and conflicting accounts. According to Kalu, the British missionary S. G. Elton was the main catalyst behind the merger. The name Grace of God Mission was adopted because they believed that Elton's conciliatory role was evidence of the 'grace of God' bringing conviction and reconciliation.[19] The consensus among my informants, however, was that it was initiated by a prophecy delivered by a visiting Yoruba Pentecostal from Lagos called Samuel Adeyemi, encouraging the merger of Riches of Christ and Jesus the Way, and promoting the idea of one united church in each urban location, with Onitsha as the centre of Nigerian Christianity. It was not intended that older denominations (Pentecostal or non-Pentecostal) should be included in this venture. Other groups subsequently joined Riches of Christ and Jesus the Way, removing their signboards as a symbolic expression of their ecumenical sentiments. Benson Ezeokeke was appointed National Chairman of Grace of God Mission, Paul Nweke, National Superintendent, and Augustine Nwodika, pastor of the headquarters church at Onitsha.

There were differing reactions to the 'New Move' among neo-Pentecostals. Some referred to it as a fresh wave of revival. Others disapproved because they felt it failed to deal with the issues that had caused divisions in the first place. One informant objected to the merger

---

[17] According to Anyaegbu ('Sabbatharianism', 187), Nweke and Nwodika took twenty-two Riches of Christ congregations with them.

[18] See Okoroafor, *William Okoye*, 118; '"Dawn of a New Anointing". Supplement on Grace of God Mission International Inc.', *Prophecy. The Messiah is Coming*, 1996; Chukwuka, *Beyond the Night*, 38.

[19] Kalu, *Embattled Gods*, 278; Kalu, 'Passive Revolution', 273.

being imposed from above and disagreed with the designation of Onitsha as the 'Christian headquarters' of Nigeria. Concern was also expressed over legalistic tendencies, including special dress codes and the prohibition of musical instruments in worship. Among NPCs who chose not to join were Save the Lost Mission and National Evangelical Mission. Some Jesus the Way Mission churches outside Onitsha also refused to join and up to today have retained their independence and their name. Meanwhile, Wilson Uzumegbunam, a former leader of SU Onitsha and Riches of Christ pastor in Aba, broke away to form All Believers Fellowship Group. So even in the midst of this ecumenical initiative, there were voices of dissent.

Unfortunately, the movement's fissiparous nature again reared its head as leadership struggles within Grace of God Mission led to further fragmentation. In 1979, Mba withdrew taking some of his pastors with him. Riches of Christ Mission continues to this day but as a relatively small denomination. It suffered a further crisis in 1988 after Mba returned from a visit to the USA a confirmed sabbatharian, prompting some of his pastors to break away to form Bread of Life Mission.[20] In 1980, Ezeokeke returned from attending Morris Cerullo's School of Ministry in the USA and subsequently left Grace of God Mission over disagreements with Nweke and Nwodika.[21] He then founded Salvation for All Mission, but had to start from scratch because most branches of the original Christ for All Mission remained with Grace of God Mission. Today, Grace of God Mission is the largest Igbo-initiated neo-Pentecostal church with direct links to the revival. It currently has more than 1,100 congregations spread all over Nigeria.[22]

Some Igbo-initiated NPCs began life outside Igboland. Igbos were among the earliest neo-Pentecostals to engage in cross-cultural mission

---

[20] Mba's form of sabbatharianism was Israelite, rather than Hebraist. He did not advocate the offering of sacrifices but taught that congregational worship should take place on Saturday rather than Sunday. He also introduced polygamy. In the late 1990s, Mba sought to return to mainstream Pentecostalism and established contact with Pentecostal Fellowship of Nigeria (PFN) President Bishop Mike Okonkwo.

[21] Morris Cerullo, an ordained AG minister, began a healing ministry in the 1950s and was associated initially with Gordon Lindsay's Voice of Healing and the US American Healing Revival (1948 to mid-1950s). His own organisation is called World Evangelism, based in San Diego, where an annual school for training ministers is held. See J. R. Zeigler, 'Cerullo, Morris (1931-)', in S. M. Burgess and Eduard M. van der Maas (eds.), *New International Dictionary of Pentecostal and Charismatic Movements*, Grand Rapids, MI: Zondervan, 2002, 472.

[22] This information was supplied by Joseph Onuchukwu, National Secretary of Grace of God Mission in 2001.

initiatives. Here I include Winter's E-2 evangelism in the category cross-cultural mission. Winter distinguishes three kinds of evangelism: same culture (E-1), culture closely related to one's own (E-2) and culture different from one's own (E-3). He differentiates between evangelism (presenting the gospel to one's own people) and missions (crossing cultural boundaries).[23] Igbo neo-Pentecostal mission initiatives were partly a consequence of the revival's strong missionary impulse. However, they were also linked to Igbo mobility and migratory habits. Population density, limited land resources and Igbo emphasis on individual achievement prompted many to cross local borders for trade purposes. Of special interest are those who planted churches in Northern Nigeria. Early attempts by revivalists in 1970 had proved largely unsuccessful, but as peace returned and the nation attained a level of stability, many Igbos migrated north for business and trade or were sent there as part of their National Youth Service Corps (NYSC) programme. Among them were Christians influenced by the revival and eager to spread the good news. Other revivalists went with the express purpose of holding evangelistic campaigns and planting churches. It is remarkable that so many were prepared to return to an area where a few years previously their relatives had been slaughtered during the 1966 pogroms. Here we concentrate on initiatives directly associated with the Civil War Revival.

I was able to study three neo-Pentecostal denominations with headquarters in the North: All Christians Fellowship Mission (ACFM), Redeemed People's Mission (RPM) and Bible Faith Mission, all started by former Igbo revivalists during the 1970s. Prior to their arrival, Assemblies of God was the most active Pentecostal church in the North. All Christians Fellowship Mission was founded by former Roman Catholic William Okoye, a trader and businessman who fought in the Biafran Army. Okoye came into contact with the revival and some of its leading protagonists when he moved to Onitsha soon after his conversion in 1971. In 1973, he became a pastor and church-planter with the newly formed Riches of Christ Mission.[24] Redeemed People's Mission was founded by Thompson Nwosu, an apprentice mechanic who also fought for Biafra. Nwosu was converted in 1970 through SU Umuahia after listening to a message preached by SU leader Felix Obiorah, co-founder of Master's Vessel Group. He then joined a SU group and became actively involved in the revival while continuing to attend his local Anglican church. In 1971, Pastor J.O. Martins invited him

---

[23] R. D. Winter, 'The New Macedonia: A Revolutionary New Era in Mission Begins', in R. D. Winter and S. C. Hawthorne (eds.), *Perspectives on the World Christian Movement. A Reader*, Pasadena, CA: William Carey Library, 1992, B-159.

[24] For a biography of William Okoye, see Okoroafor, *William Okoye.*

Figure 8. William Okoye, Abuja, c. 1996.

to join the Free Gospel Society (FGS) in Lagos and two years later transferred him to Jos as their representative in Northern Nigeria. Wilson Ezeofor founded Bible Faith Mission. After his conversion as a secondary school student in 1972 through SU Onitsha, he attended New Anointing Bible College, the training institution for prospective ministers of Riches of Christ, National Evangelical Mission and Save the Lost Mission. He then worked as a pastor with Riches of Christ prior to leaving Igboland.

The first major missionary enterprise began in Jos city in September 1973 when Nwosu was transferred there under the auspices of Free Gospel Society.[25] He launched his ministry with a citywide 'crusade' and followed this up with similar events in the major Northern cities of Zaria, Bauchi and Maiduguri. At this stage, most converts were turned over to Assemblies of God, the main Pentecostal church in the region. This changed, however,

[25] Igbos who came to the North as pastors/evangelists tended to change their names to disguise their ethnic origins in order to prevent any obstacle to the gospel so soon after the civil war. Thompson Nwosu changed his name to N. C. Thompson.

when FGS gave Nwosu permission to start churches, and in 1976, he began a Sunday morning worship service in Jos. In 1977, he resigned from FGS over the alleged immorality of its founder, and as a result, his congregation lost its premises and most of its equipment. In May 1977, Redeemed People's Mission met for the first time in a small converted 'garri' shed in a run-down district of Jos with about one hundred members (mostly Igbo but with a small number of Yorubas and indigenes). It was the third Pentecostal church to be established in Jos, after Assemblies of God and All Christians Fellowship Mission.

The year 1975 proved decisive for Igbo initiatives in the North. Ezeokeke of Christ for All Mission held an evangelistic campaign and planted a church in the Northern Muslim dominated city of Kano. He followed this with similar campaigns across the North resulting in the planting of other churches, later absorbed into Grace of God Mission when Christ for All merged with Riches of Christ. The same year also saw the launch of two other major initiatives outside Igboland. As noted in chapter 3, a young teacher called Rhoda Morah formed Aguata for Christ in 1974 as a ministry to evangelise her local community in North-Western Igboland. This eventually became a fully-fledged denomination called National Evangelical Mission (NEM) once its mission focus had shifted to Northern Nigeria. Prior to this, Morah had handed over leadership to two associates, Benjamin Ogbuezobe and Dominic Onuigwe. Ogbuezobe became overall leader, and Onuigwe, evangelism director with responsibility for overseeing their mission initiatives in the North. Onuigwe was a former associate of J. M. J. Emesim and worked closely with Hour of Freedom before joining Free Gospel Society in Lagos. Today, he is the General Overseer of National Evangelical Mission. In 1975, NEM planted the first Pentecostal church in the Northern city of Maiduguri, the current capital of Borno State, and has since become one of the largest Igbo-founded NPCs.[26]

William Okoye also launched his ministry in 1975.[27] As a trader, he regularly visited the North and often used these excursions to preach the gospel. But on this occasion, accompanied by two associates (Wilson Ezeofor and Ephraim Nweke), he conducted an evangelistic campaign in the town of Gboko, the heart of Tiv territory, and followed this with similar

[26] This was told me by Bitrus Pathel, who pastored Maiduguri NEM church from 1985 to 1986. But in a report written in 1998, Nwosu of RPM stated that NEM 'hijacked' the Free Gospel Society group he had started after a crusade he held there in 1974.

[27] This account is based on oral interviews and the following written sources: Okoroafor, *William Okoye*; Richard Nduul *et al.*, 'Rev. Okoye, Reaping the Reward of Faithfulness', *Compassion*, 1992.

Figure 9. Christian Pentecostal Mission, Aba.

events in other urban areas across the North, planting churches to cater for the many converts. Initially, they called themselves Freedom in Christ Church with Okoye as General Overseer and Ezeofor, his lieutenant. In 1976, they planted a church in Jos, which for a time became their headquarters. Leadership struggles and disagreements over the 'New Move' led to Ezeofor's resignation in 1978, and the following year he founded Bible Faith Mission in Jos. Meanwhile, Okoye changed the name of his church to All Christians Fellowship Mission, and in 1979, moved his headquarters to Abuja, the present Federal Capital of Nigeria. Today he is recognised as a pioneer of Pentecostalism in the North.

One of the more successful Igbo ventures outside Igboland began in Western Nigeria. Christian Pentecostal Mission was founded by Obiorah Ezekiel Nwogu, converted in 1970 from an Anglican and prayer house background through the advocacy of Raphael Okafor, co-leader of Hour of Freedom. At the time of his conversion, Ezekiel, as he is popularly known, was a trader with primary level education. He subsequently moved to Lagos where he joined Free Gospel Society as an evangelist. In 1977, like Nwosu of Redeemed People's Mission, Ezekiel left FGS and started the

Christian Pentecostal Mission with its headquarters in Lagos. It is currently one of the largest neo-Pentecostal denominations in Nigeria.[28]

Predisposing Conditions

I now move on to an analysis of causative factors. I focus on factors relating to origins rather than subsequent growth, even though they sometimes overlapped, and follow David Barrett by distinguishing between predisposing conditions which prepare the soil for independency and precipitating factors or 'flashpoints'.[29] As we have seen, with the emergence of charismatic fellowship groups in the early 1970s processes were already underway which would culminate in the formation of independent churches. But this transition might never have happened if other conditions had not been in place.

Sociological Factors

Barrett argues that independency is primarily a 'tribal phenomenon and can therefore legitimately be studied by means of tribal analysis'.[30] The nature of Igbo society itself facilitated the transition of charismatic fellowship groups to independent status. Barrett suggests that a society's traditional socio-political structures may encourage or discourage the formation of independent churches. Schism is less likely among groups with centralised hierarchies than among those organised in smaller independent groups.[31] In Igboland, the absence of a centralised political structure at local level allowed room for initiative and made mainline churches more susceptible to fragmentation.[32] This was one reason why Igbo NPCs emerged earlier than their counterparts in Western Nigeria where Yoruba political structures are more centralised.

A second contributory factor was the degree of social differentiation within society and church. Stark and Bainbridge argue that social

[28] 'Divine Restoration', *Pentecostal Family*, August 1999, 7. According to an alternative version, CPM was started in 1977 by Emmanuel Ugbaja, Francis Nwaka and some associates, but was subsequently handed over to Ezekiel after a financial crisis. Steward, *Churches in Nigeria*, 62-3.

[29] David B. Barrett., *Schism and Renewal in Africa*, Nairobi: Oxford University Press, 1968, 110.

[30] *Ibid.*, 58.

[31] Quoted in M. L. Daneel, *Missiology. Guide 2 (The Independent Churches in Africa)*, Pretoria: UNISA, 1982, 64. See also Barrett, *Schism*, 59, 108-9.

[32] This tendency to fragment is also reflected in the proliferation of small Igbo-initiated business/trade enterprises which litter the Nigerian landscape.

differentiation within a religious organisation increases the tendency towards sectarian schism. The potential for conflict is heightened if there are divisions between the better and worse off, and between the more or less powerful, both in terms of rewards within the wider society and within the religious organisation. Schism may occur if the relatively deprived members feel the potential advantages from breaking away outweigh the costs. Persons who lead such breakaways are usually those likely to achieve positions of authority more rewarding than those enjoyed in the parent organisation.[33] Stark and Bainbridge's thesis is influenced by relative deprivation theory, originally formulated by Charles Glock to explain the origins of new movements (both religious and secular). Glock suggests that relative deprivation can lead to social conflict and ultimately to the formation of a new social or religious group. But deprivation is not a sufficient condition for the rise of new movements. Additional conditions include a shared sense of deprivation, an absence of 'alternative institutional arrangements for its resolution', and the emergence of 'a leadership for building a movement out of the existing deprivation'.[34]

While relative deprivation was not a necessary or sufficient condition for Igbo revivalists to break away from mainline churches, it did provide a motive for secession. By the 1960s, Igbo society was stratified in terms of age, material wealth and education, and this was reflected in the mainline churches which were socially differentiated. For the poor and uneducated, access to mainline church leadership positions was restricted. The civil war was a levelling influence because many Igbos lost their possessions and were temporarily unable to continue their education, but this did not significantly affect their social status. In contrast to their counterparts in Western Nigeria with their background in the universities, most early Igbo neo-Pentecostal pioneers had only primary or secondary level education by the early 1970s and were from relatively poor family backgrounds.[35] Hence, they were closer in terms of social and educational status to some of the early AIC leaders than they were to their contemporaries in the West.[36]

[33] Stark and Bainbridge, 'Churches', 117-33; Rodney Stark and William S. Bainbridge, *The Future of Religion: Secularization, Revival and Cult Formation*, Berkeley, CA: University of California Press, 1985.

[34] C. Y. Glock, 'The Role of Deprivation in the Origin and Evolution of Religious Groups', in Robert Lee and Martin E. Marty (eds.), *Religion and Social Conflict*, New York: Oxford University Press, 1964, 27, 29.

[35] For neo-Pentecostals in Western Nigeria, see Ojo, 'Deeper Christian Life', 142-43; Ojo, *Army*, 23-45.

[36] Early Aladura leaders and members included literate clerks, traders and members of the élite, but most were without higher education. Others were poor and illiterate. It was the 1930 Revival, led by a steamroller driver called Joseph Babalola, which transformed it into a large-scale movement that

I spoke to thirty-one former revivalists who joined a neo-Pentecostal church in the 1970s. Of these, only four received education above secondary level prior to joining, and at least six went no further than primary level. Of seventeen informants who actually founded NPCs in the 1970s, five had primary level only, nine secondary and three tertiary. I also spoke to twenty-four former revivalists who chose to remain in the mainline churches during the 1970s. Of these, twenty-two had either completed or entered a tertiary level institution by 1975 (fifteen went to university and seven to a theological seminary). Some had their university education interrupted by the war but resumed after peace was restored. The evidence is inconclusive, but it does suggest that NPC pioneers were more likely to be drawn from the ranks of those with limited educational and employment prospects, who considered themselves marginalized within their local church communities. Invariably, NPC pioneers were young men on the fringes who felt excluded from positions of church leadership.

Rapid social change was another factor behind independency. I have already referred to the destabilising effects of the civil war. Urbanisation, linked to the oil boom, was also a factor. Ojo has noted this in his research into the origins of Western Nigerian charismatic movements.[37] During the early 1970s, Igbo charismatic fellowships were predominantly an urban phenomenon and the transition to denominational status took place in urban contexts, though branches were subsequently opened in rural areas. Between 1970 and 1972, there was a massive invasion of Igbo towns by people displaced due to the political upheavals of the war.[38] These urban settings, characterised by instability and fragmented communities, provided fertile ground for Pentecostal infiltration, in contrast to rural areas which were dominated by mainline churches. In the village an individual was expected to attend the family church, but in the town there was more room for manoeuvre, greater freedom to choose and fewer social restrictions. Urban migration encouraged trans-denominational mobility by loosening ties with extended kin and exposing young people to new ideas and religious options. It also precipitated crises of identity and feelings of insecurity and isolation. NPCs sought to address their messages to contemporary problems and tried to compensate for the depersonalisation of urban life. Above all, they provided new communities to replace the traditional social ties of the extended family.

Gradually, like most sect-like communities which emerge from revivalist activity, Igbo charismatic fellowship groups all underwent a process of

---

appealed to a broad sweep of the population, including many illiterate farmers. See J. D. Y. Peel, 'The Aladura Movement in Western Nigeria', *Tarikh*, 3.1, 1969, 52.

[37] Ojo, 'Deeper Christian Life', 142.

[38] Ofoegbu, 'Urbanisation', 592.

institutionalisation to cater for community demands. The transition to denominational status was linked to conversionist zeal and had a social dimension due to the intake of large numbers of under socialised recruits requiring after-care. Gradually a pastorate emerged which rapidly acquired professional status. The pressure to institutionalise increased as the youth matured and families began to join. As Ojo notes, the transition to denominational status was a response to the social needs of members.[39] Felix Obiorah, founder of Master's Vessel Church, explained how this transition occurred for them.

> At that point [our aim was] to win souls wherever we can find them - in marketplaces, in hospitals, homes, and anywhere else - and to set up Bible study and that kind of thing. And that was what we were doing. Initially, it was all young people, but when families started joining and the need became obvious that we had to care for their own needs and things like that. And then we opted to have a place of fellowship. . . . That was when we got this place. We bought a piece of land and then started building. . . . We bought the land in seventy-three and built it up around seventy-nine or so.[40]

The pressure to institutionalise was also linked to the need to survive in an increasingly competitive religious marketplace. If we recall, the 1970s was a period of unprecedented religious pluralisation as new groups arose in the wake of the civil war and people were able to choose from a growing array of religious options. If the new fellowships were to survive, they needed to provide a structure which would cater for the needs of their members.

Local Religious Demands and Global Legacies

Perhaps the most significant factor behind the genesis of neo-Pentecostal churches was the search for power to enhance life and engage in mission. If we recall, in Igbo traditional culture *ezi-ndụ* (the good life) embraces physical health, material prosperity, communal satisfaction and individual success. Barrett suggests that the 'common root cause' for independency was reaction against the failure of European missions to understand African society by distinguishing good elements from bad and recognising parallels between local culture and biblical faith.[41] Barrett's theory has been criticised for failing to explain the ongoing growth of AICs and take

[39] Ojo, 'Deeper Christian Life', 152.
[40] Interview, 6 October 2001, Umuahia.
[41] Barrett, *Schism*, 154-57.

account of the fact that not all were founded by mission church members. While I do not subscribe to Barrett's thesis as a general theory of African independency, it does have a bearing on our discussion of early Igbo NPCs which were all founded by former mission church members. The search for power to enhance life added impetus to the drive towards independency. The failure of mission church spirituality to fulfil local aspirations created a crisis of identity and precipitated a 'quest for belonging', a search for alternatives that aroused opposition from mission church leaders and contributed to the process of secession.

However, early NPCs were primarily 'mission churches' rather than 'protest groups', movements of conversion rather than secession. Igbo charismatic fellowships arose in a context of heightened evangelistic fervour, and this created tensions within mainline churches due in part to the reluctance of leaders to relinquish control and provide space for young people to participate in ministry. Eventually these tensions reached the point of rupture and protagonists felt they had no alternative but to secede. Hence, the appropriation of Pentecostal spirituality in response to mission church shortcomings, and the urge to engage in mission activity, were the two main factors which aroused opposition and hastened the transition to denominational status.

The fissiparous nature of the Protestant tradition and the multiplication of Protestant missions and denominations were also factors behind independency in Africa. As Daneel notes, it not only led to schism but also planted the idea in African minds that multiplicity of denominations was the norm.[42] If we recall, missionary rivalry was a feature of early Christian expansion in Igboland, and despite comity agreements, groups competed with one another for members. By the 1960s, the dominant Protestant denominations were Anglican, Methodist and Presbyterian, but other Protestant missions included Baptists, Qua Iboe Church, ECWA/SIM, Assemblies of God Mission and Apostolic Church. Due to different qualifications for membership and leadership, and different disciplinary regulations, it was easy to switch membership from one denomination to another.

The propensity to schism among Protestant evangelicals is partly due to their high regard for the authority of the Bible. Secession from Roman Catholic churches has been less frequent due to their concept of the holy, apostolic Church, and relative failure to circulate vernacular scriptures. According to Barrett, in most cases of independency in Africa the Bible has played a leading role.[43] This appears to be born out in our context. One of my informants expressed it rather colourfully: 'You know, Roman Catholic Church, they did a great work for their people, they took away Bible from

[42] Daneel, *Missiology*, 61.

[43] Barrett, *Schism*, 138.

them and that's why they can keep their members. . . . But Pentecostals and evangelicals, we gave the Bible to all our members, so all of them are Bible students . . . and the splits started'.[44] Despite Igboland's large Catholic community, eighteen out of twenty-one Igbo NPC founders interviewed were former members of Protestant mission churches, while only three were former Roman Catholics.[45] Out of thirty informants who joined a neo-Pentecostal church between 1972 and 1975, twenty-five were former Protestant church members, three were former Catholics, and two were from unknown church backgrounds. However, further research is required to arrive at a more accurate estimate of the proportion of Protestants and Catholics among early NPC membership.

Precipitating Factors

These underlying conditions were often insufficient to cause schism. Turner refers to precipitating factors 'which, in a situation that is ripe for such development, push things over the edge'.[46] These presuppose the presence of other more foundational enabling factors.

Charismatic Leaders Emerging from the Margins

The emergence of charismatic leaders with a new message was an important precipitating factor behind the formation of early Igbo neo-Pentecostal churches, as it has been for other AICs.[47] If we recall, the Civil War Revival was dominated initially by charismatic individuals with a new vision which they communicated to others, resulting in the creation of new 'revitalised' Christian communities. Often these compelling figures possessed charismatic qualities, such as an ability to preach and perform miracles, which validated their message in the eyes of their followers.

---

[44] Augustine Nwodika, 'Churches in the Seventies'.

[45] Omenka, *School*, 282, describes Eastern Nigeria as the most important 'Catholic stronghold' in West Africa. In 1982, the Igbo cities of Owerri, Onitsha and Enugu had by far the largest number of Catholics of all Nigerian cities. A. O. Makozi and Afolabi Ojo, (eds.), *The History of the Catholic Church in Nigeria*, Lagos: Macmillan Nigeria, 1982, 102-103.

[46] Turner, *Religious Innovation*, 11. Barrett, *Schism*, 218, refers to these precipitating factors as 'flashpoints'.

[47] Both Turner and Barrett identify the emergence of charismatic individuals as an important precipitating factor behind the emergence of AICs in other contexts (Turner, *Religious Innovation*, 11; Barrett, *Schism*, 218).

Sociologist Eileen Barker, following Wilson,[48] notes that it is at times of rapid change or unrest (economic, political, social or military upheavals) that the charismatic leader is most likely to be heard.[49] The neo-Pentecostal church movement arose at an unprecedented time of social upheaval in Igbo history and coincided with the emergence of a new generation of young leaders with charismatic qualities.

During the 1970s, there were many charismatic individuals who gained significant followings, but none more so than Edozie Mba, General Superintendent of Riches of Christ Mission.[50] In contrast to most Igbo neo-Pentecostal pioneers, Mba was born into an élite family and was brought up an Anglican in Lagos. In February 1972, he was introduced to Pentecostal spirituality through contact with Assemblies of God and Foursquare Gospel Church in Lagos, and was encouraged to enter full-time ministry by the late Benson Idahosa. According to Stark and Bainbridge, 'sect leaders usually have previous leadership experience . . . in the parent body'.[51] Most NPC pioneers, if we recall, were marginalised within their church communities but found leadership opportunities within Scripture Union. When Mba returned to the East, he became a SU evangelist in Enugu. Instead of returning to the Anglican fold, he attended Assemblies of God and attained a position of leadership. When he moved to Onitsha in December 1972 to participate in a SU citywide crusade, he encountered Hour of Freedom. Mba was a young man of outstanding qualities, and part of his appeal rested on his apparent ability to impart the power of the Spirit and perform healing. A spectacular healing in Onitsha significantly increased his popularity and by 1973, he was confirmed as the main leader of the revival. One informant summed up Mba's impact: 'In fact, when he came he just took over the leadership because you don't doubt the charisma'.[52]

Healing was an important factor in the growth of several Igbo charismatic fellowships, and those who possessed healing gifts rapidly gained large followings, especially in the wake of the civil war when access

---

[48] Bryan R. Wilson, *The Noble Savages: The Primitive Origins of Charisma*, Berkeley, CA: University of California Press, 1975, cited in Eileen Barker, 'Charismatization: The Social Production of "an Ethos Propitious to the Mobilisation of Sentiments"', in Eileen Barker, James A. Beckford and Karel Dobbelaere (eds.), *Secularization, Rationalism and Sectarianism: Essays in Honour of Bryan Wilson*, Oxford: Clarendon Press, 1993, 198.

[49] Barker, 'Charismatization', 198.

[50] This biography of Edozie Mba is based on oral interviews and the following written sources: Anyaegbu, 'Sabbatharianism', 181-89; Kalu, *Embattled Gods*, 277.

[51] Stark and Bainbridge, *Future of Religion*, 105.

[52] Interview, Benjamin Ikedinobi, 29 April 2000, Enugu.

Figure 10. Emmanuel and Chinyere Okorie, Aba, c. 2002.

to Western medicine was restricted. A ministry might receive a considerable boost because of a healing. Emmanuel Okorie, founder of Living Word Ministries (LWM), is a case in point.[53] I met him in his office at LWM's large church complex, overlooking the city of Aba. Okorie was brought up in the village of Ossah, near Umuahia, the son of a poor Methodist preacher and youngest of nine children. He was converted during the war through SU Umuahia, and in 1970 attended Wilcox Memorial Secondary School in Aba, founded by the Qua Iboe Mission and named after one its early missionaries. In 1971, Okorie was introduced to the Qua Iboe Church senior pastor in Aba, Reverend Ahunanya. Ahunanya was initially reluctant to allow Okorie to minister in his churches because of his youth and lack of theological training, even though he was a Scripture Union leader. During a visit to Ahunanya's home, Okorie prayed for his son who suffered from poliomyelitis. Ahunanya was so impressed by the boy's improvement that he allowed Okorie to hold evangelistic 'crusades' within the QIC congregations of Aba district.[54] An interesting sequel concerns Okorie's subsequent ministry in America, which was also

[53] This biography of Okorie is based on an oral interview (17 January 2002, Aba) and an article in LWM's magazine (T. Nze, 'Emma Okorie. The Man Who Sees the Invisible', *Forum*, 2001, 5-7).

[54] Okorie also claimed other notable healings through his ministry in Nigeria during the 1970s, including two resuscitations.

launched following a healing miracle. When he first arrived in 1979, he lodged with a Nigerian friend in the home of an American Pentecostal whose daughter was ill. According to Okorie, when he prayed for her she was instantly healed. Her father told his pastor, who publicised what happened, and consequently Okorie suddenly found himself in demand within the American Pentecostal community.

Igbo traditional culture has a strong tradition of religious practitioners with apparent healing abilities. For example, the *dibịa afa* (healer-diviner) is believed to possess healing powers derived from Agwu, the deity of medicine. Hence, Igbo neo-Pentecostal 'healers' have the potential to attract large followings and precipitate new movements.

Opposition from the Centre

Opposition from mainline church authorities was a significant factor behind the formation of early Igbo neo-Pentecostal churches. In fact, from an insider point of view this was the main reason for secession. This is in line with Barrett's assertion that separatism within Africa often occurs when charismatic leaders and their followers find themselves on the receiving end of persecution by mission church authorities.[55]

The early 1970s was a period of intense persecution for Igbo revivalists and many felt so alienated from their church communities that they left to form new ones. In some cases, they were literally driven out and branded as fanatics or even heretics. Some of my informants chose to remain in the mainline churches and opposed the formation of NPCs, but invariably were away at university during the persecution years, or had left temporarily to study overseas, or had transferred to a denomination more sympathetic to the revival. Out of twenty-four former revivalists who chose not to secede, twelve were away at university or theological college, two were overseas, seven switched from Anglican to Assemblies of God or ECWA (temporarily or permanently),[56] one was a Presbyterian pastor, and two moved away to work.

To minimise the possibility of bias, I interviewed representatives from both camps, though I was unable to talk to any former mainline church leaders who had opposed the revival. Cyril Okorocha's testimony is significant because he has maintained a relatively unsympathetic stance towards the neo-Pentecostal church movement despite his charismatic leanings. Okorocha was brought up in the Anglican Church and was a leader of SU Umuahia during the war. In 1970, he left Igboland to embark

---

[55] Barrett, *Schism*, 219.

[56] Those informants who switched to ECWA were based in Enugu at the time, where the ECWA pastor, Mike Bonomi, was sympathetic to the revival.

on an evangelistic tour of Western Nigeria with Mike Oye and in 1972 travelled to Britain for further studies. Okorocha has remained with the Anglican Church and when we met was Director for Mission and Evangelism of the Anglican Communion based in London. He is currently Anglican Bishop of Owerri. He told me that during the early 1970s, most Anglican priests opposed the revival and as a result, many young people were expelled or left voluntarily, initially finding refuge in Assemblies of God and other Pentecostal churches.[57]

In North-Western Igboland, most revivalists were Anglicans, the dominant church in the area. Neo-Pentecostal pioneer Augustine Nwodika claimed that persecution from Anglican authorities was the main impetus behind the formation of new churches in Onitsha.[58] The situation was similar in Southern Igboland where Anglicans and Methodists predominated. In Umuahia, the SU township group sometimes held their evangelistic guest services in St. Stephen's Anglican Church. On one occasion, the pastor told Obiorah, the Scripture Union President, to send a group of SU members out of the meeting because they had been caught 'prophesying' in their local church. When he refused, they were forced to continue the service elsewhere. Persecution by mainline church authorities was certainly a factor behind Obiorah's decision to start Master's Vessel Church, as it was for other Umuahia based NPCs, such as Canaan Gospel Centre. Following their expulsion first from the Methodist church and then from the local Anglican church, members of Canaan Gospel Centre started to attend Assemblies of God. When they were asked to leave AG over their refusal to become members, they began to meet in the primary school. Finally, they were beaten by sticks and driven out of the school by members of the local community. They then started to meet in a private home and eventually became an independent church. In the North, Igbo neo-Pentecostal pioneers also encountered opposition from mainline churches. When Thompson Nwosu started holding evangelistic campaigns under the auspices of the Free Gospel Society, some COCIN and ECWA pastors warned their members not to attend and branded him a false prophet.[59] William Okoye of All Christians Fellowship Mission also encountered opposition from non-Pentecostal churches.

Why was there this spate of persecutions? Revivalists put it down to the response of church authorities to their message and behaviour. Church leaders criticised them for their aggressive evangelistic style, their promotion of Holy Spirit baptism, their exercise of the charismatic gifts of

---

[57] Interview, 23 August 1998, Woking.

[58] Interview, 8 May 2000, Enugu.

[59] COCIN (Church of Christ in Nigeria) is one of the denominations started by the Sudan United Mission. It is the largest of the older Protestant denominations in Plateau State.

tongues and prophecy, their interdenominational stance, and their emphasis upon personal holiness. Note the following extract from a letter written by a Scripture Union member in 1971:

> We encounter a lot of persecutions. It is painful when one sees that much of the persecutions are from the so-called leaders of our churches. Some churches have banned their S.U. groups. In some cases where we have mainly new converts there has been dispersion among them - most of them have scattered. The Methodist Church at Ossah has banned the group there from the church. Presently they have attached themselves to the Anglican Church there. But what are their reasons for all such actions? That the children of God preaches salvation, calls sin, sin and would not compromise in anyway. From all the persecutions we are strengthened. If all churches or even schools reject us the market square is there for us and the Lord will certainly use us at any place provided we serve Him in all spirit and truth.[60]

However, another letter extract suggests that there was more involved than mere intransigence on the part of church authorities: 'There have been a number of clashes with the churches. In some cases, due to spurious and misguided zeal on the part of the youngsters, and in others, due to the corruption of the church dignitaries'.[61] Revivalists sometimes (rather unwisely) charged their priests with immorality and corruption, which further antagonised them.

Spirit baptism and the charismatic gifts of tongues and prophecy in particular had dangerous potential and sometimes resulted in irregular behaviour. If we recall, Spirit baptism was an early feature of the revival, but when it became a formal doctrine, due in part to the influence of Assemblies of God, it began to cause divisions within mission churches and SU fellowship groups. Note the following excerpt from a letter written in 1972:

> The S.U. groups in the East are doing well, but clashes with denominations, leading to their closing down in the churches, are now many. . . . The trouble is not with S.U. itself but with some of the Christians in her who are influenced by spiritualists and Pentecostals and insist on Water Baptism by Immersion, Holy Spirit Baptism, and other externals more than Christ. . . . We do not preach S.U. but Christ, but since S.U. is heterogeneous in denominational composition she cannot work smoothly amongst all denominations if extreme controversial

[60] Elizabeth Onukwue, Letter to Roberts, 23 May 1971.
[61] Cyril Okorocha, Letter to Roberts, 20 December 1972.

doctrines are insisted on in preaching. The only way is to work together on common grounds.[62]

The promotion of tongues as initial evidence of Spirit baptism was especially problematic. Some went further by insisting that without tongues a person was not a fully 'born-again' Christian. Note the following comments from a former revivalist: 'After the war the evil one came with all manner of false doctrine, trying to bring division among us. Men came up with the spirit of sectionalism, teaching men that people without the gift of tongues are not Christians'.[63] Prophecy, though less common, was also potentially divisive. Usually this was due to the cessationist stance of church leaders, though there were instances of excessive and irregular behaviour on the part of revivalists. In 1973 Pentecostal SU travelling secretary Muyiwa Olamijulo reported that some Igbo SU members were 'constituting a menace' by holding meetings at irregular times, and in the case of one school group by 'prophesying at night to some of the members of staff'.[64] Other SU groups were using the gift of prophecy to help members find potential spouses, prompting one former revivalist to write, 'in short S.U. became the avenue where men and women came together to chose their husbands and wives, through revelation in vision'.[65]

It was this combination of Pentecostal spirituality, aggressive evangelistic activity and radical holiness which aroused opposition from mainline church leaders and hastened the moment of rupture. However, not all mainline church leaders opposed the revival. Among those who were sympathetic was the Anglican Bishop L. M. Uzodike in Onitsha. In Raphael Okafor's journal there is a passing reference to a meeting between the Bishop and Hour of Freedom leaders: 'Three of us, Arthur, Stephen and I, as well as Mrs D. Erinne, met Bishop L. M. Uzodike and we had a very

[62] Ume Kalu, Letter to Roberts, 24 August 1972. See also Daniel Onwukwe, Scripture Union (Nigeria) Prayer Letter, October 1970: 'Firstly, we are facing problems caused by the Tongues Movement. In some quarters the S.U. image has been much damaged by the excesses of immature Christians who substituted a physical experience for the Person of the Spirit, and the gifts for the Giver. We have tried to create the right spiritual balance through circulars and injunctions, but the problem remains, especially in the Eastern States, recently out of the throes of the civil war'. Both Kalu and Onwukwe chose not to secede and join one of the NPCs. In the 1980s, Onwukwe himself testified to a personal experience of Spirit baptism.

[63] Chuma G. Obijiofor, Letter to Roberts, 24 August 1972.

[64] Muyiwa Olamijulo, SU Eastern Newsletter, No. 6, January 1973.

[65] Chuma G. Obijiofor, Letter to Roberts, 24 August 1972.

good discussion for about one hour and later he prayed for us'.[66] In Owerri, the intervention of Bishop Nwankiti prevented some of the Anglican priests from closing down SU groups meeting in their churches, and in Aba, the Methodist Superintendent also supported SU, in contrast to some of his colleagues.

The case of Enugu in North-Eastern Igboland is significant. Former revivalist Chinedu Nebo recalled the severe opposition they received from Anglican leaders. On one occasion, the priest in charge of a large Anglican church asked all those who claimed to be 'saved' and 'born-again' to stand up, and then ordered them out of his church. Many never returned.[67] Yet the movement did not splinter into many neo-Pentecostal churches as it had done in North-Western Igboland. The only neo-Pentecostal church to open a branch in Enugu during the 1970s was the Onitsha-based Riches of Christ Mission. There were two main reasons for this. Firstly, two mission church pastors were active patrons of Scripture Union during the early 1970s. Mike Bonomi and James Ukaegbu of ECWA/SIM and the Presbyterian Church respectively both welcomed the revival and allowed SU members to meet in their premises. Secondly, SU Enugu had minimal contact with the British missionary S. G. Elton, a strong advocate of church-planting. As we will see later, Elton was an important catalyst behind the formation of NPCs in North-Western Igboland. Nonetheless, many revivalists in Enugu eventually did leave the mainline churches due to the latter's anti-Pentecostal stance, and like Nebo joined Assemblies of God which had a strong base in the city.[68]

The tendency for revivalists to find a safe haven within Assemblies of God and other mission related Pentecostal churches was a pattern that recurred throughout Igboland. But AG's relationship to the revival was ambiguous and went through several stages. As a denomination, it was familiar with the concept of revival and had known periods of revivalist activity during its history.[69] It also shared similar values with civil war revivalists, such as an emphasis on experiential religion, spontaneity, otherworldliness and Biblicism, and was actively engaged in aggressive evangelism prior to the civil war. However, AG expected revival to occur within its own ranks and was initially sceptical when faced with an

---

[66] Raphael Okafor, Journal, 17 May 1971, quoted in Bolton, *Glory*, 160.

[67] Chinedu Nebo, 'Protagonists and Critics (Persecution) in the Seventies', Remembering the Seventies Conference, audiocassette, 29 April 2000, Enugu.

[68] Nebo left the Anglican Church after the war and attended AG for three years. In 1975, he travelled to the USA for further studies, where he remained until 1981. He has since become an ordained Anglican priest.

[69] See Agbo Amechi Agbo, 'Historical Development of Revival and Revivalism in the Assemblies of God Nigeria', M.Th. thesis, Theological College of Northern Nigeria, Bukuru, 1999; Ebuade *et al.*, *Assemblies of God.*

apparent outpouring of the Spirit upon the mainline churches, which it regarded as 'spiritually dead'. Like classical Pentecostals confronted with the charismatic renewal elsewhere, this had the potential to precipitate an identity crisis within AG ranks.[70]

Gradually, Assemblies of God became more receptive and benefited from its contact with the revival. AG leaders preached at SU evangelistic events and used SU as a platform for their ministries. AG also received an influx of SU members rejected by mainline churches, as well as many new converts, resulting in significant church growth. Among those who attended AG during the early 1970s were a number of key Igbo SU leaders. These included Tony Ewelike, Amauche Obijeofor (early leaders of SU Enugu), Edozie Mba, Amaechi Nwachukwu (founder of Amazing Love Assembly), Chinedu Nebo, Don Odunze (President of Family Circle Ministries), Sam Mbata (first President of Full Gospel Business Men's Fellowship International in Nigeria), and Uma Ukpai, a leading Pentecostal evangelist. The revival also stimulated a fresh outburst of charismatic and evangelistic activity within AG's institutionalised and gerontocratic structures. The example set by revivalists stimulated AG into action, and today, leaders such as Charles Osueke and Matthew Ezeigbo (present and past AG General Superintendents) look back to the early 1970s as a time of significant revival within their denomination.[71]

Although AG provided a safe haven for revivalists faced with persecution from mainline churches, its contribution was hampered by its strong denominational stance, which conflicted with SU and alienated it from emerging charismatic fellowship groups. It sought to take over the revival and contain it within its own denominational structures, insisting that SU revivalists attending AG churches should become members. Eventually, the relationship became so strained that AG tried to prevent its members from participating in SU activities for fear of losing them. In the end it severed its links with SU and the ECUs, and established the Christ's Ambassadors Student Organisation (CASOR) for students in university and secondary schools. In their turn, revivalists felt restricted and believed the freedom and unity the revival had instilled would be lost if they complied with these demands. They wished to escape the control of AG authorities (both black African and white missionary), and avoid the constraints attached to belonging to a large and established denomination.[72] AG was

[70] For example, AG North America. See Frank D. Macchia, 'God Present in a Confused Situation: The Mixed Influence of the Charismatic Movement on Classical Pentecostalism in the United States', *Pneuma*, 18.1, Spring 1996, 34-5.

[71] Agbo, 'Revival', 79.

[72] Though by this time AG Nigeria had become autonomous, the parent body in the USA still exercised influence through its missionaries active on the field.

reluctant to recognise the ministries of those who had not passed through its system and made little room for freelance evangelists. It required aspiring ministers to undergo extensive training in one of its Bible colleges and afterwards to start from the bottom.

The Removal of Restraining Influences

An important development in the transition to denominational status occurred with the removal of various restraining influences, individuals who possessed strong ecumenical inclinations and encouraged revivalists to remain in their churches despite persecution. The first was SU travelling secretary Bill Roberts, who departed the scene in late 1969. Roberts was intent on implementing SU's 'responsible church policy' and strongly opposed the exodus from mission churches, encouraging SU members instead to remain as forces for renewal. His ecumenical stance is evident in the following circular letter sent to SU area representatives in Biafra:

> We would never encourage anybody to change his denomination after experiencing blessing through an S.U. Group. I believe that when God brings revival to this land He will use fully surrendered Christians from every denomination as he has done throughout the history of the Church. . . . Hence we must be working in every denomination even if we think at the moment that our particular Church is lacking spiritual life. That is all the more reason why you should go into it wholeheartedly in order to bring back some life to that Church. We know from history that a dead Church today may be very much alive in 10 years time if you are prepared to face up to your responsibilities within your Churches rather than running away from them.[73]

Soon after Roberts' departure, some of the more mature Nigerian SU leaders left the region or departed for university, leaving the field open for younger, more radical ones to take over. Towards the end of 1970, the influential Pentecostal SU travelling secretary Mike Oye returned to his home in Western Nigeria. Like Roberts, Oye was a strong advocate of SU's interdenominational policy and encouraged those intent on leaving their churches to join one of the many existing ones rather than start new

---

During the period 1967-75 there were approximately twenty US American AG missionaries working in Igboland, out of forty-five in the whole of Nigeria. See Cimino, *Profiles*.

[73] Bill Roberts, Circular Letter to SU Area Representatives in Biafra, 20 November 1969.

ones. Among senior SU leaders to depart for university were John Onuora, Chris Onuoha (acting SU travelling secretaries), Augustus Mbanaso, and Emmanuel Ekpunobi, all of whom have remained within the Anglican Church. Perhaps the crucial factor was the departure in 1972 of Stephen and Raphael Okafor for further studies in England. As the founder of Hour of Freedom Stephen Okafor had always adopted a strong ecumenical stance and resisted the call to form new churches. When they left, Paul Nweke took over the leadership of Hour of Freedom in Onitsha and he was more receptive to the idea of planting churches. The ecumenical sentiments of these early revivalists are echoed by Hollenweger who laments the way the global charismatic movement has not lived up to its early promise and reminds his readers of the ecumenical beginnings of the Pentecostal and charismatic movements, and the ecumenical leanings of some of its leading figures.[74]

Voices from Outside

Global forces also influenced the emerging movement. The British missionary S. G. Elton was largely responsible for introducing the church-planting concept in the East, especially in North-Western Igboland. After his resignation from the Apostolic Church, Elton had teamed up with American evangelists T. L. Osborn and Gordon Lindsay in advocating this as a means of spreading the Pentecostal faith in Africa. Osborn and Lindsay were independent Pentecostal ministers, though both had previous connections with Assemblies of God (USA) and were influenced by its indigenous church principles. Osborn had consulted with AG prior to initiating a scheme for mass crusades in 1953, which would be sustained by local evangelists recruited and supported by his Association for Native Evangelism. Lindsay had previously been an AG pastor. He adopted a similar strategy to Osborn and developed his own Native Church Crusade in 1961, which supplied resources for Third-World church building programmes.[75]

---

[74] Hollenweger, *Pentecostalism*, 334-66 (see especially pp. 362-66).

[75] Initially, AG approved of Osborn's scheme but later criticised him for undermining its policy of creating self-supporting/self-financing indigenous churches, because he paid his workers more than local AG pastors. For more on Osborn and Lindsay's mission strategies and their links with Assemblies of God, see Everett A. Wilson, *Strategy of the Spirit. J. Philip Hogan and the Growth of the Assemblies of God Worldwide, 1960-1990*, Carlisle: Paternoster, 1997, 159-60; R. M. Riss, 'Osborn, Tommy Lee (1923-)', in Burgess & van der Maas (eds.), *Dictionary*, 950; D. D. Bundy, 'Lindsay, Gordon (1906-73) and Freda Theresa (1916-)', in Burgess & van der Maas (eds.), *Dictionary*, 841-42;

Elton had close links with Stephen Okafor and Hour of Freedom, but his initial attempts at persuading them to gather their converts into new churches were unsuccessful. Okafor believed that the East, with its strong attachment to mission churches, would resist the idea. The situation changed following Stephen and Raphael Okafor's departure in 1972 and Paul Nweke's succession to the leadership of Hour of Freedom in Onitsha. Nweke was more receptive because he believed that God had called him to preach *and* plant churches. In 1972, he visited Elton at Ilesha and was immediately taken under his wing. Through Elton, Nweke and Nwodika met the late Benson Idahosa and attended his New Covenant Bible School in Benin City, which further strengthened their resolve to plant churches. Idahosa's emphasis on church-planting was partly a consequence of his contact with Gordon Lindsay. Idahosa was introduced to Lindsay by Elton, and in 1971 spent a few months studying in Lindsay's Christ for the Nations Institute in the USA. On his return, he started the New Covenant Bible College, which later changed its name to All Nations for Christ Bible College.

Accounts differ as to what happened next. Here again we encounter the tendency for participants to present themselves as central figures and marginalize others. According to Nwodika, on their return to Onitsha in February 1973, they called Edozie Mba and Emeka Eze (then Vice-President of SU Onitsha) and shared their vision for starting a new church. Mba and Eze initially resisted the idea because they wanted to concentrate on evangelism, but eventually consented, and together they founded Riches of Christ.[76] Another version assigns a more central role to Mba. In Anyaegbu's account (based on a personal interview with Mba), the latter visited Onitsha in December 1972 to participate in a citywide crusade organised by Scripture Union, after completing his training at Emesim's Bible College. Following the crusade, he stayed on to conduct teaching sessions and formed a close friendship with Eze. In January 1973, Mba was invited by a SU group to speak on Holy Spirit baptism, but fell out with the leader Eliezer Okoye and apparently never associated with SU again. Meanwhile, he continued to conduct teaching sessions at Eze's house and in February 1973 opened a ministry called Riches of Christ Evangelistic Association. Soon they were joined by Nweke and Nwodika, and in 1975, after establishing branches all over Igboland, changed their name to Riches of Christ Mission.[77]

Edith L. Blumhofer, *The Assemblies of God. A Chapter in the Story of American Pentecostalism*, Volume 2, Springfield, MO: Gospel Publishing House, 1989, 67-75.

[76] Interview, 8 May 2000, Enugu.

[77] Anyaegbu, 'Sabbatharianism', 183-86.

Igbo neo-Pentecostal pioneers found submission to church authorities difficult, insisting that God had abandoned organised religion. After starting Riches of Christ, they called others to 'come out' from mainline churches, which they regarded symbolically as 'Babylon' and consequently under the judgement of God.[78] Though the new churches started as flexible organisations loosely held together by charismatic leadership, they gradually underwent a process of institutionalisation to denominational status.

Conclusion

These then were the main factors behind the formation of churches out of the original charismatic fellowship groups associated with the revival. Local and external forces facilitated the transition process. The combination of social differentiation, urban migration, decentralised political structures, local religious demands, and Protestantism's propensity to schism created a favourable environment for local initiative and secession. The pressure to institutionalise was also linked to the need to survive in a competitive religious marketplace and provide a structure to cater for local demands. In nearly every case, the actual moment of rupture was precipitated by a combination of factors. The most important from an insider point of view was opposition from mission church authorities to the revivalists' promotion of Holy Spirit baptism, practice of charismatic gifts, and aggressive evangelistic style, with its call to repentance and new birth. Hence, the formation of new Pentecostal churches was closely linked to the revival's missionary impulses. In some cases, voices from outside Igboland acted as catalysts but these never overrode local concerns. After their decision to adopt independent status, the newly formed churches rapidly attracted large followings. In the next chapter, I examine why this was so.

[78] Several former revivalists told me that the Bible text 2 Cor 6:17 was popular among NPC pioneers: '"Therefore, come out from their midst and be separate," says the Lord'.

Chapter 5

Neo-Pentecostal Church Growth, 1972-2006

> One of the reasons for the growth of Pentecostal and Charismatic churches may be that they have succeeded where western founded churches have often failed – to provide a contextualized Christianity in Africa. They are essentially of African origin . . . and fulfil African aspirations, with roots in a marginalized and underprivileged society struggling to find dignity and identity in the face of brutal colonialism and oppression. . . . But despite these important social and historical factors, fundamentally it is the ability of African Pentecostalism to adapt to and fulfil religious aspirations that continues to be its main strength (Allan H. Anderson).[1]

The new churches expanded rapidly and soon spread beyond the borders of Igboland. This chapter examines the factors behind their expansion. It also explores the way the movement's vision and values have evolved since the early 1970s in response to global flows and local demands. Like the revival itself, neo-Pentecostal expansion depended upon a balance between supply and demand. As noted in chapter 1, explanations of contemporary African Pentecostal expansion are usually situated within the broad framework of modernisation or globalisation and the more local socio-political and economic changes associated with decolonisation. In Nigeria, these processes created new religious demands which facilitated neo-Pentecostal growth. However, it was the movement's missionary impulses, generated by the revival, which were primarily responsible for neo-Pentecostal church (NPC) expansion during its formative period. Part of the movement's appeal rested on its ability to supply a repertoire of images, symbols, rituals and narratives for identity construction. Igbo neo-Pentecostals construct their identities through social interaction, ritual action and the creation of local theologies in a variety of contexts. These include fellowship meetings, group Bible teaching and preaching, communal prayer and

[1] Anderson, *Pentecostalism*, 122.

worship sessions, and mission activities. This chapter includes an analysis of these elements of neo-Pentecostal spirituality and reflects on their contribution to the movement's popularity.

Research focussed on churches in urban contexts, and we must take account of this when assessing the data.[2] Yet urban areas provide the most fertile ground for Pentecostal penetration. Even though many have established branches in rural areas, they started life in the townships and cities, and it is here they have grown most rapidly. As Ojo has noted, African neo-Pentecostal groups are especially popular in cities because their more intense religious expression compensates for the depersonalization of urban life and they address their messages to contemporary urban problems, such as unemployment, social isolation, inadequate healthcare and poor social services. They are also more likely to find the necessary economic resources for running their organisations in urban areas.[3]

Negotiating the Local and the Global

The Igbo neo-Pentecostal church movement was essentially an indigenous initiative responding to local concerns, but was also part of the global charismatic movement and as such was influenced by external forces. Irving Hexham and Karla Poewe describe charismatic Christianity as a 'global culture', because as a religious tradition it has travelled the world, maintaining its 'metacultural' dimension but taking on local colour.[4] A key question is how local populations resist, reshape or adopt the influx of images, symbols and narratives associated with global Pentecostalism. To understand the popularity of Igbo-founded NPCs we must pay attention to the local and global forces that have influenced their shape.

Neo-Pentecostal churches have responded to changing socio-economic and political contexts by adapting their message and their practices to cater for community needs. The concept of contextualisation is a key to understanding the movement's rapid growth. This process was facilitated by Pentecostalism's inherent flexibility and its ability to take on local colour, due in part to its emphasis on the 'freedom of the Spirit'. The success of any religion today, according to Harvey Cox, depends upon its

---

[2] Data for this chapter is drawn from oral interviews, church documents, magazines, newspapers and popular books.

[3] Matthews A. Ojo, 'African Charismatics', in Stephen D. Glazier (ed.), *Encyclopedia of African and African-American Religions*, London/New York: Routledge, 2001, 4.

[4] Irving Hexham and Karla Poewe, (eds.) *New Religions as Global Cultures. Making the Human Sacred*, Colorado: Westview Press, 1997, 41.

ability to 'include and transform at least certain elements of pre-existing religions which still retain a strong grip on the cultural subconscious'. Thus part of Pentecostalism's appeal lies in its capacity to combine with elements within the receptor culture, to adopt the 'language, the music, the cultural artefacts, the religious tropes . . . of the settings in which it lives'.[5] Igbo-founded NPCs generated an evolving and flexible 'actual life' theology, which helped participants refashion their identities and respond to changing contexts. This chapter includes an analysis of different theological genres that have emerged since the movement's inception, and their relationship to socio-political and economic developments.

One way they have responded to local concerns is by pursuing global connections. Hackett refers to this process as religious 'internationalism' and suggests that in Nigeria it is generally indigenous groups who seek out these connections in their pursuit of moral, religious and sometimes financial support.[6] Because of its strong global links, some scholars interpret African neo-Pentecostalism as a product of globalisation and refer to its predominantly US American origins. Thus Brouwer *et al.* deny that it is a 'genuinely African construct arising from African experience and meeting African needs', but derives primarily from the United States.[7] Underlying this is the assumption that globalisation is Westernisation (or more specifically Americanisation) and is driven by imperialistic and hegemonic ambitions. However, the Westernisation/globalisation view underestimates the capacity of local agents to select from a range of imported religious commodities to satisfy consumer demands. It also assumes that it is one particular societal model (modern Western culture) which is being globalised and ignores the multi-directional flow of people, images and goods. In the Nigerian context, cultural flows were bi-directional with Igbo neo-Pentecostals influencing their Western partners through transnational interactions.

Anthropologist Simon Ottenberg has drawn attention to Igbo receptivity to Westernisation, which he attributes to their proclivity for individual achievement and prestige.[8] While global flows from the West through

[5] Cox, *Fire*, 219, 259.

[6] Rosalind I. J. Hackett, 'New Religious Movements and Religious Self-Determination', paper for submission to Toyin Falola and J. K. Olupona (eds.), 'Religion and Society in Nigeria. Historical and Sociological Perspectives', 1986, 19.

[7] Brouwer, Gifford and Rose, *American Gospel*, 178, 151. See also Paul Gifford, 'Some Recent Developments in African Christianity', *African Affairs*, Volume 93, Issue 373, 1994, 516-20.

[8] Simon Ottenberg, 'Ibo Receptivity to Change', in W. R. Boscom and M. J. Herskovits (eds.), *Continuity and Change in African Culture*, Chicago: University of Chicago Press, 1959, 130.

media and migration influenced the shape of Igbo neo-Pentecostalism, participants made use of global resources and images to suit their own agendas and satisfy community demands. As Hexham and Poewe note, American charismatic networks do not force themselves on the rest of the world. Rather 'networks that rise spontaneously in various other countries actively seek contact with America because they regard Americans as generous'.[9] Moreover, African Christians have long harboured global aspirations and have found the West's technological superiority and material abundance particularly appealing. There were obvious benefits to be gained from US American linkages, and Igbo neo-Pentecostals eagerly seized the opportunities presented to them. American Pentecostal organisations supplied Igbo neo-Pentecostals with economic assistance, Christian literature, and opportunities for theological training and ministry. American connections were also useful for prestige and for bolstering the legitimacy of their leaders.

Several neo-Pentecostal denominations have received financial support from the USA, including William Okoye's All Christians Fellowship Mission (ACFM), Benson Ezeokeke's Salvation for All Mission and Emmanuel Okorie's Living Word Ministries (LWM). Ezeokeke, for example, is the Nigerian representative of Kingsway Fellowship International, an American Pentecostal organisation, and makes annual visits to the USA to raise money and engage in ministry. His most recent project is a 4,000 seater 'Cathedral' in Onitsha, partially funded by gifts from overseas.[10] But it is possible to make too much of the financial benefits of global connections. For instance, despite its strong US American links, Okorie states that 95 per cent of LWM's finances come from Nigeria.[11] Other NPCs with Western connections deny receiving economic assistance from overseas. These include Grace of God Mission and Christian Pentecostal Mission. Among those with no formal overseas links are Amazing Love Assembly (Enugu), Master's Vessel Church (Umuahia) and Overcomers Christian Mission (Owerri).

If we recall, Igbo NPCs did not have US American origins but did benefit from American cultural flows. Because of the civil war, most missionaries had left the region or had been unable to return. Consequently, direct foreign influence was initially restricted to Christian literature and input from the British Pentecostal missionary S. G. Elton, based in Western Nigeria. As we noted in chapter 4, Elton had linked up with American Pentecostals T. L. Osborn and Gordon Lindsay following his resignation from the British Apostolic Church, and helped to distribute

---

[9] Hexham and Poewe, *New Religions*, 45.

[10] Bishop Dr Benson C. Ezeokeke, 'Testimony and Praise Bulletin', 2000. Kingsway Fellowship International is based in Des Moines, Iowa.

[11] 'Emma Okorie Speaks to The Forum', *Forum*, 2001, 17.

their literature and promote their church-planting strategies. Osborn's writings were particularly influential. In 1971, Elton also introduced the late Benson Idahosa to Lindsay, and this proved decisive in exposing Igbo revivalists to the particular brand of Pentecostalism emanating from America. Idahosa trained at Lindsay's Christ for the Nations Institute in Texas and on his return started his own Bible College with teachers from the USA, India, England and Nigeria, which attracted some of the leading Igbo neo-Pentecostal pioneers. Idahosa also persuaded Edozie Mba, co-founder of Riches of Christ Mission, to enter full-time Christian ministry, and was an early mentor to William Okoye, founder of ACFM. Okoye's wife Helen attended Idahosa's All Nations for Christ Bible Institute, and Idahosa was the invited speaker at ACFM's first annual convention.[12]

In the mid-1970s, several leading US American evangelists visited Eastern Nigeria and forged links with Igbo neo-Pentecostal pioneers, inviting them to train in their Bible colleges. The most influential were Morris Cerullo and T. L. Osborn. Cerullo visited Western Nigeria in 1973, holding crusades in some of the major cities. One of those who attended was Thompson Nwosu who shortly afterwards was posted to Jos as an evangelist where he founded Redeemed People's Mission (RPM). Cerullo's team also organised ministry training schools in Igboland which attracted many local Pentecostal leaders. In 1975, T. L. Osborn held a series of crusades in Eastern Nigeria, attended by Igbo revivalists, including Augustine Nwodika, co-founder of Riches of Christ Mission, and William Okoye and Wilson Ezeofor before they embarked on their evangelistic ministry in the North.

In the late 1970s, Igbo neo-Pentecostal leaders began to travel to the USA, either for ministry engagements or for Bible training. Out of nineteen NPC founders interviewed, fifteen had travelled to the US during the late 1970s or early 1980s. Of these, eleven attended some form of American Bible training institution (eight attended Pentecostal institutions), and nine have maintained links with American Pentecostal ministries or churches. Benson Ezeokeke, for example, travels regularly to the USA on 'missionary trips' and during a five-week visit in 1999 had ministry engagements in eight American Pentecostal churches and three fellowship meetings. Wilson Ezeofor, founder of Bible Faith Mission (Jos), also travels to the USA and has links with American Pentecostal churches through his attendance at the International Convention of Faith Churches and Ministries. When I visited Bible Faith Mission in August 2001, they had recently hosted a team of Americans who held an evangelistic campaign in their church called the 'Dominion Conference'. Cerullo's School of Ministries attracted several NPC pioneers in the 1970s and early

[12] Okoroafor, *William Okoye*, 125.

1980s, partly because it offered scholarships to African students.[13] Okoye attended in 1981 and later acknowledged the influence of Cerullo's teaching on his ministry. Apparently, Cerullo was fond of saying, 'Because God cares we care', and Okoye adopted this motto for his church. It also influenced the choice of slogan which appears on all ACFM's church signboards: 'A Christ-Centred, Spirit-filled, Caring Church'.[14] Okoye has maintained links with the USA and travels there annually to participate in an international Pentecostal leadership conference and engage in ministry. In 1985, several American Pentecostal missionaries helped to set up the World Outreach Bible Institute in Suleja, which has become the main ACFM training centre.[15]

Two informants, Wilson Ezeofor (Bible Faith Mission) and Emmanuel Okorie (Living Word Ministries), had links with Kenneth Hagin, widely regarded as the pioneer of the US American 'Word of Faith' movement and a leading promoter of prosperity teaching. Hagin participated in the 1950s Healing Movement in America and was a member of Lindsay's Voice of Healing network before establishing an independent ministry in 1963. He founded the Tulsa-based Rhema Bible Training Center in 1974. Emmanuel Okorie credits Hagin as the inspiration behind his Living Word Training Centre in Aba, which later became Living Word Ministries. Okorie travelled to the US in 1980 and briefly attended Oral Roberts University before transferring to Hagin's Rhema Bible Training Center. He also received training at Living Word Ministries Bible School in Mount Joy, Pennsylvania, and preached in American Pentecostal churches. In 1983, while listening to a sermon preached by Hagin, Okorie apparently heard an audible voice directing him to return to Nigeria and 'teach faith to his people'. He returned to Aba in 1985 where he set up his Living Word Training Centre. Among its early teachers were three American missionaries who all attended Bible College in the USA with Chinyere Okorie. Emmanuel Okorie now has a home in Baltimore and divides his

---

[13] Igbo NPC pioneers and founders who attended Cerullo's School of Ministries in the USA included Edward Ezenwafor (Our Generation Gospel Ministries), Godwin Nwosu (Bethel Gospel Mission), Benjamin Ikedinobi (Overcomer's Bible Church), Thompson Nwosu (Redeemed People's Mission), Benson Ezeokeke (Salvation for All Mission), Chima Amadi (Holiness Evangelical Church), Samson Onwubiko (Calvary Evangelistic Mission), William Okoye (All Christians Fellowship Mission), Benjamin Ogbuozebe (National Evangelical Mission) and Mike Okonkwo (The Redeemed Evangelical Mission).

[14] Okoroafor, *William Okoye*, 131; All Christians Fellowship Mission, 'Lesson 4. Understanding the Vision and Purpose of your Church', *Membership Bible Studies*, Abuja: Christian Education Department, 2001, 19.

[15] Okoroafor, *William Okoye*, 131, 134.

time between the USA and Nigeria. He describes LWM as a 'Nigerian outfit with USA based Churches and friends'.[16]

Several neo-Pentecostal leaders have British links, and some have actually attended British educational institutions. For example, Wilson Ezeofor (Bible Faith Mission) regularly visits the UK and has close connections with Hugh Osgood, founder of Cornerstone Christian Centre (a large Essex-based church), which has helped them acquire equipment for their television ministry and finance for their school. Of all the churches I visited, the one with strongest links to Britain is Redeemed People's Mission in Jos. Since 1990, RPM's founder Thompson Nwosu has spent up to six weeks each year in the UK, preaching in different churches and raising financial support. RPM has close connections with a British-founded charismatic organisation called Supplyline which provides assistance to churches from developing countries. It has helped to raise the profile of the church in Britain and has contributed towards some of its building projects.[17]

In chapter 1, I referred to the consequences of globalisation for identity construction. Igbo neo-Pentecostalism gradually acquired a global character and consciousness through participation in transnational exchanges of ministry and exposure to Western Pentecostal literature and electronic media. However, global pressure has not resulted in a homogenous neo-Pentecostal culture such that differences between the centre and peripheries have disappeared. Rather, global flows have produced new kinds of particularism and heterogeneity, and have reinforced local identities. They have influenced Igbo neo-Pentecostal theology, rituals, methodologies and interactions through a process of 'glocalisation', blending disparate cultural forms with their own tradition, resulting in 'hybrid' forms of spirituality and religious identity. Igbo NPCs have provided access to an 'imagined community' with global dimensions and missionary ambitions. This has contributed towards their appeal, particularly among upwardly mobile adults and young people in urban contexts eager to share in modernity's 'goods' and find their footing in the modern world.

---

[16] Information from LWM literature and an interview with Emmanuel Okorie (17 January 2002, Aba).

[17] Supplyline was started by the late Arthur Wallis, a pioneer of the British charismatic movement. RPM also has links with another British-based charismatic organisation called Connections, founded by Philip Mohabir. Connections helps churches around the world with financial aid, leadership training and church planting.

Word and Worship

One way we see the interaction between the global and the local is in the content and style of Igbo neo-Pentecostal preaching and teaching ministries and the format of their worship meetings. Bible teaching and communal worship rituals are important sources for constructing and reinforcing neo-Pentecostal collective identities.

Preaching and Teaching

A major attraction of Igbo-initiated neo-Pentecostal churches is their emphasis on Bible teaching and preaching. In the Jos survey, this was the most common reason given for why members preferred their churches, alongside the lively worship styles. This stress on the Bible is understandable given the background of their founders in Scripture Union and the Civil War Revival. As Ojo has observed of similar movements in Western Nigeria, most Igbo-founded NPCs started out as non-denominational Bible study groups, a model inherited from SU in Britain, and the focus on the Bible continued when they attained denominational status.[18] This emphasis is reflected in the names they have adopted, such as Bible Faith Mission, Overcomer's Bible Church, Bible Pentecostal Life Church, Bread of Life Mission and Living Word Ministries. Several denominations also have an open Bible as part of their church logo. For Igbo neo-Pentecostals, the Bible was both a symbolic identity marker and a source for constructing new forms of individual and corporate identity.

During the 1970s, church members met frequently to study the Bible together or listen to messages delivered by their leaders. This became an important means of socialisation. Riches of Christ, for example, held meetings every day of the week. As well as Sunday worship, they organised Bible teaching sessions on Tuesday, Wednesday and Thursday evenings, while other days were set aside for prayer and evangelism. This predilection for holding meetings has continued since the 1970s, though perhaps not with the same intensity. As well as Sunday worship meetings, all the churches I visited had an Adult Sunday School and a regular weekday Bible study which members were urged to attend. Larger churches produce written Sunday school manuals, laced with Bible references. Their content suggests the influence of a global Pentecostal culture. For example, ACFM's 2001 manual contains teaching on 'new life in Christ', 'assurance of salvation', 'Holy Spirit baptism' and 'soul-

---

[18] Matthews A. Ojo, 'The Charismatic Movement in Nigeria Today', *International Bulletin of Missionary Research*, 3, 1995, 115.

winning'.[19] And Grace of God Mission's 2001 manual has chapters entitled 'Restoration', 'Faith changes destinies', 'Jesus the healer' and '33 Divine healing facts by T. L. Osborn'.[20] Churches also have weekday meetings for healing and deliverance which invariably begin with a message from the Bible.

Bible school culture was further evidence of global influences and a reflection of the importance attached to corporate Bible study. Nine denominations I visited have their own Bible schools, offering courses for both lay people and those called to full-time ministry. These are Grace of God Mission (Rock Bible College), National Evangelical Mission (New Anointing Bible College), Redeemed People's Mission (Redeemed People's Theological College), All Christians Fellowship Mission (World Outreach Bible Institute), Christian Pentecostal Mission (Pentecostal International Bible Seminary), Salvation for All Mission (Faith Bible College), Victory Christian Mission (Victory Bible College) and Amazing Love Assembly (Agape Bible College). At least two started during the 1970s: Rock Bible College and New Anointing Bible College.

A belief in the authority of the Bible is one of the implicit values of global Pentecostalism, and African Christians love to quote from it to support their beliefs. In meetings I attended the sermon was always a significant part of the programme, often lasting for over one hour and including numerous quotes from the Bible, frequently punctuated by such phrases as, 'The Bible says. . .' or 'the word of God says. . . '. Members were encouraged to bring their Bibles and often arrived with pen and paper to take notes. All but one of the meetings took place in urban areas, and here the sermons were in English, sometimes with interpretation into Igbo. There is apparently a high level of literacy in these churches and most members can understand English. In my survey, out of 105 respondents from Redeemed People's Mission, 51 per cent had been educated up to primary or secondary level and 44 per cent had tertiary level education (usually university). All the meetings I attended at RPM and Amazing Love Assembly were conducted in English without any interpretation, though many songs were in Igbo, Yoruba or Hausa.[21] Grace of God Mission meetings were also in English, but usually interpreted into Igbo. This is in contrast to some of the older AICs in urban areas. I attended two meetings in Christ Holy Church, founded during the 1940s. One meeting was in English with Igbo interpretation, but many songs were in Igbo. The

---

[19] All Christians Fellowship Mission, *New Life Sunday School*, Abuja: Christian Education Department, All Christians Fellowship Mission, 2001.

[20] Grace of God Mission Inc., *Sunday School Manual*, n.publ, February-July 2001.

[21] RPM Bukuru branch intends to start a Hausa Sunday service in addition to its English service, in order to attract more indigenes from Plateau state.

other meeting was in Igbo, though summarised in English for my benefit. I suspect that rural NPC meetings are generally conducted in the vernacular. Unfortunately, I only attended one, Christian Pentecostal Mission (CPM) in Mbubo, near Umuahia. There were approximately 100 people present and the worship was in the vernacular, but the pastor preached in English, although this again was probably for my benefit.

Igbo neo-Pentecostals have adapted the content and style of their preaching to cater for consumer demands. Preaching in Igbo NPCs is often dramatic and colourful, more a performance than a lecture and intended to entertain as well as inform. The preacher (usually a man) uses the platform as his stage, lacing his message with anecdotes and sometimes acting it out to drive his point home. British sociologist Simon Coleman refers to the 'dramatisation' of the text in Pentecostal sermon delivery, where the preacher is the 'living embodiment of the inspired Word . . . making rhetorical points through skilful oratory and dramatic body language'.[22] Sermons I witnessed were often entertaining, eliciting responses of approval and even laughter from the audience. The standard of sermons varied in quality. Those in larger churches were generally well prepared and delivered extemporaneously with considerable skill. Others were repetitious and lacked coherence and content. Some preaching styles have been influenced by American Pentecostal evangelists observed at evangelistic campaigns in the 1970s, during later visits to America, or on television and video.

Neo-Pentecostal preaching is also practical, and it is here that its main appeal lies. Those I spoke to said they expected preaching and teaching to be relevant to their lives, both in terms of problem solving and equipping for life and ministry. This is in keeping with the pragmatic nature of Igbo indigenous spirituality. Generally, the sermon is the focus of the service. This was the case with Amazing Love Assembly in Enugu, founded in 1986 by former ECWA pastor Amaechi Nwachukwu. In its *Rules and Regulations* it states, 'The most significance part of our church service is the sermon'.[23] One ALA member told me he was attracted by the in-depth Bible teaching which was practical and helped him live the Christian life. Another was impressed by the way the pastor was able to apply the Bible to everyday life. Apart from listening to Nwachukwu's sermons in church, members are encouraged to listen to his weekly 'Livingspring' radio programme and read his Bible studies in the Livingspring magazine. NPC

---

[22] Simon Coleman, *The Globalisation of Charismatic Christianity. Spreading the Gospel of Prosperity*, Cambridge: Cambridge University Press, 2000, 125.

[23] *Rules and Regulations of Amazing Love Ministries*, Enugu: Timex Enterprises, n.d., 11.

Figure 11. Amazing Love Assembly, Enugu

pastors fulfil a similar function to traditional religious leaders or the prophet-healers in the older AICs. ALA members refer to their pastor as the 'man of God' and allude to his remarkable preaching and teaching gift, his 'exemplary life' and his ability to perform healing. His sermons are invariably interpreted as messages from God. Note the following testimonies in an ALA magazine. The first is written by a student at ALA's Bible school, who was converted in 1967 but later 'slid into loose living, compromising and chasing worldly passions'.

> My testimony today is that since I came back to God and joined a living church, my eyes have been opened to the true essence of life, which is life in Jesus Christ through the incisive teachings and exemplary life of my Pastor, Rev. Amaechi Nwachukwu. His down to earth expositions of the word of God, leadership by example and pastoring in love has helped in no small measure in transforming my life and changing my value system.[24]

[24] Nweke Anyigor, 'God of a 2nd Chance', *Livingspring*, 1998, 19.

The second is written by a listener to the pastor's radio programme. 'On the 29th of September, I and my friend ran into your programme. We were thoroughly ministered to for it is a message from God meant for mature Christians'.[25]

For neo-Pentecostals, the Word itself, not just the messenger, has life-changing potential because of the ministry of the Spirit. By exposing themselves to the Word's influence, mediated by the Spirit-anointed pastor, neo-Pentecostals construct new identities for themselves. For instance, an All Christians Fellowship Mission Bible study states, 'God's word has intrinsic power - that is, it carries its power within itself. This is because it is the voice of God. . . . It therefore carries the power of God and fulfils the purpose of God'.[26] Pentecostal theologian Steven Land refers to the fusion of Spirit and Word in Pentecostal spirituality. The Spirit who inspired the Scriptures makes the Word alive and powerful today by teaching, guiding, convicting and transforming those who encounter it. 'The Word comes in words and in the power and demonstration of the Spirit'.[27] In some Igbo NPC logos, this is symbolised by an open Bible set alongside the figure of a dove, representing the Word and the Spirit. A case in point is Redeemed People's Mission in Jos where these symbols are accompanied by the Bible text: 'equipping the saints for service'. Chuks Ogoalaji, General Superintendent of Bread of Life Mission, told me that preaching is important because 'it is the Word that heals, saves, delivers and prospers the people'.[28] Coleman refers to this as the 'internalisation' of the text, where the words are believed not only 'to describe experience, but also to constitute it and cause it to occur'.[29] Igbo neo-Pentecostals talk about feeding on God's Word in order to grow. Thus Ezekiel of Christian Pentecostal Mission states, 'Christian growth is by knowledge. . . . The way a mother feeds her child is the same way God feeds us with the knowledge of His word through His divine power'.[30] And a grateful reader of Nwachukwu's teaching in *Livingspring* journal writes, 'Each time I read LSJ, it serves as a delicious meal unto my soul'.[31] Coleman describes 'eating' as a 'powerful image because it points to a notion of internalising

---

[25] Egwu Eni Ogbonna, 'Letter to Livingspring Broadcast', *Livingspring*, 1998, 10.

[26] All Christians Fellowship Mission, 'Lesson 8: Fellowship with God 1: The Word of God', *New Life Sunday School*, 32.

[27] Steven J. Land, *Pentecostal Spirituality. A Passion for the Kingdom*, Sheffield: Sheffield Academic Press, 1993, 100.

[28] Interview, 23 May 2000, Enugu.

[29] Coleman, *Globalisation*, 118, 129.

[30] Rev Dr O. Ezekiel, 'Growth', *Echoes of Joy*, April 2001, 11.

[31] Mrs Nwaka Idah, 'Talkback', *Livingspring*, 1998, 9.

truth directly, bypassing the distorting effects of both social context and intellect'.[32]

Neo-Pentecostal Bible colleges also have a practical ethos aimed at equipping students for Christian life and ministry, and reinforcing their identity as a new community distinct from the 'world'. The World Outreach Bible Institute (ACFM), for example, seeks to 'train and equip a new breed of men and women of God after the Apostolic order', while the Living Word Training Centre (LWM) claims that through a 'balanced bible-based curriculum, students are guided to apply God's word to their personal lives and ministry'.[33] Onuigbo's Victory International Bible College (Victory Christian Mission) has the rather grandiose vision of 'raising up militant soldiers of the Lord for the End-Time battle'.[34] At least two churches, ACFM and LWM, base their Bible college vision on Ephesians 4:11 (NASB): 'And he gave some as apostles, and some as prophets, and some evangelists, and some as pastors and teachers, for the equipping of the saints for the work of service, to the building up of the body of Christ'.

An examination of college curricula reveals the extent of Western evangelical and Pentecostal influences. For instance, RPM's Theological College (REPETHEC) offers courses in Theology, Bible Introduction, Hermeneutics, Homiletics, Apologetics, Missions, Nigerian Church History, Ethics, Counselling skills, Leadership Principles, Marriage and Family, Greek and Hebrew. Others college curricula contain courses that are more overtly Pentecostal. As well as conventional subjects, such as systematic theology and Bible exposition, Victory International Bible College offers courses on 'Spiritual Warfare', 'Faith Power', the 'Theology of Health' and 'Church Planting'.[35] And an Onitsha-based neo-Pentecostal ministry called 'Voice of Miracles' offers courses on 'Apostolic evangelism', 'Deliverance and Demonology', 'Gifts & Ministries', 'Miracles – Signs & Wonders', 'Breaking curses and evil covenants', and 'Giving and Prosperity'. According to its brochure, Voices of Miracles Ministry has strong links with the USA.

Initially, these colleges offered short courses to train pastors for the rapidly growing NPCs. An exception was Living Word Training Centre (LWM) which from its inception was non-denominational and attracted people from all walks of life and a variety of churches in Aba. During the

---

[32] Coleman, *Globalisation*, 128.

[33] Leaflet introducing the World Outreach Bible Institute, All Christians Fellowship Mission, Abuja; Living Word Ministries, *Annual Journal*, Aba: Living Word Ministries, 2001, 5.

[34] Victory Christian Mission, *Victory International Bible College Enugu. Hand Information Booklet*, Enugu: Brilliant Press, n.d, 3.

[35] *Ibid.*

1990s, most have responded to consumer demands by raising the profile of their training institutes, providing flexible programmes to cater for laity and full-time ministers, and employing better qualified teaching staff. REPETHEC, for example, holds its lectures during weekday evenings and offers a one-month 'Summer School'. Most students passing through Agape Bible College (ALA) are lay members, and consequently ALA holds lectures in the evenings. Both colleges have well-qualified teachers in terms of practical experience and academic excellence. For instance, Amaechi Nwachukwu, who does most of the teaching at Agape Bible College (ALA), has a Master's Degree from Wheaton College, USA. And visiting lecturers at ALA have included Ogbu Kalu, until recently a Professor at the University of Nigeria, and Yusuf Turaki, a former Professor of Theology and Social Ethics at Jos ECWA Theological Seminary (JETS) and research fellow at Yale Divinity School. David Adegboye, Principal of REPETHEC, has a Master's Degree from JETS. According to REPETHEC's brochure, the college 'is endowed with a team of committed, Spirit-filled lecturers who combine academic excellence with proven ministry experience'. Some neo-Pentecostal institutions also see themselves as vanguards against the infiltration of unbalanced teaching into the Pentecostal community. For instance, REPETHEC is concerned that church members are being exposed to 'junk' Christian literature and preachers on the electronic media, while 'sound biblical interpretation and principles have been put aside and replaced with whatever the "man of God" feels the Spirit is leading him to do'. Consequently, 'ignorance has prevailed in the church today and false doctrines are gaining firm roots'. It was out of this concern that RPM opened its college in 1994, which it claims 'caters for the needs of the church of both Pentecostal and evangelical persuasion'.[36] In 2000, REPETHEC graduated forty-three students from eighteen denominations, mainly Pentecostal but including evangelical mission churches such as ECWA, Anglican, Presbyterian, COCIN and Methodist. A recent trend is for NPC pastors to undergo further training at non-Pentecostal theological institutions.[37]

Innovative Worship Styles

While the sermon is one focus of Igbo neo-Pentecostal meetings, equal time is given to 'praise and worship'. Igbo NPCs see themselves as worshipping

---

[36] Brochure introducing the Redeemed People's Theological College, Jos.

[37] For example, pastors Cosmos Ikwe and Stephen Nyam, Jos District overseers of Redeemed People's Mission and All Christians Fellowship Mission respectively, have both completed degrees at JETS, which is affiliated to the University of Jos.

communities and engage in communal worship as a means of expressing their devotion to God and their identity as the people of God. Pentecostal worship, with its lively unstructured style and emphasis on 'freedom in the Spirit', was especially appealing compared to the more traditional, rationalistic worship of the mainline churches, and assisted the movement's assimilation into Igbo religious culture. In the Jos survey, out of 167 respondents, 88 per cent said that one reason they were attracted to their church was the quality of the worship.

The importance of worship in church life is evident in some of the names adopted by individual congregations, such as Praise Temple (ALA, Enugu), Joy Cathedral (CPM, Aba), Garden of Praise and Progress (CPM, Suleja), Chapel of Praise (Gospel Crusaders Mission, Aba) and Harmonious Worship Church (LWM, Aba). It is also reflected in the time devoted to congregational singing and choir items in their meetings. For participants, it is clearly an exhilarating and joyous experience. Larger urban-based churches follow a similar pattern during their services. The most impressive I observed was Grace Cathedral (Grace of God Mission), one of the largest Pentecostal churches in Enugu. On Sundays, it holds two morning meetings to accommodate the congregation of around 2,000. The service I attended lasted several hours and consisted of two main parts: music and the sermon. The entire congregation participated in the 'praise and worship' led by a young male soloist and a 4-piece band, all highly accomplished musicians. Choruses sung repetitively in English or Igbo were accompanied by clapping and bodily movement. The congregational singing was interspersed with offerings, testimonies and prayers which were usually spontaneous and simultaneous, allowing for greater participation. The sermon, preached by the pastor in English, was interpreted into Igbo and lasted about an hour. The second largest worship meeting I attended was at Redeemed People's Mission headquarters church in Jos, which has an average attendance of around one thousand. It followed a similar format but in addition to the worship band had a large and professional choir called the Redemption Mass Choir. Thompson Nwosu, its founder, has a regular television programme called 'The Divine Encounter', and this particular meeting was recorded for Nigerian Television (NTA). The singing was exuberant and interspersed with spontaneous prayers and testimonies. The sermon, preached in English with no interpretation, was followed by an appeal for salvation and healing, and ended with a prolonged series of offerings.

The format of neo-Pentecostal worship services and the shape of their music bear the marks of Western influence. Audiotapes, CDs and videotapes with American and British Pentecostal worships songs are widely available in Nigeria, and increasing numbers of Nigerians have access to satellite television channels which regularly relay meetings conducted by American televangelists. Songs of Western origin are often modified to suit the Igbo context or translated into the vernacular. Igbo neo-Pentecostals are enchanted by the 'modern' and where possible use electronic musical instruments in their worship, but in ways that reinforce local styles and rhythms. This blending of the global and local, the 'modern' and 'traditional', produces hybrid forms of religiosity that appeal to consumer demands.

In Igbo traditional religion, worship is communal and individual, spontaneous and experiential. Pentecostal worship is clearly very appealing in this context where a sense of divine immediacy is taken for granted. However, Igbo traditionalists engage in worship as a means of manipulating the deities to their advantage.[38] Here neo-Pentecostal piety claims to depart from the traditional model. Thus Redeemed People's Mission states, 'Very often, some gather together in worship with a view of what they will get out of it rather than what they can give to God. Until our attitudes are changed, we may not offer unto God satisfactory praise and worship'.[39] As I observed neo-Pentecostals at worship, often singing for extended periods, clapping their hands, dancing, and sometimes breaking out into emotional outbursts of prayer, their obvious enjoyment of the whole experience impressed me.

The appeal of Pentecostal worship lies in its emphasis on direct experience of the divine and its inclusive nature which encourages active participation of every member. As Anderson notes, it allows ordinary people to be 'lifted out of their mundane daily experiences into a new realm of ecstasy'.[40] In the Igbo context, collective oral prayer with worshippers praying at once is a common feature and was apparently introduced via the Civil War Revival by members of Assemblies of God. It was a novel liturgical approach for those revivalists with mainline church backgrounds, but it resonated with elements of Igbo traditional religious culture. One informant told me that when Igbos gather at traditional shrines, they simultaneously and audibly call upon God to meet their needs. It was also a common practice in prayer houses before the civil war but became more popular during the 1970s, partly as a response to the crisis. Pentecostal prayer is a form of cathartic expression. Nowhere is this more evident than when they begin to speak or sing in tongues. Cox calls this the recovery of

---

[38] Agu, *Secularization*, 400; Ikenga-Metuh, *God and Man*, 122; Okorocha, *Religious Conversion*, 206.

[39] Redeemed People's Mission, 'Lesson 3. Worship - The Life-Line of the Church', *Redeemed Adult Sunday School Lessons*, Jos: Redeemed People's Mission Inc., 1999, 8.

[40] Allan H. Anderson, 'Global Pentecostalism in the New Millenium', in Allan H. Anderson and Walter J. Hollenweger (eds.), *Pentecostals after a Century. Global Perspectives on a Movement in Transition*, Sheffield: Sheffield Academic Press, 1999, 223.

primal speech, when 'cognitive grids and perceptual barriers . . . are temporarily suspended' and people give vent to their deepest feelings.[41]

However, there is also a pragmatic element to Igbo neo-Pentecostal worship which adds to its appeal. According to Okorocha, in their traditional religion Igbo loyalty to the gods is conditional and depends upon reciprocity - they expect blessings in return.[42] Though neo-Pentecostals claim to worship God for his own sake, they also expect to receive practical benefits, and several sections of their meetings provide opportunity for this to occur. During an interlude, someone may deliver a 'prophecy' or a 'word of knowledge' for the benefit of the whole congregation or an individual. This was less common than expected, especially when compared to its prevalence within the prayer houses. I suspect this was partly a reaction against such groups, often demonised in neo-Pentecostal rhetoric, but it was also a consequence of their high regard for the Bible. I heard only five prophecies, all delivered by members of Redeemed People's Mission, though informants assured me that prophecy was quite common, especially during prayer meetings and night vigils. The most moving occurred during the first church meeting I attended after the Jos religious riots in September 2001, when many lost their lives and property, including some members of RPM. The church premises were near one of the focal points of the fighting and some members had to flee their homes to take refuge there. The message, delivered in the first person, related to the crisis and contained words of assurance that God was with them. Anderson notes that among Western Pentecostals, prophecy is normally restricted to 'forth telling' rather than 'foretelling', but in Africa, both aspects are found.[43] During the same meeting, the pastor told us about several Christian leaders who had received 'revelations' earlier in the year that something disastrous was about to happen in Jos. One of these was Igbo Pentecostal Rev. Bright Ndu, senior pastor of Footprints of Jesus Mission and Chairman of the Pentecostal Fellowship of Nigeria (Plateau State) in 2001. In an article in a local Christian magazine he refers to a dream he had five days before the crisis which he relayed to other pastors in Jos. Ndu's church premises were burnt down during the conflict.[44]

At the end of every meeting I attended opportunity was given to respond to the sermon and receive prayer. Often this included prayers for salvation, healing, deliverance and sometimes prosperity. Here the focus was on the pastor or visiting preacher who is believed to possess an ability to impart the Spirit's power. During one RPM meeting, the pastor preached a sermon

---

41 Cox, *Fire*, 82, 86.

42 Okorocha, *Religious Conversion*, 206.

43 Anderson, *Zion and Pentecost*, 280.

44 Rev. Bright Ndu, 'I saw the Jos Crisis before it happened', *Salvation*, 16 December 2001, 3.

entitled 'God's provision and prosperity'. There followed a prolonged period of prayer for three categories of people: those who found it difficult to save, those with uncompleted projects, and those who found it difficult to tithe. There was also an appeal for salvation and opportunity to receive healing prayer. During another meeting in a different branch of RPM, the pastor spoke on the need for Christians to be delivered from the effects of ancestral covenants with traditional deities if they were to fulfil their destinies. He then led the congregation in a prolonged period of deliverance prayer. I attended nine meetings at Amazing Love Assembly (Enugu), and each concluded with an opportunity for people to respond to the sermon or receive prayer, though this was not always in the form of an 'altar call' for people to come to the front. During two ALA meetings the pastor had 'words of knowledge' for members of the congregation who were then encouraged to receive prayer for healing.

Alternative Communities

Listening to the Word and participating in worship became important means for Igbo neo-Pentecostals to reinforce their collective identities and mark off their difference from the 'world'. We have identified communalism as an aspect of Igbo indigenous culture, and the failure of mission churches to fulfil Igbo communal aspirations as one reason for the popularity of the Civil War Revival and the emergence of new Pentecostal churches. I now reflect upon the communal dimension of neo-Pentecostal spirituality.

Church as Family

One reason for the continuing appeal of neo-Pentecostal churches, especially in urban contexts, is their presentation of themselves as surrogate extended families. This is reflected in the following statement taken from a neo-Pentecostal Bible study: 'The church as a community should see herself as an "extended family" of God whose bond (the blood of Jesus) is stronger than our earthly family ties'.[45] The combined effects of the civil war and urban migration created fragmented communities and weakened the role of the extended family. Government policies, as discussed in chapter 2, hampered Igbo economic recovery following the war and prevented them from benefiting fully from the prosperity of the oil boom

[45] Redeemed People's Mission, 'Lesson 1: Know the Church', *Redeemed Adult Sunday School Lessons*, 1999, 1.

years. Neo-Pentecostal churches provided access to a supportive network of relationships, independent of existing family structures.

These churches have fulfilled a similar function since the 1970s when relative prosperity gave way to rapid economic decline following the drop in international oil prices in 1981 and the implementation of SAP in 1986. Part of Pentecostalism's significance in Nigeria, according to Marshall, lies in its potential for reconstructing 'disintegrating social and economic relationships', such as collapsing patron-client networks, failing state welfare provision and the weakening of the role of the extended family.[46] In this setting, where the old resources of community have become unreliable, other modes of identification and community formation emerge. Igbo NPCs provide an alternative source of social security, with members supporting one another in moments of financial distress. Among the stated practical benefits of membership within All Christians Fellowship Mission, for example, is financial support in times of trouble and assistance with finding employment and accommodation.[47] Some NPCs have also set up self-help activities such as schools and medical services to cater for the needs of their members.

Often Igbo NPCs have home fellowship groups, which provide the context for pastoral care and practical support and reinforce collective identities. Ojo relates the success of these groups in Nigeria to the way they replicate traditional African family worship.[48] In the case of Redeemed People's Mission, home fellowship groups were set up in the 1980s, each with around fifteen people. By 1988, RPM's headquarters church in Jos had thirty-two home fellowship groups.[49] Those in RPM's Bukuru branch meet fortnightly and engage in a variety of activities, including Bible study, worship, prayer and evangelism. Christian Pentecostal Mission (CPM) has 'Family Fellowship groups' which aim to integrate members into the local church, encourage love and unity, maintain spiritual growth and give people a 'sense of belonging'.[50] These are not a recent initiative. For instance, those in the main CPM branch in Aba started soon after the inauguration of the church in 1983. Living Word Ministries has adopted a different approach. Instead of dividing the church into smaller units, they limit the size of their congregations. When they exceed

---

[46] Ruth Marshall, 'Pentecostalism in Southern Nigeria: An Overview', in Gifford (ed.), *New Dimensions*, 23.

[47] All Christians Fellowship Mission, 'Lesson 3: Importance of Local Church Membership & Benefits', *Membership Bible Studies*, 13-14.

[48] Ojo, 'Charismatic Movement in Nigeria', 117.

[49] 'Annual Progress Report', Redeemed People's Mission, 4 December 1988.

[50] 'Family Fellowship in some Lagos State Branches', *Pentecostal Family*, August 1999, 35.

250, they divide into two, thus enabling the pastor to maintain a close relationship with his people. They have also adopted the novel idea of having several churches meeting at different times in the same building, each with their own pastor.

In the Jos survey, 77 per cent of respondents stated that one reason they preferred their church was because of the love between members. Several churches have actually adopted names which reflect this community ethos. After his separation from co-leader Wilson Ezeofor, William Okoye changed the name of Freedom in Christ Church to All Christians Fellowship Mission out of a concern for unity. Okoye's ecumenical sentiments are also reflected in one of the key tenets of the new church: 'In all essential biblical doctrines, there must be unity, in non-essentials liberty, and in all things, brotherly love'. If we recall, he also adopted the motto 'Because God cares we care', and ACFM church signboards contain the slogan 'A Christ-Centred, Spirit-filled, Caring Church'.[51] Other NPCs with similar slogans include National Evangelical Mission ('The People That Love') and Salvation for All Mission ('Jesus Cares and We Care'). Another example is Amaechi Nwachukwu's Amazing Love Assembly (ALA). I stayed with Nwachukwu for two months in his large residence, known as the 'manse', and was able to observe the church community at first hand. Their motto, sung at every worship meeting and often quoted in their literature, is 'The steadfast love of the Lord never ceases', based on the Bible text Lamentations 3:22. ALA was born out of a concern for those who, for one reason or another, have failed and drifted away from the church. According to Nwachukwu, God is the 'God of the second chance', and his church welcomes those who feel alienated from the Christian community. Once they become members they are held to account by their brothers and sisters and exposed to a rigorous programme of Bible teaching, prayer and discipleship. Many aspects of ALA church life impressed me, not least the commitment of members to one another and the hospitality they showed me during my stay. At any one time, there may be up to ten young people living in the manse, and because there are church meetings everyday, there is a higher level of interaction between members than tends to be the case with the mission churches. Those I spoke to at ALA said it was the practical demonstration of love that attracted them to the church.

---

[51] Okoroafor, *William Okoye*, 122, 131; All Christians Fellowship Mission, 'Lesson 4. Understanding the Vision and Purpose of your Church', *Membership Bible Studies*, 19. The theme for ACFM's 2001 National Convention was 'That They May Be One', based on Jesus's prayer for unity in John chapter 17.

Ecclesiastical Structures

Neo-Pentecostal church government reflects Igbo patriarchal and gerontocratic extended family structures. In chapter 3, we discussed the way the revival challenged traditional gender boundaries by promoting an egalitarian fellowship and providing space for women to participate in ministry and leadership. Yet while women figured prominently in Scripture Union leadership structures, this was not replicated in the new churches which were all founded and led predominantly by men.

Since the 1970s, this trend has continued. In the denominations I visited, pastors were almost exclusively male, and women usually confined to lower levels of church administration. Christian Pentecostal Mission headquarters church in Lagos is a case in point. Out of twenty-nine zonal leaders between 1984 and 1986, twelve were women.[52] By 2001, however, there were few women in pastoral leadership, apart from wives of senior pastors. These included Mrs O. Ezekiel, wife of the General Overseer, who is CPM National/International Co-ordinator and Assistant Head Pastor of 'Believers' Cathedral (the headquarters church in Lagos), and Evangelist Mrs J. Ezeh, wife of the Imo State Co-ordinator, who is Assistant Head Pastor of CPM headquarters church in Imo State. Out of thirty-five Imo State CPM pastors in 2001, only two were women. While its literature allows for the possibility of female elders, this is not reflected in local church structures.[53] Living Word Ministries is another example. Its core leadership team has twelve members of which three are women, yet none of its branches has female pastors.[54] It is similar outside Igboland. Aside from wives of male pastors, Redeemed People's Mission has no female pastors. In 2002, Jos District of RPM consisted of sixteen churches, and all their pastors were male. It also had a District Council with thirty-one lay leaders but only five were women. RPM's membership manual contains the following statement: 'Women could be Evangelists, Missionaries, Bible Teachers, etc. but administrative or governmental headship should be that

[52] 'CPM Int'l Headquarters Long Serving Unit Leaders (1984, '85 & '86)', *Pentecostal Family*, August 1999, 36.

[53] 'CPM Branches in Imo State', *Echoes of Joy*, 35; Christian Pentecostal Mission International, 'The Church, Authority and Membership', *Membership Manual*, Lagos: Jesus Foundation Class, Christian Pentecostal Mission International, 1999, 72.

[54] See Living Word Ministries, *Annual Journal*. In 2001, the three women in LWM's leadership team are Chinyere Okorie, wife of the founder, who heads up the Living Word Training Centre; Esther Jude-Ehiemere, Director of 'We Care Ministry'; and Stella Uwaezuoke, Director of the Unique Women Fellowship.

of a man. The Lord Jesus chose 12 men to start the Church'.[55] None of the elders in RPM's Bukuru congregation are women. All Christians Fellowship Mission has a number of female pastors, but again these are mainly wives of male pastors. While this preference for male leadership reflects prevailing cultural norms, the stated intention of Igbo neo-Pentecostals is to be biblical rather than African. One exception to this trend is Bishop Mike Okonkwo of The Redeemed Evangelical Mission (TREM) who strongly supports the ordination of women and has himself publicly ordained women to the gospel ministry despite opposition from some of his Pentecostal colleagues.[56]

Neo-Pentecostal ecclesiology is also strongly authoritarian and hierarchical. In Igbo neo-Pentecostal parlance, the General Overseer or the senior pastor is often addressed as 'Daddy' or 'the man of God' and is seldom questioned or criticised. I have already referred to the revival's liberating impulse which equipped young people with tools to challenge gerontocratic authority and take on leadership roles. However, as the young founders became elders themselves, they reintroduced authoritarian structures. This is reflected in a propensity to take titles for themselves. Most of the founders of Igbo-founded NPCs I visited had the title 'Rev. Dr', four had the title 'Bishop' (Benson Ezeokeke, Wilson Uzumegbunam, Alexander Ekewuba, Amaechi Nwachukwu), and one 'Archbishop' (Victor Onuigbo). Honorary doctoral degrees have joined traditional chieftaincy titles as emblems of success within Igbo society, and these values have infected Igbo Pentecostal culture.[57] This is surprising when one considers the rejection of titles during the movement's early history. Yet some Igbo neo-Pentecostals have expressed concern over recent trends. For example, William Okoye of All Christians Fellowship Mission writes, 'The number of Bishops we have in the Pentecostal churches today is alarming, and if care is not taken, we will outnumber all the Bishops in combined mainline denominations in the next few years. Most of this is done in an effort to obtain cheap popularity and recognition'.[58] Nnaji Chukwuka, founder of Revival Time Ministries, has also expressed disapproval. He regards title-

---

[55] Redeemed People's Mission, *Membership Manual*, Jos: Redeemed People's Mission, 2003, 31.

[56] See Mike Okonkwo, 'Sustaining the Move of God', in Wagner and Thompson (eds.), *Out of Africa*, 62-3.

[57] I came across only one Igbo NPC founder from the 1970s, Felix Obiorah (Master's Vessel Church), who had obtained a doctoral degree from an accredited university. Among those who have refused such titles are Thompson Nwosu and William Okoye, founders of Redeemed People's Mission and All Christians Fellowship Mission respectively.

[58] William Okoye, *Vainglory. The Cancer of Today's Church*, Abuja: Integrity Royal Publications, 2002, 35.

seeking as an attempt by the older generation to guard their status in the face of challenges from their younger, better educated rivals: 'the "elderly" ones in defensive mood to the challenge of these youths, and the "business-preachers," sought out a kind of defence-mechanism by accepting some "old-fashioned" titles which they scorned at before. Titles like "Bishops, Archbishops, Rev. Drs"'.[59]

Yet at the level of ordinary congregational life, a democratic culture still exists. Women and young people are allowed considerable space to participate, even if denied access to senior administrative positions. They may lead worship, testify, prophesy, pray and occasionally preach during meetings. They may also take leading roles as evangelists and counsellors, as well as teach in the Bible schools and lead house fellowship groups. NPC worship meetings I attended were often led by young men or women, and all but two of the prophecies I witnessed were given by women. Opportunities to preach were rare, though I heard two sermons delivered by women, both in Amazing Love Assembly (Enugu) during its Women's Fellowship week. In the case of Living Word Ministries (Aba), Chinyere Okorie and Nnenna Ikpa are Rector and Dean respectively of Living Word Training Centre, and Esther Ehiemere is the Director of 'We Care Ministry', the social welfare wing of the church. Constance Ikwe, wife of RPM's Jos District Overseer, recently organised a prayer conference for women which was attended by Mrs Zainab Boni Haruna and Chief (Mrs) Valentina Dariya, First Ladies of Adamawa and Plateau States respectively. Women regularly lead Sunday morning worship meetings and Friday evening prayer meetings at Redeemed People's Mission Bukuru branch.

The Nuclear Family

The nuclear family is an area where Pentecostalism's potential as an agent of social transformation and cohesion is particularly evident, and this has proved highly attractive for women in particular. Marshall notes the ambiguity of Nigerian Pentecostalism in this respect. While it advocates the submission of women to men, its stress on fidelity, respect and shared family responsibilities means that women's position in the home is improved for the better.[60]

One church that lays emphasis on the nuclear family as the key to community transformation is Christian Pentecostal Mission. Through its Family Fellowship groups, annual Family Week and literature, CPM promotes family values in the church and nation. This is evident in the following extracts from an article written by the General Overseer, Obiorah

[59] Chukwuka, *Beyond the Night*, 46-7.

[60] Marshall, 'Pentecostalism', 21.

Ezekiel. Exekiel believes that many problems in society are caused by young people, often as a result of poor parental upbringing.

> What we are seeking is family values, where children will honour their parents and perform their normal duties in the home; the father takes up his normal responsibilities in the home, likewise the mother . . . . Before we can think of Divine Restoration in the church or in our nation, we must first make sure that individual members of the families that make up both the church and the nation have been divinely restored . . . . We need divine restoration in the lives of our children because occultism in our universities and other higher institutions of learning is growing at an alarming rate and when a child leaves home, the parents may not know what he will engage himself in . . . . Responsible children come from responsible homes and *vice versa.* When we give our children good home training, they will become godly children, working in the way of the Lord and bearing good fruits, hence the evils committed by youths in our nation will gradually come to a halt. And when we have godly children they will finally turn out to become godly parents and the chains of godliness will remain unbroken.[61]

Some NPCs have separate fellowship groups for men and women which encourage responsible family behaviour. This usually means the husband exercising spiritual headship over the family, but in a way that liberates rather than restricts other members. Living Word Ministries describes the impact of its Unique Women Fellowship on church life: 'Homes are daily being healed and women are becoming more effective in ministry and children upbringing. Women leaders of the stature of Ruth and Deborah have been raised here'.[62] And testimonies in LWM's magazine show the effect of its Christian Men's Forum on women's experience. One tells of how her husband used to be a 'bully' and a 'bore' but has now become a caring and romantic spouse through attending the Christian Men's Forum. Another says that when her husband started attending the group he began to involve her in his business. Most stress that the change occurred after their husbands took their place as 'spiritual' heads of the home. For example, one woman writes, 'I was far ahead of him in Christianity but like a man that he is, he has learnt fast . . . and has taken over the spiritual leadership of the family. We are all happy following him as one family in the Lord!'[63]

---

[61] Rev Dr O. Ezekiel, 'We are Seeking Family Values', *Pentecostal Family*, August 1999, 7.

[62] Living Word Ministries, *Annual Journal*, 6.

[63] '"Unique" Testimonies', *Forum*, 2001, 33.

Igbo neo-Pentecostal approaches to sexuality and marriage also reinforce collective identities and hold out benefits for youth and women in particular. Ojo notes that concern for marriage and sexuality among Nigerian neo-Pentecostals developed in the late 1970s. Before that time, most were young and single, keen to engage in evangelistic activities rather than pursue marriage, which they regarded as 'worldly'.[64] In urban contexts, where traditional ways of arranging marriages are breaking down, churches fulfil important roles. Various church groups provide a setting for meeting prospective spouses, and marriage preparation is offered as a practical benefit of church membership. For example, LWM has a mixed youth group called 'Living Youth Aflame' and a 'Unique Singles' group for 'single sisters' where 'they are groomed as leaders and also prepared for their future roles as wives and mothers'.[65] ACFM's *Membership Bible Studies* includes the following statement: 'You can wed in any of our branches. Not only that, the wedding will be announced but members will be mobilised to attend and give you gifts. Music, pre-marital counselling, bus services and video coverage will be provided free of charge'.[66]

Nigerian neo-Pentecostal churches, like their counterparts in the global North, are generally conservative in their approaches to gender and sexuality, and little opportunity is given for debate on matters such as male leadership in the home, divorce/remarriage and gay issues. Church membership manuals and written Bible studies contain little or no discussion on these issues, presumably because they regard the Bible's position as clear, unequivocal and authoritative. Igbo neo-Pentecostals forbid divorce and homosexual practice, and promote monogamy, fidelity and control of sexuality, with equal stress placed upon the responsibility of husbands to love their wives and the submission of wives to their husbands. For Igbo neo-Pentecostals, male leadership in the home does not mean domination but self-sacrifice. The growth of Pentecostalism has reinforced the conservative stance of Nigeria's evangelical constituency on family matters.

The Family Circle is an Igbo-initiated ministry founded by former revivalist and Scripture Union member Don Odunze, which promotes Christian family values. Odunze is an Assemblies of God pastor, but his ministry is financially independent and is popular among Igbo neo-Pentecostals. He organised his first marriage seminar in 1978 and has appeared regularly on television. He has also written many books on

[64] Matthews A. Ojo, 'Sexuality, Marriage and Piety among Charismatics in Nigeria', in J. L. Cox, *Rites of Passage in Contemporary Africa*, Cardiff Academic Press, 1998, 185.

[65] Living World Ministries, *Annual Journal*, 7, 55.

[66] All Christians Fellowship Mission, 'Lesson 3. Importance of Local Church Membership and Benefits', *Membership Bible Studies*, 13.

family relationships. Odunze advocates three 'divine principles' for successful marriages: monogamy, permanence (no divorce) and a determination to succeed. In African culture, a barren woman is often abandoned. However, Odunze teaches that women 'should be secure in their matrimonial homes, with or without children'. He acknowledges the importance of extended family structures, but believes that the nuclear family should take precedence.[67]

Constructing Boundaries and Maintaining Difference

Igbo Pentecostal churches express their identities by constructing symbolic boundaries to mark out their difference from the 'world' and their distance from Satan and other malign spirits. Thus in a Bible study entitled 'The Cost of Being Different', Redeemed People's Mission encourages its members to be 'different from the world in attitude and lifestyle'.[68] New birth, water baptism, Holy Communion and Spirit baptism are key identity markers that separate those who belong from outsiders, and each has ethical and spiritual conditions and consequences. For example, All Christians Fellowship Mission states, 'In baptism you take a public stand with God and righteousness. Baptism is a challenge to the powers of darkness for you have been delivered from their kingdom and now translated to the kingdom of God and as such taking a stand against the devil, his demons, sin and the world'.[69] And its stated list of conditions for Spirit baptism includes new birth and complete deliverance from involvement in demonic practices and/or 'occult' groups. ACFM then catalogues various 'occult' groups and 'demonic' practices which may infect believers and hinder reception of the Spirit: 'juju', Talisman, Yoga meditation, Guru Maharaji, Grail message, Eckanka, Rosicrucian Order (Amorc), 'White garment churches', marine spirit, witchcraft and *ogbanje* spirit.[70]

---

[67] Don Odunze, *Counsellors Handbook on Pre-Marital Counselling, Successful Marriage Techniques, the Marriage Killers*, Enugu: Family Circle Publications, 1983, 122, 112; Don Odunze and Marvin Gilbert, *Successful Family Living (An African View)*, Enugu: Donze Family Circle Publications, 1998, 170.

[68] Redeemed People's Mission, 'Lesson 21. The Cost of Being Different', *Redeemed Adult Sunday School*, Jos: Redeemed People's Mission Inc., 1998, 61.

[69] All Christians Fellowship Mission, 'Lesson 4. Our Symbol of Salvation 1: Water Baptism', *New Life Sunday School*, 16.

[70] All Christians Fellowship Mission, 'Lesson 7. The Holy Spirit Baptism', *New Life Sunday School*, 27-8. .

Ongoing obedience to biblical principles reinforces neo-Pentecostal difference. Igbo NPC texts insist on holiness for theological reasons. Thus a Bible study entitled 'Enoch: Unbroken Fellowship with God' states that 'Walking with God demands holiness'.[71] Neo-Pentecostals are also motivated by a belief that the experience of God's presence, power and blessings is conditional on personal piety. For example, Grace of God Mission's 2001 Adult Sunday School Manual contains the statement: 'God promises His presence to the obedient. . . . If we are not seeking to conform our lives to His word, we are in danger of losing His living presence in our midst'.[72] As well as positive values such as humility, honesty, purity and love, Igbo neo-Pentecostals promote holiness taboos such as modest dress codes and abstinence from smoking and alcohol consumption. CPM's membership manual contains chapters on 'Genuine Love' and 'Purity of Life', and ACFM's membership Bible studies includes sections on 'Dressing and Ornament' and 'Smoking and Drinking', which encourage modesty and abstinence. Some NPCs also teach restitution. CPM includes it among its sixteen tenets of faith, and ACFM among the twenty-one core beliefs of its Statement of Faith. ACFM defines restitution as follows: 'Restitution includes restoring where you have defrauded, stolen or slandered, paying back debts, and making confession'.[73] Finally, neo-Pentecostal identity is maintained through church discipline. This too is reflected in ACFM's membership manual:

> The Apostolic Church was strong because it was pure. Our modern Church is weak because we have compromised our position and condoned sin in the members. We must turn a new leaf. We must exercise discipline no matter whose ox is gored. . . . Discipline can be described as taking corrective measures as punishment in order to maintain the good conduct of Church members.[74]

Church names and buildings also function as Pentecostal identity markers. Csordas refers to the use of 'sacred names' by churches to

[71] Redeemed People's Mission, 'Lesson 13. Enoch: Unbroken Fellowship with God ', *Redeemed Adult Sunday School Lessons*, 1998, 39.

[72] Grace of God Mission Inc., 'Chapter One. The Presence of God', *Adult Sunday School Manual*, 2.

[73] All Christians Fellowship Mission, 'Lesson 5. Our Statement of Faith', *Membership Bible Studies*, 25.

[74] All Christians Fellowship Mission, 'Lesson 7. Church Discipline', *Membership Bible Studies*, 35.

Figure 12. Signboard for Amazing Love Assembly, Enugu.

express and reinforce collective religious identity.[75] For Igbo neo-Pentecostals, they are a means of publicly expressing core values and are usually displayed on large signboards along adjacent streets. Some church names explicitly express their identity as separated communities, such as Holiness Evangelical Church, Redeemed People's Mission and Master's Vessel Church. Church buildings, as symbolic 'holy places', are also crucial for establishing neo-Pentecostal presence and difference, and attracting potential customers. As well as the main worship centre, church premises sometimes include offices and school buildings, especially in urban areas. In Igboland, the most impressive is the recently completed His Glory Cathedral, the Onitsha headquarters of Grace of God Mission.

Former revivalists refer to a decline in Christian morality since the 1970s and a consequent reduction in difference between church and 'world', and a failure to influence the moral fibre of society despite the proliferation of NPCs. Thus Reuben Ezemadu, founder of Christian Missionary Foundation, writes:

---

[75] Thoman J. Csordas, 'Genre, Motive and Metaphor: Conditions for Creativity in Ritual Language, *Cultural Anthropology*, 2.4, November 1987, 459-60.

> For some time Nigeria has competed with Bangladesh and one or two other countries for the position of the world's most corrupt country. People however wonder why this situation should be so with Nigeria in the light of the acclaimed spiritual fervency, aggressive evangelism, rapid 'growth' of Churches, and the numerous all night prayer meetings some of which last for days and attract thousands, and in some cases, millions of the 'faithful'.[76]

In chapter 3, we noted that holiness and 'retreat from the world' were early features of the revival. However, a fall in moral standards was one reason given for the revival's decline. The contrast between the lax standards of today and the high standards of the 1970s was a common theme in participant accounts. There are references to immorality, corruption, materialism and rivalry infecting the movement and tainting both leaders and members. One former revivalist mentions neo-Pentecostal leaders engaging in court litigations, mismanagement of church funds and adultery.[77]

Some place the blame for these trends on the pastors for diluting their radical message and failing to check moral misdemeanours in their congregations. However, institutional forces contributed towards the relaxation of ethical demands. From a sect-like movement in tension with its social environment, it gradually lost its radical edge and absorbed elements from prevailing culture. Bryan Wilson identifies a loosening of rigour and a loss of a sense of dissent and protest among the consequences of denominationalism.[78] Early Igbo charismatic fellowships fitted the profile of Wilson's world-denying sects. As we have seen, their uncompromising ethical stance attracted persecution from family, friends and society in general. However, as they adopted denominational status they began to accommodate and move towards a state of low tension with their social environment. Reflecting on this, one former revivalist writes, 'We seem to have lost our message, lost our bearing, lost our focus, and even lost our identity. We have compromised where we have not been found to compromise before'.[79] This was apparent in the way some NPCs modified their message to include an emphasis on prosperity and success, an issue I deal with below, and the pursuit of status and respectability

---

[76] Reuben Ezemadu, 'Corruption, Politics, and the Church. The Nigerian Case', *The Church Leader in Africa*, 13.4, Oct.-Dec.2003, 1.

[77] Chukwuka, *Beyond the Night*, 40-8.

[78] Bryan Wilson, *The Social Dimensions of Sectarianism. Sects and New Religious Movements in Contemporary Society*, Oxford: Clarendon Press, 1990, 109.

[79] Chukwuka, *Beyond the Night*, 40.

associated with the recent tendency for leaders to take titles for themselves. The movement's moderation of its radical ethical stance was also associated with a gradual postponement of the Second Advent in neo-Pentecostal preaching and discourse. If we recall, the expectation of Christ's imminent return was a major incentive for revivalists to maintain a puritan lifestyle. However, when Christ did not appear, they gradually settled down to life in the world and abandoned their millennial outlook. They began to marry, adopt more prosperous lifestyles and consequently adapted their message.

The decline in Christian morality precipitated a renewed emphasis on holiness in some sectors of the Pentecostal fraternity during the 1990s, partly due to the influence of intercessory prayer ministries concerned about the condition of the church and the state of the nation. We will return to this when we discuss neo-Pentecostal political culture in the next chapter.

Faith, Health and Prosperity

In revivalist discourse, the relaxation of moral standards is sometimes linked to a growing emphasis on healing, deliverance and prosperity. As noted above, prayer for healing, deliverance and prosperity is a feature of Igbo neo-Pentecostal liturgy, but it has also been an important means of recruitment. Here I examine this in more depth, paying close attention to why these motifs have proved so popular.

A Holistic Understanding of Salvation

Igbo Pentecostals, like those from other African contexts, have developed a model of faith healing based on a holistic understanding of salvation and bearing a close affinity to traditional piety with its emphasis on *ezi-ndụ* (good life), which includes physical ailments, but also demonic oppression, unemployment, business failure, poverty and family relationships. More recently, they have applied healing to socio-political structures.[80] As such, they have responded to local consumer demands. This distinctive understanding of salvation is reflected in the following statement by Bishop

[80] For the application of healing by African Pentecostals, see Ojo ('African Charismatics', 5), who identifies four areas: physical healing; healing from demonic attacks (deliverance); healing from failures in life (termed 'success and prosperity'); and healing of socioeconomic/political problems. For the Igbo traditional context, see Christopher I. Ejizu, 'Healing as Wholeness: The Igbo Experience', *Africana Marbigensia*, 10.1, 1987, 9.

Mike Okonkwo of TREM: 'What I preach on the cross should give me divine health, should give me a good life-style, should make you have your home, should be able to give you good things of this life'.[81] Thompson Nwosu of Redeemed People's Mission told me why he preached a 'holistic' gospel:

> Christ has come to bring healing to our spirits, healing to our minds, healing to our circumstances; even healing to our bodies. . . . The God who saved you is also able to deliver you from that demonic operation. Some of our people come from all kinds of things, ancestral worship, demon worship, and all that. So from time to time, though they belong to church, those things react, and they go home to make sacrifices. . . . So except we convince them that we have a God who is more powerful than the spirits, they will continue to mix up Christianity with all this voodoo stuff. So I would say that my main message is that the gospel of Christ is a holistic one. It should affect every area of human life.[82]

RPM's aims and objectives include the following clause: 'to pray for healing, deliverance, prosperity, miracles and pointing individuals to the saving power of Christ'. A brochure introducing Bible Faith Mission contains the words, 'Whatever your need, come to Jesus - salvation, healing, deliverance, happy marriage, business success, knowledge of the Bible, God's abundant blessing, etc. The Church where Jesus is Lord and miracles happen'. And Overcomer's Bible Church in Onitsha offers freedom from 'tomorrow's uncertainty', oppression from unknown powers, witchcraft and barrenness.[83]

In one Sunday worship service at Redeemed People's Mission I heard two testimonies of healing. The first concerned a couple whose small child was found to have blood in his urine. Unable to find a doctor at the local hospital, they took him to the church where the pastor prayed for him. The next day they returned to the hospital where tests showed that his urine was clear. The second testimony was given by a church elder, whose brother was admitted to hospital with severe leg oedema rendering him unable to walk and in considerable pain. Despite hospital treatment his condition failed to improve, so the elder prayed for him and then discharged him. A few days later the man had a dream in which Jesus appeared to him and raised him up from his bed. The next day the oedema had subsided and he

---

[81] Geoffrey Ekenna, 'Why Pastors Live Well', *Newswatch*, 3 December 2001, 23-4. This is an interview with the Bishop.

[82] Interview, Thompson Nwosu, 31 August 2001, Jos.

[83] Overcomer's Bible Church, Leaflet advertising the 'God in Action Crusade,' Onitsha, 13-16 April 2000.

was able to walk. Testimonies like these are intended to rehearse God's blessings in a public setting, but they also serve to stimulate faith in others and act as an indirect critique of western medicine's rationalistic worldview.

Yet Pentecostal predilection for healing and deliverance does not preclude the promotion of healthy lifestyles or the use of western medicine. I came across several neo-Pentecostal church magazines containing articles on health and personal lifestyles written by medical personnel. Christian Pentecostal Mission's 2001 edition of *Echoes of Joy*, for example, has articles entitled 'You and Your Health' and 'The Concept of Mental Health'. And Living Word Ministries' *The Forum* has a feature written by Dr. Tony Ayeke entitled 'Think Health', which gives advice on dental and personal hygiene, nutrition and physical exercise. In the early 1970s, some Igbo revivalists insisted that healing should take place by faith alone without the use of medicine. But contemporary neo-Pentecostals show no such scruples. The main impediments to using western medicine are financial poverty and prohibitive medical costs rather than theological conviction. ACFM's Statement of Faith includes the following clause: 'Both human experience and Bible alike reveal the need for medical science as a means of alleviating human suffering and divine healing is not to be misconstrued as being opposed to medical science'. And a RPM Bible study entitled 'Divine Health and Healing' states, 'He [God] may choose to heal us through the application of medicine, surgery or by His divine touch. He may even choose not to remove the "thorn" in our flesh'.[84] That this has moved beyond the level of discourse to effect church life became evident while I was staying with the community of Amazing Love Assembly in Enugu. When I was sick the pastor not only prayed for me but also introduced me to two medical doctors in the congregation who gave advice on diagnosis and treatment.

Provenance and Popularity of Healing and Deliverance

Healing was a feature of the Civil War Revival and is a continuing factor in neo-Pentecostal church growth. The 1974 visit of T. L. Osborn to Eastern Nigeria resulted in a greater emphasis on healing. As well as healing from physical ailments, deliverance practices also contributed to the movement's appeal. This is again reflected in some of their congregational names, such as Deliverance Temple (Holiness Evangelical Church, Owerri), Dominion Cathedral (CPM, Aba), Liberation Centre (CPM, Aba), Victory Christian

[84] All Christians Fellowship Mission, 'Lesson 5. Our Statement of Faith', *Membership Bible Studies*, 26; Redeemed People's Mission, 'Lesson 11. Divine Health and Healing', *Redeemed Adult Sunday School Lessons*, 1998, 34.

Cathedral (Victory Christian Mission, Enugu) and Household Deliverance Church (LWM, Aba). In LWM's *Annual Journal*, Household Deliverance Church introduces itself as follows:

> As the name implies, the church remains a Household Deliverance centre. Demon possessed people have come to the fellowships and received release. Some who belonged to secret cults believe enough to denounce their past and relinquish cultic materials to the church for destruction. The barren become happy and fulfilled mothers.[85]

Ogbu Kalu suggests that deliverance was not a major emphasis during the 1970s when the focus was on 'born-again' experience and prosperity, but it began to gain prominence during the 1980s.[86] My research has shown that deliverance did take place during the early 1970s, usually in the context of evangelistic outreach, but was not stressed in the way that new birth, Spirit baptism and divine healing were. Yet today deliverance practices have become a major feature of Igbo-initiated neo-Pentecostal churches. All the churches I visited have some context where people can receive deliverance prayer. For instance, Grace of God Mission in Enugu has a 'Deliverance Service', Master's Vessel Church in Umuahia has a 'Deliverance Hour', and All Christians Fellowship Mission in Bukuru has an 'Hour of Solution' meeting.

We see a progression within Igbo neo-Pentecostalism regarding demonic infestation. As noted above, initially deliverance took place largely in evangelistic settings and even then was not prominent. However, in the mid-1970s some neo-Pentecostals became preoccupied with 'mami-wata' spirits and witchcraft. One informant said that this emphasis began within Riches of Christ, and if you were female you were liable to be branded a witch or a member of a 'mami-wata' cult. More recently, this has been elaborated in popular Nigerian Pentecostal literature which often contain testimonies of spectacular deliverances. One example from this genre is an account written by Kalu Abosi describing his deliverance from a 'mami-wata' cult in 1989 during a crusade organised by former Igbo revivalist and popular Pentecostal evangelist Uma Ukpai. In it, Abosi relates his initiation into the secret cult, his introduction to the 'Queen of the River', his conference with Satan and his eventual deliverance, all recurring themes in

---

[85] Living Word Ministries, *Annual Journal*, 42.

[86] Ogbu U. Kalu, 'The Practice of Victorious Life: Pentecostal Political Theology and Practice in Nigeria, 1970-1996', *Mission: Journal of Mission Studies*, 5.2, 1998, 238-39.

other literature of this type.[87] During the 1980s, deliverance rituals became institutionalised and incorporated into evangelistic crusades and church meetings. No longer restricted to non-Christians, deliverance was offered to church members and extended to include economic circumstances and family relationships. Currently, deliverance has been extended still further to include geographical localities, people groups and socio-political structures.

Of those churches to emerge from the Civil War Revival, Christian Pentecostal Mission has gained a particular reputation for emphasising deliverance. I interviewed two CPM pastors, and both alluded to the church's emphasis on deliverance which originated with the founder. It has a weekly 'Deliverance Hour' and a 'Faith Clinic', where it claims that 'sinners are made saints, the sick are healed, broken hearts are mended, the oppressed are freed, the demon possessed are delivered, the barren become fruitful, evil covenants are broken and hanging blessings are prayed down'.[88] Part of CPM's three-fold vision is to bring deliverance back to the Church, and Ezekiel, the founder, has been described as the man 'who popularized the destruction of demons' in Nigeria.[89] A flyer advertising a CPM crusade says, 'This is the time of restoration, deliverance for the oppressed, healing for the sick and salvation of your soul'. Ezekiel believes that every Christian has the ability to cast out demons.[90] Victor Onuigbo's Victory Christian Mission has a similar holistic understanding of healing and deliverance. During its annual 'International Convention' in Enugu, it claims to minister salvation, deliverance from poverty, unemployment, business failures and marital separation.[91]

I asked a number of NPC pastors about their experience of the deliverance ministry. Problems associated with evil spirits and targeted during deliverance sessions include bad dreams, barrenness, physical problems (such as arthritis and paralysis), psychiatric problems and bad habits. Neo-Pentecostals often link these ailments to prior involvement in witchcraft, 'mami-wata' cults and secret societies, or to curses inherited from ancestral covenants. Several Pentecostal informants stressed the need

---

[87] Kalu Abosi, *"Born Twice". From Demonism to Christianity*, Benin City: Joint Heirs Publications, n.d.

[88] *Echoes of Joy*, 50.

[89] *Ibid.*, 2; 'Supplement on Grace of God Mission', *Prophecy. The Messiah is Coming*, 15. CPM's full vision is: i) bringing deliverance back to the Church; ii) creating awareness of Christ's second coming; and (iii) preparing sons and daughters of God for glory.

[90] Rev. O. Ezekiel, 'Tips on Deliverance', *Prophecy. The Messiah is Coming*, 1996, 25.

[91] 'Victory Christian Mission Enugu', *Christian Update. PFN Enugu North*, Maiden Issue, 2001, 5.

for caution when engaging in deliverance prayer and claimed to pray 'according to the Scriptures' in order to avoid an overemphasis on demons. A member of Amazing Love Assembly told me that his church used to emphasise deliverance, but now consider the solution to most problems resides in a proper understanding of Bible. Some neo-Pentecostals are also keen to distance themselves from the more extreme forms of deliverance discourse mentioned above. Emmanuel Okorie of Living Word Ministries alludes to the danger of overemphasising demonology in a recent article on contemporary Pentecostal trends: 'Today's demonology has taken a different turn. The life of a child of God in financial distress is traced to what his forefathers did. . . . This has given jobs to advanced native doctors in the name of evangelists who just live by going from one big man's village or another delivering the land'.[92]

The appeal of Igbo neo-Pentecostal healing and deliverance approaches has partly been a response to the socio-economic climate, and the inadequacy and high cost of the health services, as Ojo has noted of African Charismatic groups in general.[93] However, their popularity also stems from their close affinity to both biblical and African cosmologies, their emphasis on the spiritual forces behind events in the material world, and the quest for power to enhance life. For Kalu, this willingness to take the African maps of the universe seriously is the main reason for their appeal.[94] Traditionally, Igbos have a strong belief in evil spirits and their potential to cause harm and prevent people from realizing their destiny and experiencing *ezi-ndụ*, as we noted in chapter 2. They also have a ritual called *ịchụ Aja*, intended to drive away evil spirits. Pentecostals accept the ontological reality of possessing spirits while at the same time demonising them. As Marshall notes, rather than sidelining problems associated with malign forces as mainline churches appear to do, they 'confront them directly, and make the vanquishing of witches, evil spirits, and other "agents of Satan" one of the central elements of church practice'.[95]

In Igbo traditional religious practice, prayer is spontaneous and pragmatic, and according to Agu, 'health, procreation, inter-personal relationships, economic problems and needs of individuals and families, welfare of the entire community and current social issues are all concrete themes of prayer'.[96] Thus neo-Pentecostal approaches to healing and

---

[92] Emmanuel Okorie, 'My Adventures with Holy Ghost Men', *Nuggets. The Apostolic People*, 23 December 2001, 2.

[93] Ojo, 'African Charismatics', 143; Ojo, 'Deeper Christian Life', 152; Ojo, 'Charismatic Movements', 104.

[94] Ogbu U. Kalu, 'Preserving a Worldview: Pentecostalism in the African Maps of the Universe', *Pneuma*, 24.2, Fall 2002, 130.

[95] Marshall, 'Pentecostalism', 22.

[96] Agu, *Secularization*, 400.

deliverance prayer fitted well with traditional aspirations. However, their intention is to be biblical rather than African. They claim to base their methodology on the Bible, and their teaching on 'divine healing' is usually full of biblical references. They also reject the healing practices of some of the older AICs which they deem unchristian and tainted by traditional culture. Note the following extract from ACFM's Statement of Faith:

> The mission while holding that divine healing is the power of the Lord Jesus Christ to heal the sick and afflicted in answer to believing prayer, believes in as well as encourages its practice in all her services, condemns healing for a fee, the use of holy water, candles, pictorial, or any other aid apart from the anointing oil as provided in James 5:14-16.[97]

From observation, healing and deliverance prayer in Igbo NPCs was sometimes accompanied by the 'laying on of hands' and anointing with oil but not the use of 'holy water', a common practice in prayer houses.[98]

Global forces through media and transnational ministry exchanges have also influenced Igbo neo-Pentecostal healing methodologies. I have mentioned the visits of American Pentecostal evangelists during the 1970s. American Pentecostal literature also proved influential. Apart from T.L. Osborn and Gordon Lindsay, other Western authors whose books on healing and demonology are readily available in Nigeria include Derek Prince, Rebecca Brown, Kenneth Hagin, Frank and Ida Hammond, and C. Peter Wagner. Global flows are partly responsible for two recent developments which have extended the practice of healing and deliverance to include economic circumstances, people groups and socio-political structures. The first relates to the 'faith gospel', which I deal with in more detail below. Here I mention Paul Gifford's assertion that the rise of deliverance theology may be a response to the failure of faith teaching. Gifford suggests that the shift from faith to deliverance is an example of African creativity in the face of current circumstances of economic collapse.[99] During the 1980s, some Igbo neo-Pentecostal preachers presented the faith gospel as the answer to financial hardship caused by economic decline. When faith failed to deliver the 'goods', deliverance from the curse of poverty was offered as an alternative remedy. This is

---

[97] All Christians Fellowship Mission, 'Our Statement of Faith', *Membership Bible Studies*, 26.

[98] For more on Igbo prayer house healing practices see Kalu, *Embattled Gods*, 293-98.

[99] Paul Gifford, 'The Complex Provenance of Some Elements of African Pentecostal Theology', in Corten and Marshall-Fratani (eds.), *Babel and Pentecost*, 73; Gifford, *African Christianity*, 338.

reflected in the following statement by a former revivalist: ‘Today’s gospel of prosperity tells us that poverty is a curse, and the poor need to have a demon of poverty cast out of them’.[100]

A second development has been an increasing emphasis on intercessory prayer and spiritual warfare. Among other strategies, this has involved ‘liberating’ or ‘redeeming’ the land from pollution caused by demonic strongholds, ancestral covenants and idolatry.[101] During the revival itself, protagonists used to engage in spiritual warfare prayer to eliminate hindrances to the spread of the gospel prior to conducting evangelistic outreaches, but this did not involve speculating on the workings of the demonic world or devising elaborate typographies. During the 1990s, however, this practice has become more sophisticated and prominent, an important mission strategy and a form of political engagement (partly a result of global flows through Christian literature from America). Popularly known as ‘strategic-level spiritual warfare’, it draws heavily on the writings of American authors like C. Peter Wagner and George Otis Jr., whose books are widely available in Nigerian Christian bookshops. I came across it when I met Joseph Umeh, a member of Redeemed People’s Mission and co-ordinator of Jos Intercessors Forum. Each week Umeh meets with a group of ‘intercessors’ to pray for Jos and obtain ‘revelation’ regarding any ‘strongholds’ that may be controlling the city. A flyer for a recent prayer conference organised by Umeh calls participants to pray for ‘Revival and Restoration of the Church’, and ‘Healing and Spiritual Liberation of the Land and the People’. A leading Nigerian proponent of this kind of prayer is former revivalist and Igbo Pentecostal Emeka Nwankpa. Nwankpa studied at the University of Ife, Western Nigeria, during the early 1970s, and one of his mentors was British Pentecostal missionary S. G. Elton, who ordained him into Christian ministry in 1981. Nwankpa helped to establish Intercessors for Nigeria and Intercessors for Africa and has since travelled the world as a teacher on such subjects as spiritual warfare prayer and Christian political responsibility.[102] Later, we will reflect further on Nwankpa’s contribution to Pentecostal prayer strategies and political engagement.

Closely linked to ‘strategic-level spiritual warfare’ is the ritual of ‘covenant-breaking’. In recent years this has supplanted deliverance as the main focus of some Igbo Pentecostal prayer ministries. Igbos believe that impediments to personal progress or communal development, or instances

---

[100] Benjamin Chuka Osisioma, *Ancient Pathway*, Enugu: Snaap Press, 1998, 53.

[101] For a summary, see Kalu, ‘Third Response’, 13-14.

[102] For a summary of Nwankpa’s teaching, see Emeka Nwankpa, *Redeeming the Land. Interceding for the Nations*, Achimota, Ghana: Africa Christian Press, 1994.

of unusual occurrences such as children dying prematurely, may be caused by ancestral covenants with traditional deities. The confession and renunciation of these ancient covenants in a corporate setting breaks their power over succeeding generations. Annual covenant-breaking rituals are currently being organised in Igbo communities, attracting Christians and non-Christians alike, including non-residents. The importance of this ritual in Igbo Pentecostal imagination is reflected in the following excerpt from an article written by neo-Pentecostal pioneer Amaechi Nwachukwu:

> The snag is that whether you know it or not, covenants do take their toll! For when you do not take divinely guided steps against covenants, they become strongholds, invariably producing curses. And no matter what you do about certain curses operating in certain individuals or families, you cannot decisively eradicate them until you get back in time to the gateways that gave access to the enemy; only there can you annul the prevailing covenants. . . . Their perpetuity is upheld by periodic re-enactment for reinforcement. . . . Satanic re-enactment takes place during new yam and other festivals, coronation ceremonies, family reunions and child dedications, but most significantly during burial and traditional marriage ceremonies. . . . Covenanters usually have a strong bond of brotherhood welding them together. This derives from the fact that they are under the same rules and regulations as stipulated by the superior partner and in most cases under oath, welding them to each other. . . . However, as many as are willing today, to break these satanic covenants can be set free from the devil's bondage. Jesus is able and willing to set them free.[103]

Emeka Nwankpa recounts the occasion of a covenant-breaking ceremony in his home village of Umuofai. In 1996, Emeka's brother Chinedu began to investigate the roots of 'idolatry' in Umuofai. Together they invited the whole village to a special meeting where they preached the gospel and called for corporate repentance and renunciation of ancestral covenants established over the previous 300 years. The community, led by the three traditional chief priests, then destroyed the nine village shrines. Nwankpa records the words of one of the priests as he stood before the shrine of a particular local deity called Amadi:

> Listen, Amadi, the people who own the land have arrived to tell you that they have just made a new covenant with the God of heaven. Therefore all the previous covenants you have made with our ancient fathers are

[103] Rev. Amaechi Nwachukwu, 'Understanding the Covenants and Breaking Strongholds', *Livingspring*, May/June 1997, 11.

> now void. The elders told me to take care of you and I have done that all these years. But today I have left you, so it is time for you to return to wherever you came from. I have also given my life to Jesus Christ, and from now on, my hands and feet are no longer here.[104]

I have heard several accounts of similar rituals taking place in Igbo communities. In one recent case former revivalist Edwin Okorougo performed a covenant-breaking ceremony in the Igbo town of Akpo. Residents were concerned about the prevalence of premature deaths, business failures, and the general lack of progress and development in their community. Traditional elders and church leaders came together to break the ancestral covenants and either transfer or renew their allegiance to Jesus Christ. My informant told me that not only has this fostered interdenominational cooperation and provided fresh opportunities to spread the gospel, but it has also helped the community to prosper economically. However, more research is needed to establish whether there is a causal link between covenant-breaking and community development.

Provenance and Popularity of Prosperity Teaching

Prosperity teaching, which links faith with the expectation of material wealth and success, has become an important element of African neo-Pentecostal identity and has contributed to the movement's appeal, particularly among young people concerned with development and progress. Some scholars have referred to the shift that has occurred within African Pentecostalism since the 1970s from an emphasis on retreat from the 'world' to a gospel of prosperity and success.[105] In the Nigerian setting, Marshall makes a distinction between 'holiness' churches, which promote a retreat from the world, and 'pentecostal' churches, which embrace a doctrine of prosperity.[106] My research suggests that from the late-1970s, some Igbo NPCs modified their message to include an emphasis on prosperity. This theological shift is reflected in the following excerpt from a talk given by former revivalist Chinedu Nebo:

---

[104] Quoted in George Otis, Jr., *Informed Intercession. Transforming Your Community Through Spiritual Mapping and Strategic Prayer*, Ventura, California: Renew Books, 1999, 27.

[105] Corten and Marshall-Fratani, 'Introduction', 5; Matthews A. Ojo, 'Healing in Sub-Saharan Africa', in Glazier (ed.), *Encyclopedia*, 143.

[106] Marshall, 'Power', 216-17.

> In those days, when we said, 'Take the whole world but give me Jesus', we meant it. But I do remember in the late '80s, when a so-called great man of God got up and challenged that song. He said we cannot tell the devil, 'Satan take the whole world, I've taken Jesus'. He said, 'no, we must get our share on this earth first'. And I do remember how people clapped their hands for him; that the world no longer belongs to the devil and the principalities of this world. We as a people are no longer aliens, no longer foreigners, no longer strangers. We have a stake here. We must grab everything we can on earth. And people clapped their hands for him.[107]

Contemporary debate centres on the provenance and merits of prosperity teaching. Some have emphasised its foreign origins and form in Africa.[108] I agree with those who stress the role of indigenous agents in transforming prosperity teaching for local consumption.[109] In the case of Igbo appropriation, existing religious preoccupations, local socio-economic context and global forces all came into play. To use an agricultural metaphor, there needed to be a fertile soil, a favourable climate and access to a ready supply of seed.

Igbo primal religious culture provided a receptive soil for prosperity teaching. Hackett notes that in West Africa, 'the preconditions for a gospel of prosperity to develop' were already there in traditional, pre-colonial societies, 'where it was common for people to associate the deities with prosperity'.[110] If we recall, the main goal of salvation in Igbo traditional religion is for viable life *(ezi-ndụ)*, which includes material prosperity. This is evident in the following excerpt from an Igbo traditional prayer:

Ma unu nyena anyị ndụ	When you do give us life
Nyekwanụ anyị ihe eji azụ ya	Please do give us also the wherewithal to maintain it.

[107] Nebo, 'Protagonists and Critics'.

[108] Paul Gifford, 'Prosperity: A New and Foreign Element in African Christianity', *Religion*, 20, 1990, 382. More recently, Gifford has adopted a more nuanced stance that is consumer- as well as producer-oriented. He argues that while it is essentially articulated in standardised American form, it is compatible with considerable local creativity. Gifford, 'Theology', 62-74.

[109] Coleman, *Globalisation*, 31; Stephen Hunt, '"Winning Ways": Globalisation and the Impact of the Health and Wealth Gospel', *Journal of Contemporary Religion*, 15.3, 2000, 332-47.

[110] Rosalind I. J. Hackett, 'The Gospel of Prosperity in West Africa', in R. H. Roberts, *Religion and the Transformation of Capitalism: Comparative Approaches*, London: Routledge, 1995, 208.

Ogolo ndụ, Ezi ndụ	Long life, viable life,
Ọmụmụ, n'ụba O.	Child-bearing and prosperity.[111]

Hence, in traditional culture prosperity is regarded as a blessing from God and poverty a curse. Due to their receptivity to change, contemporary Igbos define prosperity in terms of modern symbols such as cars and houses rather than the accumulation of wives or yams. Related to this is the Igbo emphasis on achievement, progress and prestige, where status and moral standing in the community are associated with symbols of success acquired through religious power, and the redistribution of wealth for the benefit of others.[112] However, the Igbo notion of *chi* has the potential to dampen Igbo ambitions for success by encouraging a fatalistic approach to life. The Igbo have a predestination theology which holds that a person's fate is virtually predetermined. Although this does not preclude personal responsibility, Chineke is believed to direct the destiny of individuals through *chi*.[113] Thus Chinua Achebe describes one of the characters in his novel *Things Fall Apart* as an 'ill-fated man' because he 'had a bad *chi* or personal god, and evil fortune followed him to the grave. . .'.[114] Prosperity teaching returns agency to the individual by urging those struggling with failure and apathy to change their destinies through prayer and faith. This is evident in the following sermon extract: 'A person's destiny can change through his invitation and earnest prayer to God. God did not create any man to remain stagnant, the person's past record of failure and poor background notwithstanding'.[115] And in a chapter entitled 'Faith to Change Destinies', Grace of God Mission's 2001 Sunday School Manual exhorts members to change their destinies through prayer rather than accept defeat. So there are close affinities as well discontinuities between traditional religious aspirations and prosperity teaching, with its emphasis on material acquisition through faith, and this facilitated its assimilation into Igbo culture.

Two other conditions were required for prosperity teaching to take root in Igbo soil: a suitable socio-economic climate and access to a ready supply of seed, in this case the message itself. Ojo states that in Nigeria prosperity

---

[111] Quoted in Okorocha, *Religious Conversion*, 70.

[112] Okorocha, *Religious Conversion*, 118, 192-6; Uchendu, *Igbo*, 16, 92.

[113] Ikenga-Metuh, *God and Man*, 43; C. I. Ejizu, 'Continuity and Discontinuity in Igbo Traditional Religion', in Ikenga-Metuh (ed.), *Gods in Retreat*, 141.

[114] Chinua Achebe, *Things Fall Apart*, London/Ibadan: Heinemann, 1985 (orig. publ. 1958), 13.

[115] Godwin Ugweje, 'You can Change your Destiny', excerpt from a message preached at CPM, Apapa branch, quoted in *Pentecostal Weekly*, May 14-20 2000, 6.

and success as religious ideas were 'indigenously developed as a response to the socio-economic changes of the 1980s'.[116] However, global flows through media and migration were crucial. According to informants, prosperity teaching began to lay hold of the Igbo religious landscape in the late 1970s and early 1980s. Though the decade began with severe financial hardship for the Igbos, it ended with a period of relative economic prosperity due largely to the export of oil and Igbo ingenuity.[117] If we recall, during the late 1970s Igbo neo-Pentecostal leaders began to travel to the US at the invitation of their American counterparts where they imbibed the emphasis on prosperity propagated by their sponsors. When they carried this back to Nigeria, they found it fitted well with the mood of the times and was eagerly embraced by Igbo Christians. At the same time, American Pentecostal literature was becoming more readily available. For many ordinary neo-Pentecostals, prosperity teaching promised an end to poverty and hardship, but others (primarily religious leaders and wealthy businessmen) used it to justify their increasingly lavish lifestyles during a period of economic opportunity. As Marshall asserts, 'The gospel of prosperity offers a doctrine of morally-controlled materialism, in which personal wealth and success is interpreted as the evidence of God's blessing on those who lead a "true life in Christ"'.[118] One former revivalist put it like this:

> And again the general effect of the economy in the country affected Christians. We discovered that there was a kind of materialism that was brought about by the economic and political situation in the country, with the result that everybody tried to grab as much as possible. And Christians became victims of this thing too.[119]

The economic boom came to an end in the early 1980s to be replaced by a period of economic crisis, exacerbated by the failure of the 'mega-rhetoric' of development, the introduction of SAP in 1986 and increasing exposure to global modernity. In a consumer culture, the desire for wealth and success becomes an important element in the demand for religion. Corten and Marshall-Fratani note that while globalisation opens up new avenues for material accumulation, it also incites frustration as most

---

[116] Ojo, 'Charismatic Movements', 106.

[117] Adebayo O. Olukoshi, 'General Introduction: From Crisis to Adjustment in Nigeria', in Olukoshi (ed.), *Politics*, 1.

[118] Marshall-Fratani, 'Global', 282-83.

[119] Participant, 'Round Table Discussion. Materialism in the Body of Christ in the Seventies', Remembering the Seventies Conference, audiocassette, 29 April 2000, Enugu.

people's participation in the global marketplace is reduced to 'window shopping'.[120] Prosperity teaching offered the possibility of opting into the global order and appropriating the 'goods' of modernity. Some Igbo neo-Pentecostals continued to use it to justify their excessive accumulation and maintain their status in a hostile economic environment, but the majority were more concerned with developing strategies of survival and security. The prosperity gospel promised a solution to the growing problem of financial hardship. It also addressed the African Christian identity crisis by seeking to engender self-confidence and legitimise the pursuit of success. In this sense, it has continued to be a factor in Igbo neo-Pentecostal spirituality despite changing socio-economic conditions.

The popular Nigerian magazine *Newswatch* lists two Igbo-founded neo-Pentecostal churches (Christian Pentecostal Mission and The Redeemed Evangelical Mission) among several large Nigerian Pentecostal denominations at the 'forefront of prosperity messages'. Both have their headquarters in Lagos, which provides fertile ground for such teaching.[121] While prosperity teaching was not a major emphasis within the NPCs I visited, it was undoubtedly present in some of their sermons and literature, and contributed to their appeal. Invariably, exponents buttress their arguments with biblical references. Grace of God Mission, for example, states that 'it is God's will that his people prosper spiritually, physically and financially,' and support this by citing 3 John 2.[122] Prayer for prosperity is included among the official aims of Redeemed People's Mission. As noted above, one RPM sermon I listened to was entitled 'God's provision and prosperity', based on the life of Joseph. On another occasion the pastor reminded the congregation of God's promise to give Israel 'power to make wealth' (Deut 8:18). He then prayed specifically that all those with businesses would prosper materially. However, RPM discourages financial accumulation and instead encourages members to use their money to support Christian mission, assist the poor and care for their extended families. In a Bible study entitled 'God Delights in our Prosperity', it states, 'God's primary aim is that financial prosperity should serve as a source of blessing to others and the church. . . . It is therefore evident that

[120] Corten and Marshall-Fratani, 'Introduction', 3-4.

[121] Geoffrey Ekenna, 'Who Do They Serve? Has the Church in Nigeria become a Lucrative Business Venture?, *Newswatch*, 3 December 2001, 27. Others listed include David Oyedepo's Winner's Chapel, Enoch Adeboye's Redeemed Christian Church of God, Ayo Oritsejafor's Word of Life Bible Mission, Chris Okotie's Household of God and Chris Oyakhilome's Christ Embassy.

[122] Grace of God Mission Inc., 'Chapter 2. Restoration', *Sunday School Manual*, 2001, 7. 3 John 2: 'Beloved, I pray that in all respects you may prosper and be in good health, just as your soul prospers' (NASB).

God's faithfulness in giving His children financial prosperity is not primarily for the benefit of the beneficiary'. RPM also warns against covetousness, extravagance, acquiring wealth through illegitimate means and attempts to 'commercialise' religion. Wrong ways of gaining financial prosperity, according to RPM, include the use of false weights, '419' activities, portraying God as a 'money-doubler', getting rich without working for it, gambling, drug trafficking and joining secret cults.[123] Christian Pentecostal Mission's membership manual contains a Bible study on success and material prosperity which outlines principles for receiving 'blessings from God' and includes this statement: 'Many have misconstrued prosperity to be that measure of superfluous abundance of material possessions. . . . Prosperity is not only that superfluous abundance of wealth but being able to meet one's needs through the grace of God without covetousness'.[124]

Perhaps the leading exponent of prosperity teaching among Igbo Pentecostal leaders is Bishop Mike Okonkwo, General Overseer of TREM and former President of the Pentecostal Fellowship of Nigeria (PFN). PFN describes itself as 'the coming together of Holy Spirit filled Christian Churches and Organizations who believe and practice the FULL GOSPEL MESSAGE (ACTS 2), in an independent and autonomous Christian Fellowship'.[125] Okonkwo traces the origins of prosperity teaching to divine revelation given first to US American Christians and subsequently to the Nigerian Church.[126] In a recent article, he states, 'When somebody is saved from poverty to prosperity, it is salvation. If preachers truly preach the full gospel, the people must prosper. . . . There is too much poverty in Nigeria. We need the prosperity message in Nigeria and indeed Africa'.[127] Yet most NPC leaders I interviewed expressed a commitment to a moderate form of prosperity teaching, but were critical of its overemphasis. While some still attached importance to modern symbols of affluence, such as Mercedes

---

[123] Redeemed People's Mission, 'Lesson 14. Godliness versus Love of Money', *Redeemed Adult Sunday School Lessons*, 2001, 41; Redeemed People's Mission, 'Lesson 9. God delights in our Prosperity', *Redeemed Adult Sunday School Lessons*, 1998, 26. '419' is the term used in Nigeria to denote a form of fraud addressed in that particular section of the Nigerian penal code.

[124] Christian Pentecostal Mission, 'The Secret of Blessing (Source of Material Blessing)', *Membership Manual*, 81-87.

[125] Pentecostal Fellowship of Nigeria Incorporated (P. F. N.), *Constitution*, n.d., 1-2

[126] Geoffrey Ekenna, 'Why Pastors Live Well', *Newswatch*, 3 December 2001, 23.

[127] Bishop Mike Okonkwo, 'I Won't Apologise for Prosperity Gospel', *LifeWay. The Spirit-Filled Christian Life*, Oct-Nov 2001, 54.

Benz cars, satellite televisions and large houses, others were reluctant to engage in public displays of wealth.

As in other African contexts, Igbo Pentecostals encourage hard work, self-discipline and financial responsibility, all of which are economically beneficial. Nnaji Chukwuka of Revival Time Ministries distinguishes between prosperity and materialism: 'While prosperity encourages arduousness, striving, satisfaction that leads to success in one's vocation, materialism leads to the end without means or ways'.[128] Okoye of All Christians Fellowship Mission also associates prosperity with hard work. In a booklet entitled *Youth with a Purpose*, he writes, 'If you till your land, work hard, and you are disciplined in your work habit; if you are not a lazy person that likes dozing and sleeping all the time, God will bless the work of your hands and prosper you'.[129] Understood in this sense, prosperity teaching is a motivation to economic mobility through work as well as faith. It encourages good stewardship of material resources as well as dependence on providential provision. This is summed up in an excerpt from a RPM Bible study: '[God] willingly gives His material and spiritual gifts to all who trust in Jesus. . . . His expectation is that these should be used wisely'.[130]

Problems with Deliverance and Prosperity Theologies

It is beyond the scope of this study to engage in a detailed critique of deliverance and prosperity theologies.[131] Instead I focus on the effect of these motifs upon revival and Pentecostal spirituality. Recently, criticisms have emerged from within the movement itself. According to some participants, an overemphasis on deliverance and prosperity contributed to a modification of the revival's original vision and imposed limitations on its ability to act as an agent of moral and social transformation. Oral and

---

[128] Chukwuka, *Beyond the Night*, 45.

[129] William Okoye, *Youth with a Purpose*, Enugu: Gospel Communications International, 1993, 125.

[130] Redeemed People's Mission, 'Lesson 21. Parable of the Talents', *Redeemed Adult Sunday School Lessons*, 1999, 56.

[131] For detailed analyses of prosperity theology, see D. R. McConnell, *The Promise of Health and Wealth*, London: Hodder and Stoughton, 1990; B. Barron, *The Health and Wealth Gospel*, Downers Grove: InterVarsity Press, 1987; Andrew Perriman (ed.), *Faith, Health and Prosperity. A Report on 'Word of Faith' and 'Positive Confession' Theologies*, Carlisle: Paternoster, 2003. For an analysis of its influence in Africa, see Brouwer, Gifford and Rose, *American Gospel*.

written accounts suggest that this shift had theological, missiological and ethical consequences.

Firstly, the revival gradually lost its strong Christological and eschatological edge as members became increasingly preoccupied with demons and this-worldly concerns. Thus Emmanuel Okorie, founder of Living Word Ministries, laments the loss of 'true worship of our living God' associated with an overemphasis on demons. And in an article entitled 'What leads to loss of Glory?', Christian Pentecostal Mission leader O. C. Emmanuel refers to the way Pentecostals have 'lost the vision of heaven to vision of money' by shifting their focus from God to 'earthly things'.[132] A second related consequence was a reduction in evangelistic fervour, a key component of revival spirituality. In a personal interview, former revivalist Chinedu Nebo told me, 'Instead of preaching the gospel and delivering people from sin and wickedness . . . people were more interested in saying, "Well, if you are a poor man, you have a demon of poverty; if you are sick, a demon of sickness". Every ailment on earth got a demon'.[133] And O. C. Emmanuel makes the connection between prosperity teaching and loss of evangelistic passion: 'Regrettably, today, what some men of God preach is how their hearers could live prosperous lives here on earth. . . . The Bible says we should go into all the world and preach the gospel. But regrettably, the fire of evangelism is no more burning in us'.[134]

An overemphasis on deliverance and prosperity also had ethical consequences. Reflecting on contemporary trends, Okorie states, 'Just like people hold crusades mainly on healing, many have held crusades only on demons. . . . Where is soul salvation, where is repentance? Where is new birth and new creation in Christ?'[135] In chapter 3, I referred to the revival's stress on Christian responsibility to exercise self-control, resist temptation and maintain a life free from 'sin' through repentance and faith in Christ. In recent years, there has been a spate of popular Nigerian Pentecostal literature on demonology and deliverance methodology. Some books provide long lists of demons purported to cause a variety of ethical lapses. One Igbo neo-Pentecostal author refers to demons of anger, unforgiveness, hatred, jealousy, lying, stealing, covetousness and lust, as well as territorial, political and even colonial demons. Another encourages Christians to pray against spirits of pride, adultery, drunkenness and laziness.[136] The problem

---

[132] Okorie, 'Holy Ghost Men', 2; O. C. Emmanuel, 'What Leads to Loss of Glory', *Pentecostal Family*, August 1999, 9-10.

[133] Interview, Chinedu Nebo, 4 May 2000, Enugu.

[134] Emmanuel, 'What Leads to Loss of Glory', 9-10.

[135] Okorie, 'Holy Ghost Men', 2.

[136] See Emeka Chigozie Adolf, *Deliverance of African Christians, Vol. 1*, Aba: Christ The Rock Community, 2001, 166-69; Mike Ofoegbu, *Dangerous Prayers Part 1*, Lagos: Holy Ghost Anointed Books, 1998, 24.

with overemphasizing demonic agency is that it can encourage irresponsibility with respect to individual and corporate sin, and discourage public criticism of political structures.

Prosperity teaching also contributed to a dilution of the movement's anti-materialistic holiness ethic and a decline in moral standards. If we recall, joining the 'born-again' community during the early 1970s was costly in terms of existing social relationships and economic prospects. By the 1980s, however, becoming a neo-Pentecostal pastor was more likely to be associated with economic and social mobility. Some former revivalists criticize prosperity theology for ignoring New Testament teaching on the redemptive qualities of suffering and the merits of poverty. Thus Benjamin Osisioma states, 'Paul's gospel was first and foremost the gospel of Jesus Christ. . . . It is also a gospel of suffering, pains and tears; its symbol is the cross. . . . God blesses and prospers; but there is no gospel of prosperity'.[137] Critics from within have accused prosperity teachers of 'commercialising' the gospel and turning Christian ministry into a business enterprise for personal gain. Some have certainly used the power structures in their churches to accumulate wealth, reflecting the 'big man' syndrome within Nigerian political culture. Others make a distinction between biblical prosperity and materialism. Most neo-Pentecostal leaders I encountered claim to promote a form of prosperity based on biblical principles, but reject the accumulation of wealth through immoral means. William Okoye of All Christians Fellowship Mission is one of the few Igbo Pentecostal leaders to have gained a reputation for austerity. Despite pressure from his members, he resisted for many years acquiring a Mercedes Benz car, a popular Pentecostal status symbol in Nigeria. In an interview for a Pentecostal magazine, he states:

> God wants to see us prosper and be in good health, but only according to his will. It must be through righteousness and truth. Not through 419 or any dubious means of achieving prosperity. . . . If this type of prosperity preaching ministers were commissioned and opportuned to establish at Abuja, they would turn out multi millionaires within a short period and would wreck the church also.[138]

Some former revivalists regard prosperity teaching as potentially dangerous because it encourages materialistic lifestyles, covetousness, greed and even immorality. Listen again to Okoye's reflections on current trends:

---

[137] Osisioma, *Ancient Pathway*, 56-7.

[138] 'Interview with Rev William Okoye', *Prophecy. The Messiah is Coming*, 9.

> Some ministers have succeeded in making believers to be covetous. Most of them no longer believe in total righteousness and waiting for the will of God to be done. They have also succeeded in creating in the minds of people the sense of violating the moral codes. . . . Right from Genesis to Revelation there is no place you will find the word 'go ye out into the world and seek for money or wealth', but rather you will find, 'seek ye first the kingdom of God and all its righteousness and every other thing shall be added unto you'. Instead of pastors admonishing their congregation to seek for God with all their heart, they prefer encouraging and motivating them otherwise – seeking for mundane things – the gift at the expense of the Giver to their own detriment. This has caused many believers to wax cold and unmoved about church activities. In fact, the way and manner some of these preachings are going on, if care is not taken, we will be worse off than the orthodox churches we tend to criticize.[139]

In certain sections of the neo-Pentecostal community, prosperity gradually replaced holiness and evangelistic success as the yardstick for measuring spirituality. The success of a person's ministry was gauged by the size of his church building, the quality of his car(s), the size of his bank account and the cut of his clothes.

Missionary Communities

Perhaps the most important factor behind Igbo neo-Pentecostal expansion, especially during the 1970s, was its missionary impulse. I have noted this in relation to the revival itself and as a factor behind the genesis of the neo-Pentecostal church movement. Here I examine the missionary dynamic of the neo-Pentecostal community.

The Gift of the Spirit

Igbo neo-Pentecostal mission strategy was specifically linked to the experience of Spirit baptism, the hallmark of Pentecostal identity and the defining impulse behind global Pentecostal expansion.[140] Anderson refers

---

[139] *Ibid.*, 8.

[140] Gary B. McGee, 'Pentecostal and Charismatic Missions', in James M. Phillips and Robert T. Coote (eds.), *Toward the 21st Century in Christian Mission*, Grand Rapids, MI: Eerdmans, 1993, 46; Paul Pomerville, *Introduction*

to the Spirit poured out at Pentecost as a missionary Spirit and the church full of the Spirit as a missionary community.[141] When interviewed, Igbo neo-Pentecostals from the 1970s consistently referred to Spirit baptism as a pivotal event in their Christian experience and one that propelled them into intense mission activity, often in the face of stiff opposition. Usually this added a new dimension to their ministry and an expectation that supernatural 'sign and wonders' would accompany the preaching of the gospel. I interviewed fourteen Igbo neo-Pentecostals who said they had an experience of Spirit baptism during the 1970s. Of these, eleven said it had a significant impact upon their ministries, giving them increased power and courage to bear witness to the gospel or enabling them to perform healings and exorcisms. When asked how they knew they had received the Spirit, all said that it was when they began to speak in tongues.

Spirit baptism has continued to occupy an important position in neo-Pentecostal discourse and experience since the 1970s. Grace Cathedral (Grace of God Mission, Enugu), for example, has a weekly meeting for people to receive prayer for 'Holy Ghost Baptism'. I interviewed fifteen people who have joined a NPC since the 1970s, and all claimed to have received the gift of tongues. In the Jos survey, out of 167 respondents, 72 per cent said they spoke in tongues. There is, however, some disagreement concerning the doctrine of Spirit baptism. Most teach that it is an experience subsequent to conversion for missionary empowerment. Thus in their 'Articles of Faith and Doctrine', Redeemed People's Mission state that 'the baptism of the Holy Spirit is a definite and separate experience of God's grace whereby the believer is endued with power from on High, enabling him to have power for service (Acts 1.5, 8; 2.4)'.[142] And All Christians Fellowship Mission's 'Statement of Faith' includes the following: 'The Baptism of the Holy Ghost is the endowment of power from on high upon the clean, sanctified believer. . . . When we receive the gift of the Holy Ghost it is accompanied with the initial sign as the disciples had on the day of Pentecost i.e. speaking with tongues as the Spirit gives utterance'. ACFM also outlines some consequences of Spirit baptism, which along with 'tongues' include 'divine power', 'boldness in testimony and service', 'spiritual insight into the word of God' and 'tremendous prayer ability'.[143] Amazing Love Assembly, on the other hand, teaches that Spirit baptism occurs at conversion. It does not discourage speaking in

---

to Missions: an Independent-Study Textbook, Iring, TX: ICI University Press, 1987, 100.

[141] Anderson, *Pentecostalism*, 207.

[142] Redeemed People's Mission, *Membership Manual*, 41.

[143] All Christians Fellowship Mission, 'Lesson 5. Our Statement of Faith', *Membership Bible Studies*, 26; All Christians Fellowship Mission, 'Lesson 7. The Holy Spirit Baptism', *New Life Sunday School*, 28.

tongues, but denies that it is the only evidence of receiving the Spirit.[144] Nevertheless, I interviewed eight ALA members, including the senior pastor, and all but one said they spoke in tongues. If we recall, Spirit baptism was a contentious issue during the revival and contributed to the emergence of NPCs. It was the promotion of tongues as initial evidence which first created problems. Contemporary practice that has also proved controversial includes teaching people to speak in tongues and simultaneous praying in tongues without interpretation during meetings.

In his exploration of the implicit values in Pentecostal missions, Russell Spittler notes the prevalence of spontaneous 'Spirit-born' ventures in Pentecostal history.[145] Sometimes Igbo neo-Pentecostal pioneers claimed to receive specific directions from the Spirit before embarking on mission initiatives. One example was ACFM founder William Okoye who left Riches of Christ Mission to form an independent evangelistic team after receiving 'strong impressions' from the Spirit to preach and plant churches in the North. Later, he set up his headquarters in Abuja, the Federal Capital of Nigeria, a move prompted by a dream received during an extended period of fasting and prayer. Okoye was among the pioneers of Pentecostalism in Abuja and now has one of the largest churches in the city.[146] This dream appears in several ACFM publications and represents an important landmark in the church's history. As noted in chapter 3, dreams can be an important means of legitimising the message of charismatic religious leaders. While they were common in older AICs, they were not a regular feature of Igbo neo-Pentecostal activity. Okoye's dream was probably an exception among NPC pioneers, but its prominence within ACFM publications suggests that it was often retold and circulated among members as a means of legitimising his ministry in Abuja.

Some NPC leaders promote a 'latter rain' theology as motivation for mission. Proponents of this teaching, which is based on Joel chapter 2, believe that there will be an outpouring of the Holy Spirit in revival immediately prior to Christ's Second Advent. Its roots within the movement can be traced to the early 1970s and the influence of the British Pentecostal S. G. Elton who had links with the US American 'Latter Rain Movement'. Elton apparently referred to the Civil War Revival as the latter rain of God's Spirit. He also promoted this teaching in his pamphlet *Herald of His Coming*, distributed widely in Nigeria. In Igbo neo-Pentecostal texts, references are made to the 'former and latter rains', 'the last Days', 'restoration', the 'Great Move of The Holy Spirit', the 'glorious

---

[144] 'Concluding Thoughts on Baptism with the Holy Spirit', *Livingspring*, May/June, 1997, 8.

[145] Russell P. Spittler, 'Implicit Values in Pentecostal Missions', *Missiology: An International Review*, 16.4, October, 1988, 415.

[146] Okoroafor, *William Okoye*, 68-70, 123-27.

church' and the 'millennial rule of Christ'. In its adult Sunday School Manual, Christian Pentecostal Mission states, 'The purpose of this restoration is to empower His people for the end-time world wide aggressive evangelism. The Lord is about to send both the former and latter rains upon the earth for an overwhelming harvest of souls into his kingdom'.[147] Associated with this is a belief that there will be a transfer of wealth to the church to assist the evangelisation process. Thus Grace of God Mission states:

> God is doing a great work of restoration in these last Days. As the Church is marching towards the 2nd coming of Christ and the millennial rule of Christ, God's miracles, favour and divine intervention, sickness which has been long will suddenly disappear as the Holy Spirit restores and repairs His temple. There will be a transfer of wealth and knowledge to God's people, people will be ready to use their wealth to propagate the gospel as God restores His glory. In these latter days, the Church will be transformed from weak and powerless people to a glorious Church. Eph. 5:27.[148]

Lay Ministry

Evangelistic fervour was a significant factor in early Igbo neo-Pentecostal church expansion. If we recall, most started as charismatic ministries led by individuals with strong evangelistic gifts. More important, though, was the effect of the Pentecostal impulse upon the laity. This has been an important factor in global Pentecostal growth since its inception, largely due to the levelling influence of Spirit baptism.[149] During the 1970s, Igbo neo-Pentecostal churches encouraged every member to be a witness, based on their experience of Spirit baptism rather than education, training or worldly rank. In Riches of Christ Mission, for example, church meetings provided the venue for equipping members as effective witnesses, and before long, some were offering themselves for full-time ministry. What was important was evidence of new birth, Spirit baptism and a clear conviction of a divine call. However, from its inception Riches of Christ had its own Bible school, and prospective candidates were usually required

---

[147] Christian Pentecostal Mission, 'Introduction', *Sunday School Adult Bible Class Manual*, 5.

[148] Grace of God Mission Inc., 'Chapter 2. Restoration', *Sunday School Manual*.

[149] Anderson, 'Global Pentecostalism', 222; McGee, 'Pentecostal and Charismatic Missions', 46.

to attend a four-month 'crash programme' before being sent out to preach and plant churches. This stands in stark contrast to the often prolonged training required by mainline churches and mission-related Pentecostal churches.

The attention given to mission and evangelism within contemporary neo-Pentecostal churches is evident in their mission statements and membership manuals which encourage all members to participate in evangelistic activity. Thus All Christians Fellowship Mission describes itself as a 'missionary church', and its four-fold vision includes a commitment to 'Mission, Evangelism and church planting'. Its mission statement contains the following clause: 'This ministry has a very strong sense of mission and believes that it is only as the church fulfils its missionary obligation that it justifies its existence. Evangelism is our supreme task'.[150] The church is a member of the Nigerian Evangelical Missions Association (NEMA) and has its own mission department, seeking to work among unreached people groups.[151] Redeemed People's Mission's mission statement includes the phrase: 'to uphold, teach, practice and preach the gospel of Christ in Nigeria and all over the world'. Its membership manual outlines its mission policy which includes the setting up of a 'Missions Department', the recruitment and support of 'missionaries' and the planting of local churches in 'unreached' areas.[152] For Christian Pentecostal Mission, evangelism is 'the primary task given to the Church in expanding the Kingdom of God,' and for Amazing Love Assembly, its 'number one priority'.[153] In the Jos survey, out of 167 respondents, 65 per cent said they were attracted by their church's commitment to evangelism, and 30 per cent said they belonged to their church's evangelism team.

To what extent has this missionary vision, so clearly articulated in the churches' membership manuals, been implemented at the grassroots? Some neo-Pentecostals (including former revivalists) refer to a decline in

---

[150] All Christians Fellowship Mission, 'Lesson 6. Our Church Family Values', *Membership Bible Studies*, 33; All Christians Fellowship Mission, 'Lesson 4. Understanding the Vision and Purpose of your Church', *Membership Bible Studies*, 20-1.

[151] NEMA was established in Jos in 1982 by six Nigerian indigenous missionary societies (EMS/ECWA, Calvary Ministries, His Grace Evangelical Movement, Christian Missionary Foundation, Christ Ambassador Evangelical Team, and Community Missions Board of COCIN) to encourage and co-ordinate missionary activity within Nigeria and beyond. By 2005, it had over ninety member agencies and churches working in about forty countries with some 4,000 Nigerian missionaries worldwide.

[152] Redeemed People's Mission, *Membership Manual*, 22-27.

[153] Christian Pentecostal Mission, 'Christian Commitment', *Membership Manual*, 78; Amazing Love Ministries, *Rules and Regulations*, 25.

evangelistic passion and missionary activity since the 1970s. This is evident from a feature in a neo-Pentecostal magazine entitled 'Fading Priority', which contrasts the passion for 'saving the souls of men' in the 1970s with the problem-centred approach today and its focus on promoting material wealth and success.[154] I have already noted the detrimental effects of deliverance and prosperity on evangelistic fervour. It was also a consequence of ageing and the routinisation of charisma associated with the revival's decline. In the early 1970s, many young revivalists were unable to obtain employment or pursue further education. This was due to a combination of factors, including an inability to pay fees and poor administration following the war. However, strong adventist beliefs also deterred some from pursuing secular education. Instead, driven by their youthful energy and the revival's intense charismatic impulses and millennial outlook they seized the opportunity to preach the gospel on a full-time basis. But as they settled down to the responsibilities of marriage, employment or college they no longer found they had the time or energy to engage in aggressive evangelism. Today, few neo-Pentecostals admit to being unemployed and most claim to be engaged in some form of occupation or study programme. Evangelism, while not abandoned, is no longer a priority. In the Jos survey, out of 105 respondents in Redeemed People's Mission, 75 per cent claimed to have a job, while 12 per cent said they were either students or 'applicants'.

Mission Strategies

During the 1970s, some neo-Pentecostal churches employed an aggressive strategy of crusade evangelism and church planting, though this enthusiasm for expansion was not shared by all, and consequently they have not all experienced the same growth in terms of new congregations. Among the more successful were Riches of Christ Mission, Grace of God Mission, Christian Pentecostal Mission, All Christians Fellowship Mission, Redeemed People's Mission, Save the Lost Mission and National Evangelical Mission. Anderson refers to church planting by indigenous evangelists as a fundamental principle of Pentecostal mission strategy which has resulted in thriving churches being planted in many parts of the world without the help of foreign missionaries.[155] Nigeria was no exception. Initially, those who pursued a church-planting strategy targeted urban areas, holding extended evangelistic campaigns, planting churches from their converts and then using these as a platform for penetrating rural areas and financing further crusades. Outside Igboland, Igbo neo-

[154] Chidi Arinze Okafor, 'Fading Priority', *Echoes of Joy*, 14.
[155] Anderson, *Pentecostalism*, 216.

Pentecostal pioneers claimed to target areas where there was no strong evangelical or Pentecostal presence and to mobilise local Christians to evangelise their own communities. Thus in 1975, National Evangelical Mission planted the first Pentecostal church in the Northern city of Maiduguri (the present capital of Borno state), but chose to bypass the city of Jos where there was already a Pentecostal presence. All Christians Fellowship Mission also avoided areas where there were existing Pentecostal churches, claiming that its early policy was not to 'steal' members from other Protestant groups. ACFM was the first 'full Pentecostal' church in the towns of Lokoja, Zaki-Biam, Kabba and Abuja, and the second in Jos, after Assemblies of God.[156] NPC pioneers distinguished between 'living churches' and those they felt were not actively engaged in evangelism or preaching a 'full gospel'. This is how Wilson Ezeofor explained his rationale for starting Bible Faith Mission in Jos:

> My main vision at that time was to plant living churches. What I mean by that is to plant churches that will be vibrant, where the true gospel, where the gospel will be preached without compromise, making sure that people are born-again, filled with the Holy Spirit, and healed if they need healing. A church that preaches the full gospel. That was my main vision, to plant churches like that all over Plateau, all over Nigeria.[157]

Church planting has intensified since the 1970s and most NPCs now pursue this strategy. For example, Amazing Love Assembly (Enugu) began to plant new churches in 2000, having existed for thirteen years as a single congregation. Within a year it had started three new branches in the Igbo towns of Abakaliki, Awka and Okigwe. Grace of God Mission, which has actively pursued a church-planting policy since its inception, intends to establish churches in all the states of Nigeria. By 1996, it had come close to achieving this objective by planting branches in all of Nigeria's thirty-six states apart from Lagos, Oyo, Ogun and Kwara.[158] National Evangelical Mission has also continued its policy of planting churches in the North. Either it enters new territory through invitation or because it believes a locality has been insufficiently evangelised. Sometimes a new venture is initiated by a vision. NEM pastor Bitrus Pathel told me of the occasion when he received a vision of a mountain with over-ripe millet and no one to harvest it. He was also given the name of a village he had not heard of

---

[156] Okoroafor, *William Okoye*, 85-93.

[157] Interview, 25 September 2001, Jos.

[158] 'Supplement on Grace of God Mission', *Prophecy. The Messiah is Coming*, 14.

before and on enquiry discovered it was located on a mountain. NEM has since planted a church there.

Local evangelistic strategies identified by respondents include personal witnessing, church-based evangelistic events, open-air 'crusades', hospital and prison visitation, and the use of media technologies. Christian Pentecostal Mission in Aba, for example, has an 'Evangelical Group', which engages in a variety of evangelistic activities.[159] It has also launched a new initiative called 'Operation 7000 souls' (to encourage members to become 'soul-winners') and has created a Hotel Outreach Department. NPCs target hotels mainly because prostitutes use them to ply their trade. During his tenure as PFN Chairman (Abia State), CPM pastor John Ezeh coordinated the 2001 visit of the German evangelist Reinhard Bonnke to Aba. Amazing Love Assembly (Enugu) lists among its methods: evangelism in cities, personal evangelism, mass evangelism, literature evangelism, TV evangelism, radio evangelism and crusades. As noted above, it has recently embarked on a new venture, sending 'missionaries' to evangelise and plant churches in surrounding towns.

NPCs have increasingly employed Western techniques and technologies to propagate the gospel. I have mentioned their preference for 'crusade' evangelism and church planting. Media evangelism has also been a feature from the movement's inception. Initially this was limited to print media, and in particular the use of tracts as evangelistic tools. More recently, like other African neo-Pentecostals, they have employed electronic media to spread their message.[160] Igbo neo-Pentecostals were using radio and television as far back as the early 1980s. Paul Nwachukwu of Grace of God Mission and Tony Okeke of Save the Lost Mission both had TV outreaches, and William Okoye of ACFM had a regular slot on Capital Radio Abuja. In recent years, this approach has become more widespread. Leaders from at least six of the NPCs I visited have appeared on Nigerian television, and several others have their own radio programmes. CPM in Aba has a TV programme called 'Moment of Joy', RPM (Jos) has a TV outreach called 'Divine Encounter' (a recording of its Sunday worship meeting), and ALA (Enugu) has a weekly radio programme called 'Livingspring'. It is usually the larger denominations that have TV programmes, and invariably the founder or senior pastor who delivers the message. The use of audio and videotapes has also become a popular strategy, giving rise to the 'cassettisation' of modern religious culture. Together these techniques have increased the movement's visibility, raised

[159] The 'Evangelical Group' of CPM, Aba, includes the following sections: Jesus Harvesters, Hospital Ministration, Exploiters Squad, Visitation Team, and Bus and Morning Cry. *Echoes of Joy*, 31.

[160] During my field research in Nigeria, I myself appeared on television twice and radio once in the company of Igbo neo-Pentecostals.

the profiles of its leaders, and allowed neo-Pentecostal messages to be spread over wide geographical areas and heterogeneous populations.

Another factor behind Igbo neo-Pentecostal expansion has been its commitment to power-oriented evangelism. As Pentecostal missiologist Gary McGee has noted, Pentecostals expect 'signs and wonders' to accompany gospel preaching.[161] I have referred to the importance of healing for Igbo neo-Pentecostal growth and only touch on it here. Preaching a 'full gospel' was an indispensable part of NPC methodology, and power-oriented evangelism was a significant factor in attracting crowds to evangelistic campaigns and recruiting new members. When ACFM founder William Okoye conducted his inaugural crusade in the Middle Belt town of Gboko in 1975, it drew large crowds partly because posters and loudspeakers advertising the event promised not only forgiveness for sinners but healing and deliverance for the sick and oppressed. When reports began to circulate of significant healings on the first night, many more turned up.[162] Igbo neo-Pentecostal accounts of past glories are replete with examples of healing miracles and conversions. During his 30th anniversary celebration as a 'minister of the gospel', Thompson Nwosu of Redeemed People's Mission referred to the many notable conversions and miracles that accompanied his early ministry as evidence that God was with him.[163] Such accounts serve to legitimise Pentecostal ministries in the eyes of their followers, but obviously need to be treated with caution.

In Igbo neo-Pentecostal mission initiatives outside Igboland, commitment to indigenous principles has met with limited success, especially when compared to the mission churches and Assemblies of God (AG). As noted in chapter 2, Assemblies of God has a strong indigenous church policy, though this has not always been successful, especially in urban areas. In Jos city, for example, most members of AG congregations are southerners, though the Jos District Superintendent in 2001 was from the local Berom ethnic group. Outside Jos, and especially in rural areas, indigenes predominate. Initially, NPCs appealed to the poorer and less-educated strata of society. They have a mix of ethnic groups among their membership, including settlers and indigenes, though Igbos remain in the majority. Indigenous membership is strongest in rural congregations and those urban areas where mission churches are weak. Thus in RPM

[161] Gary B. McGee, 'Pentecostals and their Various Strategies for Global Mission: An Historical Assessment', in M. A. Dempster, B. D. Klaus and D. Petersen (eds.), *Called and Empowered: Global Mission in Pentecostal Perspective*, Peabody, MA: Hendrickson, 1991, 215.

[162] Okoroafor, *William Okoye*, 77-81; Nduul *et al.*, 'Rev. Okoye', 5.

[163] Rev N. C. Thompson, 'Account of Rev N. C. Thompson's Stewardship, presented at his 30th Anniversary as a Minister of the Gospel', Jos, 4 November, 2001.

branches outside Plateau State and in rural congregations most members are indigenes. But in Jos, where mission churches are particularly strong, RPM, ACFM and Bible Faith Mission congregations are dominated by Igbos and attract few indigenes. Out of 105 respondents from three RPM congregations in Jos District, 58 per cent were Igbos, 23 per cent belonged to other southern ethnic groups (mainly Yoruba), 3 per cent were indigenes from Plateau State, and 14 per cent were from other Northern or Middle Belt ethnic groups. The Jos District Overseer of ACFM, himself a Northerner, told me that his city congregation has a mix of ethnic groups, including Esan (Edo State), Isoko (Delta State), Efik/Ibibio (Akwa Ibom State), Yoruba (Western States), Ngas and Berom (Plateau State), but again the proportion of local indigenes was small. It was difficult to determine numbers of indigenes joining these churches, but overall they have remained low in proportion to congregational sizes. Most church leaders are from the South, though there are a number of indigenes in leadership positions. For example, in 1998 Redeemed People's Mission consisted of six districts (Jos, Yola, Bauchi, Gembu, Jalingo, Eastern), presided over by six District Superintendents (three Igbos, one from Delta State in the South, and two Northerners).[164] All Christians Fellowship Mission tries to employ indigenous leaders but this is not always possible. In Benue State, for example, 90 per cent of ACFM pastors are from the local Tiv ethnic group.

Igbo NPCs have made little impression on Muslim populations, especially in recent years as inter-religious tensions have escalated. All the leaders I spoke to in NEM, RPM and ACFM were agreed on this. Thompson Nwosu of RPM said that he found it easier to influence Muslims with the gospel early in his ministry because they were less antagonistic compared to today. Over the years, some Muslims have come to the church for prayer, but few have become members. RPM's limited success has partly been because they lack an effective rehabilitation programme. Those Muslims who convert to Christianity do so at risk to their lives and usually have to leave their communities. One example is a Muslim lady who approached a RPM pastor wishing to convert to Christianity. She told him that Jesus Christ had appeared to her in a dream and this had prompted her to begin to read the New Testament. After her conversion, she began to talk to her Muslim friends about Christ and was subsequently disowned by her husband and her father. ACFM reports a similar failure to influence its Muslim neighbours. Its Jos congregation had one Fulani Muslim convert in 2001. Unfortunately he was forced to leave his home and is now attending Bible school. Through his witness, two others were converted, but one was apparently killed by his local community. In the Jos survey, out of 167

[164] Redeemed People's Mission, Annual Progress Report, 6 December 1992.

Figure 13. Signboard for All Christians Fellowship Mission, Abuja, showing its global and ecumenical vision.

respondents there were four (2 per cent) former Muslims, but only one was converted through their present church and none were local indigenes or Hausa-Fulanis. When asked whether there were any converted Muslims in their churches, most respondents said they knew of less than three. Due to recent developments, there is a lack of confidence in inter-religious dialogue as a viable strategy for peace and reconciliation. Neo-Pentecostals tend to regard Muslims as their enemies and consequently adopt an aggressive style of evangelism to reach them.

A recent trend is for some churches to pursue a 'global vision', reflected in a penchant for inserting the word 'international' into their names and an image of the globe on their logos. Examples include Grace of God Mission International, Christian Pentecostal Mission International and Salvation for All Mission International. The headquarters of Grace of God Mission in Onitsha is called Grace Cathedral - World Outreach Centre, and Salvation for All Mission's headquarters is called Faith Cathedral, International Outreach Church. Christian Pentecostal Mission has an International Bible Seminary, and the General Overseer of Save the Lost Mission calls his ministry Tony Okeke World Outreach. The impulse behind this is the global mission to which they believe God has called them, as Asamoah-Gyadu has noted of their Ghanaian counterparts, and their belief that God has blessed them with resources to evangelise the African continent.[165] So Paul Nwachukwu of Grace of God Mission states, 'Africa is the hope of the world, and Nigeria is the Jerusalem of Africa'.[166] All Christians Fellowship Mission is another church with a global vision. It has its 'International Headquarters' in Abuja and has apparently established contact with over two hundred 'evangelism-orientated' churches and ministries in approximately one hundred nations.[167] ACFM's church logo, displayed in their literature and on their signboards, contains the symbol of a globe with Africa at the centre and the text: 'Making disciples of all nations'.[168] Several denominations have established branches abroad. Living Word Ministries has branches in the USA and has recently opened one in London. Grace of God Mission has branches in Cameroon and Cote d'Ivoire. Christian Pentecostal Mission has branches in Greece and England, as well as Ghana, Cameroon and Benin, and its vision is to open branches in every African nation.

Church Growth Patterns

Church growth is difficult to measure. Statistics are prone to exaggeration, and congregational sizes vary considerably from under fifty to several thousand. For example, Grace of God Mission's congregation in Dadin Kowa, on the outskirts of Jos, had about ten people when I attended, and its main congregation in Enugu had approximately two thousand. All Christian Fellowship Mission's Bukuru branch had less than ten people when I attended, while its Jos District headquarters had approximately two hundred. Moreover, many members join through transfer from other denominations rather than conversion. In the Jos survey, out of 167 respondents only 33 per cent joined their church through conversion, while 58 per cent transferred from another denomination. In addition, some churches have started as schisms from existing ones. Having said this, growth rates, at least in their initial stages, have been impressive both in terms of congregational sizes and new branches. For instance, Christian Pentecostal Mission, started in 1977 with about sixteen members, by 2001 had established 240 branches across Nigeria. These were distributed as follows: Lagos State (thirty-four branches); Ogun/Ondo/Oyo States (twelve); Edo/Delta States (forty); Anambra/Enugu/Abia/ Imo/Ebonyi States (eighty-seven); Rivers State (twenty-six); Akwa Ibom/Cross River

---

[165] Asamoah-Gyadu, *African Charismatics*, 100.

[166] Quoted in 'Supplement on Grace of God Mission', *Prophecy. The Messiah is Coming*, 19.

[167] Okoroafor, *William Okoye*, 181.

[168] Based on Matt 28:19.

States (eight); Kwara (two); Northern States (twenty-eight); Ghana (one). Some of its urban congregations number several thousand.[169] Grace of God Mission, started in 1978, by 2001 claimed to have approximately 1,100 branches and over 500,000 adherents.[170] A more recent example is Living Word Ministries in Aba which began in 1987 and by 2001 had planted seventy-five new congregations. Most are located in the city of Aba, but in 2001, LWM also had branches in Umuahia, Onitsha, Owerri, Port Harcourt and three in the USA. LWM congregations grow to around 250 before they divide.[171]

The majority of churches have experienced most of their growth within Igboland or Southern Nigeria, but in the case of National Evangelical Mission, All Christians Fellowship Mission and Redeemed People's Mission, they have flourished predominantly in the North. NEM, which began in 1975, is the largest with approximately two hundred branches, and several of its urban congregations have over 1,000 members. According to informants, the first church planted by NEM in the Northern city of Maiduguri had approximately 1,500 members in 1986, and its branch at Zaki-Biam had an average attendance of over 1,000 in 1992. ACFM had eight branches by 1979. This had grown to forty by 1996 and approximately eighty by 2001. These are distributed in seven districts: Abuja (approximately fifty branches), Gboko (approximately twenty branches), Jos (five), Lokoja (two), Kaduna (one), and Eastern (at least three). Apart from some branches in Abuja district, most congregations are not large. Thus ACFM's Jos district headquarters church, planted in 1976, by 2001 had between 200 and 250 members. RPM established at least five branches by 1979 and during the 1980s planted churches in nine different states, mostly in the North. By 2001, it had established seventy-nine branches. RPM headquarters church in Jos, which opened in 1977 with approximately 100 members, initially grew quickly and by 1987 had an average attendance of over 1,000. However, since then attendance has fluctuated and by 2000 it had dropped to 800. This fall in attendance was partly a result of several schisms RPM has experienced over the years, but it has also planted out at least three other congregations in Jos from among its membership.[172]

---

[169] Statistics from *Pentecostal Family*, August 1999, 7; Christian Pentecostal Mission, 'Branches and their Addresses', *Adult Sunday School Manual*, 59-65.

[170] Statistics based on interview with Joseph Onuchukwu, National Secretary of Grace of God Mission, and 'Supplement on Grace of God Mission', *Prophecy. The Messiah is Coming*, 14.

[171] Living Word Ministries, *Annual Journal*, 9.

[172] Thompson, 'Account', 6-8; Redeemed People's Mission Annual Progress Reports, 1986 to 2000.

Fragmented Communities

Not all new churches were a result of mission initiatives. One reason for the proliferation of NPCs has been the movement's fissiparous nature, a characteristic of global Pentecostalism generally. Schismatic tendencies soon overtook the fledgling movement. At least twenty-four Igbo-founded NPCs started during the 1970s and seven were the result of schism. These included Redeeming Time Pilgrims Mission (Owerri), Jesus the Way Mission (Onitsha), Gospel Crusaders Mission (Aba), Fullness of Christ Mission (Udi), All Believers Fellowship Group (Aba), Holy Ghost Ministry (Awka) and Bible Faith Mission (Jos). Ironically, some Pentecostals trace this trend to the so-called 'New Move', intended as an ecumenical initiative. It was after this that new groups began to multiply at an alarming rate. NPC proliferation has continued since the 1970s, and many new denominations were also secessions from existing ones. Most of those I visited have experienced several breakaways during their relatively brief histories. At least six new churches have started as secessions from Grace of God Mission, at least two from Christian Pentecostal Mission, three from Redeemed People's Mission, and at least three from Holiness Evangelical Church.

Church proliferation has reached epidemic proportions in recent years. For example, by 2001 there were over forty-seven neo-Pentecostal denominations in Anambra State, most founded by Igbos and many with branches in the major city of Onitsha.[173] In Enugu, there were more than thirty-five neo-Pentecostal denominations or ministries by the year 2000, many started during the 1990s. Along a one and a half kilometre stretch of Agbani Road, Enugu, there are over thirty churches situated in different buildings. Some of the buildings contain several churches located on different floors.[174] The same trend is present in the North. For instance, in the small town of Bukuru, Plateau State, there are branches from at least thirty-eight neo-Pentecostal denominations, many started by members of ethnic groups from Southern Nigeria.[175]

[173] Information based on personal observation and Pentecostal Fellowship of Nigeria (PFN) membership, quoted in F. Ude, 'The Pentecostal Fellowship of Nigeria in Anambra', M.A. thesis, Evangel Theological Seminary, Jos, 2000, 95-7.

[174] Information based on PFN membership, personal observation, and a recent issue of Nigeria's *Newswatch* magazine (3 December 2001, 23-4).

[175] Information based on PFN membership and personal observation.

Causes of Schism

Some factors that contributed towards the fragmentation of neo-Pentecostal denominations are different from those that caused them to break away from mission churches in the first place. For example, reaction to the mission churches and the quest for a more satisfying expression of Christianity were no longer decisive issues. However, other factors came into play. Here I draw on John Wilson's sociological model of religious schism to explore the reasons behind the movement's fragmentation.[176]

Wilson suggests that certain organisational structures are more susceptible to easy fragmentation. Schism is more likely to occur where a movement falls at either end of the continuum between highly centralised organisation and decentralisation.[177] As they attained denominational status, NPCs adopted increasingly authoritarian ecclesiastical structures which conflicted with traditional Igbo democratic culture. One reason given for the schism within Riches of Christ Mission was Mba's autocratic leadership style and reluctance to delegate responsibility to fellow leaders.[178] A more recent example occurred within Redeemed People's Mission when Deputy General Superintendent, Kenneth Eze, who had been a pastor in the church since 1977, left to form Living Spring Assembly in 1999. A few years prior to his departure, Eze had transferred to the headquarters church to work directly under Thompson Nwosu, the General Superintendent. This coincided with Nwosu taking more control of the organisation, a move that strained the relationship and eventually led to schism.[179]

The concept of structural strain is the 'keystone' of Wilson's model of analysis. The major source of structural strain is the disjuncture that may occur in a religious group between norms and values. For Wilson, a schismatic group 'is a movement which has its origins in a dispute over norms and allegations that the main group has departed from those

---

[176] John Wilson, 'The Sociology of Schism', in Michael Hill (ed.), *A Sociology Yearbook of Religion in Britain*, London: SCM Press Ltd, 1971, 1-20. Wilson bases his theory on Neil Smelser's *Theory of Collective Behaviour* (London: Routledge & Kegan Paul, 1962), a model derived from the analysis of social movements.

[177] Wilson, 'Schism', 10-11.

[178] Anyaegbu, 'Pentecostal/Evangelical', 57 (based on a personal interview with Paul Nweke).

[179] Interview, Thompson Nwosu, 31.8.01, Jos. In a recent interview in a Christian newspaper, Eze explains his departure from RPM as a response to the call of God to start a new church (*VineyardNEWS*, 2.6, September 2005, 7).

implicated in the values of the original movement'.[180] There was considerable ideological conformity among early leaders and members of Igbo-founded NPCs. They were committed to Pentecostal spirituality, radical holiness and aggressive evangelism. However, actual practice sometimes deviated from stated values. The behaviour of Edozie Mba is a case in point. A further reason given for the early schism within Riches of Christ was Mba's alleged immoral conduct which was inconsistent with the church's strong ethical values.[181] Another example was Okeke's Save the Lost Mission. Okeke's original calling was as an evangelist, but when Save the Lost Mission began to plant new churches, he found himself distracted by administrative duties. Okeke felt the church had departed from its original vision and eventually left temporarily to resume his evangelistic activities on an independent basis. Something similar occurred when Okoye and Ezeofor broke away from Riches of Christ to embark on their evangelistic venture outside Igboland, a move initially opposed by the leaders, but which was compatible with the original missionary objectives of the church.[182] These examples support Barrett's assertion that motives behind further schism within African independency rest on a conviction that the separatist body has betrayed its original vision.[183]

Wilson refers to the blockage of mobility among the laity and their exclusion from positions of power as another source of structural strain.[184] Some of the leadership tussles that were symptomatic of Igbo NPCs had their origins in status frustration. The schisms within Grace of God Mission, for example, occurred largely because some pastors who relinquished their leadership roles to join the merger in 1976 felt excluded from positions of power in the new organisation. This was also a reason behind the rift between Ezeofor and Okoye of Freedom in Christ Church (later, All Christians Fellowship Mission). Ezeofor started Bible Faith Mission in 1979 because he felt frustrated with his subordinate position.[185] Another related source of structural strain stemmed from the individualistic orientation and pneumatic emphasis of neo-Pentecostal spirituality. The stress on personal charisma and spiritual revelation encouraged individual autonomy and competing claims to authority which facilitated the fragmentation of the movement.

Structural conduciveness and conditions of strain may exist without necessarily resulting in schism. For schism to occur there needs to be a precipitating factor to provide a stimulus for direct action and a mobilising

---

[180] Wilson, 'Schism', 5.

[181] Anyaegbu, 'Pentecostal/Evangelical', 57.

[182] Okoroafor, *William Okoye*, 68-9.

[183] Barrett, *Schism*, 197.

[184] Wilson, 'Schism', 7, 9.

[185] Okoroafor, *William Okoye*, 114-21.

agent to organise the dissident group.[186] In almost every case I came across it has been pastors within existing churches who have acted as 'mobilising agents' for secession. Factors that precipitated schism included personality clashes, sexual and financial misdemeanours, doctrinal disagreements and new visions. One example is Christ Love Mission, founded in 1986 by Mose Akwuobi after he quarrelled with Peter Maduako, his senior pastor in Central Christian Fellowship Mission (CCFM).[187] Several churches started after founders came under discipline in their former churches for immoral behaviour. Thus Fullness of Christ Mission, another breakaway from CCFM, started after its founder was disciplined for alleged immorality.[188] A more recent example occurred in 1999 when a senior pastor of Grace of God Mission also came under discipline and left to form his own ministry. Doctrinal disagreement was not a common cause of schism but did occasionally occur. The most infamous case concerns Edozie Mba again. If we recall, in 1988 he introduced sabbatharian doctrines into Riches of Christ, prompting the resignation of most of his pastors who broke away to form Bread of Life Mission. Finally, some seceded on the pretext of receiving new visions for ministry and mission. I have already mentioned the case of William Okoye. A less commendable example involved Lawrence Odunze, a leading pastor with Grace of God Mission, who in 1988 claimed to receive a 'vision' to open his own ministry and promptly 'hijacked' the Awka branch of the church, renaming it Royal Pentecostal Mission.[189]

Consequences of Schism

Church historians, missiologists and sociologists have noted the detrimental effects of schism on the spirituality and social impact of religious movements.[190] As Leslie Newbigin observes, when schism occurs, 'something essential to the true being of the Church is lost'.[191] The consensus is that the ecumenical impulses of revivals invariably give way to sectarian tendencies, which though presented in terms of church growth actually result in a loss of momentum and a decline in social influence.

---

[186] Wilson, 'Schism', 14-15.

[187] Anyaegbu, 'Pentecostal/Evangelical', 84.

[188] *Ibid.*, 80.

[189] *Ibid.*, 87-8.

[190] See for example, Lovelace, *Spiritual Life*, 289, 305; Hollenweger, *Pentecostalism*, 334, 366; Leslie Newbigin, *The Household of God: Lectures on the Nature of the Church*, London: SCM, 1957, 39; Steve Bruce, *God is Dead. Secularization in the West*, Oxford: Blackwell, 2002, 22, 24.

[191] Newbigin, *Household of God*, 108.

A recent article in a Nigerian Pentecostal magazine entitled 'The Break-Away Syndrome in Pentecostal Churches' reflects a growing concern among Nigerian Pentecostals about the divisive nature of their movement. This concern is shared by former Igbo revivalists who look back with nostalgia to the early 1970s when there was genuine unity among the 'brethren'. They identify schism and disunity as both cause and symptom of the revival's decline and decay. Participant accounts and church documents identify a number of consequences of fragmentation and disharmony. Firstly, disunity hinders cooperation in mission and results in the duplication of efforts to propagate the gospel. Thus All Christians Fellowship Mission states, 'We promote respect for the universal body of Christ thereby eliminating the competitive spirit among ministers of the gospel and churches and unnecessary duplication of efforts'.[192] Secondly, it compromises the church's message and threatens its credibility and integrity within society. In 1997, a group of Christians (including former Igbo revivalists), calling themselves the Congress of Christian Ethics in Nigeria (COCEN), wrote the Nigeria Covenant to express their conviction that Christian ethics must permeate every sphere of Nigerian society. In this, they state their belief in a united Christian community as the 'conscience of the nation' and reject sectarianism because it weakens the 'testimony and purpose of the Church'.[193] Finally, disunity reduces effectiveness in the political arena. This was the main impetus behind the formation of the Pentecostal Fellowship of Nigeria, a topic we return to in the next chapter.[194]

The issue of religious unity has a bearing upon the so-called secularisation thesis and the challenge posed to it by rational choice theorists. Secularisation theorists, like Steve Bruce, argue that the sectarianism hastens secularisation by weakening the dominant religious tradition and driving religion out of the public domain.[195] Against this, rational choice theorists argue that competitive pluralism increases religious vitality.[196] While the fragmentation of Igbo neo-Pentecostalism has

---

[192] All Christians Fellowship Mission, 'Lesson 6. Our Church Family Values', *Membership Bible Studies*, 33.

[193] Congress on Christian Ethics in Nigeria, *Nigeria Covenant*, Jos: CAPRO Media, 1997, 16. The Congress of Christian Ethics (COCEN) was established in 1994. Among its early leaders were James Ukaegbu, Peter Ozodo, William Okoye and Mike Oye, all former revivalists.

[194] Pentecostal Fellowship of Nigeria, *Constitution*, 3. Significantly, one of the themes of PFN's 1991 annual conference was 'Strength in Unity'.

[195] Bruce, *Secularization*, 22, 24.

[196] See for example, Rodney Stark, and Roger Finke, *Acts of Faith: Explaining the Human Side of Religion*, Berkeley and Los Angeles: University of California Press, 2000.

arguably increased levels of participation in its networks by expanding the religious marketplace, the foregoing critique suggests that it has reduced its ability to act as an agent of social and moral transformation.

Conclusion

This chapter has examined contributory factors behind the expansion of Igbo-founded neo-Pentecostal churches. The inherent flexibility of Pentecostal spirituality has enabled them to adapt their message and methodology to suit local contexts and cater for consumer demands. Their emphasis on the Bible, innovative worship styles, community ethos and proclamation of a holistic gospel have appealed to those faced with disintegrating social and economic relationships, and accustomed to a universe alive with spiritual forces. Each of these elements contributed to the construction of Igbo neo-Pentecostal identity. By establishing links with Western Pentecostal organisations, they are providing opportunity for people to opt into the global order and find their footing in the modern world. Hence, both local and global forces have influenced the shape of neo-Pentecostal spirituality. Perhaps the most significant factor behind neo-Pentecostal church growth, particularly in its formative period, has been its orientation towards mission which betrays its origins within the Civil War Revival. However, not all new churches were a result of mission initiatives. From the mid-1970s, the movement gradually lost its ecumenical vision, resulting in fragmentation and schism. And in its haste to respond to local consumer demands, it modified its message to include an emphasis on prosperity and deliverance, and relaxed its radical stance on ethical issues. This has had implications for its ability to act as an agent of socio-political transformation. To this we now turn.

Chapter 6

Revivalists, Pentecostals and Public Zeal

> While ministries of social welfare are a necessary part of the church's *diakonic* ministry, they need to be complemented by social action in order to express the kind of service that God intends to render to world in his reign of love, justice, and shalom. Programs of social action recognise that the church's ministry, like Jesus' own kingdom ministry, is always carried out in a socio-political context. . . . The church as a social institution needs to desacralize the state and its system of laws as the ultimate source of human rights by reminding political authorities of their God-given obligation to guarantee justice for all peoples (Murray Dempster).[1]

This chapter analyses the movement's record of engagement in the public arena from its origins in the civil war to the present. It focuses on two aspects of Christian service, identified by Dempster as social welfare and social action. Social welfare involves caring in practical ways for victims of injustice. Social action seeks to change basic conditions in society that cause human need through politics.[2] While the movement's political role will form the primary focus, I will also examine its record of social and humanitarian engagement. The movement went through several stages. While its civil war phase contained the seeds of a theology that provided an ideological basis for engagement through prayer, political activism and social initiatives, participants failed to build upon this after the war. Since the late 1980s, however, a shift has occurred towards a more proactive engagement with socio-economic and political realities.

---

[1] Murray A. Dempster, 'Evangelism, Social Concern and the Kingdom of God', in Dempster, Klaus and Petersen (eds.), *Called and Empowered*, 35.

[2] *Ibid.*, 33-36.

Ruth Marshall, following Copans, warns of falling into the traps of 'political reductionism' or 'symbolic expansionism' in political analysis of religious movements.[3] On the one hand is a tendency to concentrate on the 'narrow sphere of elite politics' and focus on leaders' public statements, while paying scant attention to popular forms of Christian belief and practice. Consequently, the political is stripped of its symbolic and expressive aspects. On the other hand, local studies of popular Christianity, 'while drawing attention to other idioms of protest and political action', are prone to expand the realm of the political so that it becomes too broad.[4] Following Marshall, I focus on points of interaction between the religious and political domains - be they institutional, symbolic or expressive - through an analysis of revivalist and Pentecostal discourse and praxis. Data is drawn from official church documents, leaders' statements, private correspondence, oral interviews and popular literature. I have also observed Pentecostals in action as they engage with their socio-political context in a variety of ways.

The study of the beliefs (or theology) of religious movements is crucial. As Gifford rightly observes, religion offers a 'reading of the world, of history, of society, of time, of space, of power, of authority, of justice and of ultimate truth' that are all issues for socio-political analysis.[5] Theology acts as an ideological construct which has socio-political implications and side effects. In response to an ongoing context of crisis, the Civil War Revival and its Pentecostal progeny generated a theology 'from below' which helped participants adapt to changing contexts and refashion their identity in terms of a missionary fellowship with ambitions to transform their local communities.

Scripture Union and the Politics of Biafra, 1960-70

During Nigeria's First Republic (1960-66), mission churches adopted a quietist rather than a prophetic stance and failed to develop a theology that included social concern and political action. Ojo identifies this as a serious lapse, especially as many political leaders were Christians or products of

---

[3] Jean Copans, *La Longue Marche de la Modernité Africaine: Savoirs, Intellectuels, Democratie*, Paris: Karthala, 1990, 294-95, cited in Ruth Marshall, '"God is not a Democrat": Pentecostalism and Democratization in Nigeria', in Paul Gifford (ed.), *The Christian Churches and the Democratisation of Africa*, Leiden: E. J. Brill, 1995, 239-44.

[4] Marshall, 'God is not a Democrat', 240-41.

[5] Gifford, *African Christianity*, 26.

mission education.[6] An article in the September 1968 edition of the *Nigerian Christian* laments this tendency towards political acquiescence.

> What should be the function of the Church and Christians in a nation afflicted by a crisis? It has been stressed *ad nauseam* by many critics that the Church must accept part responsibility for the unhappy situation which this country faces today. For a long time the Church in Nigeria has been afraid to minister to the nation, to stand courageously by the truth and to speak out objectively. What we have been getting are the woolliness that hedges political intrigues, the sectional feelings that obscure the truth and the naivety and platitudes that characterise the flippant.[7]

The same article refers to the Church accumulating 'huge sums of money' to build a modern cathedral, while thousands die daily from lack of food, shelter and clothing. It also criticizes the mission churches for remaining silent during the 'evil days which preceded Jan 15, 1966', a reference to the First Republic.[8]

Immediately prior to the outbreak of civil war some mainline church leaders did try to prevent hostilities by writing to military governors to express their belief in one Nigeria and urge a resolution through peaceful means.[9] Yet when war broke out Christian leaders on both sides tended to support their respective governments, causing a rift within the Christian Council of Nigeria, the main Protestant ecumenical body. In Western Nigeria, few Christian leaders were critical of the Federal cause, partly because General Yakubu Gowon, the Nigerian head of state, was known to be a highly respected Christian. Leading Nigerian churchmen denied it was a religious war, objected to the involvement of Western Christian agencies in the Biafran relief effort, and labelled their counterparts in Eastern Nigeria 'rebels'.[10]

---

[6] Ojo, 'Church', 26.

[7] *Nigerian Christian*, 2.9, September 1968, 1. The *Nigerian Christian* is a monthly newspaper produced by the Christian Council of Nigeria (CCN), an organisation established in 1948 to unite Protestant denominations.

[8] S. A. Banjo, 'He told me to keep quiet', *Nigerian Christian*, 1.3, June 1967, 3.

[9] 'Church Leaders meet in Benin. Letter to Military Governors', *Nigerian Christian*, May 1967, 4. This action was initiated by the Igbo Roman Catholic Bishop of Port Harcourt and involved leading churchmen from Eastern and Western Nigeria.

[10] Ojo, 'Church', 26; M. Y. Nabofa, 'Christianity in Nigeria: Its Role in Nation-Building', in J. A. Atanda, Garba Ashiwaju and Yaya Abubakar, *Nigeria Since Independence. The First 25 Years, Volume IX, Religion,* Ibadan:

Igbo Christian leaders were generally supportive of the Biafran cause, especially during the early stages, and there were few voices of dissent. One of the more prominent was Presbyterian Dr Francis Akanu Ibiam who represented Biafra in the international arena and became Special Adviser to Ojukwu, the Biafran leader. Most Biafrans saw it as a war of survival and a clash between Christian Biafra and Islamic Nigeria. This was a crucial factor in the mobilisation of recruits and helped to shape their identity as Christian agents defending their communities against a Muslim *Jihad.* It was reinforced by Biafran propaganda and the popular press, which identified Biafra with biblical Israel and presented Ojukwu as a Moses figure, while it demonised Gowon and Harold Wilson, the British prime minister, for his support of the Federation.[11]

Most revivalists also supported the concept of Biafra, particularly during the early stages of the war following the pogroms in the North and the declaration of independence. From their point of view, an independent state was the only viable option and they were ready to fight for its survival after the Federation's declaration of war. None of my informants said they were opposed to the decision to secede, and significant numbers took active roles in support of the Biafran cause as soldiers or in a non-combative capacity as intelligence officers, propagandists and arms producers. Not all were 'born-again' Christians or Scripture Union members at the time, though the majority were mission church members. For most of the war, Igbo SU leaders believed that an independent Biafra was God's will and an answer to their problems, though they favoured a peaceful resolution. Initially they prayed for victory, but towards the end of the war they prayed for peace and for God's will to be done. When defeat finally came in January 1970, most accepted it as God's will and were grateful to have survived. In the following letter extract, a member of SU Umuahia struggles to resolve the tension arising from his twin beliefs in the justness of the Biafran cause and God's providential control.

> It has been a struggle to me personally to accept again the concept of 'One Nigeria' and somehow I have been very pessimistic about the future of that association. There is however no doubt that the war ended when and how it did at the Lord's intervention, which means that He considers it best for us to go back to Nigeria.[12]

Despite their relative marginalisation in the politics of Biafra, Igbo revivalists were not politically acquiescent. In 1968, Scripture Union in

---

Heinemann, 105; A. E. Ekoko and L. O. Amadi, 'Religion and Stability in Nigeria', in Atanda, Ashiwaju and Abubakar, *Nigeria*, 118.

[11] Kalu, *Embattled Gods*, 271; Walls, 'Religion and the Press', 210-11.

[12] Matthias Eluwah, Letter to Bill Roberts, 23 March 1970.

Biafra wrote a letter to London headquarters expressing concern over the latter's quietist approach and appealing to them to protest against the British government's policy of arms sales to Nigeria.[13]

> Other Christian bodies have been speaking up trying to bring peace through Christian understanding and not through arms. . . . They are doing all in their power to relieve our suffering people by bringing in food and drugs. They are fighting to make all nations concerned in this Nigeria - Biafra War, especially the big powers behind this War, to stop the arms conflict and supply, and to depend on peace talks for settlement. Yet the SU, part of the Christian body which should help to effect this, seems to be quiet. We would anyway suppose that the cause of your apparent quiet is that you do not yet understand the real situation over here, and Biafra's stand in it, despite the wide publicity it has been given by our Foreign Ministry, the Christian Council of Churches, the Vatican Council, Doctor Ibiam in his last tour of Britain, the countries that have accorded us diplomatic recognition, and through the unsuccessful Kampala talks. . . . God has shown us with many signs and in many wonderful ways, through this war, that He wants us to stay and remain as Biafra. . . . We know that Satan through many agents usually tries, of course unsuccessfully, to prevent God's plans from being carried out, so it is all our duty to effect God's wish through His Spirit and with His power. Though the Spirit prepares the soil the planting must be done through human agents, that is through us, to effect God's plan. So you should join us in our fight for peace, please, if you have not done so before now. May we add, before you misunderstand us, that we know you might have been contributing very much in prayers for peace in our land. Thank you for that and we shall still value more of your prayers very much. But prayer alone is not enough. We all know that action speaks better than words and feelings, not that we are discrediting the power of sincere prayer to God, not at all. The Christians and people of Nigeria and Biafra are suffering much right now. From Eph 6.10-20 we see the sort of war the Christian is fighting and how he is to overcome. It is a war that must be won with all the armour used effectively. None is to be left out because the enemy who is very powerful and crafty (Eph 6.12) will use our weak points to destroy us. This applies to us suffering Biafrans and Nigerians. The devil is strong but God is stronger and we shall win if we trust Him fully and use effectively all the armour He has given us. This war is not left, then, to few members of the Christian

---

[13] The British government's support for Nigeria by supplying arms was critical to the outcome of the war as Federal Nigeria did not produce weapons of its own.

body, but all must fight the war to make sure there are no weak points somewhere, so you are equally in this Nigeria - Biafra war as well as we are, just as we shall be ready to help you in time of need in anyway possible. So do not depend on prayer alone. Act please. Let the Spirit of God make you bold (Acts 4.29, Eph 6.20) and use the power He has given you to speak out for peace in West Africa and other disturbed areas of the world. Be bold and press your Home Government to stop supplying one side with arms but to take a Christian stand and make peace. Be bold to speak against Russia's stand in this war. Be bold to appeal to the heads of Governments of Biafra and Nigeria that the only way to peace is through peaceful negotiations not by arms conflict. Be bold to team up with the World Christian Council of Churches, the Vatican Council, the International Red Cross and other Christian bodies to attack the common enemy - the devil. Stand for Christ boldly in all courses and you will always overcome. Encourage other SU Missions in America, Canada, and West Africa especially, to help settle this our trouble by contributing their quota in prayers, peace campaigns, and relief of the suffering masses in our area. We hope you could please ask brother Bill Roberts to tell you his observations about our sufferings. First, the 'Refugee' problem is great and hunger is the greatest tragedy, so that many unsaved souls are perishing. Second, the effect of the war - Air raids have claimed many lives and maimed many others. Third, the sick, both in hospital and at home, have few drugs and medicines to cure them. Fourthly, the SU and other Christians here need tracts with which to witness, Pamphlets and Books to keep us meditating on God's Word, SU Cards and Notes and Guides to help us grow spiritually. So please we do hope that you will do all you can to get our suffering people some Relief in form of food, drugs, clothings and Christian literature. We know, please, that it is difficult to transport things to Biafra, but we shall like you to contact the International Red Cross planes, the Christian Council planes and other bodies that have been sending relief by air or any other means to us.[14]

This text contains the seeds of a political theology, based on a dualistic worldview and a belief in invisible forces controlling material events. The authors, all young people on the margins of the mainline churches, were convinced that the fate of Biafra rested on the outcome of a spiritual battle between good and evil. Satan may try to frustrate God's plans, but will not succeed if Christians exercise faith and engage in spiritual warfare. While they believed in God's sovereign will, they were not fatalists. They reminded their readers that Christians, as God's agents, can influence

[14] SU Biafra, Letter to Scripture Union London, 8 July 1968.

earthly affairs through prayer *and* political activism. Prayer alone is insufficient. Christians have a responsibility to speak out against injustice and if necessary confront state governments. They should also supply relief materials to relieve the 'suffering masses,' and Christian literature to stem the flow of 'unsaved souls' perishing without Christ. So while the authors interpreted the political situation in terms of spiritual causality, they believed this to be entirely compatible with socio-political action.

Revivalists were also unafraid to challenge power élites at local level. Reference has already been made to Uchenna Emezue's account of revivalist activity in Ossah village and the clash between SU young people and their elders in church and community on the occasion of the New Year traditional 'swearing ceremony'. In this instance, the combined effects of their 'born-again' conversion, exposure to the Bible, corporate prayer and Christian fellowship enabled the young protagonists to challenge the authority of their elders in a public setting.[15]

Revivalists, Pentecostals and Post-War Politics, 1970-79

During the 1970s, mainline churches maintained their silence during the Gowon regime, despite an escalation in government corruption.[16] Generally, Pentecostals also adopted a quietist approach and were suspicious of political involvement. I found little evidence that Igbo revivalists or Pentecostals actively pursued positions of political power or sought to influence government through direct action. Rather, they believed that a combination of prayer and evangelism was sufficient to transform economic, social and political landscapes. This negative attitude is hinted at in the following letter extract: 'I'm writing to you from the University of Nigeria Nsukka. I was admitted here to do a 3 year programme in Political Science. Don't think I'm going into Politics! . . . I'd never be a professional politician'.[17]

One reason for their reluctance to engage in direct political activity was relief that the war was over and gratitude to Gowon for preventing genocide and for his prosecution of the 'three Rs' (Reconciliation, Rehabilitation and Reconstruction). Another reason was their roots in the evangelical spirituality of Scripture Union which emphasised evangelism rather than socio-political critique, and the influence of Keswick which focused on the personal rather than systemic and structural effects of sin.[18] Gifford refers

[15] Emezue, 'New Year's Victory', 1969.

[16] Ojo, 'Church', 26.

[17] Uchenna, Emezue, Letter to Roberts, 28 September 1973.

[18] Pat Williams and Toyin Falola, *Religious Impact on the Nation State*, Aldershot: Avebury, 1995, 164; David Bebbington, 'The Decline and

to Africa's revival Christianity as 'private, personalized and otherworldly'. As such, it does not engage in social analysis nor challenge oppressive systems.[19] One informant stated, 'Christians would look at that kind of thing and all they were interested in really was bringing the politicians to Christ. But that a Christian could actually themselves go into this, no, that didn't occur to them'.[20] Strong adventist beliefs and retreatist attitudes also discouraged political activism. Revivalists and Pentecostals were preoccupied with winning souls and preparing the faithful before Christ's imminent return and consequently had little interest in socio-political critique. A stress on retreat from the 'world' led many to consider participation in politics 'unchristian' and to shun political ambitions. Politics was regarded as 'worldly' and evil, tainted by its association with traditional religion and 'occult' forces, and linked to corruption and violence. One informant said that during the 1970s revivalists believed that successful politicians acquired 'power' through engaging the services of traditional religious practitioners or establishing connections with secret 'occult' societies. The reluctance to participate in the political process was reinforced by memories of the First republic and events leading up to the civil war. However, the primary reason for their quietist approach was their marginalised position in society. Most were young, relatively poor, and outsiders in the political process. The revival in the East was primarily a movement of the youth and the urban poor, rather than the élite or the middle class. Even if inclined to engage in critical dialogue, they would probably not have been in a position to be heard.

Despite a lack of overt political activity, there was evidence of political resistance expressed through a denunciation of gerontocratic power, oral and written discourse, and intercessory prayer. Marshall refers to the way Nigerian Pentecostalism, with its central theme of rebirth, creates 'autonomous spaces' of practice which 'defy the oppressive logic of current power monopolies', and formulates strategies for survival.[21] By setting up symbolic boundaries with an amoral world, Igbo Pentecostals developed counter-cultural lifestyles and acquired a set of democratic values, based on participation and competition, which awaited release into public space. As we saw in chapter 3, the 'born-again' experience enabled young revivalists to challenge gerontocracy at local level. While this was felt primarily among Christians, sometimes it overflowed into the community as 'born-again' youth contested the authority of local elders and traditional religious

---

Resurgence of Evangelical Social Concern 1918-1980', in John Wolfe (ed.), *Evangelical Faith and Public Zeal. Evangelicals and Society in Britain 1780-1980*, London: SPCK, 1995, 78-9.

[19] Gifford, 'Prosperity', 380-81.

[20] Interview, Frances Lawjua Bolton, 4 October 2002, London.

[21] Marshall, 'Power', 215.

practitioners. In the following oral narrative, former revivalist and neo-Pentecostal pioneer Samson Onwubiko describes the challenge he posed to traditional religionists soon after his conversion to Christianity in the early 1970s. He begins by referring to a meeting with his grandfather, the local chief priest.

> He reminded me of all the places we went to, the things we did, the groves we went to, the sacrifices we made, all the covenants made here and there. I said, 'Yes, those things were true, but no longer do I belong to them again. I belong to Jesus. He died for me and paid my price, so I owe nobody anything anymore'. So I spent time and prayed and God helped me. Now after another one year he watched me. Nothing happened to me. He called his grandchildren and said to them, all his years as a chief priest of the gods nobody has ever stood against the gods and ever lived. But his grandson has stood against the demons and they all ran away. . . . And that he has watched me. No headache, no fever, no sickness of any kind as a result of that. And that he has now come to conclude that the God I have discovered is the true God. As a result of that he was not going to hand over the gods to any of his children before he dies, that he was going to destroy them before he died. And then he said, 'Look at that grove there, the toughest so far, because all the land over there, nobody ever goes in there to do any farm work'. He said, 'You go, drive the demons, build your church there'. So that's how I got there.[22]

As the head of the *umụnna* (kinship group), Onwubiko's grandfather had considerable local political power and was responsible for the distribution of land. But he derived this power from his position as the living representative of the ancestors and the custodian of the village deities. By defying the deities and transferring his allegiance to the church, Onwubiko posed a direct challenge to his grandfather's political authority.

The formation of the Christian Students' Social Movement (CSSM) in 1977 reflected a growing concern among some Nigerian Pentecostals about the lack of national political awareness within their movement. CSSM was partly a response to the perceived threat posed by Muslim attempts to extend the jurisdiction of *Shari'a* courts and add *Shari'a* Law to the 1979 Constitution. It was also a reaction to the cultural revival associated with FESTAC '77 (Festival of Arts and Culture), which Pentecostals believed would open the door to demonic activity because of its celebration of Nigeria's traditional religious heritage. Though CSSM was started in Western Nigeria, its early leaders were Austin Ukachi and Emeka

---

[22] Interview, 10 October 2001, Amachara.

Nwankpa, both Igbo neo-Pentecostals and former students at the universities of Ibadan and Ile-Ife respectively, and Igbo revivalist Reuben Ezemadu, founder of Christian Missionary Foundation.[23] According to Ojo, CSSM has sought to 'enlighten charismatics on the possibility of their influence in national life by linking prophecy with politics'.[24] During the late 1970s, through its conferences and its monthly Prayer Bulletin, it alerted Christians to the 'dangers' of socialism, Islam and cultural revival, provoked prayer for the nation, and encouraged Christians to speak out on political issues. In its early bulletins, it represented the political arena as a sacralised public space controlled by spiritual forces. Yet CSSM remained committed to a belief in the power of evangelism to transform the economic and socio-political situation of Nigeria. This is reflected in the following extract from a manual on Christian social responsibility written in 1980: 'Social reform therefore must always start with the individual by seeking to bring him into a saving relationship to Christ'.[25]

Corruption, Religious Politics and Democratisation, 1979-2006

From the late 1970s, government corruption and mismanagement, economic recession and austerity measures were recurring themes within Nigerian political and economic culture. This generated an upsurge in civil disobedience, which in turn led to political repression by increasingly authoritarian regimes. Other themes that dominated the next two decades were the escalation of religious violence between Muslims and Christians, and the contested democratisation programme.

Despite the upsurge in civil society resistance during the early 1980s, Igbo Pentecostals tended to refrain from public political critique or acts of civil disobedience. This did not necessarily mean political acquiescence or conservatism, but a pursuit of change within the limits of law and order, and a strong respect for the 'powers' ordained by God. In moments of crisis, they preferred to resort to prayer and trust in providential intervention. This is reflected in the following extract from a message preached by William Okoye of All Christians Fellowship Mission and published in the National Concord newspaper shortly after the contested 1979 elections, which ushered in the Second Republic and the corrupt Shagari administration. It contains a number of themes that recur in

[23] Austin Ukachi, a member of Scripture Union in Biafra during the war, was the first President of CSWSM. Emeka Nwankpa was the Coordinating Secretary of CSSM from 1977-1981.

[24] Ojo, 'Church', 27. See also Ojo, *Army*, 105-15.

[25] Christian Students Social Movement, *Working Manual No.2, Christian Social Responsibility*, Ile-Ife: CSSM, 1980, 7.

Pentecostal political discourse: a belief in the efficacy of prayer and the rule of God over the affairs of this world; the biblical injunction to submit to governing authorities; the association of political office with corruption; and the impotence of politicians to solve Nigeria's problems.

> We want to say without any shadow of doubt that the President, the State Governors and all the elected civilians who took over the rule of this country from the military are God approved and appointed (Romans 13:1-8). . . . Some people will say that many of these people came to power through corrupt means. They may have, but did not hundreds of thousands of God fearing people in this country pray and fast, some for a whole week, that God will give us people after His own heart to rule us? If you are a true child of God and you believe that God answers prayers, then God is in this or else you will be saying that God has disappointed you. . . . We must also make it crystal clear that no political party, politician or person has the solution to the problems of the country.[26]

Igbo Pentecostals were still preoccupied with personal salvation and regarded politics as immoral. The advent of prosperity teaching in the early 1980s compounded the tendency for some to adopt a conservative non-critical stance. Gifford identifies this as one reason why liberation theology and socio-political critique have been uncharacteristic of African Pentecostalism generally. It offers 'no incentive to economic analysis and socio-political involvement', but reassures the prosperous that 'wealth is their due' and is unrelated to unjust structures.[27] Jeff Haynes identifies another reason for the apolitical effects of prosperity teaching. Because African Pentecostals believe earthly events are contingent on the outcome of a cosmic battle between Satan and God, and redemption and prosperity are in God's and the individual's hands, they neither expect governments to supply their needs nor hold them responsible for deteriorating socio-economic conditions.[28]

The 1980s saw the resacralisation of public space as religion re-emerged as a feature of Nigerian political culture. This was largely due to the strong presence of resurgent Islam and Christian revivalism which, according to Paul Freston, has made Nigeria 'globally unique in terms of evangelical

---

[26] Message by William Okoye of ACFM, 'God is above all - Jesus is Lord of all', *National Concord*, quoted in Okoroafor, *William Okoye*, 165-66.

[27] Gifford, 'Prosperity', 380-81, 373, 382.

[28] Jeff Haynes, *Religion and Politics in Africa*, London & New Jersey: Zed Books, 1996, 204.

politics'.[29] Muslim-Christian tensions reached new heights during the Second Republic (1979-83) and were accompanied by an escalation of violence between Muslims and Christians. The manipulation of religion, exacerbated by the *Shari'a* debate, was a feature of the 1978 elections, when Muslims and Christians were urged to vote along religious lines. This generated public demonstrations on both sides. But the most notable crisis occurred in the Northern city of Zaria when a clash between Muslim and Christian students at Ahmadu Bello University killed six students and was quelled only when the army intervened. The re-emergence of religious politics was also linked to the deepening economic crisis caused by the decline in oil revenues in the early 1980s and the introduction of the Structural Adjustment Programme (SAP) in 1986. This intensified intra-ethnic and religious tensions as different factions competed for their share of the national cake. Since then, the increasing consciousness of religion as a factor in Nigerian politics has heightened the geo-political problems of the country and deepened the North-South divide, making Nigeria the focus of one of the 'most important Muslim-Christian political clashes in any nation-state today'.[30]

Islamic resurgence and a succession of Muslim military rulers transformed the political landscape so that politics was increasingly played out in a pluralistic setting.[31] Yet while Christianity was no longer associated with the centre of power, Pentecostals were beginning to discover their political potential. According to Cleary, marginal groups become mainstream political actors when they reach a critical size.[32] Although at this stage Pentecostal political theology was underdeveloped, the presence of large numbers of 'born-again' Christians, particularly in the North, acted as a counterbalance to Islamic resurgence.

A shift to a Pentecostal theology of political engagement occurred in the late-1980s and was precipitated by a number of factors. Firstly, President Ibrahim Babangida enabled religion to become a platform to express political issues, and consequently it attained a new level of political prominence. Religious groups were the only civil associations tolerated by his regime (1985-1993), and religious leaders were the only leaders able to

---

[29] Paul Freston, *Evangelicals and Politics in Asia, Africa and Latin America*, Cambridge: Cambridge University Press, 2001, 182.

[30] *Ibid.*, 181.

[31] Ogbu U. Kalu, 'Faith and Politics in Africa. Emergent Political Theology of Engagement in Nigeria', paper presented as the Paul B. Henry Lecture, Paul Henry Institute, Calvin College, Grand Rapids, Mich., 2003, 8.

[32] Edward L. Cleary, 'Introduction: Pentecostals, Prominence, and Politics', in Edward L. Cleary and Hannah Stewart-Gambino (eds.), *Power, Politics, and Pentecostals in Latin America*, Boulder, CO: Westview Press, 1998, 13.

speak freely without risking incarceration.[33] Secondly, concern over the moral state of the nation and the alleged incompetence of Nigeria's political leaders provoked some Igbo neo-Pentecostals to socio-political critique. In a book published in 1985, William Okoye of All Christians Fellowship Mission expressed moral outrage at the way Nigeria had been ruled since independence and traced the country's national problems to ungodliness and the failure of the Church to fulfil its responsibility.[34] However, the main 'trigger' issue, according to Haynes, was the 'fear of Islamization', which galvanised Pentecostal political activity and led to their involvement at national level.[35] This was exacerbated by Babangida's decision to join the Organisation of Islamic Countries (OIC) in 1986 and the attempt to extend the jurisdiction of *Shari'a* courts in the 1988-9 Constituent Assembly. Christian opposition to the OIC was based on the assumption that it undermined the nation's secular status, in contravention of the 1979 Constitution, and the fear that it would enlarge Muslim monopoly of public space. Christians accused Babangida's government of favouring Northern interests, adopting pro-Islam policies and failing to protect Christians in the North from attacks by Muslims. Between 1986 and 1993, major Muslim-Christian clashes occurred in Kafanchan, Kaduna, Katsina, Funtua, Kano, Zaria (1987); Katsina, Bauchi, Kano (1991) and Zangon-Kataf (1992). Some of the most aggressive attacks by Muslims were a direct response to Pentecostal activities. The 1987 conflict, which started at a college of education in Kafanchan, Kaduna State, was especially shocking and changed the Nigerian religious landscape. Many churches were destroyed, and many thousands of (mainly Christian) lives were lost.

Significantly, the Muslim challenge revived the Protestant ecumenical impulse of the 1960s.[36] The Christian Association of Nigeria (CAN), founded in 1976, became the main vehicle for Christian political engagement and by 1987, had 'resolved that Christians must be directly involved in politics'.[37] CAN consists of five groupings: the Catholic Secretariat of Nigeria (CSN), the Christian Council of Nigeria (CCN), the Organization of African Instituted Churches (OAIC), the Pentecostal Fellowship of Nigeria (PFN) and TEKAN/ECWA. Its radical stance was a

---

[33] Falola, *Violence*, 224.

[34] William Okoye, *The Role of the Church in Nation Building*, 1985, cited in Okoroafor, *William Okoye*, 169. Okoye's book received a sympathetic review in the May 15 1985 edition of the National Concord newspaper.

[35] Haynes, *Religion and Politics*, 206.

[36] If we recall, Protestant ecumenism in the 1960s culminated in the church union project, an unsuccessful attempt to unite the Anglican, Methodist and Presbyterian churches.

[37] CAN, *Leadership in Nigeria (To Date): An Analysis*, Kaduna: CAN Northern Zone, 1987, 73, cited in Falola, *Violence*, 224.

response to Islamic domination of public space and oppressive military regimes, and a wish to protect Christian interests in a hostile environment. As early as 1985, it was making public statements critical of the military and demanding a return to civil rule. Its 1988 manifesto encouraged Christians to vote for the leaders of their choice, to become politically aware, to expose corruption among political leaders, and not allow their vote to be influenced by bribery, ethnic sentiments or religious intolerance.[38]

The Pentecostal Fellowship of Nigeria (PFN), founded in 1986, soon became an influential voice within CAN. Originally an apolitical organisation, it too re-evaluated its political stance in response to impending Islamization.[39] Groups that came together to form PFN included Christian Pentecostal Mission, The Redeemed Evangelical Mission (TREM) and Uma Ukpai Evangelistic Association, all founded by former Igbo revivalists. All the Pentecostal churches that emerged from the Civil War Revival are currently members of PFN, and some of their leaders have occupied senior positions within both organisations. William Okoye (ACFM) was Charter Chairman of PFN Abuja Chapter in 1990 and an Executive member of CAN. K. Chukuemeka (RPM) was Chairman of Plateau State PFN and General Secretary of Jos Local Government CAN in 1987. Paul Nwachukwu, General Superintendent of Grace of God Mission, was PFN Vice-President (Eastern Zone) in 2002. The fragmentation of the NPC church movement militated against it becoming a political force in Nigeria. PFN has helped it to present a united front in the public arena and promote political awareness among its members. It claims to be the 'mouthpiece for the Pentecostal Movement in Nigeria' and has helped to counter Islamic domination.[40]

Christian resurgence contributed to a rise in religious violence as Muslim domination of the North gradually came under threat. In 2001, I experienced firsthand a violent clash between Muslims and Christians while teaching in the Northern city of Jos. The crisis began four days before the September 11th terrorist attacks in the USA, but received little international media coverage despite extensive loss of life and destruction of property. For ten days, we were confined to our college campus while Christians and Muslims fought each other for territorial and political control of Jos District. The crisis caught people by surprise, because Jos was known as a peaceful city and had never experienced anything like it before. Both mosques and churches were destroyed, and over 3,000 Muslims and Christians lost their lives. Thousands of others were

---

[38] *Ibid.*

[39] Haynes, *Religion and Politics*, 218.

[40] P.F.N., *Constitution*, 2.

Figure 15. Church destroyed during the 2001 Jos religious riots.

brutalised, raped and maimed.[41] The large Igbo community was one of the targets of Muslim insurgence.

Written and oral texts produced at the time give an insight into Igbo Pentecostal approaches to politics and inter-religious conflict.[42] They contain several recurring themes. Blame for the crisis is levelled either at Muslims for seeking to establish Islamic hegemony or the Devil and his demons for disturbing the peace of the state. Christians should expect persecution and suffering, and rely upon divine protection rather than military intervention. Finally, while it is understandable for Christians to be angry, they should refrain from religious hatred. Prayer, righteousness and sacrificial love are the proper 'weapons of warfare' for religious conflict. The consensus among Pentecostals interviewed at the time was that they would not instigate violence against Muslims, unless provoked or as a means of defence. None of my informants said they were actively involved in violent encounters, though some Igbo Pentecostals lost their lives and property. In an interview for a local Christian newspaper,

[41] These estimated figures are based on data collected by Rebecca Dali, a research student at the University of Jos and a member of the faculty of the Theological College of Northern Nigeria.

[42] Sources included sermons I listened during NPC meetings in the aftermath of the crisis, oral interviews and personal conversations, and interviews published in local Christian newspapers.

Thompson Nwosu of Redeemed People's Mission refers to the case of Monday Nwosu, an Igbo member of staff at the University of Jos:

> He was conveying members of his family in their car to Rukuba Barracks (Jos) when suddenly he decided to go back and check for their first child, a lady who was not around while they left for the Barracks. He left his wife and the other children in the car almost near to the Rukubu Barracks and went to their Masalacin Yidi area for their child when he was cornered by Muslim fanatics and slaughtered. The widow and the eight children are here with me in this house.[43]

In the aftermath of the crisis, Igbo Pentecostal pastor Emmanuel Nwajei called for Christians to be more politically proactive:

> I am concerned that Christians are behind in political participation. . . . We must rise up to the challenge and get involved in politics to fight those who think they own the monopoly of life. . . . The time for passive silence is over. While we are not encouraging our people to violence, we are however asking them not to fold their hands.[44]

While Christian political activism in Africa has often produced acts of heroism and sacrifice, there are potentially disturbing possibilities. Philip Jenkins warns of a 'new Christendom', based in the global South and characterised by intolerance and conflict, as religious identification takes precedence over allegiance to secular nation-states.[45] Faced with growing demands by Muslim activists for an Islamic state and adoption of *Shari'a* law, Nigerian churches may be tempted to retaliate by 'asserting their own religious beliefs through legislation' and calling for the creation of 'Christian' states.[46] After the Jos religious riots, Nwajei called for precisely this as the solution to Muslim attempts to monopolise public space in Plateau State.[47] Jenkins believes that international politics in the coming decades is likely to revolve around inter-faith conflicts. The potential for conflict becomes more intense when one religious tradition seeks to declare

---

[43] Rev. N. C. Thompson, 'Jos Religious Crisis. Many members of my Church were killed', *Salvation*, 16 December 2001, 2.

[44] 'Jos Religious Crisis. Declare Plateau a Christian State', *Salvation*, December 16 2001, 13, 19.

[45] Jenkins, *Next Christendom*, 12-3.

[46] *Ibid.*, 153. By 2001, nine of Nigeria's thirty-six states had imposed *Shari'a* religious law in whole or in part.

[47] 'Jos Religious Crisis', 19.

a particular nation is or should be Christian or Muslim. Linked to this is the fact that both Islam and Christianity are missionary religions with aspirations to convert the entire globe, and both have traditions of seeking to impose their views through political actions.[48] In the case of Nigeria, evangelism is sometimes used as a means of establishing a support base for Christian candidates. The close association between evangelisation and politics presents potential problems for Igbo Pentecostals as they seek to develop a viable political theology.

The other theme to dominate Nigerian political culture from the mid-1980s was the contested democratisation programme which culminated in the election of the Christian President Olusegan Obasanjo in 1999. Any discussion of the political role of contemporary African Pentecostals must include their relationship to Africa's 'second liberation', which began in the late 1980s as people tried to free themselves from oppressive political systems.[49] The failure of African states to redeem their promises of democratisation and development opened the way for alternative forms of authority and legitimacy. Church leaders began to play a more active role in the democratisation process. Conferences were convened to hasten the transition to democracy, often presided over by mainline church leaders. In Zaire, for example, the Roman Catholic Archbishop of Kisangani presided over the 1991 national conference, an attempt to halt the slide into anarchy. In Malawi, the 1992 Lenten pastoral of the Catholic bishops marked the beginning of opposition to President Banda's dictatorial regime. And in Ghana, the Christian Council of Ghana, the main Protestant ecumenical body, was deeply involved in the transition to democratic rule during the 1990s, issuing memoranda and holding meetings across the country.[50] While no such conference was held in Nigeria, nevertheless churches emerged as major organs of civil society.

Gifford has argued that in general it is Africa's mainline churches that have acted as agents of democratisation, while the newer Pentecostal churches have provided support for Africa's dictators for pragmatic reasons. When they enter the political arena, their intention is to obtain practical benefits for themselves rather than challenge government corruption and mismanagement.[51] In Nigeria, this was not strictly so. While Igbo Pentecostal political consciousness during the 1980s still remained at the level of discourse rather than direct action, in the early 1990s, they became a more significant political force. For instance, in January 1993, William Okoye preached a sermon in which he castigated

[48] Jenkins, *Next Christendom*, 164, 168-69.

[49] Paul Gifford, 'Introduction: Democratisation and the Churches', in Gifford (ed.), *Christian Churches*, 1.

[50] Gifford, 'Democratisation', 1; Gifford, *African Christianity*, 71.

[51] Gifford, 'Democratisation', 5; Gifford, *African Christianity*, 341-42.

political leaders who deny others their rights, oppress and exploit them, and then use their powers to silence them. The address was broadcast on Nigerian television and radio.[52] While it is doubtful that Pentecostals significantly influenced the transition process during the Babangida regime, except through prayer, the annulment of the 1993 elections and General Abacha's subsequent intervention stimulated them into action.[53] As the church became a major pro-democracy group within civil society, Pentecostals began to play a more active role in the politics of transition. Kalu suggests that Pentecostals actually 'radicalized' the politics of mainline churches during the 1990s.[54]

Some Igbo Pentecostals have adopted a critical public stance towards Nigeria's ethical and political problems. In chapter 5, I mentioned the Congress of Christian Ethics (COCEN), established in 1994 during the Abacha military regime (1993-1998) by Nigerian Christians (including former Igbo revivalists and Pentecostals), alarmed at the 'flood of corruption inundating Nigerian society'. In 1997, COCEN produced the Nigeria Covenant and sent copies to Christians and political leaders throughout the nation. The Nigeria Covenant calls upon Christians to respect and obey their leaders, encourages active participation in politics, and recognises the validity of civil disobedience and passive resistance as long as it does not involve violence or the destruction of property. It also pledges to resist all forms of injustice and corruption in society.[55]

Igbo Pentecostals see the hand of God behind the election of President Obasanjo in 1999, and it has boosted their confidence to act as an organ of civil society. Okoye of ACFM, for example, refers to Obasanjo's appointment as evidence of God's mercy and providential intervention in the affairs of the nation, setting it free from 'those who believe that Nigeria is their personal property'.[56] Freston suggests that theology is but one factor among many that influence Christian political action. Other variables, such as ecclesiastical position and international connections, must be taken into account.[57] Some Igbo Pentecostal leaders now head up large organisations with global links which makes them less susceptible to

---

[52] Okoroafor, *William Okoye*, 178-79.

[53] For example, Emeka Nwankpa participated in an extended (forty days) period of 'fasting and prayer' on Nigeria's 30th independence anniversary in 1990, a time of national crisis, and believes this had a significant impact on the transition process. Nwankpa, *Redeeming the Land*, 107-108.

[54] Kalu, 'Faith and Politics', 10.

[55] Congress on Christian Ethics in Nigeria, *Nigeria Covenant*, Jos: CAPRO Media Print Production, n.d., 3, 5, 16.

[56] William Okoye, *Clash of the Champions. Battle for the Soul of Nigeria*, Abuja: Integrity Royal Publications, 2000, ii-iii.

[57] Freston, *Evangelicals and Politics*, 148.

intimidation. Membership of PFN has helped to raise their profile in the political arena. During his recent tenure as PFN National President, Igbo Pentecostal Bishop Mike Okonkwo wrote in Nigerian newspapers, and the Nigerian press regularly solicited his opinions on national issues. He also had the ear of state governors. As well as calling for government intervention to prevent Muslim attacks on Christians in the North, PFN stated publicly its support for Obasanjo's anti-corruption campaign and made several public statements in the run-up to the 2003 elections, calling for prospective candidates to refrain from using illegitimate means to gain votes. Apart from Okonkwo, other Igbo Pentecostal leaders have also attained positions of political influence. These include Paul Nwachukwu, General Overseer of Grace of God Mission, and Okoye of ACFM, who was recently appointed Chaplain to President Obasanjo. Okoye is also a member of the presidential advisory council on youth affairs and a committee member for the Nigerian Political Reforms Programme (NPRC), a Presidential initiative for reforming Nigerian political culture. Jenkins refers to the danger that African churches who participated in democratic revolutions provide uncritical support for new regimes.[58] Obasanjo has his critics among Pentecostals, but they recognise the problems he faces keeping the country united and understandably fear a return to Islamic hegemony.[59]

Social Welfare and Development Initiatives

Political activism is not the only avenue for promoting social reform. Dempster suggests that the church can promote social change by initiating social programmes as 'instruments of human justice'.[60] While marginalisation reduced the movement's political potential during the 1960s and 1970s, it did not prevent participants from engaging in social welfare activities. By the end of 1967, the situation in Biafra had reached crisis proportions, and the relief operation was one factor that alleviated tensions within the enclave. Catholic and Protestant churches both played a leading role, along with various secular aid agencies. All Protestant relief work in Biafra was performed under the auspices of the World Council of Churches (WCC). By July 1968, there were more than 650 camps set up for over a million refugees.

[58] Jenkins, *Next Christendom*, 154.

[59] A notable Pentecostal critic is Pastor Tunde Bakare of the Latter Rain Assembly in Lagos, who has made several public statements predicting the failure of Obasanjo's regime.

[60] Dempster, 'Evangelism', 37.

In October 1968, Scripture Union became involved in the relief effort when SU travelling secretary Bill Roberts was appointed Protestant representative in Umuahia Province, where there were ninety-two refugee camps with an average of 400 people each. Unfortunately corruption was a problem. Drivers hijacked vehicles carrying supplies, and relief stores became the target of unscrupulous officials. This prompted the WCC to ask Roberts to recruit honest young people to assist with relief distribution by acting as escorts, and by the end of the war there were about sixty SU members employed in different aspects of relief work.[61] Yet when peace was restored, revivalists failed to build upon this outburst of social activity by developing lasting strategies for social reform. Beyond providing support for one another within their local fellowship groups, and later within their new church structures, their understanding of mission did not extend to practical social programmes aimed at improving their respective communities. Their urgent task was to evangelise the world before the imminent return of Christ. Here there are parallels with global Pentecostalism where intense eschatological expectation, particularly in its early stages, militated against the implementation of social welfare projects.[62]

During the 1980s, despite a decline in adventist beliefs, there was little change in Igbo Pentecostal attitudes to social welfare as an integral part of Christian mission. This was partly due to their status as an emerging movement, preoccupied with issues of consolidation and identity. It was also due to their focus on the 'prosperity gospel' and deliverance theology as the principle remedies for prevailing social ills. Some churches did start schools during the 1980s, but these were mainly intended to cater for the needs of their members or to evangelise children. They were an attempt to contextualise Christianity in an increasingly secular and technological environment, where educational standards are generally considered to be in decline. Thus Master's Vessel Church (MVC) in Umuahia established a nursery school in 1981. Due to demands from parents, disillusioned with state education, MVC started a primary school in 1991 and more recently has opened a secondary school. According to MVC co-founder Felix Obiorah, 80 per cent of the children come from other churches in the community. During the 1990s, most of the larger Pentecostal denominations followed suit by opening their own schools. The most sophisticated and largest educational institutions I observed belonged to Living Word Ministries (LWM) in the city of Aba, southern Igboland. Its vision for setting up Christian schools came out of a concern for children

---

61 Roberts, SU Prayer Letter No. 15, 7 November and 8 December 1968.

62 Murray A. Dempster, 'Christian Social Concern in Pentecostal Perspective: Reformulating Pentecostal Eschatology', *Journal of Pentecostal Theology*, 2, 1993, 59.

and young people 'who were attending secular schools and soaking in all manner of unbiblical doctrines'.[63] The nursery/primary sections of the Living Word Academy were established in 1988 with an initial student body of 236 pupils and a faculty of 13 teachers. By 2001, the primary section had four separate campuses in Aba with approximately 3,000 pupils and 230 members of staff. LWM started a secondary school in 1995. It considers its schools to be tools for evangelism, as well as for equipping young people to face the challenges of contemporary Nigerian society.

Some NPCs provide medical facilities for their members and the wider community, though this is a relatively recent development. Redeemed People's Mission has a clinic run by the medical director of ECWA Evangel Hospital, a member of the church. Christian Pentecostal Mission has a clinic called Joy Health Counselling Unit, also run by medical staff within its membership. Again the most extensive medical services I observed belonged to Living Word Ministries which has established four hospitals in Aba, with sophisticated equipment and staffed by church members. They also have an arrangement with a medical centre in America where they use video conferencing to update Nigerian doctors on current medical practice. According to LWM founder Emmanuel Okorie, it has gained a reputation for high standards of care and its hospitals are the best in Aba. Members also have the freedom to pray for and preach the gospel to in-patients.

Igbo Pentecostals have begun to take seriously their responsibility to combine evangelism with responsible social action, reflecting recent trends within global Pentecostalism.[64] Apart from schools and hospitals, which in some cases are serving the community as well as the local membership, some churches have opened social welfare departments to care for the poor and needy. Thus ACFM has started the 'Christ Compassion Ministry'. At present church members visit the sick in hospitals, prison inmates, prostitutes in hotels and people living on the streets, but the church also has plans to build a hospital (Christ Compassion Hospital) and rehabilitation homes for street people. LWM's social welfare arm is called 'We-Care Ministry', set up in 1989. Initially it concentrated on caring for prisoners, but since then has diversified its ministry to include other sectors of society. However, I found little evidence that these churches are actively seeking to address the HIV/AIDS epidemic, which is rapidly becoming the most pressing social problem in Nigeria.

[63] Living Word Ministries, *Annual Journal*, 47.

[64] Dempster, 'Christian Social Concern', 52.

A Pentecostal Theology of Politics and Social Concern

Igbo Pentecostal socio-political theology developed as participants realised the movement's political potential, responded to critical moments in Nigeria's post-colonial history and interacted with their local communities. Contrary to Gifford's assertion that much of Africa's Christianity (i.e. the Pentecostal sector) dismisses the contemporary political situation as theologically irrelevant, many Igbo Pentecostals are very conscious of it.[65] While they lack a formalised political theology, it is implicit in their discourse and praxis. Theirs is an enacted theology which emerges through action as well as reflection. But rather than pursue a path of civil disobedience, contemporary Igbo Pentecostals have developed other strategies of socio-political engagement. I have noted the dangerous possibilities associated with the tendency for Pentecostals to link evangelisation with political activity. As I examine Igbo Pentecostal political theology I will reflect upon its potential for promoting good governance, justice and reconciliation in a nation torn apart by religious and ethnic divisions.

Nigeria's End-Time Destiny

Contemporary Igbo Pentecostal political theology is based on a particular eschatological reading of history that regards Africa (and Nigeria in particular) as inheriting a global 'end-time' leadership role, both spiritually and politically. This is reflected in Igbo Pentecostal leader Mosy Madugba's account of Christian history from its origins in the Middle East through to the Reformation in Europe, the US American Pentecostal movement and Africa's current reformation. Madugba, who is Director of Spiritual Life Outreach in Port Harcourt, believes that it is Africa's turn to take over the baton for the last leg of the relay race.[66] Nigeria's special role is affirmed by Nnaji Chukwuka, founder of Revival Time Ministries:

> Nigeria is a great nation, with a great history, and a great responsibility for African leadership. . . . Nigeria is indeed the giant of Africa. As I look at our position within the comity of nations I see that God has a blessed agenda for us – to take the nations for Him. . . . We have the

---

[65] Gifford, *African Christianity*, 333.

[66] Mosy U. Madugba, *Africa's Time of Recovery*, Port Harcourt: Spiritual Life Publications, 2000, 24-37.

human resources; we have the economic resources and we have the spiritual endowment.[67]

Marshall-Fratani has argued that by describing their mission in these terms Nigerian Pentecostals are appropriating the language and imagery of the state and projecting into the national public space a 'highly political agenda'.[68] There are parallels here with Nigeria's foreign policy. According to Osaghae, this has been informed by a 'perception of leadership', referred to by Nigerian scholars as the nation's 'manifest destiny', which stresses her responsibility for the liberation and development of Africa.[69]

Okoye of All Christians Fellowship Mission compares Nigeria with ancient Israel. Despite her destiny as 'one of the most enviable nations of the world', she has squandered her opportunities and 'wandered in the wilderness of corruption, waste and poverty' for forty years, but is poised to enter her 'own land of greatness and prosperity'. The crucial question is whether Nigeria's destiny will be thwarted by Satan, the actions of evil people in government and the failure of the church. Okoye calls upon Nigerians to replace attitudes that hinder progress, such as greed, indiscipline and violence, with more positive ones, such as selflessness and hard work, and exhorts Christians to 'take advantage of what God is doing to move this nation in the direction that God has ordained Nigeria to go'.[70] The crucial role of the church in Pentecostal political theology reflects its strong eschatological content, linked to an emphasis on the kingdom of God and the Holy Spirit. Thus Emeka Nwankpa states, 'In the kingdom of the Lord Jesus Christ, the Holy Spirit is the Chief Instructor and the Chief Spokesman. . . . The kingdom of the Lord Jesus Christ must operate in us now. . . . We should be sharing in the exercise of His authority over the earth now, over situations, over circumstances and over nations'.[71]

Some Igbo Pentecostals promote a form of Christian Zionism, linked to a pre-millennial worldview and influenced by global Pentecostal flows. Associated with this is the idea that God has a special 'end-time' role for Israel and will prosper any nation that supports her. As far back as the

---

[67] Chukwuka, *Beyond the Night*, 52-55.

[68] Marshall-Fratani, 'Global', 306.

[69] Osaghae, *Nigeria*, 29.

[70] William Okoye, *Nigeria at 40. God's Message to the Nation*, Abuja: Integrity Royal Publications, 2000, 4-13; William Okoye, *God's Purpose for Nations. Satan's Deceit Exposed*, Abuja: Integrity Royal Publications, 2001, 21.

[71] Emeka Nwankpa, *Translated into the Kingdom of Christ*, Lagos: Touchstone, 1983, 37, 41.

early 1980s, Okoye of ACFM was urging Nigeria's political leaders to restore diplomatic relations with Israel as a necessary pre-condition for attracting God's blessings upon the nation, and Madugba currently heads up the Nigerian branch of the International Christian Embassy Jerusalem (ICEJ). ICEJ was established in 1980 by Christian supporters of Israel, after the international community condemned Israel for declaring united Jerusalem the capital of the Jewish state, and thirteen nations moved their embassies to Tel Aviv. Gifford argues that Christian Zionism is a product of developments in America's recent history, rather than reflection on the Bible, and leads to uncritical support for Israel's policies.[72] But Okoye of ACFM bases his support for Israel on God's words to Abraham in Gen 12:3 - 'And I will bless those who bless you, and the one who curses you I will curse. And in you all the families of the earth shall be blessed' (NASB).[73]

One implication of Christian Zionism is opposition to Islam. Consequently, it does little to improve relations between Nigeria's Christian and Muslim communities. Pentecostal political discourse with its language of domination, its call to take the nation(s) for Jesus and its support for Israel has the potential to exacerbate Christian-Muslim tensions, precipitate violence and encourage the use of political process to impose beliefs and values, thus coming dangerously close to resembling Jenkins' new 'Christendom'. But this would be a misreading. While Islamists aspire to change society by creating a theocracy, Igbo Pentecostals believe that the rule of the kingdom must transform individuals through the Spirit before it can permeate society. Note the following extract from a Redeemed People's Mission Bible study:

> God's rule is rejected in the world but Jesus has proclaimed the arrival of that Kingdom in which God will affirm His royal authority and establish His rule among men. God's rule starts in the hearts of those who belong to Him (Col.1:13). The church should submit as a servant to God's rule through the word before she can become the instrument of His rule on earth.[74]

Okoye of ACFM warns particular groups not to expect special favour from a Christian President. Obasanjo is the 'president of all Nigerians', Okoye

---

[72] Gifford, 'Theology', 74-5; Gifford, *African Christianity*, 199-201.

[73] William Okoye, *The Role of the Church in Nation Building*, cited in Okoroafor, *William Okoye*, 163.

[74] Redeemed People's Mission, 'Lesson 1. Know the Church', *Redeemed Adult Sunday School Lessons*, 1999, 3.

insists, and 'there should be no partiality and tribalism, because we are all one'.[75]

Within Igbo Pentecostal texts there are the seeds of a political theology which has the potential to promote justice and reconciliation in a pluralistic setting. It would be wrong to expect churches to abandon their ambition to spread the gospel, for they see this as crucial for transforming society. If carried out in an aggressive fashion, without sensitivity to local culture and customs, this will inevitably provoke opposition. In the remainder of the chapter I examine three elements of Pentecostal theology and praxis that offer a possible way ahead for the development of a viable Christian approach to politics and social concern in Nigeria.

The Model Citizen and the Prophetic Church

In their desire to influence society and precipitate revival, some Igbo Pentecostal churches aspire to a 'prophetic' role by nurturing a Christian counterculture and speaking publicly on political issues through sermons or print and electronic media. Kalu states that only a 'spiritually-alive prophetic church' offers hope amidst Africa's political stagnation.[76] One such example is All Christians Fellowship Mission whose four-fold vision includes a commitment to minister to the political leadership through a 'prophetic ministry'. ACFM encourages its members to act as 'model citizens' by obeying the rule of law, paying taxes, registering to vote, confronting evil and acting as 'salt and light'.

> Speak out against evil in our land and insist on seeing that the right thing is done no matter what it will cost you. . . . Live exemplary lives; live a decent Christian life at all times beginning from your family, to the church and the society at large. . . . As salt prevents decay, so also be a crusader against abuses, corruption and all forms of injustice and desist from them yourself, then others will no doubt imitate you.[77]

Christian Pentecostal Mission's prophetic stance is reflected in its conception of the church as the 'conscience' of society: 'Whoever is led by God to advise or warn government officials should do so. God expects a

---

[75] Okoye, *God's Purpose*, 21.

[76] Ogbu U. Kalu, *Power, Poverty and Prayer: The Challenges of Poverty and Pluralism in African Christianity, 1960-1996*, Frankfurt: Peter Lang, 2000, 102.

[77] All Christians Fellowship Mission, 'Lesson 4. Understanding the Vision and Purpose of your Church', *Membership Bible Studies*, 21-2.

good ministry like ours to be a watchman, the conscience of the society. When they do the right thing, God will fulfil his promise and there will be an outbreak of revival'.[78] CPM believes that national ills caused by the actions of evil people will only be cured by maintaining a high standard of 'family values', rather than through government intervention.

In their hermeneutic, some Pentecostals stress the resonance between African and biblical worldviews, and lay the blame for Africa's present socio-economic ills on the actions of rulers and subjects. They believe that government leaders can use witchcraft to secure political office, and both individual and communal problems can result from ancestral covenants entered into by their forefathers. Nwankpa, for example, links Pentecostal political engagement to a theology of the land, drawn from biblical motifs and Pentecostal literature, which resonates with traditional religious beliefs.[79] During periods of socio-political distress, Igbos traditionally look to the land and their relationship with the earth deity, Ala. Offences against her are believed to bring dire consequences on individuals, families and communities.[80] Nwankpa refers to 'sins' that 'pollute the land' and provide access to malignant spirits, such as 'idol worship', ritual sacrifice, sexual immorality (including homosexuality), divorce, abortion, drug trafficking, prostitution, assassination gangs and political insurgents. Rather than oppose evil through violent action, Nwankpa encourages Christians to develop alternative lifestyles: 'Redeeming the land actually involves changing the tide, going against the usual run of things, doing the will of God even when it appears unpopular, opposing decisions of the world that run counter to God's will'.[81] Nwankpa also links land redemption to confession and repentance, and as part of his strategy asks elders and local Christians to publicly confess the sins of their communities.[82] There are affinities here with traditional piety, which, as discussed in chapter 3, associates moral probity with the acquisition of power and divine favour. Some Pentecostals apply the metaphor of healing to Nigeria's socio-political ills and hold her citizens responsible for allowing access to evil spirits through corporate sin. Consequently, repentance is promoted as a necessary condition for God to cleanse and heal the land.

One way that Igbo Pentecostals have sought to influence society is by promoting biblical values through print media. Since Obasanjo's election as President, Okoye of ACFM has written a series of booklets addressing problems in the church and the nation, which the government has circulated

[78] O. Peters, 'The Big Happy Family and Challenges Ahead', *Pentecostal Family*, August 1999, 14.

[79] Nwankpa, *Redeeming the Land.*

[80] Kalu, 'Practice', 247.

[81] Nwankpa, *Redeeming the Land*, 17, 76-97.

[82] *Ibid.*, 85-6.

free-of-charge throughout Nigeria. In one, Okoye states, 'the Church needs to join hands with the government in re-orienting the society through Bible based wholistic teachings'.[83] Another way they have sought to influence society is by encouraging their members to seek political office if called by God. The Enugu-based Amazing Love Assembly, for example, allows members to participate in politics, as long as they do so 'with all honesty for the glory of God and for the benefits of God's society'.[84] Madugba envisions a 'recovery army', consisting of Christians in influential positions who will restore Africa's fortunes, and Nwankpa has established a national programme, known as the SALT programme, to train 'servant leaders' to apply biblical standards to government and all levels of public life.[85] However, I was unable to discover any examples of Igbo Pentecostals holding public office.

One problem with 'joining hands with the government' to promote biblical values and encouraging Christians to seek political office is that it can interfere with the church's prophetic stance which depends upon maintaining a certain critical distance from the seats of power. Jenkins warns against churches refusing to acknowledge the flaws of a regime just because it is Christian.[86] As long as the emphasis is on nurturing servant leaders and encouraging religious-based values to permeate Nigerian political culture, rather than establishing Christian domination, then this strategy is compatible with NPC ambitions to act as 'salt and light'.

Intercession and Spiritual Warfare

Intercessory prayer, sometimes linked to prophecy, is the second and most important strategy for socio-political engagement employed by Igbo neo-Pentecostals. Prayer was a major aspect of Pentecostal political engagement as far back as the late 1970s, but during the 1990s this strategy has become more pronounced and has included a strong emphasis on holiness, deliverance and spiritual warfare. For instance, All Christians Fellowship Mission operates a 24-hour fasting and prayer programme for Obasanjo's administration and the nation, and in March 2000, Christian Pentecostal Mission held a five-day fasting and prayer programme to 'address the prevalent religious disturbances in the country'.

---

[83] Okoye, *Clash of the Champions*, 27-8.

[84] Amazing Love Ministries, *Rules and Regulations*, 24.

[85] Madugba, *Africa's Time of Recovery*, 65-6. The acronym SALT stands for Sundoulos African Leadership Training Program. *Sundoulos* in the Greek language means 'fellow servants of the same Lord' (Matt 18:28).

[86] Jenkins, *Next Christendom*, 154.

In Igbo Pentecostal discourse, politics is spiritualised and presented in terms of a religious contest between good and evil. God originally gave dominion over the earth to humankind, but they relinquished control to Satan and his cohorts through disobedience. Contemporary Nigerian politics operates within a sacralised public space inhabited by numerous spiritual entities, and cultic power is often employed to buttress political clout. Thus Okoye of ACFM states that in contrast to some previous governments, who have employed 'occult' forces to gain power, the 'power base' of the present Obasanjo administration is 'spiritual and not demonic'. He then calls upon Christians to provide a spiritual foundation through prayer in order to combat the enemies of the government and the efforts of Islamic fundamentalists.[87] Marshall refers to the political implications of Pentecostal belief in the existence of spiritual forces behind material events. For many Nigerians, identifying the government as a source of oppression can only mean passive acceptance, because any form of confrontation will lead to further oppression. Having access to deliverance practices returns 'agency to the individual', even if it may not prevent problems in the future or solve present ones.[88]

Former revivalists Emeka Nwankpa and Mosy Madugba are among those who have popularised Pentecostal intercessory prayer through their conferences and literature. As noted in chapter 5, Nwankpa helped to establish Intercessors for Nigeria and Intercessors for Africa. As co-ordinator of the Ministers Prayer Network, Madugba has organised annual International Ministers and Christian Leaders prayer conferences in Port Harcourt since 1997. The 2003 conference was said to have attracted up to 18,000 Christians. Nwankpa and Madugba suggest a number of strategies Christians can employ to 'redeem the land' from the hand of Satan, partly gleaned from American Pentecostal literature, and their books contain biblical quotations and anecdotal evidence to support their teaching.[89] There is a strong ethical element reflected in an emphasis on holiness and reconciliation as necessary conditions for effective intercession. They also promote a violent form of spiritual warfare to wrest control over governments from malign spirits and believe that ordinary Christians can change the destinies of nations through prayer. Note the following excerpt from a prayer spoken at the Nigeria 2000 Prayer and Leadership

[87] Okoye, *Clash of the Champions*, 20-22, 26.

[88] Marshall, 'Pentecostalism', 22-23.

[89] Especially popular are the writings of C. Peter Wagner and George Otis Jr., leading proponents of 'Strategic-level spiritual warfare'. See for example, C. Peter Wagner (ed.), *Territorial Spirits. Insights on Strategic-Level Spiritual Warfare from Nineteen Christian Leaders*, Chichester: Sovereign World, 1991. Strategies include identificational repentance, spiritual mapping, breaking covenants and prophetic prayer.

Conference in Port Harcourt organised by Madugba and attended by Emeka Nwankpa, Austin Ukachi, James Ukaegbu, and Charles Osueke, all former Igbo revivalists: 'And Lord, we bring the thrones, the seats of power, the seats of government, the instruments of power in the nations, we bring them and command that they bow before the name of the Lord Jesus. We pray that your name may be glorified. We ask that your will be done in the nations as it is in Heaven'.[90] Nwankpa stresses the potency of 'prophetic' prayer: 'When you pray prophetically, you are in the place of governmental authority. . . . Prophetic praying is very powerful. It can change laws. It can cancel what politicians have said'.[91] There is also a strong emphasis on predictive prophecy. Madugba refers to a prophecy given during a prayer meeting in 1998 predicting the removal of two prominent political leaders. Within three weeks General Sani Abacha died suddenly in his sleep, and a month later Chief Abiola, winner of the annulled 1993 Presidential election, died in prison.[92]

There are potential dangers attached to the use of spiritual warfare prayer as a strategy for political engagement. Firstly, attributing socio-political and economic ills solely to malignant spirits may divert attention from structural causes and corrupt leaders, and discourage a life of activism in politics. Yet, as Marshall observes, a belief in the efficacy of prayer and deliverance in relation to politics does not necessarily encourage people to ignore the real root of problems. It is possible to hold the government responsible for social ills, 'while at the same time laying the blame for daily problems at the door of Satan'.[93] Secondly, a subtle shift can sometimes occur in spiritual warfare prayer towards regarding people rather than Satan as enemies, and this can lead to an aggressive approach to mission which reinforces local antagonisms, especially in a Muslim context.

A Practical Theology of Compassion

While prophetic witness and prayer remain priorities, gradually a praxis-oriented theology of social concern is emerging which extends beyond church boundaries. This is reflected in the following statement from a Redeemed People's Mission Bible study: 'We are to have compassion on the needy and the less privileged. . . . The church should be at the forefront of measures that would alleviate suffering and poverty. . . . The church also

[90] Nigeria 2000, 'Rebirth of the Apostolic & Prophetic Era', 4th International Ministers & Christian Leaders Prayer & Leadership Conference, videocassette, 2000, Port Harcourt.

[91] Nwankpa, *Redeeming the Land*, 65, 69.

[92] Madugba, *Africa's Time of Recovery*, 1, 16-17.

[93] Marshall, 'Pentecostalism', 22-23.

has a duty towards those who are not believers'. Like other elements of Pentecostal socio-political theology, this has evolved through interaction with local contexts and reflection upon the Bible and Christian tradition. The breakdown of the extended family in urban areas and the lack of a viable state welfare system have left particular groups vulnerable to poverty and neglect. This has stimulated action on the part of some Pentecostals. Living Word Ministries' 'We-Care Ministry', for example, was born out of concern for prison inmates and motherless babies, but has extended its vision to include widows, old people without family support, unemployed youth, abandoned mentally ill, the homeless and the poor in general. It also has a rehabilitation programme for drug addicts and alcoholics, and provides free medical care in its hospitals for the poor.

Igbo Pentecostals draw upon biblical and historical models and motifs to shape their social vision and motivate their members. All Christians Fellowship Mission's social vision is reflected in the name given to its new headquarters, the Cathedral of Compassion. Its 2001 membership manual states, 'This mission essentially is an outreach of compassion. . . . It is also important to know that Jesus himself was motivated and driven by compassion throughout his earthly ministry (Matt. 9:35-38)'. Grace of God Mission's 'Dorcas Ministry' was named after the woman in Acts with a reputation for helping the poor, and Nwachukwu, the General Superintendent, was influenced by the example of Western missionaries: 'The white missionaries came, they spent a lot of money . . . built schools, built hospitals, everything. It is our duty now to do the same thing for other African countries. . . . It is our duty to take the gospel to our own people, to build hospitals and schools too'.[94] Redeemed People's Mission also uses biblical precedent *and* Christian tradition to promote social action, citing the examples of Jesus, as well as the nineteenth century evangelical social reformer William Wilberforce and George Muller, the founder of Christian orphanages. According to RPM literature, love should be the main motive - love for Christ, expressed through obedience, and love for the needy – but the expectation of eschatological rewards is also a valid incentive.

Conclusion

My research suggests that during the civil war, revivalist spirituality contained the seeds of a socio-political theology which included prayer, political activism and humanitarian concern. But during the 1970s, participants failed to build upon this due to their preoccupation with evangelising the lost before the imminent return of Christ, their focus on the personal rather than structural effects of sin, their consciousness of their

[94] Interview, 12 May 2000, Onitsha.

marginal position in society, and their belief that politics was a dirty business, tainted by association with cultic powers and linked to corruption and violence. In the 1980s, prosperity teaching, deliverance theology and the movement's fragmentation further militated against Pentecostal socio-political engagement. All these factors imposed limitations on the movement's effectiveness as an agent of social transformation. However, given their particular theological beliefs and restricted access to the corridors of power, there is an inner logic to Pentecostal preference for prayer as the principle tool for political engagement. And from the movement's inception, currents of latent resistance, expressed through counter cultural lifestyles and the creation of 'autonomous spaces' of practice, suggest a political consciousness that belies its acquiescent image.

Since the late 1980s, Igbo Pentecostals have developed a socio-political theology of engagement that moves beyond prayer and deliverance, though this was initially precipitated by a concern to protect their own interests in a hostile environment characterised by Islamic hegemony. The formation of PFN has helped them present a united front in the public arena. But the close link between evangelisation and political activity in current Pentecostal practice has potential to exacerbate Christian-Muslim tensions and create what Jenkins has referred to as a 'new Christendom', especially now that Nigeria has a President with 'born-again' credentials. My research suggests, however, that Pentecostal leaders are encouraging members to influence society through prophetic witness, responsible citizenship, puritan lifestyles, intercessory prayer and acts of compassion, rather than violent activism or political force, which holds out promise for the future. Whether these values are able to permeate Pentecostal culture at the grassroots remains to be seen.

Chapter 7

The Revival's Legacy and the Future of Nigerian Pentecostalism

This book set out to tell the story of the Civil War Revival and its Pentecostal progeny from its origins in the late 1960s to the beginning of the new millennium. In doing so, it provides the first comprehensive account of the movement in Eastern Nigeria and clarifies the extent of its intersections and interactions with other sectors of the Nigerian Christian movement, as well as its relationship to global Pentecostalism. While not wishing to rehearse points already made, I will briefly recapitulate before proceeding to some general conclusions concerning the movement's enduring impact. This will involve broadening our discussion to include other sectors of the Nigerian neo-Pentecostal movement, as well as the older mainline churches. We will end by considering the future of Nigerian neo-Pentecostalism and exploring ways in which it might benefit from reflecting on its roots in the Civil War Revival.

The success of the revival, as we have argued, depended upon a balance between supply and demand. Colonial legacies, Western missionary endeavours, decolonisation and civil war not only created new religious demands, but they contributed to the formation of a missionary fellowship able to exploit the disorder of Igbo society and the failure of existing religious options to fulfil traditional aspirations. Following Okorocha, we have suggested that the traditional search for power to enhance life (*ezi-ndụ*) is the key to determining the shape of Igbo Christian conversion.[1] During the colonial era, mission Christianity, influenced by Enlightenment thinking, precipitated a crisis of identity and left a legacy of 'split-level' Christianity which encouraged dual allegiance to church and traditional cult as local Christians searched for power to solve pressing problems. This identity crisis was exacerbated by the reluctance of mission churches to relinquish control and cultivate indigenous church communities. To some extent, the various local Christian initiatives and innovations that burst upon the scene from 1914 alleviated these dilemmas. But as their charismatic impulses subsided, they either lost their radical edge and became vulnerable to bureaucratisation, or developed hybrid forms of spirituality that bore little resemblance to biblical Christianity. By the

[1] Okorocha, *Religious Conversion*, 206, 278.

1960s, neither the mission related Pentecostal churches, nor the prayer houses, posed a significant threat to the hegemony of mainline mission churches. Nonetheless, they were important because they introduced many revivalists to Pentecostal spirituality and injected a Pentecostal flavour into the fledgling movement.

The legacies of colonialism, decolonisation, civil war, and subsequent political instability and economic decline, created a series of crises comparable in their impact to the colonial conquest and contributed to the appeal of the Civil War Revival and its Pentecostal progeny. My study suggests that it was precisely because they bore the brunt of the suffering during the civil war that the Igbo response to the revival during the 1970s was so dramatic compared to their counterparts in Western Nigeria. But it was the revival's missionary impulse, forged in the furnace of the civil war and the SU fellowship groups, which was principally responsible for its success. Membership of this dynamic egalitarian missionary fellowship, with its strong Christological, pneumatological and eschatological focus, provided a means for Igbos to reconstruct individual and collective identities shattered by the war. These identities were reinforced by the erection of moral and symbolic boundaries (separating insiders from outsiders), participation in communal activities, and the creation of local theologies. Because so much depended upon the activities of itinerant preachers, we explored the issue of religious motivation. The revival generated a theology 'from below' which evolved through interaction with local contexts and global flows, and reflection upon the Bible and Christian tradition. This provided the ideological basis for revivalist activity, and awakened a 'passion for the kingdom' which propelled those touched by the 'Spirit' into the margins of society.

This missionary imperative was largely responsible for shaping the revival's moral and social ethic. The revival was both context sensitive and counter cultural, and contained strong currents of accommodation and resistance. The mobilisation of neglected forces and appropriation of Pentecostal spirituality alleviated the dilemma of dual allegiance and contributed to the cultivation of indigenous mission-oriented communities, intent on responding to consumer demands. Other features of the revival, such as multiple conversions, puritan lifestyles, the erosion of boundaries (based on ethnicity, colour, denominational affiliation and gender), and an emphasis on healing flowed from this missionary impulse. The emergence of neo-Pentecostal churches was also closely linked to the revival's missionary impulse and the influence of Scripture Union. Despite its commitment to ecumenical and evangelical ideals, SU set in motion certain trends that hastened the fragmentation of the movement. The combined effects of radical Biblicism, born-again conversion and evangelistic zeal, all defining marks of SU identity, supplied revivalists with tools to challenge gerontocracy in church and community, and precipitated the emergence of autonomous charismatic fellowship groups. While local socio-economic realities and global religious legacies provided a favourable environment for secession, opposition from mainline church authorities to the revivalists' promotion of Holy Spirit baptism, practice of charismatic gifts, and presentation of the gospel (with its call to repentance and new birth), hastened the moment of rupture and the transition of charismatic fellowships to denominational status.

Neo-Pentecostal church growth also depended upon a balance between supply and demand. The inherent flexibility of Pentecostal spirituality enabled the new churches to adapt their message and their methodology to suit local contexts affected by global flows. Their emphasis on the Bible, innovative worship styles, community ethos and proclamation of a holistic gospel appealed to those faced with disintegrating social and economic relationships and accustomed to a universe alive with spiritual forces. Each of these elements contributed to the construction of Igbo neo-Pentecostal identity. But the most significant factor behind neo-Pentecostal church growth, particularly in its formative period, has been its orientation towards mission, which betrays its origins within the Civil War Revival.

Yet the movement has undergone significant changes since the 1970s, partly as a result of global influences. By establishing links with US American and European Pentecostal organisations, as we discussed in chapter 5, neo-Pentecostal churches have provided access to an 'imagined community' with global dimensions and missionary ambitions. Here we agree with Gifford who regards the new churches as one of Africa's 'best remaining ways of opting into the global order', especially as it has tended to be bypassed by other global networks.[2] Yet it is possible to overemphasize the influence of global connections. Gifford stresses the American origins of African neo-Pentecostal churches and interprets them primarily as products of globalisation or 'Americanisation'.[3] This study concurs with those who emphasise local agency over global influences.[4] In the Nigerian setting, cultural flows were bi-directional, with indigenous neo-Pentecostals influencing their Western partners through transnational interactions, a trend that is likely to continue as Nigerian Pentecostals plant churches in Europe and the USA. And while global cultural and ideological flows through media and migration affected the shape of Igbo initiated neo-Pentecostalism, participants made use of global resources and images to suit their own agendas and satisfy consumer demands. Global

[2] Gifford, *African Christianity*, 321.

[3] *Ibid.*, 39-44, 314-22; Gifford, 'Developments', 516-20; Brouwer, Gifford and Rose, *American Gospel*, 178, 151.

[4] For example, Marshall-Fratani, 'Power', 21; Hackett, 'Charismatic/ Pentecostal, 263; David Maxwell, 'Review Article. In Defence of African Creativity', *JRA*, 30, 2000, 176; Ojo, 'Charismatic Movements', 92.

forces stimulated local initiative and heterogeneity. However, the urge to engage in mission and evangelism was not primarily a result of external influences, as Gifford supposes, but a response to local reflection on the Bible, current socio-political contexts and the promptings of the Spirit.[5] Finally, our study has shown that a decline of this missionary impulse, combined with a paradigm shift from holiness to prosperity teaching and a propensity to schism, have imposed limitations on the movement's potential as an agent of transformation. During the 1990s, a further shift has occurred towards a theology of socio-political engagement, which has raised the movement's profile and exacerbated tensions within Nigeria's pluralistic society.

The Enduring Impact of the Civil War Revival

The Nigerian neo-Pentecostal movement, which had its roots in the Civil War Revival, has transformed the local religious landscape in a variety of ways. While this has been felt primarily within the Pentecostal fraternity, more recently its influence has spread to the older mission churches. What follows is an attempt to delineate the enduring impact of the movement. The revival's missionary impulse has contributed to the resacralisation of the Nigerian Christian landscape by precipitating multiple conversions and a proliferation of new denominations. This has resulted in a significant enlargement of Nigeria's evangelical constituency, increased plurality and an expanding religious marketplace, leaving the religious consumer with a dazzling array of options to choose from. Pentecostalism, which before the 1970s was a relatively minor presence, has now become the dominant expression of Nigerian Christianity, especially in urban areas. For example, in the 1970s there were only three Pentecostal denominations in the city of Jos. By 2005, this had grown to over 110, of which approximately 90 are neo-Pentecostal denominations (post-1970).[6] Here we disagree with Harvey Cox, who regards the older classical African initiated churches as the African expression of the worldwide Pentecostal movement.[7] In Nigeria, it is the newer post-1970 Pentecostal churches which now dominate the religious scene.

The revival's legacy is partly to be explained by its particular blend of spirituality, which combined devotion to the Word with openness to the Spirit. As an evangelical movement influenced by Scripture Union, it injected a Bible reading culture into the local landscape through the

[5] Gifford, *African Christianity*, 332.

[6] Joseph Kingswem, *Ideal Christian Directory for Plateau State*, Jos: Ideal Companionship Communications Company, 2005.

[7] Cox, *Fire*, 246.

introduction of daily Bible reading notes and Bible study groups, supplemented by a strong emphasis on preaching and teaching. This has provided a robust biblical foundation to the neo-Pentecostal movement, which earlier Pentecostal waves sometimes lacked. The churches that emerged from the revival continue to hold the Bible in high regard, encouraging their members to listen to sermons, attend Adult Sunday schools and mid-week Bible studies, and read the Bible for themselves. Most of the larger neo-Pentecostal denominations have their own Bible schools, which cater for pastors and laypeople. These have progressively become more sophisticated, with better qualified teachers and more flexible programmes.

Due to local demands and external influences, the revival also acquired a distinctive Pentecostal flavour which has helped to check the secularising influence of Enlightenment thinking spread through global flows. It has also alleviated the dilemma of split-level Christianity, which encouraged dual allegiance to church and traditional cult or occult society among those who retained an 'enchanted' worldview. Relief from sickness, poverty and the effects of witchcraft could now be sought in the Pentecostal prayer meeting rather than the prayer house or traditional shrine. In chapter 1, I referred to the more inclusive definition of Pentecostalism adopted by Hollenweger and Anderson. They use the term to describe any church or movement which stresses the experience of the Spirit and the practice of spiritual gifts.[8] All the churches that emerged from the Civil War Revival were Pentecostal in nature. Because of the inherent flexibility of Pentecostal spirituality, this has contributed towards Christianity's absorption into Nigerian soil through a process of inculturation from below, rather than one imposed from above by academic theologians.

Anderson refers to Pentecostalism's capacity to make itself at home in almost any context due to its emphasis on the 'freedom in the Spirit', which allows participants the flexibility to develop culturally relevant expressions.[9] Nowhere is this more apparent than in the church meetings, where traditional hymn-singing, formal prayers and the recitation of written creeds have given way to less structured, oral, spontaneous and emotional forms of worship, more in tune with the pragmatic and experiential nature of African indigenous piety. One of the enduring legacies of the revival has been the widespread diffusion of Pentecostal worship across the Nigerian religious landscape. According to informants, what distinguishes Pentecostal from non-Pentecostal worship is the space given to the Spirit to operate in church meetings without human interference. Rather than be

---

[8] Hollenweger, *Pentecostals*, 149; Anderson, *Zion and Pentecost*, 26-7, 35-37.

[9] Anderson, *Pentecostalism*, 283.

constrained by written liturgy or human control, Pentecostals claim to rely upon the direction and power of the Holy Spirit. Hollenweger refers to the oral nature of Pentecostal liturgy, which appeals to 'oral people', not necessarily the illiterate, but those whose main medium of expression is the oral form. For Hollenweger, the most important element of an oral worship is the active participation of every member.[10] Nigerian neo-Pentecostals, as we have noted, include the educated élite and people from middle-class backgrounds, but they remain essentially oral people. Nigerian neo-Pentecostal worship, with its short choruses, spontaneous prayers, personal testimonies, interactive sermons, and its emphasis on spiritual gifts (especially speaking in tongues), has a democratising effect on the congregation and encourages the active participation of every member.

Pentecostal worship as a divine encounter is also expected to bring tangible results in the lives of those who participate. This, as we noted in chapter 5, is especially appealing in contexts such as Nigeria where spiritual power is a prevailing cultural theme. Sermons are invariably followed by prolonged periods of simultaneous and audible prayer, and space is provided for participants to respond to the message. This is usually accompanied by an opportunity to publicly confess Christ or receive ministry for healing and deliverance. Because Pentecostal spirituality affirms the immediacy of God's presence, participants are encouraged to express their feelings to God in prayer and to anticipate practical solutions to their pressing problems. But worship is also to be enjoyed for its own sake as a celebration of God's love. Nigerian Pentecostals, like their global counterparts, expect to experience the 'real presence of Christ in worship'.[11] This is in sharp contrast to the more traditional, rationalistic and restrained forms of worship found in some of the mainline churches. Nigerian Pentecostals insist that through the Spirit they can know the power and love of God as an experience which touches the depths of their being and expresses itself in emotional outbursts and bodily movements. 'Praise and worship', as we noted in chapter 5, form a substantial part of most Pentecostal church meetings, and are accompanied by levels of enthusiasm and intensity often missing from mainline churches. Repetitive chorus-singing, rhythmic dancing and clapping, shouting, and emotional praying are regular features of Nigerian Pentecostal worship. This subtle blend of pragmatic and expressive spirituality resonates with traditional African forms of worship, in which audible prayers, singing, drumming, dancing, and expressions of emotion are considered normal, and participants expect to receive practical benefits in return for their devotion.

---

[10] Hollenweger, *Pentecostalism*, 270.

[11] Robert E. Webber, *Worship Old and New*, Grand Rapids, MI: Zondervan, 1994, 128.

Yet Pentecostal worship is vulnerable to routinisation, especially when its charismatic impulses have subsided. Spontaneity, freedom and vitality can be replaced by predictability and control. Hollenweger warns that oral liturgy can become as fixed and dull as written liturgy 'when it becomes dominated by a few individuals and is no longer the open-ended expectant experience of the whole congregation'.[12] Despite claims to the contrary, neo-Pentecostal worship in Nigeria often follows a predictable pattern. In one church I attended regularly, worship usually began with the singing of a hymn from Ira Sankey's *Sacred Songs and Solos*, followed by short choruses, a period of simultaneous and audible prayer, two offerings, the sermon, and an extended time of prayer for those wishing to respond to the message. Another charge levelled against contemporary Nigerian Pentecostals is that their worship meetings sometimes lack spiritual depth and reality. Modern choruses have little theological content and are often accompanied by music played too loudly, making it difficult to follow the words unless one has already memorized them. This can mean that the mind is not fully engaged in the act of worship, which can become little more than an emotional rollercoaster. One also finds in some churches that while much is promised in the sermons and prayers, little is delivered in terms of spiritual power and problem-solving. This is linked to the emphasis on experience and divine immediacy in Pentecostal spirituality, which places pressure on worship leaders and pastors to produce instant results. Former revivalist and co-founder of CAPRO Bayo Famunore put it like this:

> We make a lot of noise but there is an irritating emptiness. Somehow we have come to confuse noise with power. Our meetings are filled with a lot of ecstatic sounds and weird noises. We have not learnt that it is the Spirit who groans in prayer for us so we begin to grunt, hiss and make all kinds of noise to show how passionate we are in prayer! Our meetings are filled with tongues but lack sincerity; filled with noises but sadly lacking in power, suffused with emotion but no passion.[13]

A second enduring legacy of the revival has been its orientation towards mission. The impulse behind this, as we have noted in chapter 3, was the movement's emphasis on the Word and the Spirit. The Bible provided ingredients for evangelistic discourse, shaped the revivalists' conception of the missionary task and presented evangelistic models for them to emulate. But their efforts were grounded in the conviction that the Holy Spirit was both the motivating power behind all such activity and the primary agent of

---

[12] Hollenweger, *Pentecostalism*, 272.

[13] Bayo Famonure, *Revive Us Again*, n.publ., 2004, 50.

conversion. Among the revival's main contributions was the normalisation of aggressive power-oriented evangelism in Christian expression. Previously restricted to a few Pentecostal groups on the margins, personal evangelism, open-air evangelistic campaigns, altar calls, spiritual warfare, public prayers for healing and deliverance, and the use of the media to propagate the gospel have become regular features of the Nigerian religious landscape. The Pentecostal impulse released by the revival also contributed to the democratisation of Christianity and the involvement of the laity in mission initiatives. While institutionalisation has caused the reappearance of clericalism, evangelism is still regarded as a lay responsibility by Nigerian neo-Pentecostals. Every member, by virtue of their experience of the Spirit, is a potential evangelist, with the ability to preach the gospel, heal the sick and cast out demons. This is reflected in Redeemed People's Mission's membership manual which contains the following clause: 'We believe that every born-again, Spirit-filled member can be used by God to perform miracles of healing, deliverance, etc. Everyone can be a minister'.[14] Mission as the prerogative of the laity, regardless of age, gender or denominational affiliation, remains one of the lasting legacies of the revival.

Yet there is one element of the revival's missionary legacy which did not endure and is only now being recovered. During the civil war, Scripture Union involvement in the relief operation suggests that early revivalists had a holistic conception of mission which combined evangelism with responsible social action. While post-war revivalists intensified their evangelistic efforts, for reasons discussed in chapter 6, they failed to build upon this outburst of social activity by developing lasting strategies for social reform. During the 1980s, there was little change in neo-Pentecostal attitudes to social welfare as an integral part of Christian mission. Yet there are signs that this is changing. Faced with poverty on an unprecedented scale, Nigerian neo-Pentecostals have begun to engage in social action by opening social welfare departments, clinics and hospitals to care for the poor and needy, echoing the social responsibility of their revivalist predecessors.

The urge to cross ethnic and national boundaries to spread the gospel was another legacy of the revival's missionary impulse. As we noted in chapter 3, the first non-denominational indigenous mission agencies in Nigeria, and indeed the whole of West Africa, were directly linked to the revival in Eastern and Western Nigeria. As early as 1973, Igbo revivalists were crossing ethnic boundaries to engage in mission initiatives. In chapter 4, we referred to the examples of Thompson Nwosu, William Okoye and Wilson Ezeofor, all converts of the Civil War Revival. But it was groups

[14] Redeemed People's Mission, *Membership Manual*, 21.

like CAPRO and Christian Missionary Foundation who set the agenda and stimulated widespread interest in cross-cultural missions among Nigerian Pentecostals and evangelicals, as well as in other African countries. Thus today Nigerian Christians are working among unreached people groups both within Nigeria and abroad under the auspices of indigenous charismatic missionary enterprises, or they are engaging in missionary programmes organised by their local churches. For example, Pastor Cosmos Ikwe, Jos District Superintendent of Redeemed People's Mission, takes a team of evangelists and medical personnel at least twice a year to work among a people group in the Katsina Ala area of Benue State, about 250 kilometres south of Jos. Known as the Redeemed People's Mission Rural Medical Project, it was started in 1999. Teams visit remote village communities where there are no government medical facilities, and offer free treatment, clothing and counselling. They also preach the gospel and open churches.[15] Anderson has referred to the lessons that can be learnt about inter-faith dialogue from the Pentecostal and Charismatic movements because they are so often at the forefront of encounter with other faiths.[16] In Nigeria, neo-Pentecostals, like Joe Olaiya and Emmanuel Kure, are among those leading the way in Muslim evangelism. Olaiya is the founder of Living Faith Foundation in the partly Islamic Kaduna State and has worked for many years among the Muslim communities of Northern Nigeria. Kure is the coordinator of the Throneroom Ministry and a former CAPRO chapter coordinator for Kafanchan, the scene of serious Muslim/Christian conflicts in 1987. He too has been closely involved in mission initiatives in Northern Nigeria and has witnessed many Christian conversions among Hausa-Fulani Muslim communities. Neo-Pentecostals are also at the forefront of recruiting and preparing indigenous workers for missionary service. Mission agencies, such as CAPRO and CMF, have organised conferences to stimulate mission awareness and have established schools of missions to train cross-cultural missionaries.

But there are several dangers attached to this drive to evangelise and plant churches. Firstly, the urge to engage in aggressive evangelism by organising evangelistic 'crusades', employing what Ojo refers to as militaristic popular speech,[17] and publicly demonising other religions, can prove counterproductive, especially in Islamic contexts with a history of violent Christian/Muslim conflicts. In some neo-Pentecostal churches, Sunday sermons and all night prayer vigils are relayed by loudspeakers to the surrounding community in the belief that this will facilitate the penetration of the gospel. It is more likely to exacerbate existing tensions

---

[15] *Redemption Encounter*, 1.1, 2005, 8.

[16] Anderson, *Pentecostalism*, 283.

[17] Ojo, 'African Charismatics', 5.

between the two religious communities. In these contexts, Muslims need to see God's love and power demonstrated to them in practical ways before they will respond positively to the gospel message. Murray Dempster refers to the church's missiological responsibility to act as a Christian social witness, thus 'making the truth visible'. The gospel requires 'the validation of a living community that translates proclaimed truth into social practice'.[18] Missiologist Paul Hiebert suggests that Christian invitations to Muslims to follow Christ should be accompanied by 'demonstrations of God's power'. These include 'the passing signs of healing of those who are sick, and provision for those who are destitute. And they should surely include the more permanent signs of righteousness and transformed lives'.[19] Joe Olaiya of Living Faith Foundation echoes these sentiments when he recommends that evangelism in a Muslim context should be supplemented by an emphasis on holiness and righteousness, intercessory prayer and fasting, and a demonstration of the power of God in diverse human situations.[20] In their interactions with Muslims, neo-Pentecostals would also do well to develop an alternative discourse (at least in public) that avoids the potentially provocative language of spiritual warfare and Christian domination, though this will not be easy in the current climate.

A second problem associated with Nigerian Pentecostal missionary activity and the drive to plant churches is that it can result in parochialism and rivalry, which in turn hinders ecumenical cooperation. One symptom of this is the duplication of efforts by indigenous mission agencies, prompting some Nigerian mission leaders to call for cooperation and

---

[18] Dempster, 'Evangelism', 29-30.

[19] Paul G. Hiebert, 'Power Encounters and Folk Islam', in J. Dudley Woodberry (ed.), *Muslims & Christians on the Emmaus Road*, Monrovia, CA: MARC, 1989, 56. Missiologists make a distinction between formal and folk (or high and low) Islam. The high form focuses on the obedience and worship of God; the low form on power and the manipulation of spiritual entities for human purposes. Both types are found in Nigerian Muslim communities. See J. Dudley Woodberry, 'The Relevance of Power Ministries for Folk Muslims', in C. Peter Wagner & F. Douglas Pennoyer (eds.), *Wrestling with Dark Angels. Toward a Deeper Understanding of the Supernatural Forces in Spiritual Warfare*, Ventura, California: Regal Books, 1990, 313-331; Dean Gilliland, 'Response', in Wagner & Pennoyer (eds.), *Wrestling with Dark Angels*, 332-337.

[20] Joe Olaiya, 'Praying to See God's Promises', in Wagner and Thompson (eds.), *Out of Africa*, 116-17.

partnership among different organisations.[21] We also see this in the way some Pentecostals insist on opening branches in close proximity to existing denominations and often without their consent, despite PFN's attempts to control the proliferation of new churches and branches. One of the driving forces behind Pentecostal rivalry is the pursuit of money. For some, opening a church and becoming a 'President and Founder' has become a lucrative business venture, especially when tithing is presented as a condition of membership and prosperity teaching is propagated from the pulpit. For these pastors, the city is more attractive than the village, and they concentrate their activities on areas already saturated with churches.

Thirdly, the reintroduction of clericalism and authoritarian structures can inhibit innovation and initiative. This was already beginning to happen during the 1970s, when neo-Pentecostal pastors William Okoye and Wilson Ezeofor left Riches of Christ Mission to pursue their vision of preaching the gospel in the North, but it has continued as a source of frustration for other aspiring evangelists. One young pastor told me that he has recently set aside his desire to work as an evangelist and church planter because his vision conflicted with the leaders of his denomination. Another chose to resign from his position as a Pentecostal pastor and join a mainline denomination, because of the latter's willingness to sponsor his mission activities. Due to insecurity and an unwillingness to relinquish control, senior Pentecostal pastors are sometimes reluctant to hand over responsibility to their subordinates or allow them space to develop their ministries.

Finally, the pressure to produce results in terms of converts and church growth can cause Pentecostal pastors to seek power through alternative means. There are numerous stories of church leaders allegedly employing occult techniques to work miracles and attract large followings.[22] Igbo Pentecostal pastor Okwudili Ononugbo describes giving a lift to a young Muslim cleric who offered to assist him to acquire power so that he would be able to register 5,000 members within a year. The man claimed that many AIC prophets and apostles were among his clientele. Ononugbo believes that the obsessive urge to perform 'signs and wonders' has had a detrimental effect upon genuine church growth.[23]

---

[21] Segun Adekoya, 'Training to Contend the Emerging Error', *Occupy*, Vol.16, Nos 3 & 4, 1997, 9. Until recently, Adekoya was the principal of NEMI (Nigeria Evangelical Missionary Institute), the training arm of NEMA.

[22] In 2000, there was a story reported in the media of a NPC pastor in Onitsha accused of burying a dead body and various cult objects under his pulpit in the belief that this would attract large crowds to his meetings.

[23] A. Okwudili Ononugbo, 'His Offer Dazed Me', *Occupy*, 16.3 & 4, 1997, 7.

Another legacy of the revival which flowed directly from its missionary impulse was its radical holiness and social ethic. At the height of its popularity it posed a significant challenge to the moral and social fabric of Nigerian society, fractured by disintegrating social and economic relationships due to modernisation, increasing urban migration and the civil war crisis. The idiom of new birth linked to a call to radical repentance, rejection of traditional religious practices, and a promise of power for ethical renewal, captured the Igbo imagination and provided the basis for the construction of new forms of identity. It also resonated with local aspirations and the quest for power to enhance life, which in traditional discourse was linked to moral probity. The social implications and consequences of the revival were associated both with its emphasis on individual conversion and its missionary impulse. The shared experience of new birth, and mutual membership of a dynamic missionary fellowship intent on evangelising local communities, eroded denominational and ethnic barriers, and challenged gerontocratic, gender, and colour boundaries in church and society. The revival's relationship to modernity was equivocal, with participants engaging in a bargaining process of accommodation and resistance. On the one hand, its emphasis on new birth and rupture with the past hastened the breakdown of traditional communal obligations, already set in motion by other modernising forces such as Western education and urbanisation, and encouraged progress and socio-economic mobility. On the other hand, it resisted the secularist agenda and moral relativism associated with Western modernity by adopting a literalist approach to the Bible, which affirmed the immediacy of God's presence and the activity of lesser spirits, and embraced an ethic of radical holiness.

In their formative years, the new churches shared this ethic. By constructing moral and symbolic boundaries, they marked out their difference from the 'world' and protected their members from the dangers of materialism, corruption and immorality. Yet these boundaries have gradually been eroded as the revival's charismatic and missionary impulses have subsided, resulting in a reduction in distance from the world and a loss of counter cultural potential. This is reflected in an excerpt from the 2005 inauguration address of the National Chairman of Scripture Union (Nigeria):

> It is on record that most of our church leaders today, both orthodox, Pentecostal and Evangelical are products of the SU Movement in the 70s. It is disturbing that despite the great increase in the number of Pentecostal

and Evangelical churches and organizations, our country is getting more corrupt and moral decay is in the increase.[24]

One symptom of this moral decline is growing materialism within the churches. In some quarters, prosperity teaching has gained ascendancy as neo-Pentecostal leaders, responding to pressures from global consumer culture and demands to alleviate local conditions of poverty, have promoted the cross as a source for material prosperity, to the neglect of its significance as a symbol of suffering and its potential for ethical renewal and social transformation. Consequently, prosperity has sometimes replaced holiness, Christian service, and evangelistic success as the yardstick for measuring spirituality.[25] Yet as Maxwell has shown in his work on Zimbabwe,[26] many Nigerians regard prosperity teaching as a means of avoiding destitution rather than accumulating wealth. Linked to this is the provision of local support networks and safe havens, especially in urban communities fractured by disintegrating social and economic relationships. By promoting family values, based on biblical rather than traditional principles, and by encouraging marital fidelity, hard work, economic discipline and shared domestic responsibilities, neo-Pentecostal churches hold out benefits for women in particular and foster upward mobility.

However, while boundaries separating Pentecostals from the 'world' have been eroded, others have been strengthened. Denominational barriers, separating neo-Pentecostals from other church communities, have become more pronounced to the detriment of the revival's original ecumenical impulse, and clericalism, linked to male-dominated authoritarian ecclesiastical structures, has been re-introduced, resulting in a reduction in the revival's democratic impulse. This is reflected in a recent tendency for neo-Pentecostal pastors to take titles, such as 'Rev. Dr.' or 'Bishop', and the exclusion of women from senior administrative positions. It is surprising how quickly they have adopted the institutional structures of the churches they criticized so stridently in the 1970s.

This study has also explored the movement's socio-political theology and record of engagement with the wider society. Despite its early promise, one of its weaknesses was its failure to develop a viable theology

[24] Engineer Rich Onyeaso, 'Inauguration Speech', *Plumbline. Journal of the Pilgrims Ministry SU (Nigeria)*, 2005, 36.

[25] Femi Adeleye, former national director of NIFES, refers to prosperity teaching as a 'different gospel' (*Preachers of a Different Gospel*, Kampala: International Fellowship of Evangelical Students (IFES), 1999).

[26] David Maxwell, 'Delivered from the Spirit of Poverty?: Pentecostalism, Prosperity and Modernity in Zimbabwe', *JRA*, 28.3, 1998, 351, 369.

of politics and social concern which moved beyond prayer and evangelism. This imposed limitations on its potential as an agent of social transformation. Yet since the late 1980s, the movement has become more politically active, for reasons discussed in chapter 6, and has been at the forefront of developing a socio-political theology of engagement, linked to a call to corporate repentance, social critique and humanitarian engagement, which has challenged the mainline churches to emulative action. This is both an attempt to counter Islamic hegemony in the public space, an effort to inject Christian-based democratic values into Nigerian political culture, a strategy for disarming the 'powers' impeding the progress of local communities, and a genuine desire to help the poor and marginalized.

The Pentecostalisation of the Mainline Churches

This Pentecostal impulse which originated in the revival is now spreading to the older churches whose leaders once rejected it. There are several reasons for this. Firstly, the older churches hope to stem the flow of young people leaving to join the new churches in a quest for a more meaningful and practical spirituality. This exodus began in the 1970s but has continued unabated during successive decades and has challenged the mainline mission churches to emulative action as a means of retaining their members. Secondly, some former revivalists, who have embraced Pentecostal spirituality but have chosen to remain in the mainline churches, have since attained positions of influence within these organisations.[27] They have been joined by younger pastors, equally open to Pentecostal spirituality and eager to spread it among their members. Together these groups are labelled 'Reformists' by Ojo in his typology of African charismatics because they seek to precipitate revival and renewal within their existing non-Pentecostal denominations.[28] Their Pentecostal experience has been sustained and renewed by their membership of renewal groups like the Evangelical Fellowship in the Anglican Communion (EFAC), the Presbyterian Young People's Association and the Baptist Student Fellowship (BSF), and their participation in the activities of parachurch organisations like Scripture Union and the Fellowship of Christian Students (FCS). Thirdly, former revivalists and neo-Pentecostals have become popular speakers at denominational and interdenominational events. For example, Gbile Akanni, a leading Yoruba neo-Pentecostal, was

---

[27] Examples include Anglican Bishops Cyril Okorocha (Owerri), Ken Okeke (the Niger), Peter Onekpe (Ika), E. A. Awosoga (Ijebu), G. L. Lasebikan (Ondo) and Gideon Olajide; and Rev James Ukaegbu, former Moderator of the Presbyterian Synod and Director of Missions.

[28] Ojo, 'African Charismatics', 4.

among the invited speakers at the 2005 COCIN pastors' annual retreat, and Peter Ozodo, co-founder of CAPRO, was the guest speaker at the inaugural Youth Convention of TEKAN, a confederation of twelve different mainline denominations.[29] Gbile Akanni also holds clergy retreats for mainline denominational leaders. The October 2005 retreat was attended by the General Secretary of the Nigerian Baptist Convention, the President of COCIN and the Anglican Bishop of Jos, among others. Recently I attended two Christian gatherings in Jos organised by PFN and addressed by the senior pastors of two of the largest neo-Pentecostal denominations in Africa, Pastor Enoch Adeboye of the Redeemed Christian Church of God and David Oyedepo of Living Faith Church. Both meetings were attended by members from the older mainline churches, including the Governor of Plateau State (a member of COCIN). Finally, members at the grassroots are responding to a fresh wave of spiritual renewal within the institutionalised structures of the older churches, reminiscent of the early 1970s. The difference is that today many of their leaders are sympathetic to the renewal and, unlike their predecessors, are determined to cherish it rather than drive it out of the church. Thus a major paradigm shift is occurring in the spirituality of the mainline churches, which is changing Nigeria's Christian religious landscape and blurring the distinction between Pentecostal and non-Pentecostal churches.[30]

The 'Pentecostalisation' of the older churches has affected them in a number of ways. Firstly, it has challenged their theology and encouraged a Bible reading culture among the membership which was not there before. Sermons, prayers and songs have a strong Christological focus and are liberally interspersed with phrases like 'the name of Jesus' and 'the blood of Jesus', though one suspects that the theological content of these terms is not always understood. There is a greater emphasis on the new birth and openness to the work of the Spirit as a conscious experience, even if this is not always understood in terms of a formal doctrine of Spirit baptism subsequent to conversion. Linked to this is receptivity to spiritual gifts, such as speaking in tongues, prophecy and healing, and a determination by some to integrate them into the life of the church. Where once they were prohibited, the public use of these gifts is now tolerated and even encouraged in some congregations, though they have not yet become a

[29] The acronym TEKAN stands for 'Tarayar Ekklesiyoyin Kristi a Nigeria' (The Fellowship of the Churches of Christ in Nigeria), made up of denominations linked to the different branches of the former Sudan United Mission.

[30] For similar developments within the Ghanaian context, see Cephas N. Omenyo, '"From the Fringes to the Centre": Pentecostalization of the Mainline Churches in Ghana', *Exchange. Journal of Missiological and Ecumenical Research*, 34.1, 2005, 39-60.

normal feature of church life. One informant told me that during a recent interview for the Presbyterian ministry he was asked whether he spoke in tongues and whether he would encourage its practice in his church. In the past, an affirmative answer would have disqualified him from becoming a Presbyterian pastor. But this is no longer the case. Many pastors in the older churches now encourage people to be born-again and receive Holy Spirit baptism, and provide opportunity for members to receive prayer for healing and deliverance. Some allow the use of 'olive oil' for healing prayer, a ritual directly imported from the Pentecostal churches. These trends are reflected in a recent book written by Igbo Anglican priest Paul Chinedu Akunne entitled *Having Power with God.* Akunne is a member of several parachurch organisations, including Scripture Union, EFAC, Ministers Prayer Network and Full Gospel Businessmen's Fellowship International. His book encourages Christians to seek the power of the Holy Spirit for victory over sin, Satan, sickness and poverty, and insists that spiritual gifts, such as healing, prophecy and speaking in tongues, are available today. Akunne himself claims to exercise the gifts of prophecy and healing in his pastoral and evangelistic ministry.[31]

Secondly, Pentecostal spirituality has affected the worship and ministry styles of the older churches. Many now engage in worship using modern electronic instruments and contemporary songs of Western and local origin. 'Gospel bands', similar to those found in black American Pentecostal churches, are employed alongside more traditional choirs during Sunday worship. Hand-clapping, drumming and dancing, simultaneous audible prayer, 'night vigils' and communal 'praise and worship' sessions are now regular features of many non-Pentecostal churches. An Anglican priest told me that churches in his diocese now hold monthly 'free worship' sessions and quarterly 'night vigils' to cater for the needs of their young people. Other beliefs and practices introduced through Pentecostal contact include adult baptism by immersion (in denominations where only infant baptism was offered), healing and deliverance prayer, tithing and prosperity teaching. A typical Sunday service at COCIN Headquarters Church in Jos, for example, begins with a session of modern 'praise and worship' led by a gospel band. This is followed by the singing of a traditional hymn and a period of simultaneous and audible prayer. The church choir performs while the offering is being taken. The sermon, lasting about an hour, is preached extemporaneously in a style similar to those I have observed in Pentecostal churches. The pastor uses the platform as a stage, punctuating his message with exclamations of 'Praise the Lord' and 'Hallelujah',

---

[31] Paul Chinedu Akunne, *Having Power with God*, Lagos: Ikechbenjamin Christian Publishers, 2004; interview, Paul Chinedu Akunne, 3 April 2006, Bukuru. The Forward to Akunne's book is written by Henry C. Ndukuba, the Anglican Bishop of Gombe.

sometimes breaking out into song, and lacing his message with anecdotes and practical application. This is followed by an extended altar call and an opportunity for the audience to respond to the sermon.[32]

Several senior clergy have gained reputations as evangelists with ministries of healing and deliverance. One of these is Yoruba Baptist pastor Job Ade Alabi, who since the late 1980s has exercised an itinerant ministry as an evangelist mainly among churches linked to the Nigerian Baptist Convention. During 'revival' meetings and evangelistic campaigns, he preaches the gospel, exhorts his audience to be born-again, and prays for their healing and deliverance. Another is Rev. Gilmon Ruwanzafi, COCIN Director of Personnel, whose ministry of healing and deliverance has been officially recognised by his denomination. But ministry is not restricted to ordained clergy. Increasingly, lay men and women are being allowed space to preach, lead worship and Bible studies, and engage in counselling. Asamoah-Gyadu refers to this as the 'democratisation of ministry', which is linked to the biblical idea of the priesthood of all believers and the universal availability of the Spirit.[33] One of the liveliest prayer meetings I attended was led by a lay member (a medical doctor) of COCIN in Jos. Many of the Pentecostal ingredients were there: simultaneous audible prayer for personal needs, short choruses sung repetitively in Hausa and English, and intercessory/spiritual warfare prayer for the church and for Plateau State.

Thirdly, the Pentecostal impulse has challenged the mainline churches in the area of mission and evangelism. Members of renewal groups like EFAC are often those most committed to evangelism and church-planting and most active in organising and implementing social welfare programmes. Revival meetings, open-air 'crusades', and healing and deliverances services are becoming popular within the mainline churches and, as with the Pentecostal churches, are being advertised through electronic and print media. Particularly significant is the recognition now given to lay ministries within the older churches. Some have teams specializing in intercessory prayer, evangelism, deliverance, counselling, prison and hospital visitation, and youth work. As a result, lay members are discovering their gifts and an increasing number are entering the ordained ministry.

However, there are potential problems ahead as the renewal movement moves from the fringes to the centre, especially in the Anglican Church where clergy sympathetic to the renewal are now in the majority. In some quarters, their attempts at taking over responsibility for leading the

---

[32] One of the pastors at COCIN headquarters church in Jos, David Pofi, used to attend weekly Bible studies at Redeemed People's Mission and was President of the Fellowship of Christian Students at Kaduna Polytechnic during the 1980s.

[33] Asamoah-Gyadu, *African Charismatics*, 127.

movement are being resisted by lay leaders who feel sidelined and marginalized. This is causing friction within the churches.

The Future of Nigerian Pentecostalism

Some observers believe that the Nigerian church is currently experiencing a revival of unprecedented dimensions which will transform the nation and alter the shape of global Christianity. This is the opinion of the contributors to a recent book on Nigerian church growth co-edited by C. Peter Wagner and Joseph Thompson.[34] For example, Paul Adefarasin, founder of the Lagos-based church House on the Rock, writes:

> To say that the explosion of Christianity and the number of Bible believing-churches in Nigeria are remarkable would be an understatement. Nigeria, a country too often associated with vices and corruption, has a different side. It is seen by many as the epicentre of one of the greatest moves of God in recent Church history.[35]

And in the same volume, Joe Olaiya states: 'The current revival in the nation of Nigeria comes in fulfilment of the promise of God to raise up a mighty army that will take the gospel far beyond the boundaries of our nation'.[36] Yet others, such as former revivalist and co-founder of CAPRO Bayo Famunore, are not so optimistic.

> The church in Nigeria is presently going through a very interesting stage. Indeed the church has a semblance of revival, but it is just a semblance. All over the country, there are large gatherings taking place on a monthly basis, sometimes on a weekly basis. . . . These prayer meetings attract tens of thousands of devotees. Most of the time, the prayer meetings take place in the night. So they are termed all-night prayer meetings or night vigils. Quite a number of the new Pentecostals go from night vigil to night vigil. Teachers of the word attract thousands to their meetings and many of those who attend these meetings are one and the same people. This is the era of going to conferences. . . . Taking a critical look at our insatiable penchant for conference attendance, it will be discovered that

---

[34] Wagner and Thompson (eds.), *Out of Africa*. The book's back cover contains the following statement: 'A model for worldwide revival is alive and thriving in Nigeria!'

[35] Paul Adefarasin, 'The Kingdoms of this World', in Wagner and Thompson (eds.), *Out of Africa*, 135-36.

[36] Olaiya, 'God's Promises', 118.

> many things are wrong. At a number of these night vigils, we spend more time dancing to the latest beats in towns than actual praying. . . . We groan and cry to God for 'breakthrough'. By that we mean a great provision in terms of finances or some earthly property.[37]

If we return to the definition of revival proposed in chapter 1, we find that current developments fall short on a number of counts. Firstly, while numerical growth in terms of congregational size and new churches is impressive, much of it is due to transfer of membership from older churches and the schismatic tendencies of the neo-Pentecostal church movement, rather than conversion. Secondly, despite recent calls for a return to holiness, the current Pentecostal wave has not substantially raised levels of morality within the churches, which continue to be characterised by leadership struggles, disunity, materialism and a variety of ethical lapses. Thirdly, contemporary evangelism is largely restricted to organised programmes and initiatives, and there is little evidence that the numerous conferences, 'revival' meetings and evangelistic campaigns have resulted in a widespread sense of sorrow for sin within or beyond the Christian community. Neither are there signs of a large-scale turning to Christ among non-Christian populations, whether Muslim or traditionalist.[38] Finally, despite having the largest evangelical community on the continent, Nigeria remains among the world's most corrupt nations, with the gulf between the rich and the poor becoming ever wider.[39]

Yet even if we were to concede that Nigeria is experiencing revival, there is no room for complacency. Indeed, there are dangers that the neo-Pentecostal movement may lose its cutting edge unless it makes certain adjustments. There has been a recent appeal by scholars, responding to criticisms of contemporary global Pentecostalism, for Pentecostals to look to their origins as a source for theological and spiritual renewal, and recognise its formative years as the heart of the movement, not just its infancy.[40] Given changing contexts, history cannot supply exact models for

---

[37] Famonure, *Revive us again*, 43-4.

[38] Although there have been reports of whole villages in the North turning from Islam to Christianity, sometimes without any human intervention. See Emmanuel Nuhu Kure, 'Bringing Light to the Muslims', in Wagner and Thompson (eds.), *Out of Africa*, 184.

[39] In 2005, Nigeria was the 6th most corrupt nation out of 159 surveyed, according to Transparency International. But it was also singled out as the most improved country in Africa.

[40] For example, Hollenweger, *Pentecostalism*, 397-400; Land, *Pentecostal Spirituality*, 26; William D. Faupel, *The Everlasting Gospel. The Significance of Eschatology in the Development of Pentecostal Thought*, Journal of

emulation, but it can provide inspiration for re-visioning. Nigerian neo-Pentecostals would benefit from reflecting on their own roots in the Civil War Revival and regarding it as a potential resource for renewing the movement's distinctive identity and witness. For this to occur, the movement needs to recover its early missionary passion which propelled those touched by the Spirit into the margins of society (where they not only preached the gospel but engaged in acts of sacrificial service). During the revival, as we noted in chapter 3, the Pentecostal spirit was understood primarily as an empowering for mission, and spiritual gifts, such as prophecy and healing, were valued as tools for evangelism and Christian service. Anderson warns that the experience of the Spirit and spiritual gifts can be detrimental to a healthy and holistic Christian life if they merely become a means of personal 'spiritual' gratification.[41] Nigerian neo-Pentecostals need to (re-)experience the Holy Spirit as the missionary Spirit who impelled their predecessors to cross social, ethnic and national boundaries to preach the gospel and plant churches, often at great cost to themselves in terms of socio-economic prospects and sometimes in the face of stiff opposition.

They also need to rediscover the radical potential of new birth and Holy Spirit baptism for ethical renewal, ecumenical initiative and social transformation, which in revivalist discourse flowed from this missionary impulse. The revival's moral and social ethic speaks powerfully to contemporary Nigerian Pentecostalism, which has been fractured by schism, rampant denominationalism, clericalism and tribalism. Practical holiness and 'love for the brethren', rather than the love of money or social status, were consistent themes in revivalist discourse and practice. Both were energised by openness to the Holy Spirit, an eagerness to obey biblical commands, and a determination to fulfil Jesus' missionary mandate in the light of his imminent return. Their reasoning was that for mission to be successful, preaching should be accompanied by community lifestyles consistent with the gospel and reflecting Christ's sacrificial love. As leaders emerged, they were recognised on the basis of their charismatic gifting, character and capacity to serve others, rather than their theological training, ordination credentials or social status. Their preference was for democratic rather than hierarchical authority structures and they rejected the use of titles so prevalent in mainline churches and traditional culture. The common designation for revival leaders was 'brother' or 'sister' rather than 'Rev Dr', 'bishop' or 'apostle'. If the movement is to rediscover its distinctive identity and regain its position as a counter-cultural force in Nigeria's pluralistic society, it needs to recognise and re-appropriate the

---

Pentecostal Theology Supplement Series 10, Sheffield: Sheffield Academic Press, 1996, 309.

[41] Anderson, *Pentecostalism*, 284.

revival's liberating and democratising impulse which challenged the dominant order of the day, characterised by gerontocratic and patriarchal structures in church and community, and opened up space for men and women, regardless of ethnic and social status, to work and worship alongside each other in the ministry of the gospel. This is what Anderson refers to as a 'Pentecostal theology of liberation', where the freedom associated with the experience of the Spirit has the potential to recreate an inclusive community which transcends boundaries based on race, gender and social class.[42]

The shift towards a theology and praxis of socio-political engagement within some sectors of Nigerian neo-Pentecostalism is a welcome development. Yet there are several problems associated with this new socio-political consciousness which call for attention if the movement is to recover its cutting edge. Firstly, the potential for the Pentecostal community to promote good governance and community development in contemporary Nigeria is compromised by the discrepancy between the values it preaches and those it practices. As Ojo has noted, it needs to remove the public perception of corruption within its constituency as a result of reported cases of financial and sexual impropriety among its hierarchy.[43] Secondly, the close link between evangelisation and political activity in current Pentecostal practice has the potential to exacerbate Christian-Muslim tensions and create what Jenkins has referred to as a 'new Christendom'. However, as we noted in chapter 6, Pentecostal leaders are encouraging members to influence society through prophetic witness, responsible citizenship, puritan lifestyles, intercessory prayer and acts of compassion, rather than violent activism or political force. Whether these values are able to permeate Pentecostal culture at the grassroots remains to be seen. To fulfil their prophetic calling, Pentecostals must maintain their critical distance from government, even if they risk becoming unpopular and marginalized. Finally, while recent attempts to implement social welfare programmes are to be commended, Nigerian neo-Pentecostals have failed to adequately address the HIV/AIDS epidemic, which is rapidly becoming a social problem of catastrophic proportions. Attention has been focussed on prayer rather than efforts to influence public morality or provide treatment and support for those affected. Most NGOs addressing the AIDS issue are linked to mainline mission churches or parachurch

---

[42] *Ibid.*, 261, 270.

[43] Matthews A. Ojo, 'Pentecostalism, Public Accountability and Governance in Nigeria', Paper presented at the workshop on 'Pentecostal-Civil Society Dialogue on Public Accountability and Governance', Lagos, October 18 2004, 11.

organisations.[44] Yet the sheer size of the Pentecostal community and the influence of its leaders demand a more proactive response. As Ojo observes, pastors are held in high esteem by their congregations and this can be used to pass down religious and social values. Churches can promote abstinence and cultivate faithfulness in marriage as an intervention strategy.[45] They can also provide support networks for those living with HIV/AIDS both within their communities and outside. A belief in God's ability to heal in response to prayer is not incompatible with medical intervention and practical care.

The growth of Nigerian Pentecostalism, as we noted in chapter 1, is rapidly becoming a phenomenon of global significance. The migratory patterns of Nigerian Pentecostals and the global missionary vision of their leaders have resulted in the spread of Nigerian initiated Pentecostal denominations to Europe and the USA, where some have experienced rapid growth. Many Nigerian Pentecostals regard the 'dark continent' of Europe in particular as a potential mission field in need of reconversion and believe that it is their responsibility to bring the gospel back to those who originally provided it. Jenkins refers to the prospect of a 'revitalized Christian presence on European soil' due to immigrant populations or 'new Europeans', and predicts that African congregations represent the 'future face of Christianity in Western Europe'.[46] Yet many of these African initiated churches are failing to attract significant followings from white indigenous communities and are directing their missionary activities to their fellow Africans instead. This is especially the case in the United Kingdom. For instance, the London-based Kingsway International Christian Centre (KICC), founded by Nigerian Pastor Matthew Ashimolowo, is largely made up of people of African and Caribbean stock. Another example is the Redeemed Christian Church of God, arguably the largest and fastest-growing Pentecostal denomination in Nigeria. Its missionary vision is to plant a church within five minutes of every home worldwide. In 1985, it planted its first church in Britain, and by 2002, it had approximately 100 branches, mostly situated in London and the Midlands. But its membership in Britain is predominantly Nigerian. A survey of its largest congregation, the 1,200 strong Jesus House started in West London by Pastor Agu Irukwe, showed that 96 per cent of its members were of African origin and

---

[44] For example, in the city of Jos there are several Christian organisations involved in HIV/AIDS programmes, including 'Spring of Life' (ECWA) and Faith Alive Foundation, founded in 1996 by a Delta Igbo medical doctor called Chris Isichei, a member of a local Baptist church.

[45] Ojo, 'Pentecostalism', 10.

[46] Jenkins, *Next Christendom*, 98.

90 per cent were Nigerian.[47] If these immigrant churches are to attract more white indigenous members they need to adapt their message, their worship and preaching styles, and their recruitment strategies to satisfy consumer demands quite different from those they are used to in Africa. As Jenkins notes, they will have to treat 'White habits and worldviews with due respect and sensitivity: to practice inculturation, in fact'.[48] To be fair, some Nigerian church leaders are aware of this. Matthew Ashimolowo, for example, has recently begun a Breaking Barriers Crusade to recruit white members. An alternative approach is for Nigerian 'missionaries' to encourage renewal and revival by working with existing white-led churches rather than starting new ones.

According to projections, by 2025 Nigeria will be the 5th most populous nation in the world. While religious patterns are harder to quantify, the present size of Nigeria's neo-Pentecostal community and its global ambitions guarantee that it will remain a major player in world Christianity for some time to come. It may even contribute to the revitalisation and reshaping of Christianity in the North. But this will depend upon its ability to adapt its message and methods for local consumption while at the same time maintaining its counter-cultural edge.

---

[47] See Stephen Hunt, 'The "New" Black Pentecostal Churches in Britain', Paper presented at CESNUR 14th International Conference, Riga, Latvia, August 29-31, 2000; Sola Fola-Alade, 'Missionary to London', 120-33. Another large RCCG congregation is Trinity Chapel in the London borough of Newnham, started by Pastor Sola Fola-Alade and five others in 1996. Pastor Fola-Alade describes himself as a 'long-term missionary' to London. Seven years later his church had grown to around 700 members, many of whom hold influential positions in the community. Yet his account makes no mention of the ethnic mix of the congregation. For an important study of African Christians in Europe, see Gerrie ter Haar, *African Christians in Europe*, Nairobi: Acton, 2001.

[48] Jenkins, *Next Christendom*, 177.

Appendix

Jos Survey Tables

RPM = Redeemed People's Mission – 105 respondents
BFM = Bible Faith Mission – 40 respondents
ACFM = All Christians Fellowship Mission – 22 respondents

Table 1. Why do you prefer your present church to others?

	RPM	%	BFM	%	ACFM	%	Total	%
Group totals	**105**		**40**		**22**		**167**	
Bible teaching	93	89	35	88	19	86	147	88
Worship	95	90	36	90	16	73	147	88
Sermons	77	73	38	95	16	72	131	78
Love	83	79	32	80	13	59	128	77
Spiritual gifts	76	72	35	88	16	73	127	76
Prayer	69	66	31	78	15	68	115	69
Holiness	70	67	29	72	16	73	115	69
Mission	70	67	28	70	11	50	109	65
Use of money	57	54	26	65	8	40	91	54
Pastoral care	47	45	28	70	11	50	86	51
Use of English	48	46	21	53	12	55	81	49
Problem solving	35	33	26	65	10	46	71	43
Healing	34	32	25	63	9	41	68	41
Prosperity	24	23	21	53	11	50	56	34
Ethnic mix	5	5	5	12	3	14	13	8
Not stated	1	1	0	0	0	0	1	1

Table 2. What is your ethnic group?

Church	N	Igbo (%)	Other Southern groups (%)	Indigenes (Plateau State) (%)	Other Northern groups (%)	Not stated (%)
RPM	105	58	23	3	14	2
BFM	40	42	42	12	0	4
ACFM	22	41	41	5	9	4
Total	167	52	30	5	10	3

Table 3. Did you join your church through conversion or transfer?

Church	N	Conversion (%)	Transfer (%)	Not stated (%)
RPM	105	31	64	5
BFM	40	45	45	10
ACFM	22	18	55	27
Total	167	33	58	9

Table 4. What was your religion prior to joining your church?

Church	N	Christian %	Islam %	ATR %	Other %	Did not state %
RPM	105	86	2	7	2	3
BFM	40	95	2	3	0	0
ACFM	22	91	5	4	0	0
Total	167	89	3	5	1	2

Table 5. What was your church affiliation prior to joining?

Church	N	Mainline (%)	Catholic (%)	Mission Pentecostal (%)	AIC (%)	Other NPC (%)	Did not state (%)
RPM	105	26	17	9	16	18	14
BFM	40	41	18	3	15	3	20
ACFM	22	33	33	0	0	0	34
Total	167	33	19	6	13	11	18

Table 6. Do you know of any indigenes who have joined your church?

Church	N	None (%)	1-5 (%)	6-10 (%)	> 10 (%)	Unsure of number (%)	Did not state (%)
RPM	105	12	21	12	21	12	22
BFM	40	13	15	10	37	10	15
ACFM	22	4	32	32	9	5	18
Total	167	10	24	19	22	10	16

Table 7. Do you know of any Muslims converted in your church?

Church	N	None (%)	1-3 (%)	4-6 (%)	7-10 (%)	>10 (%)	Number not stated (%)	Did not state (%)
RPM	105	22	27	4	4	1	9	33
BFM	40	40	28	2	2	0	10	18
ACFM	22	0	59	14	0	4	5	18
Total	167	24	32	5	4	1	9	25

Table 8. Redeemed People's Mission - age and education

	N	Primary 6/ Secondary (%)	Tertiary (%)	None of above (%)	Not stated (%)
Males					
11-20	0	0	0	0	0
21-30	13	46	54	0	0
31-40	20	50	45	5	0
41-50	20	55	45	0	0
51-60	5	60	20	20	0
61-70	1	0	100	0	0
Total(male)	60	50	45	3	2
Females					
11-20	1	100	0	0	0
21-30	18	44	44	6	6
31-40	17	60	40	0	0
41-50	7	57	43	0	0
51-60	2	50	50	0	0
61-70	0	0	0	0	0
Total (female)	45	53	43	2	2
Total (both)	**105**	**51**	**44**	**3**	**2**

Bibliography

Oral interviews included Nigerian Christian pastors and leaders, church founders, church members, academic staff and Western missionaries. Most interviews were tape-recorded and transcripts made. With a few exceptions, written sources are limited to works cited.

Primary Sources

Interviews

(m = male)
(f = female)
David Adegboye (m), pastor, RPM, 6.9.01, Jos.
Felix Adejoh (m), NEM, 30.12.01, Ayangba.
Emmanuel Agonmo (m), lecturer, University of Nigeria, 29.4.00, Enugu.
Chris Agu (m), pastor, LWM, 14.10.01, Aba.
Emmanuel Akinola (m), Anglican, 8.4.06, Bukuru.
Paul Chinedu Akunne (m), pastor, Anglican, 3.4.06, Bukuru.
Chris Alagbu (m), pastor, ALA, 3.5.00, Enugu.
Kenneth Amadi (m), pastor, AG Nigeria, 21.11.01, Bukuru.
Francis Amaechi (m), pastor, NEM, 15.5.00, Onitsha.
Hygienus Anigbo (m), ALA, 2.5.00, Enugu.
Leo Anorue (m), pastor, RPM, 18.9.01, Bukuru.
Austin Authur (m), pastor, Grace of God Mission, 25.11.01, Jos.
Frances Lawjua Bolton (f), member, Anglican, 23.5.99 and 4.10.02, London.
Elias Chukwu (m), founder, Pentecostal Life Bible Church, 21.12.01, Bukuru.
Nnenna Chukwuma (f), Great Commission Movement, 26.5.00, Enugu.
Chung Pam Chu (m), District Superintendent, AG Nigeria, 26.9.01, Jos.
Evans Daniel (m), Abia State Co-ordinator, CPM, 14.10.01, Aba.
Prince David (m), pastor, Christ Holy Church, 30.11.01, Jos.
Kenneth Eboh (m), General Overseer, Holiness Evangelical Church, 16.11.01, Owerri.
Joseph Egboh (m), Principal, ECWA Bible College, 12.1001, Aba.
Aso Egwu (m), pastor, RPM, 12.12.01, Jos.
Alexander Ekewuba (m), founder, Overcomer's Christian Mission, 17.1.02, Owerri.
Zion Ekpeh (m), pastor, Grace of God, 9.5.00, Enugu.
Emmanuel Ekpunobi (m), Principal, Anglican Training Centre, 24.10.01, Awka.
Anselm Ekwebelem (m), pastor, ALA, 25.5.00, Enugu.
Mathias Eluwah (m), Anglican, 13.10.01, Aba.

Rosebud Eluwah (f), Anglican, 13.10.01, Aba.
Uchenna Emezue (m), Canaan Gospel Centre, 11.10.01, Umuahia.
Aureola Enwezer (f), Anglican, 24.5.00, Enugu.
Emeka Enwezor (m), Anglican, 24.5.00 and 9.1.02, Enugu.
Comfort Essien (f), former SU travelling secretary, Qua Iboe Church, 18.1.02, Etinan.
Edet Etuk (m), Qua Iboe Church, 18.1.02, Etinan.
Eze N. Eze (m), Academic Dean, TCNN, Presbyterian, 1.12.01, Bukuru.
Wilson Ezeofor (m), founder and President, Bible Faith Mission, 25.9.01, Jos.
Benson Ezeokeke (m), founder and Bishop, Salvation for All Mission, 11.5.00, Onitsha.
Bayo Famunore (m), co-founder, CAPRO, 21.12.01, Jos.
Anne Goodchild (f), Anglican, 19.4.01, Birmingham.
Peter Game (m), Connections, 11.11.01, Bukuru.
Emeka Ibekwe (m), District Pastor, Christian Pentecostal Mission, 16.10.01, Umuahia.
Maxwell Onyemaechi Ibenyenwa (m), ECWA, 17.5.00, Enugu.
Charles Igwilo (m), Great Commission Movement, 25.5.00, Enugu.
Martins Iheaka (m), pastor, Gospel Crusaders Mission, 14.1001, Aba.
Isaac Ihukwumere (m), AG Nigeria, 12.10.01, Aba.
Donatus Ikechukwu (m), evangelist, Christ Holy Church, 9.9.01, Bukuru.
B. C. Ikedinobi (m), General Overseer, Overcomer's Bible Church, 12.5.00, Onitsha.
Mrs. B. C. Ikedinobi (f), pastor, Overcomer's Bible Church, 12.5.00, Onitsha.
Emenike Ikegbune (m), Chief Librarian, University of Nigeria, 2.1.02, Nsukka.
Godwin Ikwunze (m), pastor, St Joseph's Chosen Church of God, 8.10.01, Umuahia.
Meshak Ilobi (m), 28.4.00, Enugu.
D. O. Iwuagwu (m), Apostle and District Overseer, Apostolic Church, 23.10.01, Enugu.
Tshally Jeff-Onyegbule (m), pastor, ALA, 9.5.00, Enugu.
Michael Kalu (m), NEM, 30.12.01, Anyangba.
Ume Kalu (m), Presbyterian, 17.10.01, Amachara.
Mrs. Jenny Kelsey (f), former CMS missionary, 3.10.02, Emsworth.
Joshua Mallam (m), pastor, Anglican, 26.6.05, Jos.
Augustine Mbamalu (m), District Overseer, Grace of God Mission, 19.11.01, Jos.
Augustus Mbaneso (m), former National Chairman, SU Nigeria, 12.1.02, Umuahia.
Chukwendu Mgbeahaike (m), Gospel Crusaders Mission, 13.10.01, Aba.
Ikechukwu Nduka (m), pastor, Presbyterian, 26.6.05, Jos.
B. O. Ndumele (m), pastor, Divine Abosso Apostolic Faith Church, 11.1.02, Umuahia.
Chinedu Nebo (m), Anglican priest and Professor, Enugu State University of Technology, 4.5.00, Enugu.
Chijioke Nlem (m), Archdeacon, Anglican, Jos, 12.10.05, Jos.
Godwin Nnaji Chukwuka(m), founder, Revival Time Ministry, 29.4.00, Enugu.
S. C. Nnodim (m), Bishop, AFC, 6.1.02, Enugu.
Amaechi Nwachukwu (m), founder and Bishop, ALA, 6.6.00, Enugu.
Paul Nwachukwu (m), General Superintendent, Grace of God, 12.5.00, Onitsha.
Kenechukwu Nwanisobi (m), pastor, ALA, 17.10.01, Enugu.
Augustine Nwodika (m), General Superintendent, Throne of Grace, 8.5.00, Enugu.
Mrs. C. U. Nwokoro (f), wife of founder, Last Days Messengers, 17.10.01, Okigwe.

Godwin Nwosu (m), pastor, RPM, 10.10.01, Umuahia.
Thompson Nwosu (m), General Superintendent, RPM, 31.8.01, Jos.
Stephen Nyam (m), District Overseer, ACFM, 22.11.01, Jos.
Felix Obiorah (m), General Overseer, MVC, 6.10.01, Umuahia.
Pius Obuegbe (m), pastor, ACFM, 29.8.01, Bukuru.
Emmanuel Odiaka (m), Director of Evangelism, Grace of God, 12.5.00, Onitsha.
Don Odunze (m), founder, Family Circle Centre, 22.10.01, Enugu.
J. Ogbansiegbe (m), General Overseer, Christian Fellowship Group, 12.10.01, Aba.
Bartholemew Ogbonna (m), pastor, TREM, 8.1.02, Enugu.
Onyinye Ogbonna (m), ECWA, 6.10.01, Azuiyi-Oloko.
Rufus Ogbonna (m), pastor, Qua Iboe Church, 12.4.00, Ochadamu.
Ifeyinma Orajekwe (f), ECWA, 1.5.00, Enugu.
Emmanuel Orji (m), AG Nigeria, 10.1.02, Umuahia.
Chuks Ogoalaji (m), General Superintendent, Bread of Life Mission, 23.5.00, Enugu.
Raphael Okafor (m), co-founder, Hour of Freedom, & Archdeacon, Anglican, 8.5.00 and 7.1.01, Enugu.
Stephen Okafor (m), co-founder, Hour of Freedom, 16.12.98, London.
Ken Okeke (m), Anglican Bishop of the Niger (Onitsha), 17.12.98, London.
Tony Okeke (m), founder, Save the Lost Mission, 20.10.01, Enugu.
Emmanuel Okorie (m), President, LWM, 17 January 2002, Aba.
Ben Okoroafor (m), pastor, AG Nigeria, 22.10.01, Enugu.
Cyril C. Okorocha (m), Anglican Bishop of Owerri, 23.8.98 and 8.2.99, Woking.
Eliezer Okoye (m), founder, Travelling Gospel Team, 13.5.00, Onitsha.
Mike Okoye (m), Assistant General Overseer, ACFM, 2.9.01, Jos.
William Okoye (m), founder and General Overseer, ACFM, 28.10.01, Abuja.
Emmanuel Oladipo (m), SU International Secretary, 18.11.99, Bletchley.
Muyiwa Olamijulo (m), former SU travelling secretary, & District Overseer, AFC, 17.1.02, Ikot Enwang.
Joseph Onuchukwu (m), National Secretary, Grace of God, 23.5.00, Enugu.
Victor Onuigbo (m), founder and Archbishop, Victory Christian Mission, 1.5.00, Enugu.
Uche Onuoha (m), evangelist, ALA, 5.5.00, Enugu.
Udobata Onunwa (m), Canon, Anglican, 11.1.00, 25.1.01, 23.3.04, Birmingham.
John Onuora (m), former SU travelling secretary, Anglican, 30.4.00, Enugu.
Mrs. J. Onuora (f), Anglican, 23.10.01, Enugu.
Obed Onuzo (m), Anglican, 25.1.01, Birmingham.
Samson Onwubiko (m), General Overseer, Calvary Evangelistic Mission, 10.10.01, Umuahia.
Dan Onwukwe (m), former SU General Secretary, Anglican, 15.1.02, Owerri.
Samson Onyeoziri (m), Senior Pastor, Canaan Gospel Centre, 11.10.01, Umuahia.
S. O. Orji (m), General Secretary, Christ Ascension Church, 7.1.02, Enugu.
Charles O. Osueke (m), General Superintendent, AG Nigeria, 19.10.01, Enugu.
Ndubueze Oti (m), pastor, AG Nigeria, 19.10.01, Enugu.
Mike Oye (m), former SU travelling secretary, Methodist, 6.5.00, Enugu.
Peter Ozodo (m), co-founder, CAPRO, 1.10.01, Jos.

Bitrus Pathel (m), pastor, NEM, 18.11.01, Bukuru.
W. B. Roberts (m), former SU travelling secretary, Anglican, 23.7.99, Cullompton.
Jane Sutton (f), former SU travelling secretary, 10.9.99, Newbury.
Okebugwu Ubani (m), pastor, LWM, 16.10.01, Umuahia.
Nicholas Udemba (m), District Superintendent, Christ Holy Church, 5.1.02, Enugu.
John Ugah (m), General Overseer, Jesus the Way Mission, 7.6.00, Enugu.
Timothy Uhiara (m), Vice-President, MVC, 16.10.01, Umuahia.
James Ukaegbu (m), pastor, Presbyterian, 10.10.01, Umuahia.
Joseph Umeh (m), Jos Intercessors Forum & RPM, 19.12.01, Jos.
N. O. Umeh (m), Bishop, Christ Holy Church, 6.12.01, Jos.
Mrs. N. O. Umeh (f), Christ Holy Church, 6.12.01, Jos.
F. C. Uwa (m), Senior Pastor, Living Faith Church, 15.5.00, Onitsha.
Gideon Uzoma (m), pastor, CPM, 6.12.01, Jos.
Wilson Uzumegbunam (m), founder, All Believers Fellowship Group, 13.10.01, Aba.
Andrawus Yusuf (m), pastor, COCIN, 26.7.05, Jos.

Unpublished Documentary Sources

All Africa Conference of Churches *et al.*, 'The Church Making a Difference in the 21st Century', Communiqué of AACC/CIRCLE/CATI/EATWOT/OAIC Joint Theological Conference, Mbagathi, Nairobi, 14-18 August 2000: Resolution 12.

All Christian Fellowship Mission
Leaflet introducing the World Outreach Bible Institute, Abuja.

Apostolic Church
M. M. Anyachor, 'Welcome to Igbo Field of the Apostolic Church, Nigeria', 3 May 1998.
G. S. Selby, Letter to author, 14 April 2001.

Mbaneso, A. U.
'First Scripture Union (Nigeria) Summit 16th October 1999', Keynote Address by the National Chairman, Camp of Faith, Okigwe.

Okeke, David C.
'Report: Ufuma Praying Band', 1972.

Redeemed People's Mission
Annual Progress Reports, 1986-2000.
'Redeemed People's Mission at 25, Goodwill Message from the General Superintendent', 1998.
Brochure introducing the Redeemed People's Theological College, Jos.
N. C. Thompson, 'Account of Rev. N. C. Thompson's Stewardship, presented at his 30th Anniversary as a Minister of the Gospel, on Sunday, 4th November 2001'.

Roberts, W. B. (Private Papers)
Written testimonies, Igbo SU members, 1969.
Letters from Igbo SU members to Roberts, 1969-1973.
Letters from SU Umuahia to SU London, 1968-1969.
W. B. Roberts, SU Prayer Letters, September 1967 to March 1970.
W. B. Roberts, Letter to SU Group Area Representatives, 20 November 1969.

W. B. Roberts, Pilgrims of the Scripture Union, Newsletters, Nos. 1-3, 1967 to 1968.
Muyiwa Olamijulo, 'Report of Visit to the East Central State', 1970.
Muyiwa Olamijulo, Eastern Newsletter No.6, January 1973.
SU (Nigeria), Annual Reports, and Minutes of Executive Committee Meetings and Council Meetings, 1967 to 1970.
Daniel N. Onwukwe, SU (Nigeria) Prayer Letter, October 1970.
Salvation For All Mission International
Bishop Dr. Benson C. Ezeokeke, 'Testimony and Praise Bulletin', 2000.
Scripture Union Archives (Milton Keynes, England)
Minutes of SU Overseas Committee meetings, January 1966-November 1969.
Minutes of SU London Council meeting, 28 November 1970.

Published Documentary Sources

Abosi, Kalu, *"Born Twice". From Demonism to Christianity, Vol. 1*, Benin City: Joint Heirs Publications, n.d.

Adolf, Emeka Chigozie, *Deliverance of African Christians, Vol.1*, Aba: Christ The Rock Community, 2001.

All Christians Fellowship Mission, *Teaching the Whole Counsel of God. New Life Sunday School*, Abuja: Christian Education Department, All Christians Fellowship Mission, 2001.

– *Teaching the Whole Counsel of God. Membership Bible Studies*, Abuja: Christian Education Department, All Christians Fellowship Mission, 2001.

Amazing Love Assembly, *Rules and Regulations of Amazing Love Ministries*, Enugu: Timex Enterprises, n.d.

Bolton, Frances Lawjua, *And We Beheld His Glory. A Personal Account of the Revival in Eastern Nigeria in 1970/'71*, Harlow: Christ the King Publishing, 1992.

Christian Pentecostal Mission International, *Membership Manual*, Lagos: Jesus Foundation Class, Christian Pentecostal Mission International, 2000.

– *Sunday School Adult Bible Class Manual*, Lagos: National Council of Christian Education, Christian Pentecostal Mission International, 2001.

Chukwuka, Nnaji Godwin, *Looking Beyond the Night*, Enugu: Snaap Press, 1997.

Cimino, Ralph L., *Lifting Hands to Plant the Church. A Compilation of the Profiles of the Assemblies of God Missionaries in Nigeria*, n.publ., 1998.

Congress on Christian Ethics in Nigeria, *Nigeria Covenant*, Jos: CAPRO Media Print Production, n.d.

Christian Students Social Movement, *Working Manual No.2, Christian Social Responsibility*, Ile-Ife: CSSM, 1980.

Famonure, Bayo, *Revive Us Again*, n.publ., 2004.

Grace of God Mission Inc., *Sunday School Manual*, n.publ, February – July, 2001.

Living Word Ministries, *Annual Journal*, Aba: Living Word Ministries, 2001.

Kingswem, Joseph, *Ideal Christian Directory for Plateau State*, Jos: Ideal Companionship Communications Company, 2005.

Madugba, Mosy U., *Africa's Time of Recovery*, Port Harcourt: Spiritual Life Publications, 2000.

Nwachukwu, Amaechi, *How Born-again are the Born-agains?*, Enugu: Livingspring Communications, 2002.

Nwankpa, Emeka, *Translated into the Kingdom of Christ*, Lagos: Touchstone, 1983.

– *Redeeming the Land. Interceding for the Nations*, Achimota, Ghana: Africa Christian Press, 1994.

Odunze, Don, *Counsellor's Hand Book on Pre-marital Counselling, Successful Marriage Techniques, The Marriage Killers*, Enugu: Donze Family Circle Publications, 1983.

Odunze, Don and Marvin Gilbert, *Successful Family Living (An African View)*, Enugu: Donze Family Circle Publications, 1998.

Ofoegbu, Mike, *Dangerous Prayers Part 1*, Lagos: Holy Ghost Anointed Books, 1998.

Ogbansiegbe, Godson C. D., *The Manual of the Christian Fellowship Group*, n.publ., n.d.

Okoroafor, Peter A., *William Okoye: Called To Serve*, Abuja: The Whole Gospel Publications, 1996.

Okoye, William, *Youth with a Purpose*, Abuja: The Whole Gospel Publications, 1993.

– *Clash of the Champions. Battle for the Soul of Nigeria*, Abuja: Integrity Royal Publications, 2000.

– *Nigeria at 40. God's Message to the Nation*, Abuja: Integrity Royal Publications, 2000.

– *God's Purpose for Nations. Satan's Deceit Exposed*, Abuja: Integrity Royal Publications, 2001.

– *Vain Glory. The Cancer of Today's Church*, Abuja: Integrity Royal Publications, 2002.

Osborn, T. L., *Soulwinning Out Where The Sinners Are*, 7th ed., Tulsa: Osborn Foundation, 1966.

Pentecostal Fellowship of Nigeria, *Pentecostal Fellowship of Nigeria Incorporated (P.F.N.) Constitution*, n.publ., n.d.

Redeemed People's Mission, *Redeemed Adult Sunday School Lessons*, Jos: Redeemed People's Mission Inc., 1998-2001.

– *Membership Manual*, Jos: Redeemed People's Mission Inc., 2003.

Roberts, W. B., *Life and Death among the Ibos*, London: Scripture Union, 1970.

Victory Christian Mission, *Victory International Bible College Enugu. Hand Information Booklet*, Enugu: Brilliant Press, n.d.

Westgarth, J. W., *The Holy Spirit and the Primitive Mind. A Remarkable Account of a Spiritual Awakening in Darkest Africa*, London: Victory Press, 1946.

Newspapers and Magazines

Christian Update. PFN Enugu North, Maiden Issue, 2001.

Church Leader in Africa, The, Oct.-Dec.2003.

Church of England Newspaper, 22 August 1969 & 9 January 1970.

Compassion, The, 1992.

Daily Telegraph Magazine, The, 23 August 1968.

Echoes of Joy, April 2001.

Forum, The, 2001.
Glad News, 2000.
Life of Faith, 10 January 1970.
LifeWay. The Spirit-Filled Christian Life, Oct-Nov 2001.
Livingspring, 1997 & 1997.
Newswatch, 3 December 2001 & 8 August 2005.
Nigerian Christian, April 1967-April 1969.
Nuggets. The Apostolic People, Nos 17-35, July-December, 2001.
Occupy, 16.3 & 4, 1997.
Pentecostal Family, The, August 1999.
Pentecostal Weekly, 2000.
Plumbline. The Journal of the Pilgrims Ministry S.U. (Nigeria), 1992 & 2005.
Prophecy. The Messiah is Coming, 1996.
Salvation, 16 December 2001.
Tell, 1 May 2006.
Time Magazine, 23 August 1968.
VineyardNEWS, September 2005.

Secondary Sources

Achunike, Hilary C., *Dreams of Heaven. A Modern Response to Christianity in North Western Igboland 1970-1990*, Enugu: Fourth Dimension, 1995.

Adefarasin, Paul, 'The Kingdoms of this World', in Wagner and Thompson (eds.), *Out of Africa*, 134-50.

Adeleye, Femi, *Preachers of a Different Gospel*, Kampala: International Fellowship of Evangelical Students (IFES), 1999.

Afigbo, A. E., 'The Missions, the State and Education in South-Eastern Nigeria, 1956-71', in Fasholé-Luke *et al.* (eds.), *Christianity*, 176-92.

– 'The Age of Innocence: the Igbo and their Neighbours in pre-Colonial Times', The 1981 Ahiajoku Lecture, 1981.

– *Ropes of Sand. Studies in Igbo History and Culture*, New York: University Press, 1981.

– (ed.), *Groundwork of Igbo History*, Lagos: Vista Books, 1991.

Agbasiere, J. T., *Women in Igbo Life and Thought*, London/New York: Routledge, 2000.

Agu, Charles Chikezie, *Secularization in Igboland. Socio-religious Change and its Challenges to the Church Among the Igbo*, Frankfurt: Peter Lang, 1989.

Akpan, N. U., *The Struggle for Secession 1966-1970*, London: Frank Cass, 1976.

Akunne, Paul Chinedu, *Having Power with God*, Lagos: Ikechbenjamin Christian Publishers, 2004.

Alioha, G. M., *The Grain of Mustard Seed (The History of Assemblies of God, Nigeria)*, Aba: Assemblies of God Press, 1975.

Aluko, S. A., 'How many Nigerians? An Analysis of Nigeria's Census Problems, 1901-63', *Journal of Modern African Studies*, 3.3, 371-92.

Anderson, Allan H., 'Global Pentecostalism in the New Millenium', in Allan H. Anderson and Walter J. Hollenweger (eds.), *Pentecostals after a Century. Global Perspectives on a Movement in Transition*, Sheffield: Sheffield Academic Press, 1999, 209-23.

– *Zion and Pentecost. The Spirituality and Experience of Pentecostal and Zionist/Apostolic Churches in South Africa*, Pretoria: University of South Africa Press, 2000.

– *African Reformation. African Initiated Christianity in the 20th Century*, Trenton, NJ: Africa World Press, 2001.

– *An Introduction to Pentecostalism*, Cambridge: Cambridge University Press, 2004.

Anderson, Benedict, *Imagined Communities: Reflections on the Origin and Spread of Nationalism*, London: Verso, 1991.

Anderson, D. M., and D. M. Johnson, 'Revealing Prophets', in D. M. Anderson and D. M. Johnson (eds.), *Revealing Prophets: Prophecy in Eastern African History*, London: James Currey, 1995, 1-26.

Anyaegbu, J. O., 'The Growth and Development of Pentecostal/Evangelical Movements in Igboland: A Case Study of North-West Igboland, 1965-1990', M. A. thesis, University of Nigeria, Nsukka, 1991.

– 'Sabbatharianism in Igboland 1916-1990', Ph.D thesis, University of Nigeria, Nsukka, 1993.

Anyachor, Monday Mboko, *History of the Apostolic Church in Igboland*, Owerri: Ihem Davis Press, 1988.

Anyanwu, U. D., 'Gender Question in Igbo Politics', in Anyanwu and Aguwa (eds.), *Igbo*, 113-20.

– and J. C. U. Aguwa (eds.), *The Igbo and the Tradition of Politics*, Enugu: Fourth Dimension, 1993.

Appiah-Kubi, Kofi, and Sergio Torres (eds.), *African Theology en Route*, Maryknoll: Orbis, 1979.

Arnold, Guy, *Modern Nigeria*, London: Longman, 1977.

Asamoah-Gyadu, J. Kwabena, *African Charismatics. Current Developments within Independent Indigenous Pentecostalism in Ghana*, Leiden: E. J. Brill, 2005.

Awe, Bolanle, 'Conflict and Divergence: Government and Society in Nigeria', *African Studies Review*, 42.3, 1999, 1-20.

Ayandele, E. A., *The Missionary Impact on Modern Nigeria, 1842-1914. A Political and Social Analysis*, London: Longman, 1966.

Badru, Pade, *Imperialism and Ethnic Politics in Nigeria*, Trenton, NJ: Africa World Press, 1998, 92.

Barker, Eileen, 'Charismatization: The Social Production of "an Ethos Propitious to the Mobilisation of Sentiments"', in Eileen Barker, James A. Beckford and Karel Dobbelaere (eds.), *Secularization, Rationalism and Sectarianism: Essays in Honour of Bryan Wilson*, Oxford: Clarendon Press, 1993, 181-201.

Barrett, David B., *Schism and Renewal in Africa*, Nairobi: Oxford University Press, 1968.

– 'Interdisciplinary Theories of Religion and African Independency', in David B. Barrett (ed.), *African Initiatives in Religion*, Nairobi: East African Publishing House, 1971, 146-59.

Bastion, Jean-Pierre, 'Pentecostalism, Market logic and Religious Transnationalism in Costa Rica', in Corten and Marshall-Fratani (eds.), *Babel and Pentecost*, 163-80.

Bastion, Misty L., '"Bloodhounds who have no friends": Witchcraft and Locality in the Nigerian Popular Press', in Jean and John Comaroff (eds.), *Modernity and its Malcontents: Ritual and Power in Postcolonial Africa*, Chicago: University of Chicago Press, 1993, 129-66.

– 'Married in the water: Spirit Kin and other Afflictions of Modernity in Southeastern Nigeria', *JRA*, 27.2, 1997, 116-35.

– 'A Tale of Two Visionaries: Father Edeh, Sister Kate and Visions of the Everyday in Southeastern Nigeria', unpublished paper presented at the symposium 'Prophets, Visionaries and their Publics in the Afro-Atlantic World', University of Maryland-College Park, October 9 and 10, 1998.

Bayart, Jean-Francois, *The State in Africa: The Politics of the Belly*, London: Longman, 1993.

Bays, Daniel H., 'Christian Revival in China 1900-1937', in Blumhofer and Balmer (eds.), *Modern Christian Revivals*, 161-79.

Bebbington, David, *Evangelicalism in Modern Britain: A History from the 1730s to the 1980s*, London: Unwin Hyman, 1989.

– 'The Decline and Resurgence of Evangelical Social Concern 1918-1980', in John Wolfe (ed.), *Evangelical Faith and Public Zeal. Evangelicals and Society in Britain 1780-1980*, London: SPCK, 1995, 175-97.

Beckford, James A., 'Accounting for Conversion', *British Journal of Sociology*, 29.2, June 1983, 249-62.

Bediako, Kwame, 'The Roots of African Theology', *International Bulletin of Missionary Research*, 13, April 1989, 8-65.

– *Christianity in Africa: The Renewal of a Non-Western Religion*, Edinburgh: Edinburgh University Press, 1995.

– 'Types of African Theology', in Christopher Fyfe and Andrew F. Walls (eds.), *Christianity in Africa in the 1990's*, University of Edinburgh: Centre of African Studies, 1996, 56-69.

Berger, Peter L., 'The Desecularization of the World: A Global Overview', in Peter L. Berger (ed.), *The Desecularization of the World. Resurgent Religion and World Politics*, Washington: Ethics and Public Policy Center, Grand Rapids, MI: Eerdmans, 1999, 1-18.

Beyer, Peter, *Religion and Globalization*, London: Sage, 1994.

Black, Jeremy, and Donal M. MacRaid, *Studying History*, New York: Palgrave, 2000.

Blumhofer, E. L., *The Assemblies of God. A Chapter in the Story of American Pentecostalism, Vol. 2*, Springfield, MO: Gospel Publishing House, 1989.

– and Randall Balmer (eds.), *Modern Christian Revivals*, Urbana and Chicago: University of Illinois Press, 1993.

Bundy, D. D., 'Lindsay, Gordon (1906-73) and Freda Theresa (1916-)', in Burgess & van der Maas (eds.), *Dictionary*, 841-42.

Bourdillon, M. F. C., 'Anthropological Approaches to the Study of African Religion', in Jan Platvoet, James Cox and Jacob Olupona (eds.), *The Study of Religions in Africa, Past, Present and Prospects. Proceedings of the Regional Conference of the International Association for the History of Religions, Harare, 1992*, Zimbabwe, Cambridge: Roots and Branches, 1996, 139-54.

Brouwer, Steve, Paul Gifford and Susan D. Rose, *Exporting the American Gospel: Global Christian Fundamentalism*, London: Routledge, 1996.

Bruce, Steve, 'Religion and Rational Choice: A Critique of Economic Explanations of Religious Behavior', *Sociology of Religion*, 54, 1993, 193-205.

– *God is Dead. Secularization in the West*, Oxford: Blackwell, 2002.

Burgess, S. M., and Eduard M. van der Maas (eds.), *New International Dictionary of Pentecostal and Charismatic Movements*, Grand Rapids, MI: Zondervan, 2002.

Carwardine, Richard, 'The Second Great Awakening in Comparative Perspective: Revival and Culture in the United States and Britain', in Blumhofer and Balmer (eds.), *Modern Christian Revivals*, 84-100.

Castells, Manuel, *The Power of Identity*, Oxford: Blackwell, 1997.

Cerulo, Karen A., 'Identity Construction: New Issues, New Directions', *Annual Review of Sociology*, 23, 1997, 385-409.

Chuta, Sunday Chibuzo, 'Africans in the Christianization of Southern Igboland, 1875-1952, Ph.D thesis, University of Nigeria, Nsukka, 1986.

Clarke, P. B., 'The Methods and Ideology of the Holy Ghost Fathers in Eastern Nigeria 1885-1905', in Kalu (ed.), *History*, 36-75.

Cleary, Edward L., 'Introduction: Pentecostals, Prominence, and Politics', in Edward L. Cleary and Hannah Stewart-Gambino (eds.), *Power, Politics, and Pentecostals in Latin America*, Boulder, CO: Westview Press, 1998, 1-24.

Coleman, Simon, *The Globalisation of Charismatic Christianity. Spreading the Gospel of Prosperity*, Cambridge: Cambridge University Press, 2000.

Corten, André, and Ruth Marshall-Fratani (eds.), *Between Babel and Pentecost. Transnational Pentecostalism in Africa and Latin America*, London: Hurst & Company, 2001.

– 'Introduction', Corten and Marshall-Fratani (eds.), *Babel and Pentecost*, 1-21.

Cox, Harvey, *Fire from Heaven. The Rise of Pentecostal Spirituality and the Reshaping of Religion in the Twenty-First Century*, Reading, Massachusetts: Addison-Wesley, 1995.

Crowther, Samuel, and J. C. Taylor, *The Gospel on the Banks of the Niger*, London: Seeley, Jackson & Co., 1859.

Csordas, Thomas J., 'Genre, Motive and Metaphor: Conditions for Creativity in Ritual Language, *Cultural Anthropology*, 2.4, November, 1987, 445-59.

Curley, Richard T., 'Dreams of Power: Social Process in a West African Religious Movement', *Africa*, 53, 1983, 20-37.

Daneel, Marthinus L., *The God of the Matopo Hills*, The Hague: Mouton and Company, 1970.

– *Missiology. Guide 2 (The Independent Churches in Africa)*, Pretoria: UNISA, 1982.

– 'African Initiated Churches in Southern Africa: Protest Movements or Mission Churches?', in Donald M. Lewis (ed.), *Christianity Reborn. The Global Expansion of Evangelicalism in the Twentieth Century*, Grand Rapids, MI: Eerdmans, 2004, 181-218.

Danfulani, Umar Habila Dadem, 'Religious Conflict on the Jos Plateau: The Interplay between Christianity and Traditional Religion During the Early Missionary Period', *Swedish Missiological Themes*, 89.1, 2001, 7-40.

Dempster, Murray A., 'Evangelism, Social Concern and the Kingdom of God', in Dempster, Klaus and Petersen (eds.), *Called and Empowered*, 22-43.

– 'Christian Social Concern in Pentecostal Perspective: Reformulating Pentecostal Eschatology', *Journal of Pentecostal Theology*, 2, 1993, 51-64.

– B. D. Klaus and D. P. Petersen (eds.), *Called and Empowered: Global Mission in Pentecostal Perspective*, Peabody, MA: Hendrickson, 1991.

– B. D. Klaus and D. P. Petersen (eds.), *The Globalization of Pentecostalism: A Religion Made to Travel*, Oxford: Regnum, 1999.

DomNwachukwu, Peter Nlemadim, *Authentic African Christianity. An Inculturation Model for the Igbo*, Frankfurt: Peter Lang, 2000.

Droogers, André, 'The Normalisation of Religious Experience: Healing, Prophecy, Dreams, and Visions', in Karla Poewe (ed.), *Charismatic Christianity as a Global Culture*, Columbia, SC: University of South Carolina, 1994, 33-49.

Ebuade, R. I. *et al.*, *The Growth of the Assemblies of God in Nigeria*, Aba: Assemblies of God Press, 1989.

Echema, Austin, *Corporate Personality in Traditional Igbo Society and the Sacrament of Reconciliation*, Frankfurt: Peter Lang, 1995.

Ejizu, Christopher I., 'Continuity and Discontinuity in Igbo Traditional Religion', in Ikenga-Metuh (ed.), *Gods in Retreat*, 133-56.

– 'Healing as Wholeness: The Igbo Experience', *African Marbigensia*, 20.1, 1987, 3-17.

– 'Endurance of Conviction: The Persistence of the Traditional World-View in Igbo Christian Converts', *Neue Zeitschrift fur Missionswissenschaft*, 43.2, 1987, 125-35.

Ekechi, F. K., 'Colonialism and Christianity in West Africa: The Igbo Case, 1900-1915', *Journal of African History*, 12, 1971, 103-15.

– *Missionary Enterprise and Rivalry in Igboland 1857-1914*, London: Frank Cass, 1972.

Ekoko, A. E., and L. O. Amadi, 'Religion and Stability in Nigeria', in J. A. Atanda, Garba Ashiwaju and Yaya Abubakar, *Nigeria Since Independence. The First 25 Years, Volume IX, Religion*, Ibadan: Heinemann, 1989, 110-33.

Ekwueme, Martina Ukaoma, 'Independent Churches in Igbo Historiography', M.A. thesis, University of Nigeria, Nsukka, 1989.

Ellis, Stephen, and Gerrie ter Haar, 'Religion and Politics in Sub-Saharan Africa', *The Journal of Modern African Studies*, 36.2, 1998, 175-201.

Epelle, E. M. T., 'The Sects', *West African Religion*, nos. 13-14, Sept-Dec. 1972, 43-51.

Fabian, Johannes, 'Six Theses Regarding the Anthropology of African Religious Movements', *Religion*, 11, 1996, 109-26.

Falola, Toyin, *Violence in Nigeria. The Crisis of Religious Politics and Secular Ideologies*, Rochester, New York: University of Rochester Press, 1998.

– *The History of Nigeria*, Westport, Connecticut: Greenwood Press, 1999.

– and Julius Ihonvbere, *The Rise and Fall of Nigeria's Second Republic 1979-84*, London: Zed Books, 1985.

Fasholé-Luke, Edward W. *et al.* (eds.), *Christianity in Independant Africa*, London: Rex Collings, 1978.

Faupel, William D., *The Everlasting Gospel. The Significance of Eschatology in the Development of Pentecostal Thought*, Sheffield: Sheffield Academic Press, 1996.

Fiedler, Klaus, *The Story of Faith Missions*, Oxford: Regnum, 1994.

Fola-Alade, Sola, 'Missionary to London', in Wagner and Thompson (eds.), *Out of Africa*, 120-33.

Forde, Daryll, and G. I. Jones, *The Ibo- and Ibibio-Speaking Peoples of South-Eastern Nigeria*, London: Oxford University Press for the International African Institute, 1950.

Friedman, Jonathan, *Cultural Identity and Global Processes*, London: Sage, 1994.

Freston, Paul, *Evangelicals and Politics in Asia, Africa and Latin America*, Cambridge: Cambridge University Press, 2001.

Galadima, Bulus and Yusufu Turaki, 'Christianity in Nigeria. Part II', *Africa Journal of Evangelical Theology*, 20.2, 2001, 177-208.

Gbulie, Ben, *The Fall of Biafra*, Enugu: Fourth Dimension, 1989.

Giddens, Anthony, *Sociology*, 4th ed., Cambridge: Polity Press, 2001.

Gifford, Paul, 'Prosperity: A New and Foreign Element in African Christianity', *Religion*, 20, 1990, 373-88.

– 'Some Recent Developments in African Christianity', *African Affairs*, Volume 93, Issue 373, 1994, 513-34.

– 'Introduction: Democratisation and the Churches', in Gifford (ed.), *Christian Churches*, 1-35.

– *African Christianity. Its Public Role*, London: Hurst & Company, 1998.

– 'The Complex Provenance of Some Elements of African Pentecostal Theology', in Corten and Marshall-Fratani (eds.), *Babel and Pentecost*, 62-74.

– *Ghana's New Christianity. Pentecostalism in a Globalizing African Economy*, Bloomington & Indianapolis: Indiana University Press, 2004.

– (ed.), *New Dimensions in African Christianity*, Nairobi: AACC, 1992.

– (ed.), *The Christian Churches and the Democratisation of Africa*, Leiden: E. J. Brill, 1995.

Gilliland, Dean, 'Response', in C. Peter Wagner & F. Douglas Pennoyer (eds.), *Wrestling with Dark Angels. Toward a Deeper Understanding of the Supernatural Forces in Spiritual Warfare*, Ventura, California: Regal Books, 1990, 332-337.

Glazier, Stephen D. (ed.), *Encyclopedia of African and African-American Religions*, London/New York: Routledge, 2001.

Glock, C. Y., 'The Role of Deprivation in the Origin and Evolution of Religious Groups', in Robert Lee and Martin E. Marty (eds.), *Religion and Social Conflict*, New York: Oxford University Press, 1964, 24-36.

Graf, William D., *The Nigerian State. Political Economy, State Class and Political System in the Post-Colonial Era*, London: James Currey, 1988.

Hackett, Rosalind I. J., 'Power and Authority in Nigeria's Independent Churches', *West African Religion*, 20.1/2, 1983, 37-54.

– 'New Religious Movements and Religious Self-determination', Paper for submission to Toyin Falola and J. K. Olupona (eds.), 'Religion and Society in Nigeria. Historical and Sociological Perspectives', 1986, 1-26.

– 'Thirty Years of Growth and Change in a West African Independent Church: A Sociological Perspective', in Rosalind I. J. Hackett (ed.), *New Religious Movements in Nigeria: A Current Perspective, African Studies 5*, New York: Edwin Mellen Press, 1987, 161-77.

– 'Enigma Variations: the New Religious Movements in Nigeria today', in Andrew F. Walls and Wilbert R. Schenk (eds.), *Exploring New Religious Movements. Essays in Honour of Harold W. Turner*, Elkhart, Indiana: Mission Focus, 1990, 131-42.

– 'The Gospel of Prosperity in West Africa', in R. H. Roberts, *Religion and the Transformation of Capitalism: Comparative Approaches*, London: Routledge, 1995, 199-214.

– 'Charismatic/Pentecostal Appropriation of Media Technologies in Nigeria and Ghana', *JRA*, 28.3, 1998, 259-77.

Hanciles, Jehu, 'Conversion and Social Change: A Review of the "Unfinished Task" in West Africa', in Donald M. Lewis (ed.), *Christianity Reborn. The Global Expansion of Evangelicalism in the Twentieth Century*, Grand Rapids, MI: Eerdmans, 2004, 157-80.

Hannerz, Ulf, *Cultural Complexity. Studies in the Social Organization of Meaning*, New York: Columbia University Press, 1992.

Hastings, Adrian, *A History of African Christianity 1950-1975*, Cambridge: Cambridge University Press, 1979.

– *The Church in Africa 1450-1950*, Oxford: Clarendon Press, 1994.

– 'African Christian Studies, 1967-1999: Reflections of an Editor', *JRA*, 30.1, 2000, 30-44.

Haynes, Jeff, *Religion and Politics in Africa*, London & New Jersey: Zed Books, 1996.

Held, David, and Anthony McGrew (eds.), *The Global Transformations Reader. An Introduction to the Globalization Debate*, Cambridge: Polity Press, 2000.

Hexham, Irving, and Karla Poewe, (eds.) *New Religions as Global Cultures. Making the Human Sacred*, Colorado: Westview Press, 1997.

Hiebert, Paul G., 'Power Encounters and Folk Islam', in J. Dudley Woodberry (ed.), *Muslims & Christians on the Emmaus Road*, Monrovia, CA: MARC, 1989, 45-60.

Hine, Virginia H., 'Bridge Burners: Commitment and Participation in a Religious Movement', *Sociological Analysis*, 31, 1970, 61-6.

Hollenweger, Walter J., *The Pentecostals*, Minneapolis/London: SCM Press, 1972.

– *Pentecostalism: Origins and Developments Worldwide*, Peabody, MA: Hendricksons, 1997.

Horton, Robin, 'African Conversion', *Africa,* 41.2, 1971, 91-112.

– 'On the Rationality of Conversion, Part 1', *Africa,* 45.3, 1975, 219-35.

Hunt, Stephen, '"Winning Ways": Globalisation and the Impact of the Health and Wealth Gospel', *Journal of Contemporary Religion*, 15.3, 2000, 331-47.

– 'The "New" Black Pentecostal Churches in Britain', Paper presented at CESNUR 14th International Conference, Riga, Latvia, August 29-31, 2000.

Hunter, James D., 'What is Modernity? Historical Roots and Contemporary Features', in Philip Sampson, Vinay Samuel and Chris Sugden (eds.), *Faith and Modernity*, Oxford: Regnum, 1994, 12-28.

Iannaccone, Laurence R., 'Voodoo Economics? Reviewing the Rational Choice Approach to Religion', *Journal for the Scientific Study of Religion*, 34.1, 1995, 76-89.

Ibrahim, Jibrin, 'Religion and Political Turbulence in Nigeria', *Journal of Modern African Studies*, 29.1, March, 1991, 115-36.

Ifeka-Moller, C. V., 'White Power: Social-Structural Factors in Conversion to Christianity, Eastern Nigeria, 1921-26', *Canadian Journal of African Studies*, 8.1, 1974, 55-72.

Ifere, S. E., *God's Response to Nigeria. The Story of NIFES*, Jos: NIFES Press, 1995.

Igenoza, Andrew Olu, 'Contextual Balancing of Scripture with Scripture: Scripture Union in Nigeria and Ghana', in G. O. West and Musa W. Dube (eds.), *The Bible in Africa. Transactions, Trajectories and Trends*, Leiden: E. J. Brill, 2000, 292-309.

Igwe, G. E., *Church Union in Nigeria*, Umuahia: Ark, 2000.

Ihonvbere, Julius, and Timothy Shaw, *Illusions of Power. Nigeria in Transition*, Trenton, NJ: Africa World Press, 1998.

Ike, Chukwuemeka, *Sunset at Dawn*, Glasgow: Williams Collins & Co., 1976.

Ikenga-Metuh, Emefie E., *God and Man in African Religion: A Case Study of the Igbo of Nigeria,* London: Geoffrey Chapman, 1981.

– 'Critique of Explanations of Conversion in Black Africa', in Ikenga-Metuh (ed.), *Gods in Retreat*, 257-79.

– *African Religions in Western Conceptual Schemes: The Problem of Interpretation (Studies in Igbo Religion)*, Onitsha: Imico, 1991 (orig. publ. 1987).

– *Comparative Studies of African Traditional Religions*, 2nd ed., Onitsha: Imico, 1992.

– (ed.), *The Gods in Retreat. Continuity and Change in African Religions*, Enugu: Fourth Dimension, 1986.

Ikeobi, G.C., 'Catholic Response to the Challenge of "Prayer Houses" - Origins of the "Tuesday Prayer" in Onitsha', in V. A. Nwosu (ed.), *The Catholic Church in Onitsha. People, Places and Events (1985-1985)*, Onitsha: Etukokwu Press, 1985, 262-75.

Ilesanmi, Simeon O., *Religious Pluralism and the Nigerian State*, Athens, OH: Ohio University Press, 1997.

Ilogu, Edmund, *Christianity and Ibo Culture*, Leiden: E. J. Brill, 1974.

Inyama, Emma O. 'Trends in Traditional Rulership in Igboland', in Anyanwu and Aguwa (eds.), *Igbo*, 216-31.

Isichei, Elizabeth, 'Seven Varieties of Ambiguity: Some Patterns of Igbo Response to Christian Missions', *JRA*, 3, 1970, 209-27.

– *The Ibo People and the Europeans. The Genesis of a Relationship - to 1906*, London: Faber & Faber, 1973.

– *A History of the Igbo people*, London: Macmillan Press, 1976.

– *History of Nigeria*, London: Longman, 1983.

– *A History of Christianity in Africa. From Antiquity to the Present*, Grand Rapids, MI: Eerdmans, 1995.

Iwuagwu, Augustine O., 'The "Spiritual" Churches in the Eastern States of Nigeria (a Selected Study)', Ph.D. thesis, University of Ibadan, 1971.

Jenkins, Paul, 'The Roots of African Church History: Some Polemic Thoughts', *International Bulletin of Missionary Research*, 10, April 1985, 67-71.

Jenkins, Philip, *The Next Christendom. The Coming of Global Christianity*, Oxford: Oxford University Press, 2002.

Johnson, Douglas, *Contending for the Faith: A History of the Evangelical Movement in the Universities and Colleges*, Leicester: IVP, 1979.

Johnson, Douglas M., and David M. Anderson, 'Revealing Prophets', in Douglas M. Johnson and David M. Anderson (eds.), *Revealing Prophets; Prophesy in Eastern African History*, London: James Currey, 1995, 1-26.

Johnstone, Patrick, and Jason Mandryk, *Operation World 21st Century Edition*, Carlisle: Paternoster, 2001.

Jules-Rosette, Bennetta, 'Tradition and Continuity in African Religions. The Case of New Religious Movements', in Jacob K. Olupona (ed.), *African Traditional Religions in Contemporary Society*, New York: Paragon House, 1991, 150-60.

Kailing, Joel B., 'Communication and the Development of Religious Culture: Pentecostal Evangelicalism in Nigeria's Igboland', Ph.D. thesis, University of Kentucky, 1993.

Kalu, Ogbu U., 'The Task', in Kalu (ed.), *History*, 1-9.

– 'Color and Conversion: The White Missionary Factor in the Christianization of Igboland 1857-1967', *Missiology: An International Review*, 18.1, January, 1990, 61-73.

– *The Embattled Gods: Christianization of Igboland 1841-1991*, Lagos/London: Minaj, 1996.

– 'The Third Response: Pentecostalism and the Reconstruction of Christian Experience in Africa, 1970-1995', *Journal of African Christian Thought*, 1.2, December, 1998, 3-16.

– 'The Practice of Victorious Life: Pentecostal Political Theology and Practice in Nigeria, 1970-1996', *Mission: Journal of Mission Studies*, 5.2, 1998, 229-55.

– *Power, Poverty and Prayer: The Challenges of Poverty and Pluralism in African Christianity, 1960-1996*, Frankfurt: Peter Lang, 2000.

– 'Preserving a Worldview: Pentecostalism in the African Maps of the Universe', *Pneuma*, 24.2, Fall 2002, 110-37.

– 'Passive Revolution and its Saboteurs: African Christian Initiative in the Era of Decolonization', in Brian Stanley (ed.), *Missions, Nationalism, & the End of the Empire*, Grand Rapids, MI: Eerdmans, 2003.

– 'Faith and Politics in Africa. Emergent Political Theology of Engagement in Nigeria', paper presented as the Paul B. Henry Lecture, Paul Henry Institute, Calvin College, Grand Rapids, MI, 2003, 1-15.

– 'Doing Mission through the Post Office: The Naked Faith People of Igboland, 1920-1960', unpublished paper, University of Nigeria, Nsukka, 1-18, n.d.

– (ed.), *The History of Christianity in West Africa*, London: Longmans, 1980.

Kenny, Joseph, 'Sharia and Christianity in Nigeria: Islam and a "Secular" State', *JRA*, 26.4, 1996, 338-64.

Kirk-Greene, A. H. M., *Crisis and Conflict in Nigeria. A Documentary Sourcebook 1966-1970*, 2 Vols., Ibadan: Oxford University Press, 1971.

Kukah, Matthew Hassan, 'The Politicisation of Fundamentalism in Nigeria', in Gifford (ed.), *New Dimensions*, 183-206.

Land, Steven J., *Pentecostal Spirituality. A Passion for the Kingdom*, Sheffield: Sheffield Academic Press, 1993.

Larbi, E. Kingsley, *Pentecostalism. The Eddies of Ghanaian Christianity*, Dansoman, Accra-Ghana: Centre for Pentecostal and Charismatic Studies, 2001.

Lechner, Frank J. and John Boli (eds.), *The Globalization Reader*, Oxford: Blackwell, 2000.

Lofland, John, and Rodney Stark, 'Becoming a World-Saver: A Theory of Conversion to a Deviant Perspective', *American Sociological Review*, 30, 1965, 862-75.

Lofland, John, and Norman Skonovd, 'Conversion Motifs', *Journal for the Scientific Study of Religion*, 20, 1981, 373-85.

Lovelace, Richard F., *Dynamics of Spiritual Life: An Evangelical Theology of Renewal*, Exeter: Paternoster, 1979.

Ludwig, Frieder, 'Elijah II. Radicalisation and Consolidation of the Garrick Braide Movement 1915-1918', *JRA*, 23.4, 1993, 296-317.

Macchia, Frank D., 'God Present in a Confused Situation: The Mixed Influence of the Charismatic Movement on Classical Pentecostalism in the United State', *Pneuma*, 18.1, Spring 1996, 33-54.

Madiebo, A., *The Nigerian Revolution and Biafran War*, Enugu: Fourth Dimension, 1980.

Makozi, A. O. and Afolabi Ojo, (eds.), *The History of the Catholic Church in Nigeria*, Lagos: Macmillan, 1982.

Marshall-Fratani, Ruth, 'Pentecostalism in Southern Nigeria: An overview', in Gifford (ed.), *New Dimensions*, 7-32.

– 'Power in the Name of Jesus: Social Transformation and Pentecostalism in Western Nigeria "Revisited"', in Terence O. Ranger and Olufemi Vaughan (eds.), *Legitimacy and the State in Twentieth-Century Africa*, London: Macmillans, 1993, 213-46.

– '"God is not a Democrat": Pentecostalism and Democratization in Nigeria', in Gifford (ed.), *Christian Churches*, 239-60.

– 'Mediating the Global and Local in Nigerian Pentecostalism', *JRA*, 28.3, 1998, 278-315.

Martin, David, *Pentecostalism: The World Their Parish*, Oxford: Blackwell, 2002.

Maxwell, David, '"Delivered from the Spirit of Poverty?": Pentecostalism, Prosperity and Modernity in Zimbabwe', *JRA*, 28.3, 1998, 350-73.

– *Christians and Chiefs in Zimbabwe. A Social History of the Hwesa People c.1870s-1990s*, Edinburgh: Edinburgh University Press, 1999.

– 'Review Article. In Defence of African Creativity', *JRA*, 30, 2000, 468-81.

– 'Introduction. Christianity and the African Imagination', in David Maxwell with Ingrid Lawrie (eds.), *Christianity & the African Imagination. Essays in Honour of Adrian Hastings*, Leiden: E. J. Brill, 2002, 1-24.

McClung, L. Grant, Jr., 'Pentecostal/Charismatic Perspectives on a Missiology for the Twenty-First Century', *Pneuma*, 16.1, Spring 1994, 11-21

McConnell, D. R., *The Promise of Health and Wealth: A Historical and Biblical Analysis of the Modern Faith Movement*, London: Hodder and Stoughton, 1990.

McGee, Gary B., *This Gospel shall be Preached. A History and Theology of Assemblies of God Foreign Missions to 1959*, Springfield, Missouri: Gospel Publishing House, 1986.

– 'Pentecostal and Charismatic Missions', in James M. Phillips and Robert T. Coote (eds.), *Toward the 21st Century in Christian Mission*, Grand Rapids, MI: Eerdmans, 1993, 41-53.

– 'Pentecostals and their Various Strategies for Global Mission: An Historical Assessment', in Dempster, Klaus and Petersen (eds.), *Called and Empowered*, 203-24.

McGrath, Alister E., *The Future of Christianity*, Oxford: Blackwell, 2002.

Melton, Gordon J., *The Encyclopaedia of American Religions*, Tarrytown, NY: Triumph Books, 1991.

Meyer, Birgit, '"Make a Complete Break with the Past": Memory and Post-Colonial Modernity in Ghanaian Pentecostal Discourse', in Richard Werbner (ed.), *Memory and the Postcolony. African Anthropology and the Critique of Power*, London and New York: Zed Books, 1998, 182-208.

– *Translating the Devil. Religions and Modernity among the Ewe in Ghana*, Edinburgh: Edinburgh University Press, 1999.

– 'Commodities and the Power of Prayer: Pentecostalist Attitudes Towards Consumption in Contemporary Ghana', in Meyer and Geschiere (eds.), *Globalization*, 151-76.

– and Peter Geschiere (eds.), *Globalization and Identity. Dialectics of Flow and Closure*, Oxford: Blackwell, 1999.

– and Peter Geschiere, 'Globalization and Identity: Dialectics of Flow and Closure. Introduction', in Meyer and Geschiere (eds.), *Globalization*, 1-15.

Nabofa, M. Y., 'Christianity in Nigeria: Its Role in Nation-Building', in J. A. Atanda, Garba Ashiwaju and Yaya Abubakar, *Nigeria Since Independence. The First 25 Years, Volume IX, Religion*, Ibadan: Heinemann, 1989, 98-109.

Nafziger, E. Wayne, 'The Economic Impact of the Nigerian Civil War', *Journal of Modern African Studies*, 10.2, July 1972, 223-45.

Ndubuisi, C. I., 'Evangelical Pentecostalism in Southern Igboland, 1930-90', M.A. thesis, University of Nigeria, Nsukka, 1991.

Ndubuisi, C. S., 'Fifty Years of Assemblies of God Mission In Igboland, 1930-80', Ph.D. thesis, University of Nigeria, Nsukka, 1992.

Neill, Stephen, *The Unfinished Task*, London: Lutterworth Press, 1953.

Newbigin, Lesslie, *The Household of God*, London: SCM Press, 1953.

Niebuhr, H. R., *The Social Sources of Denominationalism*, New York: World Publishing, 1957.

Nkwoka, Anthony O., 'The Role of the Bible in the Igbo Christianity of Nigeria', in West and Dube (eds.), *Bible in Africa*, 326-35.

Nock, A.D., *Conversion, the Old and the New in Religion from Alexander the Great to Augustine of Hippo*, Oxford: Clarendon Press, 1933.

Nwala, T. Uzodinma, *Igbo Philosophy*, Ikeja-Lagos: Lantern Books, 1985.

Nwabughuogu, A. I., 'Economic Aspects of Igbo Political Evolution', in Anyanwu and Aguwa (eds.), *Igbo*, 157-71.

Nwanunobi, C.O., 'Sects as an Urban Phenomenon in Contemporary Eastern Nigeria', *Anthropos*, 75, 1980, 117-28.

Nwoga, Donatus Ibe, 'Nka na Nzere: The Focus of Igbo World View', *Ahiajoku Lecture Series*, Owerri: Culture Division, Ministry of Information, Culture, Youth and Sports, 1984, 45-77.

– *The Supreme God as Stranger in Igbo Religious Thought*, Owerri: Owerri Hawk Press, 1984.

Nwolise, O. B. C., 'The Social Consequences of the Civil War in Biafra', in T. N. Tamuno (ed.), *Nigeria Since Independence, Vol.III, The Civil War Years*, Zaria: Nigeria Since Independence History Project, 1984, 21-59.

Nwosu, V. A., *Prayer Houses and Faith Healing*, Onitsha, n.publ., 1971.

– 'The Growth of the Catholic Church in Onitsha Ecclesiastical Province', in Makozi and Ojo (eds.), *History*, 38-53.

– 'The Era of Archbishop Charles Heerey 1931-1967', in V. A. Nwosu (ed.), *The Catholic Church in Onitsha. People, Places and Events (1985-1985)*, Onitsha: Etukokwu Press, 1985, 42-68.

Nzimiro, F. I., *Studies in Ibo Political Structures. Chieftaincy and Politics in Four Nigerian States*, London: Frank Cass, 1972.

Ofoegbu, Ray, 'Urbanisation and the Rise of Modern Igbo Enterprise', in Afigbo (ed.), *Groundwork*, 570-99.

Ogbalu, F. Chidozie, and E. Nolue Emenanjo, (eds.), *Igbo Language and Culture*, Ibadan: Oxford University Press, 1975.

Ohadike, Don C., *Anioma. A Social History of the Western Igbo People*, Athens: Ohio University Press, 1994.

Ohonvbere, Julius O., and Timothy Shaw, *Illusions of Power. Nigeria in Transition*, Trenton, NJ: Africa World Press, 1998.

Ojo, Matthews A., 'The Growth of Campus Christianity and Charismatic Movements in Western Nigeria', Ph.D. thesis, University of London, 1987.

– 'Deeper Christian Life Ministry: A Case Study of the Charismatic Movements in Western Nigeria', *JRA*, 18.2, 1988, 141-62.

– 'The Contextual Significance of the Charismatic Movements in Independent Nigeria', *Africa,* 58.2, 1988, 175-92.

– 'The Charismatic Movement in Nigeria Today', *International Bulletin of Missionary Research*, 3, 1995, 114-18.

– 'Charismatic Movements in Africa', in Christopher Fyfe and Andrew F. Walls (eds.), *Christianity in Africa in the 1990's*, University of Edinburgh: Centre of African Studies, 1996, 92-110.

– 'The Dynamics of Indigenous Charismatic Missionary Enterprises in West Africa', *Missionalia,* 25.4, December 1997, 537-61

– 'The Church in the African State: The Charismatic/Pentecostal Experience in Nigeria', *Journal of African Christian Thought*, 1.2, December 1998, 25-32.

– 'Sexuality, Marriage and Piety among Charismatics in Nigeria', in James L. Cox (ed.), *Rites of Passage in Contemporary Africa: Interaction between Christianity and African Traditional Religion*, Cardiff: Cardiff Academic Press, 1998, 180-87.

– 'African Charismatics', in Glazier (ed.), *Encyclopedia*, 2-6.

– 'Pentecostalism, Public Accountability and Governance in Nigeria', Paper presented at the workshop on 'Pentecostal-Civil Society Dialogue on Public Accountability and Governance', Lagos, October 18 2004.

– *The End-Time Army. Charismatic Movements in Modern Nigeria*, Religion in Contemporary Africa Series, Trenton, NJ: Africa World Press, 2006.

Okorocha, Cyril C., *The Meaning of Religious Conversion in Africa. The Case of the Igbo of Nigeria*, Aldershot: Avebury, 1987.

– 'Religious Conversion in Africa: its Missiological Implications', *Mission Studies*, 9.2, 1992, 168-82.

– 'Reconciliation: What Price? Some Biblical and Practical Reflections from Africa', in Barbara Butler (ed.), *Open Hands. Reconciliation, Justice and Peace Work around the World*, Bury St. Edmunds, Suffolk: Kevin Mayhew, 1998, 185-200.

Olaiya, Joe, 'Praying to See God's Promises', in Wagner and Thompson (eds.), *Out of Africa*, 100-119.

Olukoshi, Adebayo O., (ed.), *The Politics of Structural Adjustment in Nigeria*, London: James Curry, 1993.

– 'General Introduction: From Crisis to Adjustment in Nigeria', in Olukoshi (ed.), *Politics*, 1-15.

Omenka, Nicholas Ibeawuchi, *The School in the Service of Evangelization. The Catholic Educational Impact in Eastern Nigeria 1886-1959*, Leiden: E. J. Brill, 1989.

Omenyo, Cephas N., '"From the Fringes to the Centre": Pentecostalization of the Mainline Churches in Ghana', *Exchange. Journal of Missiological and Ecumenical Research*, 34.1, 2005, 39-60.

Onunwa, Udobata, *Studies in Igbo Traditional Religion*, Obosi, Anambra: Pacific, 1990.

Onwuejeogwu, M. A., 'The Igbo Culture Area', in Ogbalu and Emenanjo (eds.), *Igbo*, 1-10.

Oriji, John Nwachimereze, *Traditions of Igbo Origin. A Study of Pre-Colonial Population Movements in Africa*, Frankfurt: Peter Lang. 1994.

Osaghae, Eghosa E., *Nigeria since Independence. Crippled Giant*, London: Hurst & Co., 1998.

Otis Jr., George, *Informed Intercession. Transforming Your Community Through Spiritual Mapping and Strategic Prayer*, Ventura, California: Renew Books, 1999.

Ottenberg, Simon, 'Ibo Receptivity to Change', in W. R. Boscom and M. J. Herskovits (eds.), *Continuity and Change in African Culture*, Chicago: University of Chicago Press, 1959, 130-43.

– 'Statement and Reality: The Renewal of an Igbo Protective Shrine', *International Archives of Ethnography*, 51, Amsterdam, 1968, 143-62.

Pan African Conference of Third World Theologians, December 17-23, 1977, Accra, Ghana, 'Final Communiqué', in Appiah-Kubi and Torres (eds.), *African Theology*, 189-95.

Peel, J. D. Y., *Aladura: A Religious Movement among the Yorubas*, London: Oxford University Press, 1968.

– 'The Aladura Movement in Western Nigeria', *Tarikh*, 3.1, 1969, 48-55.

– *Religious Encounter and the Making of the Yoruba*, Bloomington & Indianapolis: Indiana University Press, 2000.

Perriman, Andrew, (ed.), *Faith, Health and Prosperity. A Report on 'Word of Faith' and 'Positive Confession' Theologies*, Carlisle: Paternoster, 2003.

Pomerville, Paul A., *Introduction to Missions: an Independent-Study Textbook*, Iring, TX: ICI University Press, 1987.

Rambo, Lewis R., 'Current Research on Religious Conversion', *Religious Studies Review*, 8.2, April 1982, 146-59.

– *Understanding Religious Conversion*, New Haven/London: Yale University Press, 1993.

Ranger, Terence O., 'Religious Movements and Politics in Sub-Saharan Africa', *African Studies Review*, 29.2, 1986, 1-69.

– 'Religion, Development and African Christian Identity', *Neue Zeitschrift fur Missionswissenshcaft*, 42.1, 1986, 44-68.

– and I. Kimambo, *The Historical Study of African Religion*, Berkeley: University of Calfornia Press, 1972.

Rawlyk, George A., 'Writing about Canadian Religious Revivals', in Blumhofer and Balmer, (eds.), *Modern Christian Revivals*, 208-26.

Riss, R. M., 'The Latter Rain Movement of 1948', *Pneuma*, 4.1, Spring 1982, 32-45.

– 'Osborn, Tommy Lee (1923-), in Burgess and van der Maas (eds.), *Dictionary*, 950.

Salamone, Frank A., 'Continuity of Igbo Values After Conversion: A Study in Purity and Prestige', *Missiology*, 3.1,1975, 33-43.

Sanneh, Lamin, *West African Christianity: The Religious Impact*, London: Hurst & Co., 1983.

Schreiter, Robert, *Constructing Local Theologies*, Maryknoll: Orbis, 1985.

Snow, David A., and Richard Machalek, 'The Sociology of Conversion', *Annual Review of Sociology*, 10, 1984, 167-90.

Spittler, Russell P., 'Implicit Values in Pentecostal Missions', *Missiology: An International Review*, 16.4, October, 1988, 409-24.

Stanley, Brian, 'The East African Revival: African Initiative Within a European Tradition', *The Churchman*, 92.1, 1978, 6-22.

– *The Bible and the Flag*, Leicester: IVP, 1990.

– 'Christian Missions and the Enlightenment: A Reevaluation', in Brian Stanley (ed.), *Christian Missions and the Enlightenment*, Grand Rapids, MI: Eerdmans, 2001,

Stark, Rodney and William S. Bainbridge, 'Of Churches, Sects and Cults: Preliminary Concepts for a Theory of Religious Movements', *Journal for the Scientific Study of Religion*, 18.2, 1979, 117-33.

– *The Future of Religion: Secularization, Revival and Cult Formation*, Berkeley, CA: University of California Press, 1985.

Stark, Rodney, and Roger Finke, *Acts of Faith: Explaining the Human Side of Religion*, Berkeley, CA: University of California Press, 2000.

Stark, Rodney, and Laurence R. Iannacone, 'A Supply-side Reinterpretation of the Secularization of Europe', *Journal for the Scientific Study of Religion*, 33, 1994, 230-52.

Steward, Benjamin, *Historical Background of Churches in Nigeria*, Lagos: Interwale Press, 1984.

St. Jorre, John de, *The Nigerian Civil War*, London: Hodder and Stoughton, 1972.

Sundkler, Bengt, *Bantu Prophets in South Africa*, London: Oxford University Press, 1961.

Sylvester, Nigel, *God's Word in a Young World. The Story of Scripture Union*, London: Scripture Union, 1984.

Tasie, G. O. M., 'Christian Awakening in West Africa 1914-1918. A Study in the Significance of Native Agency', *West African Religion*, 16.2, 1975, 32-42.

ter Haar, Gerrie, *African Christians in Europe*, Nairobi: Acton, 2001.

Thomson, Alistair, Michael Frisch and Paula Hamilton, 'The Memory and History Debates: Some International Perspectives', *Oral History*, Autumn 1994, 33-43.

Tippett, Alan R., 'Conversion as a Dynamic Process in Christian Mission', *Missiology: An International Review*, 2, 1977, 203-21.

Troeltsch, Ernst, *The Social Teaching of the Christian Churches*, New York: Macmillan, 1931.

Turaki, Yusufu, *An Introduction to the History of SIM/ECWA in Nigeria, 1893-1993*, Jos: Challenge Press, 1993.

Turnbull, T. N., *What God Hath Wrought. A Short History of the Apostolic Church*, Bradford, n.publ., 1959.

Turner, Harold W., 'A Typology for Modern African Religious Movements', *Journal of Religion and Religions*, 1.1, 1967, 1-34.

– *African Independent Church*, 2 Vols., Oxford: Clarendon Press, 1967.

– 'Primal Religions and Their Study', in Victor C. Hayes (ed.), *Australian Essays in World Religions*, Adelaide: Australian Association for the Study of Religions, 1977, 27-37.

– *Religious Innovation in Africa. Collected Essays on New Religious Movements*, Boston, Mass.: G. K. Hall & Co., 1979.

Turner, V. W., *The Ritual Process: Structure and Anti-Structure*, Chicago: Aldine, 1969.

– 'Betwixt and Between: the Liminal Period in *Rites de Passage*', in William A. Lessa and Evon Z. Vogt (eds.), *Reader in Comparative Religion: an Anthropological Approach*, New York: Harper Collins, 1979, 234-43.

Ubah, C.N., 'Religious Change among the Igbo during the Colonial Period', *JRA*, 18, February 1988, 71-91.

Uchendu, Victor C., *The Igbo of Southeast Nigeria*, New York: Holt, Rinehart and Winston, 1965.

Ude, F., 'The Pentecostal Fellowship of Nigeria in Anambra', M.A. thesis, Evangel Theological Seminary, Jos, 2000.

Udo, E. A., 'The Missionary Scramble for Spheres of Influence in South-eastern Nigeria 1900-52', in Kalu (ed.), *History*, 159-81.

Ukah, Asonzeh F. K., 'Advertising God: Nigerian Christian Video-Films and the Power of Consumer Culture', *JRA*, 33.2, 2003, 203-31.

van Allen, Judith, '"Sitting on a Man": Colonialism and the Lost Political Institutions of Igbo Women', Roy Richard Grinker and Christopher B. Steiner (eds.), *Perspectives on Africa. A Reader in Culture, History and Representation*, Oxford: Blackwell, 1997, 536-49.

van Dijk, Rijk, 'Young Born-Again Preachers in Post-Independence Malawi: the Significance of an Extraneous Identity', in Gifford (ed.), *New Dimensions*, 55-79.

– 'Young Puritan Preachers in Post Independence Malawi', *Africa*, 62.2, 1992, 159-80.

– 'Pentecostalism, Gerontocratic Rule and Democratization in Malawi: the Changing Position of the Young in Political Culture', in Jeff Haynes (ed.), *Religion, Globalization and Political Culture in the Third World*, New York: St. Martin's Press, 1999, 164-88.

– 'Christian Fundamentalism in Sub-Saharan Africa: The Case of Pentecostalism', Occasional Paper, Centre of African Studies, University of Copenhagen, February 2000, 1-23.

– and Peter Pels, 'Contested Authorities and the Politics of Perception: Deconstructing the Study of Religion in Africa', in Richard Werbner and Terence Ranger (eds.), *Postcolonial Identities in Africa*, London & New Jersey: Zed Books, 245-70.

Vaughan, I. J., *Nigeria. The Origins of Apostolic Church Pentecostalism, with Particular Reference to the Years 1931-52 together with some Personal Reminences of I. J.Vaughan*, n. publ., 1991.

Verstraelen, Frans J., 'History of Christianity in Africa in the Context of African History – Four Recent Contributions Compared', *Exchange. Journal of Missiological and Ecumenical Research*, 31.2, April 2002, 171-99.

Wagner, C. Peter, 'Introduction', in Wagner and Thompson (eds.), *Out of Africa*, 7-18.

– (ed.), *Territorial Spirits. Insights on Strategic-Level Spiritual Warfare from Nineteen Christian Leaders*, Chichester: Sovereign World, 1991.

– and F. Douglas Pennoyer (eds.), *Wrestling with Dark Angels. Toward a Deeper Understanding of the Supernatural Forces in Spiritual Warfare*, Ventura, California: Regal Books, 1990, 313-31.

– and Joseph Thompson (eds.), *Out of Africa*, Ventura, California: Regal Books, 2004.

Walls, Andrew F., 'Religion and the Press in "the Enclave" in the Nigerian Civil War', in Fasholé-Luke *et al.* (eds.), *Christianity*, 207-16.

– 'Africa and Christian Identity', *Mission Focus*, 6.7, 1978, 11-13.

– 'Missionary Vocation and the Ministry: the First Generation', in Kalu (ed.), *History*, 22-35.

– *The Missionary Movement in Christian History. Studies in the Transmission of Faith*, Maryknoll: Orbis, 1996.

– 'Christian Scholarship in Africa in the Twenty-first Century', *Transformation. An International Dialogue on Mission and Ethics*, 19.4, October 2002, 217-28.

Ward, Kevin, '"Tukutendereza Yesu": The Balokole Revival in Uganda', in Z. Nthamburi (ed.), *From Mission to Church: A Handbook of Christianity in East Africa*, Nairobi: Uzima Press, 1991, 113-44.

– '"Taking Stock": The Church Missionary Society and its Historians', in Kevin Ward and Brian Stanley (eds.), *The Church Missionary Society and World Christianity 1799-1999*, Grand Rapids, MI: Eerdmanns, 15-42.

Webber, Robert E., *Worship Old and New*, Grand Rapids, MI: Zondervan, 1994.

Webster, James B., *The African Churches among the Yoruba 1888-1922*, Oxford: Clarendon Press, 1964.

Williams, Pat, and Toyin Falola, *Religious Impact on the Nation State*, Aldershot: Avebury, 1995.

Williams, Sarah, 'Problem of Belief: The Place of Oral History in the Study of Popular Religion', *Oral History*, Autumn 1996, 27-34.

Wilson, Bryan, *Religious Sects. A Sociological Study*, London: World University Library, 1970.

– *Magic and Millenium. A Sociological Study of Religious Movements and Protest among Tribal and Third-World Peoples*, London: Heinemann, 1973.

– *Religion in Sociological Perspective*, Oxford: Oxford University Press, 1982.

– *The Social Dimensions of Sectarianism. Sects and New Religious Movements in Contemporary Society*, Oxford: Clarendon Press, 1990.

Wilson, Everett A., *Strategy of the Spirit. J. Philip Hogan and the Growth of the Assemblies of God Worldwide, 1960-1990*, Carlisle: Paternoster, 1997.

Wilson, John, 'The Sociology of Schism', in Michael Hill (ed.), *A Sociology Yearbook of Religion in Britain*, London: SCM Press, 1971, 1-20

Winter, R. D., 'The New Macedonia: A Revolutionary New Era in Mission Begins', in J. D. Winter and S. C. Hawthorne (eds.), *Perspectives on the World Christian Movement. A Reader*, Pasadena, CA: William Carey Library, B-157-175, 1992 (orig. publ. 1981).

Woodberry, J. Dudley, 'The Relevance of Power Ministries for Folk Muslims', in Wagner & Pennoyer (eds.), *Wrestling with Dark Angels*, 313-331

Woodward, Kathryn, 'Concepts of Identity and Difference', in Kathryn Woodward (ed.), *Identity and Difference*, London: Sage, 1997, 8-59.

Worsfold, James E., *The Origins of the Apostolic Church in Great Britain, with a Breviate of its Early Missionary Endeavours*, Wellington, New Zealand: Julian Literature Trust, 1991.

Yates, Timothy E., *Christian Mission in the Twentieth Century*, Cambridge: Cambridge University Press, 1994.

Young III, Josiah U., *African Theology: A Critical Analysis and Annotated Bibliography*, Westport, Connecticut: Greenwood Press, 1992.

Index